Shared Book Reading and Children's Social-Emotional Competence

Rotem Schapira • Dorit Aram
Editors

Shared Book Reading and Children's Social-Emotional Competence

Springer

Editors
Rotem Schapira
The Academic College Levinsky-Wingate
Tel Aviv, Israel

Tel-Aviv University, Tel Aviv, Israel

Dorit Aram
Constantiner School of Education
Tel Aviv University
Tel Aviv, Israel

ISBN 978-3-032-14687-8 ISBN 978-3-032-14688-5 (eBook)
https://doi.org/10.1007/978-3-032-14688-5

This Springer imprint is published by the registered company Springer Nature Switzerland AG
The registered company address is: Gewerbestrasse 11, 6330 Cham, Switzerland

We dedicate this book to our children and grandchildren, as well as to all the children of the world. We hope that books will be an integral part of your lives, and that you will contribute to making the world a better place—creating a society in which people are sensitive to one another and embrace each other with loving eyes and open hearts.

Acknowledgments

We warmly thank all the contributors to this book for their inspiring research, which has deepened and enriched the understanding of the contribution of shared book reading to children's socio-emotional competencies. We are also grateful to the parents, teachers, students, and children who took part in the studies. With appreciation, we extend special thanks to our mentor and source of inspiration, the late Professor Iris Levin, whose wisdom and vision opened for us the gateway into the world of storybook reading research.

Contents

Chapter 1
Introduction

Rotem Schapira and Dorit Aram

Contents

Early childhood is a formative period for the development of essential socio-emotional abilities. During these years, children learn to recognize and label emotions, express them in socially appropriate ways, and begin to regulate their emotional responses. They also develop empathy, perspective-taking, and prosocial behaviors such as sharing, helping, and cooperating (Denham, 2023; Eisenberg et al., 2015). These early competencies serve as foundations for more complex forms of social understanding and self-regulation (Thompson, 2015). They also provide essential foundations for children's well-being, enriching peer relationships both in the present and later in life, and supporting school adjustment, academic achievement, and mental health (Denham, 2007; Jones et al., 2015).

According to Bronfenbrenner's (1979, 1995) bioecological model, children develop within multiple nested systems, ranging from the microsystem (e.g., family, preschool) to the macrosystem (e.g., culture, societal values). Within these proximal contexts, children learn about the emotional and social world through their daily interactions with the people around them. They are exposed to behavioral and verbal messages—how to recognize and interpret feelings, what counts as a supportive

R. Schapira (✉)
The Academic College Levinsky-Wingate, Tel Aviv, Israel

Tel- Aviv University, Tel-Aviv, Israel
e-mail: rotem.schapira@l-w.ac.il

D. Aram
Constantiner School of Education, Tel Aviv University, Tel Aviv, Israel
e-mail: dorita@tauex.tau.ac.il

R. Schapira, D. Aram (eds.), *Shared Book Reading and Children's Social-Emotional Competence*, https://doi.org/10.1007/978-3-032-14688-5_1

or considerate reaction, and how adults respond to challenges in expressing emotions and engaging with others. Parents provide the earliest context for emotion socialization; however, research emphasizes the central role of teachers, given that preschoolers spend a significant portion of their daily lives in educational settings, where opportunities to engage with emotions are abundant (Denham, 2023).

Emotion socialization in early childhood is shaped to a considerable extent by adults through three interrelated processes: (1) modeling, as children observe how adults express, regulate, and communicate emotions, provides powerful implicit lessons about what is considered acceptable emotional behavior; (2) contingency, reflected in adults' supportive or dismissive responses to children's expressions of emotion, conveys messages about the value and legitimacy of emotions and can either validate or discourage children's emotional experiences; and (3) direct teaching takes place when adults engage children in explicit conversations about feelings, their causes, and possible strategies for coping, thus providing children with a language for emotions and tools for regulation. Together, these processes form dynamic and reciprocal cycles: children's emotional expressions shape adult responses, which in turn influence children's developing understanding of emotions and their broader socio-emotional competence (Gottman et al., 1997; Morris et al., 2007; Denham, 2023).

Shared Book Reading (SBR) is a pathway of emotional socialization, particularly within direct teaching. While long recognized as a powerful tool for fostering language and literacy (Mol et al., 2008; Dowdall et al., 2020), SBR also offers rich opportunities for socio-emotional learning. Over the past three decades, studies have shown that SBR can enhance children's understanding of emotions, empathy, prosocial behavior, and mental state language. Through stories, children encounter emotions and perspectives, identify with characters, and reflect on the causes and consequences of emotional events. Adults support this process by highlighting emotional cues, asking open-ended questions, and guiding perspective-taking (Grazzani et al., 2016; Ornaghi et al., 2015; Schapira & Aram, 2020). More broadly, literature serves as a vehicle for evoking empathy and social cognition (Miller, 2001), with narrative fiction allowing readers to simulate diverse emotions and interpersonal experiences (Mar et al., 2009). Children's books are particularly suited to this task. They frequently portray characters' emotions, intentions, and beliefs, as well as everyday social interactions and challenges, thus inviting discussion about socio-emotional issues (Cassidy et al., 1998).

Indeed, children's books contain a striking density of mental state terms—about one every three sentences (Dyer et al., 2000)—underscoring their potential as tools for socio-emotional growth. Bruner's (1986, 1990) dual landscape model highlights how narratives unfold both in the Action landscape (observable events) and the Consciousness landscape (thoughts and emotions underlying behaviors). Adults differ in the extent to which they emphasize these landscapes and link stories to children's experiences (Price et al., 2009; Kuchirko et al., 2016; Tompkins et al., 2017), shaping the depth of emotional dialogue during SBR. Finally, the very context of shared reading—whether at home or in preschool—provides a calm, intimate setting that encourages psychological closeness, attentive listening, and meaningful dialogue between adults and children, as well as among peers. These conditions enable connections between stories and children's personal experiences, allowing emotions to be explored and reflected upon within a safe and supportive environment.

This book brings together recent research findings that illuminate SBR within the context of socio-emotional development. The book is divided into three parts: the first examines the nature of adult child discourse during SBR and its relation to children's socio-emotional development; the second explores interventions that promote parent–child book reading; and the third addresses interventions implemented within educational settings.

Part I: Mental State Discourse During SBR

Book reading offers a powerful context for mental state discourse—that is, conversations about emotions, thoughts, beliefs, intentions, and behaviors. Such discussions help children express themselves, deepen their understanding, and develop skills for regulating their feelings and actions. *Deckert and Lenhart* compared parent–child mental discourse across four media types—books, audiobooks, TV shows, and movies—and found that conventional joint book reading was both the most frequent shared activity and the richest in conversations about emotions, cognitions, and social behavior. Importantly, book reading elicited significantly more mental discourse than any other medium, including audiobooks.

Indeed, beyond the frequency, research highlights the importance of the nature of parent–child conversations during shared reading (Aram & Shapira, 2012; Pillinger & Vardy, 2022). *Aram and colleagues* in the chapter focused on the content of the books, investigating whether the type of protagonist—human versus animal—affects the richness of adult–child discourse. Across two studies, with preservice teachers and with parents, they found that books featuring human characters generated more elaborate, emotionally focused, and personally relevant adult–child conversations than those with animal protagonists. Parents also engaged more in comparative discussions about siblings and family roles when the protagonists were human.

Recognizing the power of cultural contexts in shaping caregivers' socialization goals, *Carmiol and Schröder* examined mother–child SBR in Costa Rica and Germany. Their study highlighted how book reading serves as a vehicle for both emotional socialization and the transmission of cultural values. They show that while mothers in both countries emphasized autonomy, Costa Rican mothers used a higher proportion of emotion terms and more explicitly framed books as tools for teaching moral and social norms. *López-Escribano* demonstrates the strength of SBR in a meta-analysis of 13 recent studies examining adult-child SBR in the home setting. The studies showed that children who engaged more frequently and more richly in SBR displayed higher levels of emotional understanding, empathy, prosocial behavior, and theory of mind.

Beyond everyday adult–child SBR practices, bibliotherapy is an intentional use of books as a tool to support emotional growth, psychological well-being, and therapeutic healing (Jack & Ronan, 2008). In their chapter, *Sofri and Ziv* present a new research tool, the Story Processing Assessment (SPA), designed to evaluate how children process and reflect on stories through the lens of bibliotherapy, and how this processing can foster emotional reflectivity, socioemotional development, and school readiness.

Taken together, the studies in Part I suggest that SBR is not only a frequent and engaging activity but is also a uniquely rich context that offers opportunities to support and promote children's socio-emotional growth.

Part II: SBR Interventions at Home

The qualities of children's books, combined with research showing their capacity to elicit rich mental state discourse between adults and children, and evidence linking book-reading practices with children's socio-emotional competencies, have motivated intervention studies. These studies focus on training parents to engage in elaborated mental-state discourse with their children during SBR.

Clifford and her colleagues report on a 1-year follow-up of a 6-week SBR intervention. Parents were trained to engage in rich reading and reminiscing with their preschool children. Results showed that parents and children in the intervention group continued to use richer mental-state discourse than those in the control conditions. However, although the researchers found that enriched conversations were positively associated with children's socio-emotional skills 7 months after the intervention, they were not related to children's socio-emotional skills at the time of school entry. Therefore, the researchers discuss the complexity of linking such a short intervention to long-term socio-emotional outcomes.

Many interventions aim to support children and families at risk. In this regard, *Dirks and Wauters* present two interventions that taught parents how to use storybooks to notice and discuss emotion words, facial expressions, and characters' perspectives, and connect stories to their children's experiences. Parents reported that they gained strategies and applied them during book reading with their children. *Garner and her colleagues* elaborate and present a narrative review of studies on the benefits of mental state discourse during SBR across diverse child and family risk contexts. Specifically, they refer to the mental discourse in reading with children experiencing autism, Down syndrome, prematurity, and histories of maltreatment. They also refer to parents' economic disadvantage and parental psychopathology. Moreover, they describe a pilot intervention with addicted mothers during rehabilitation.

Part III: Interventions in Educational Settings

Beyond interventions focusing on parents and families, an increasing number of SBR programs have been implemented within early childhood educational settings. In these contexts, teachers and caregivers guide mental state discourse during SBR while children engage as active participants.

Barnes and colleagues investigated read-aloud practices in Head Start Pre-Kindergarten classrooms. The program incorporates daily read-aloud of 48 picture books across thematic units, with each book read multiple times and accompanied by guided teacher support. Findings indicated that children demonstrated dual growth in language and socio-emotional domains. Moreover, they showed reduced behavioral problems. *Schapira's* chapter presents a 6-week SBR intervention designed to foster preschoolers' empathy, implemented by novice teachers. Findings showed that children's empathy increased and boys—who initially demonstrated lower empathic abilities—made greater progress compared to girls. Alongside gender differences, cultural contexts also play a role in shaping how children respond to SBR interventions. This is evident in the Persona Doll Approach, implemented in kindergartens, which directly addresses diversity, bias, and shared life. *Ziv and Verete* present the use of child-like dolls representing children from diverse cultural, religious, and ethnic backgrounds. The dolls' "voices" introduce stories and dilemmas drawn from real-life experiences, while children are invited to co-create the unfolding narratives. Through this co-woven storytelling process, children not only gain mirrors of their own identities but also windows into the lives of others, fostering empathy, reducing prejudice, and opening "sliding glass doors" toward a more inclusive perspective.

Just as cultural contexts shape how children engage with SBR, the developmental stage is also critical. *Grazzani and Scotti's* chapter presents one of the first large-scale interventions for toddlers (ages 2–3). Teachers led group readings of specially designed picture books, followed by guided discussions on emotions and prosocial behaviors (e.g., helping, sharing, and comforting). Compared to control groups that (1) discussed only the books' plot or (2) played free play, children in the intervention showed greater gains in emotional competence, prosocial behavior, and language. These findings show the effectiveness of SBR in promoting socio-emotional development from early childhood. Last, *Sun and colleagues* reviewed 17 intervention studies with children aged 0–8 and showed that SBR enhances social-emotional competence in both home and educational settings. While home interventions yielded somewhat greater impact, preschool programs offered broader scalability, underscoring the complementary roles of families and educators.

To summarize, SBR offers a platform for engaging conversations about emotions, relationships, and social experiences. Through these interactions, adults support children's understanding of both the text and the social world it reflects. The studies in this book enrich our knowledge of how adults and children engage with books, how these interactions relate to children's socio-emotional development, and how this everyday practice can be promoted in diverse cultural and developmental contexts. Books touch the inner worlds of adults and children, resonating with their emotions and experiences. It is well known that books contain a wealth of information. Likewise, the discourse on socio-emotional development is vast, encompassing a wide range of children's skills and behaviors.

There is more to explore about what actually occurs in this everyday interaction between adults and children—how it resonates within the children's inner world and to what extent it promotes their development. More attention is needed to the mechanisms that illuminate which aspects of the interaction (e.g., frequency of mental-state talk, emotional richness of texts, parental modeling) are most influential.

Also, several areas remain less explored. More studies are needed with very young children in infancy and toddlerhood, as well as with diverse populations. Likewise, the role of fathers, grandparents, siblings, and educators outside of formal preschool settings has been largely overlooked. Cross-cultural and multilingual contexts, including diglossia and bilingualism, also warrant more systematic investigation. Furthermore, longitudinal research is required to clarify whether and how early SBR predicts later socio-emotional adjustment. Finally, in the current global context, the potential of SBR to support resilience in contexts of poverty, displacement, and socio-political crisis remains a particularly urgent avenue for study. We hope that this book will open new avenues for future research in this important field.

References

Aram, D., & Shapira, R. (2012). Parent-child shared book reading and children's language, literacy, and empathy development. *Rivista italiana di educazione familiare, 2*, 55–65. http://www.fupress.com/rief

Bronfenbrenner, U. (1979). *The ecology of human development*. Harvard University Press.

Bronfenbrenner, U. (1995). The bioecological model from a life course perspective: Reflections of a participant observer. In P. Moen, G. H. Elder Jr., & K. Lüscher (Eds.), *Examining lives in context: Perspectives on the ecology of human development* (pp. 599–618). American Psychological Association. https://doi.org/10.1037/10176-017

Bruner, J. S. (1986). *Actual minds, possible worlds*. Harvard University Press.

Bruner, J. S. (1990). *Acts of meaning*. Harvard University Press.

Cassidy, K. W., Ball, L. V., Rourke, M. T., Werner, R. S., Feeny, N., Chu, J., & Perkins, A. (1998). Theory of mind concepts in children's literature. *Applied Psycholinguistics, 19, 463–470.* https://doi.org/10.1017/S0142716400010274

Denham, S. A. (2007). Dealing with feeling: How children negotiate the worlds of emotions and social relationships. *Cognition, Brain & Behavior, 1*, 48. https://denhamlab.gmu.edu/Publications%20PDFs/Denham%202007.pdf

Denham, S. A. (2023). *Development of emotional competence in young children*. Guilford Publications.

Dowdall, N., Melendez-Torres, G. J., Murray, L., Gardner, F., Hartford, L., & Cooper, P. J. (2020). Shared picture book reading interventions for child language development: A systematic review and meta-analysis. *Child Development, 91*(2), e383–e399. https://doi.org/10.1111/cdev.13225

Dyer, J. R., Shatz, M., & Wellman, H. M. (2000). Young children's storybooks as a source of mental state information. *Cognitive Development, 15*, 17–37. https://doi.org/10.1016/S0885-2014(00)00017-4

Eisenberg, N., Eggum-Wilkens, N. D., & Spinrad, T. L. (2015). The development of prosocial behavior. In D. A. Schroeder & W. G. Graziano (Eds.), *Oxford library of psychology. The Oxford Handbook of Prosocial Behaviour* (pp. 114–136). Oxford University Press.

Grazzani, I., Ornaghi, V., Agliati, A., & Brazzelli, E. (2016). How to foster toddlers' mental-state talk, emotion understanding, and prosocial behavior: A conversation-based intervention at nursery school. *Infancy, 21*(2), 199–227. https://doi.org/10.1111/infa.12107

Gottman, J. M., Katz, I. F., & Hooven, C. (1997). *Meta-emotion: How families communicate emotionally*. Erlbaum.

Jack, S. J., & Ronan, K. R. (2008). Bibliotherapy: Practice and research. *School Psychology International, 29*(2), 161–182. https://doi.org/10.1177/0143034308090058

Jones, D. E., Greenberg, M., & Crowley, M. (2015). Early social-emotional functioning and public health: The relationship between kindergarten social competence and future wellness. *American Journal of Public Health, 105(11), 2283–2290.*

Kuchirko, Y., Tamis-LeMonda, C. S., Luo, R., & Liang, E. (2016). 'What happened next?': Developmental changes in mothers' questions to children. *Journal of Early Childhood Literacy, 16*(4), 498–521. https://doi.org/10.1177/1468798415598822

Mar, R. A., Oatley, K., & Peterson, J. B. (2009). Exploring the link between reading fiction and empathy: Ruling out individual differences and examining outcomes. *Communications, 34*, 407–428. https://doi.org/10.1515/COMM.2009.025

Miller, H. M. (2001). A dose of empathy. *The Reading Teacher, 54*, 380–381.

Mol, S. E., Bus, A. G., de Jong, M. T., & Smeets, D. J. H. (2008). Added value of dialogic parent–child book readings: A meta-analysis. *Early Education and Development, 19*(1), 7–26. https://doi.org/10.1080/10409280701838603

Morris, A. S., Silk, J. S., Steinberg, L., Myers, S. S., & Robinson, L. R. (2007). The role of the family context in the development of emotion regulation. *Social Development, 16*(2), 361–388. https://doi.org/10.1111/j.1467-9507.2007.00389.x

Ornaghi, V., Grazzani, I., Cherubin, E., Conte, E., & Piralli, F. (2015). 'Let's Talk about Emotions!'. The effect of conversational training on preschoolers' emotion comprehension and prosocial orientation. *Social Development, 24*(1), 166–183. https://doi.org/10.1111/sode.12091

Pillinger, C., & Vardy, E. J. (2022). The story so far: A systematic review of the dialogic reading literature. *Journal of Research in Reading, 45*(4), 533–548. https://doi.org/10.1111/1467-9817.12407

Price, L. H., Van Kleeck, A., & Huberty, C. J. (2009). Talk during book sharing between parents and preschool children: A comparison between storybook and expository book conditions. *Reading Research Quarterly, 44*(2), 171–194. https://doi.org/10.1598/RRQ.44.2.4

Schapira, R., & Aram, D. (2020). Shared book reading at home and preschoolers' socio-emotional competence. *Early Education and Development, 31*(6), 819–837. https://doi.org/10.1080/10409289.2019.1692624

Thompson, R. A. (2015). Relationships, regulation, and early development. *Handbook of child psychology and developmental science, 1–46.* https://doi.org/10.1002/9781118963418.childpsy306

Tompkins, V., Bengochea, A., Nicol, S., & Justice, L. M. (2017). Maternal inferential input and children's language skills. *Reading Research Quarterly, 52*(4), 397–416. https://doi.org/10.1002/rrq.176

Part I
Mental State Discourse during Shared Book Reading

Chapter 2
Shared Book Reading as a Unique Opportunity for Parent–Child Talk About Mental States

Katharina Deckert and Jan Lenhart

Contents

Introduction

The media are an integral part of our everyday lives. A German survey called the *miniKIM-study 2023* (Medienpädagogischer Forschungsverbund Südwest, 2023) reports that even 2- to 5-year-old children are already exposed to a variety of different media types, including *books*, *audiobooks*, *TV shows*, and *movies*, with *books* still being the most popular type of media in many families. Exposure to media can have many advantages for young children, for example, increasing their vocabulary, listening comprehension skills, and cultural knowledge (e.g., Sénéchal & LeFevre, 2003; West et al., 1993). Some theories even propose that media exposure can support the development of children's (and adults') social cognition (Kidd & Castano, 2013; Mar, 2018; Oatley, 1999; Zunshine, 2006). Social cognition represents a broad umbrella term and is defined as "the processing of stimuli relevant to understanding agents and their interactions" (Happé et al., 2017, p. 244). It encompasses many different skills, including theory of mind, knowledge about emotions, and empathy. Theory of mind can be defined as the process of understanding and representing one's own and others' mental states (Happé et al., 2017). During early

K. Deckert · J. Lenhart (✉)
University of Bamberg, Bamberg, Germany
e-mail: katharina.deckert@uni-bamberg.de; jan.lenhart@uni-bamberg.de

R. Schapira, D. Aram (eds.), *Shared Book Reading and Children's Social-Emotional Competence*, https://doi.org/10.1007/978-3-032-14688-5_2

childhood, children acquire increasing knowledge about their own and others' desires, beliefs, access to knowledge, and false beliefs (Wellman, 2002). Knowledge about emotions encompasses various facets, including recognizing facial expressions and their emotion-specific classification, verbal expression of emotions, and understanding the causes of emotions (Petermann & Gust, 2016). Empathy reflects the ability to adopt others' emotions (Happé et al., 2017). All those skills are undoubtedly important for interpersonal communication, cooperation, and for academic performance such as listening and reading comprehension (Dore et al., 2018).

Moreover, although media exposure alone might suffice for adolescents and adults to increase their skills and knowledge, research on young children's learning from media emphasizes the importance of parental mediation of media content and parent–child interaction during media usage (e.g., Lenhart et al., 2019, 2020; Nathanson et al., 2013; Schapira & Aram, 2019). Accordingly, in the present study, we examined not only different types of media (*books*, *audiobooks*, *TV shows*, and *movies*) and contexts of *media use* (alone, together with parents) but also the frequency of parent–child talk about fictional characters' emotions and cognitions during and after media exposure across the different types of media and contexts. In the following section, we start with an overview of social cognition and its relation to media exposure. Then we turn to social cognition as a theme in media content. We conclude by discussing *parent–child conversations* about social cognition during *media use* for different types of media.

Effects of Media Exposure and Parent–Child Conversations About Mental States on Social Cognition

Although general cognitive development and real-life experiences undoubtedly play a major role in individuals' social-cognitive development, exposure to media might also help to improve social cognition (for an overview, see Mar, 2018). For instance, in his recently proposed SPaCEN (Social Processes and Content Entrained by Narrative) framework, Mar (2018) argues that media (or more precisely media in narrative form) foster social cognition via two routes: via social content and processes. First, narratives provide social information and role models that can be observed and learned from. Children, for example, might learn from narratives that using the "n" word for people of color is inappropriate and hurtful. They might also learn that talking about feelings and problems is not girlish but beneficial for all genders. Second, narratives might improve social-cognitive processes by providing opportunities to slip into the shoes of story characters. This role-taking is thought of as a simulation that runs in minds (Oatley, 1999). Just like a pilot who learns how to fly in a flight simulator before steering a real airplane, narratives provide the possibility to practice social situations in a safe context by simulating story characters' minds (Oatley, 2016). Similar to expertise development in various domains, improvements (particularly for social processes) are assumed to be incremental, requiring cumulative exposure to appropriate narratives (Mar, 2018).

On an empirical level, mere exposure to stories and their effect on social cognition has been mostly studied with adults so far. For adults, meta-analyses of correlational studies report small associations between story reading and social cognition (Mumper & Gerrig, 2017; Wimmer et al., 2024). Similarly, meta-analyses of experimental studies found small effects of story reading on social cognition (Dodell-Feder & Tamir, 2018; Wimmer et al., 2024). For children, the empirical evidence base is less extensive. On a correlative level, performance on theory-of-mind tasks has been shown to be positively associated with exposure to children's *books* (Adrian et al., 2005; Lenhart & Richter, 2024; Mar et al., 2010), *audiobooks* (Lenhart & Richter, 2024), and *movies* for children (Mar et al., 2010). In contrast, for children's *TV shows*, most studies found negative (Nathanson & Fries, 2014; Nathanson et al., 2013) or null correlations (Lenhart & Richter, 2024; Mar et al., 2010). In addition, experimental studies found that reading *books* with children improved children's performance on standard theory-of-mind tasks (e.g., Cates & Nicolopoulou, 2019).

Moreover, correlational research has shown that *parent–child conversations* about mental states (i.e., characters' cognitions and emotions) are associated with diverse indicators of children's social-cognitive development. Parents' mental state talk during book reading is related to children's performance in theory-of-mind tasks (Adrian et al., 2005, 2007; Symons et al., 2010), their emotion recognition (Taumoepeau & Ruffman, 2006, 2008), their empathy and prosocial behavior (Schapira & Aram, 2019), and their own use of mental state language (Taumoepeau & Ruffman, 2006, 2008). In addition, several experiments found that adult–child talk about social-cognitive themes during book reading increased children's social-cognitive learning compared to a no-reading control group or reading the *books* without conversations about mental states (Grazzani et al., 2016; Tompkins, 2015). These findings highlight that—at least for younger children—social-cognitive content in media and *parent–child conversations* accompanying *media use* might be beneficial for children's social-cognitive development and explain differences between different types of media.

Social-Cognitive Themes in the Media

Turning to media content, a few studies have looked at social-cognitive themes included in children's *books*. An indicator of social-cognitive themes and contents is frequent occurrences of mental/internal state references (e.g., *think, feel*; Cassidy et al., 1998; Dyer et al., 2000; Dyer-Seymour et al., 2004; Farkas et al., 2020). Cassidy et al. (1998), for example, analyzed the *books* that US middle-class parents of 47 preschoolers read to their children and analyzed the mental state references as well as the presence and types of false beliefs in the plot. They found that 78% of the *books* contained one or more references to internal states and that 34% of the *books* included false beliefs. The most common were references to states such as feeling (80%), thinking (55%), wanting (46%), and knowing (35%). False beliefs resulted mostly from a lack of information (42%) or a deception of others (31%). In addition, Dyer et al. (2000) showed that mental state words occurred on average every three sentences in US *books* marketed for children between 3 and 6 years and that many *books* included several different mental state terms. Although the relative distribution of mental state categories seems to differ somewhat, the total frequency of mental state references in children's *books* appears to be rather similar across different cultures (Dyer-Seymour et al., 2004; Farkas et al., 2020).

To our knowledge, there are no such studies examining the frequency and diversity of mental state terms in audio media or audiovisual media. From a theoretical perspective, the social-cognitive content of different types of media should be similar (Mar, 2018). Written texts clearly represent the most abstract of narrative forms, which provides readers with a purely symbolic and nonrepresentational portrayal of the social world and its characters, whereas audio media and audiovisual media provide direct visual and auditory representations (Mar & Oatley, 2008). As children's *books* typically include many pictures, these differences might be less pronounced in media that are produced for children.

Parent–Child Conversations About Mental States During Media Use

Due to the prominence of social-cognitive content, children's *books* (and potentially other media designed for children) might serve as an especially fruitful context for *parent–child conversations* about mental states. However, children's *books*, audio media, and audiovisual media might differ regarding the context of consumption, namely whether the child consumes the media alone or together with his/her parents, and regarding the frequency of *parent–child conversations* about mental states during media consumption.

Indeed, according to the most recently published study of 2- to 5-year-old children's media usage in Germany (Medienpädagogischer Forschungsverbund Südwest, 2023), *books* are typically read together with parents, while *audiobooks* are often used by the child alone. The study did not differentiate between *TV shows* and *movies* but shows that audiovisual media are situated between the audio media and *books* regarding their context of usage. Given that most children at this age are not able to read yet, it makes sense that book reading typically requires an adult to do so, while the child can use audio media and audiovisual media on his/her own. Moreover, even if audio media and audiovisual media are used together with parents, they might still be less suitable for parent–child interaction and discussion during their usage. When reading a book, it is easy to pause in order to ask questions or to discuss certain content. However, when listening to an audiobook or watching a TV show or movie, it is less convenient to interrupt the presentation in order to talk about certain content. Agreeing with this assumption, experimental studies have shown that quality and quantity of parent language directed at children was considerably reduced during TV viewing compared to play or book reading sessions (Lavigne et al., 2015; Nathanson & Rasmussen, 2011), and observational research revealed that parents' sentences were shorter and parental input was less frequent when the TV was turned on (Tanimura et al., 2007). Thus, it seems likely that audio media and audiovisual media stimulate less parent–child talk about social-cognitive themes as well.

The Present Study

Given that conversational interactions are of fundamental importance for children's social-cognitive development (de Rosnay & Hughes, 2010) and parental mediation of media content seems to be crucial for children's learning from media (e.g., Lenhart et al., 2019, 2020; Nathanson et al., 2013; Poulain et al., 2019; Schapira & Aram, 2019), it is important to look at *parent–child conversations* about mental states across different types and contexts of *media use*. Accordingly, the aims of the present study were to gain an insight into preschool children's *media use* concerning (a) the use of different types of media (*books, audiobooks, movies, TV shows*), (b) the context of *media use* (alone, together with the parents), and (c) *parent–child conversations* about mental states accompanying *media use*. To do so, we conducted a questionnaire study with preschool children's parents.

Method

Sample

Six kindergartens in Bavaria, Germany, agreed to participate in the study. The kindergartens were provided with informed consent forms and a parent questionnaire for each child between the ages of 3½ and 6 years. A total of 71 kindergarten children (57.7% female) and their parent(s) participated in the study. The children were between 41 and 81 months old (M = 59.62 months, SD = 11.21). Most children (98.6%) and their parents (90.1%) were born in Germany, indicating an underrepresentation of participants with a migration background compared to the entire German population (Statistisches Bundesamt, 2022b). The children had between zero and five siblings, and most families (90.1%) spoke only German at home. Only 4% of the fathers stated that they did not graduate from school. A total of 38% of the mothers and 42% of the fathers reached a *(Fach-)Hochschulreife* (the option to obtain a university degree) as their highest educational qualification. In comparison with the 30- to 35-year-old women and men in the German population, the maternal and paternal educational levels in the present study were somewhat lower (Statistisches Bundesamt, 2022a). The parental questionnaire was completed mostly by the mother (mother: 78%, mother and father: 18%, father: 4%).

Parent Questionnaire

A three-part questionnaire was used to collect demographic data as well as data on media consumption habits and *parent–child conversations* about mental states accompanying *media use*. In the first part, parents were asked to provide information on parents' and children's country of origin, number of siblings, the language spoken at home, and parents' level of education. Parents were then asked to indicate which parent had completed the questionnaire. The second part asked about children's media usage concerning four popular types of media. Parents were asked how many minutes a day (broken down by weekday and weekend) their children spent watching children's *TV shows* and *movies*, reading *books*, and listening to *audiobooks*. The questions were asked separately for two contexts of *media use*, namely together with the parents and for the child on his/her own.

The third part asked about *parent–child conversations* about mental states during and after media exposure. It was divided into questions on the different types of media (*TV shows*, *movies*, *books, audiobooks*) and further subdivided into the context of *media use* (alone, together with parents). For each type and context of *media use*, eight scenarios of parental mediation of social cognition were described (e.g., "When my child watches *TV shows* alone, we talk about the characters' feelings afterwards." or "When my child and I listen to *audiobooks* together, I encourage my child to put himself/herself in the characters' perspectives"). Three items focused on characters' emotions ("talk about the characters' feelings", "talk about the fact that characters sometimes pretend to have feelings that they don't actually feel", "encourage the child to put himself/herself in the characters' feelings"). Four items focused on characters' cognitions ("talk about characters' diverse desires", "talk about characters' diverse perspectives/beliefs", "talk about characters' false beliefs/ lack of knowledge", "encourage child to put himself/herself in the characters' perspectives"). Finally, an item focused on social behavior ("talk about how some characters behave well socially (or not)"). Parents were asked to indicate on a 5-point Likert scale (1 = *never*, 2 = *rarely*, 3 = *sometimes*, 4 = *often*, 5 = *almost always*) how often they engaged in conversations about these topics with their children.

Data Preparation and Analysis

Parents were asked to provide the amount of time their children used a certain media type per day during the week and at the weekend in minutes, both alone and together with their parents. This information was then converted into the time that children used a certain media type in a specific context on an average day by multiplying the time for a weekday by five and the time for a weekend day by two. These scores were then added together and divided by seven. When processing the data, it became apparent that some information provided by the parents was imprecise (e.g., "15–20 minutes", "1 movie per weekend", etc.). Whenever possible, numerical coding was still done. For example, if a range of minutes was provided, the mean was used as an approximation or if an amount of TV show episodes or *movies* was provided, 20 and 60 min, respectively, were used as an approximation. However, for some of the other statements, numerical coding was not feasible. Here duration of *media use* had to be coded as missing.

In addition, some parents did not complete the questionnaire on *parent–child conversations* as instructed. In some instances, parents indicated that their child never used one particular kind of media, but they provided data for their conversations in this situation. As we were interested in actual and not hypothetical conversations (as indicated in the instruction to the parents), we recoded responses on these *parent–child conversations* as 1 (= *never*) because these children were "non-users" of these media types and could therefore not engage *in parent–child conversations* accompanying this media type.

Data analysis was carried out with the statistics program JASP (version 0.16.4.0). For significance tests, the significance threshold was set at $p < .05$, and all tests were conducted two-tailed. To compare differences concerning the frequency of *parent–child conversations* between individual media types and contexts, t-tests for dependent samples were calculated. Cohen's d is reported as an effect size measure, with d between 0.20 and 0.50 representing small effects, d between 0.50 and 0.80 representing medium effects, and $d \geq 0.80$ representing large effects.

Results

Children's Media Use

Table 2.1 provides an overview of the numbers of "users" and "non-users" of specific media types in specific contexts, as well as information on the average usage duration in minutes per day. A comparison of the media types and contexts shows that almost all families were "users" of *books*, together and alone. The other media types also showed high usage rates but were used less frequently. In particular, children rarely watched *movies* alone, and parents and children seldom listened to *audiobooks* together.

Concerning the duration of children's daily media exposure, the highest number of minutes was reported for children watching *TV shows* alone, followed by parent–child book reading (see Table 2.1). The lowest durations were reported for children watching *movies* alone and listening to *audiobooks* together with their parents

Table 2.1 Children's media use and parent–child conversations about mental states in different media types and contexts

Media type	Context	users	Non-users	Media use (min)			Conversations ("users")		Conversations ("users" and "non-users")	
		n	*n*	*n*[a]	*M*	*SD*	*M*	*SD*	*M*	*SD*
TV shows	Alone	53	18	71	29.33	28.64	2.67	0.90	2.39	1.03
	Together	49	22	67	15.12	14.72	3.32	0.85	2.87	1.14
Movies	Alone	15	56	71	8.74	22.02	2.94	0.91	1.74	1.11
	Together	42	29	66	13.23	18.36	3.41	0.76	2.65	1.28
books	Alone	59	12	66	18.54	17.72	2.65	1.00	2.49	1.09
	Together	65	6	66	23.57	19.76	3.57	0.82	3.49	0.93
Audio-books	Alone	50	21	66	18.21	21.87	2.40	0.87	2.20	1.00
	Together	27	44	67	6.70	14.41	3.18	0.90	2.17	1.25

Note. Media usage is reported in minutes per day. *Parent–child conversation* ranges from 1 (*never*) to 5 (*almost always*). "Non-users" are children whose parents indicated "0 minutes" for this media type in this context. "Users" are children whose parents indicated that they use this media type in this context

[a]Sample sizes differ for the duration of *media use* from the total sample size of 71 due to non-numeric statements that could not be transformed into numeric values. The sample sizes can also differ from the sample sizes reported for "users" and "non-users" because answers such as twice per week clearly indicate a "user" but represent a missing value for the duration of *media use*

because many parents indicated zero minutes for these types and contexts of *media use*.

Parent–Child Conversations About Mental States During Media Use

To get a differentiated look at *parent–child conversations* about mental states for different media types and contexts, we analyzed the frequency of those conversations for "users" as well as for the whole sample, consisting of "users" and "non-users," separately. The values for the whole sample indicate the general frequency of media-associated *parent–child conversations* about mental states. Those frequencies are affected by the general use of media types in specific contexts as well as by the occurrence of mental-state conversations during actual *media use*. The values for the "users" look only at differences in mental-state conversations between families that actually use a specific media type in a certain context. Descriptive statistics for the whole sample ("users" and "non-users") as well as for "users" only are reported in Table 2.1.

Looking at the whole sample ("users" and "non-users") (see Fig. 2.1), it is apparent that *parent–child conversations* during and after media consumption occurred more frequently when children and parents used media together than when children used media alone (together vs. alone: *TV shows*: $t(70) = 3.82$, $p < .001$, $d = 0.45$,

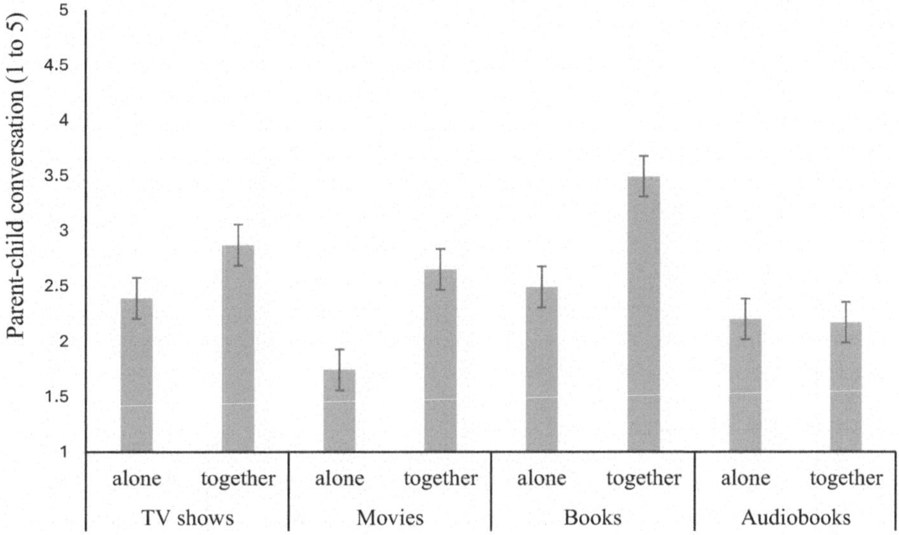

Fig. 2.1 Parent–child conversations about mental states during or after media exposure for the different media types and contexts in the whole sample. *Note.* The figure depicts mean values and standard errors of the means

95% CI for *d* [0.21, 0.70]; *Movies*: $t(70) = 6.55$, $p < .001$, $d = 0.78$, 95% CI for *d* [0.51, 1.04]; *Books*: $t(70) = 8.26$, $p < .001$, $d = 0.98$, 95% CI for *d* [0.69, 1.26]). *Audiobooks* were the only exception to that rule ($t(70) = 0.20$, $p = .846$, $d = -0.02$, 95% CI for *d* [−0.21, 0.26]), probably explained by the fact that parent–child *audiobook* consumption occurred only rarely compared to children's autonomous use of *audiobooks*. Similarly, the low number of children watching *movies* alone resulted most probably in very low numbers of *parent–child conversations* about mental states for this kind of *media use*. Moreover, *books* were accompanied by most *parent–child conversations*—in particular when parents and children engaged in book reading together (*books* together vs. other media types used together: *TV shows* together: $t(70) = 5.64$, $p < .001$, $d = 0.67$, 95% CI for *d* [0.41, 0.93]; *Movies* together: $t(70) = 5.86$, $p < .001$, $d = 0.70$, 95% CI for *d* [0.43, 0.95]; *Audiobooks* together: $t(70) = 8.78$, $p < .001$, $d = 1.04$, 95% CI for *d* [0.75, 1.33]).

Looking at the subsample of "users" only (see Fig. 2.2), the difference between the two contexts of *media use*, namely, if children and parents consumed media together or alone, was apparent again. When children and parents used media together, *parent–child conversations* during and/or after *media use* occurred much more frequently (together vs. alone: *TV shows*: $t(36) = 4.94$, $p < .001$, $d = 0.81$, 95% CI for *d* [0.44, 1.18]; *Movies*: $t(12) = 3.11$, $p = .009$, $d = 0.86$, 95% CI for *d* [0.21, 1.49]; *Books*: $t(54) = 7.93$, $p < .001$, $d = 1.07$, 95% CI for *d* [0.73, 1.40]; *Audiobooks*: $t(20) = 3.25$, $p < .004$, $d = 0.71$, 95% CI for *d* [0.22, 1.18]). In contrast to the whole sample, the difference was also observable for *audiobooks*.

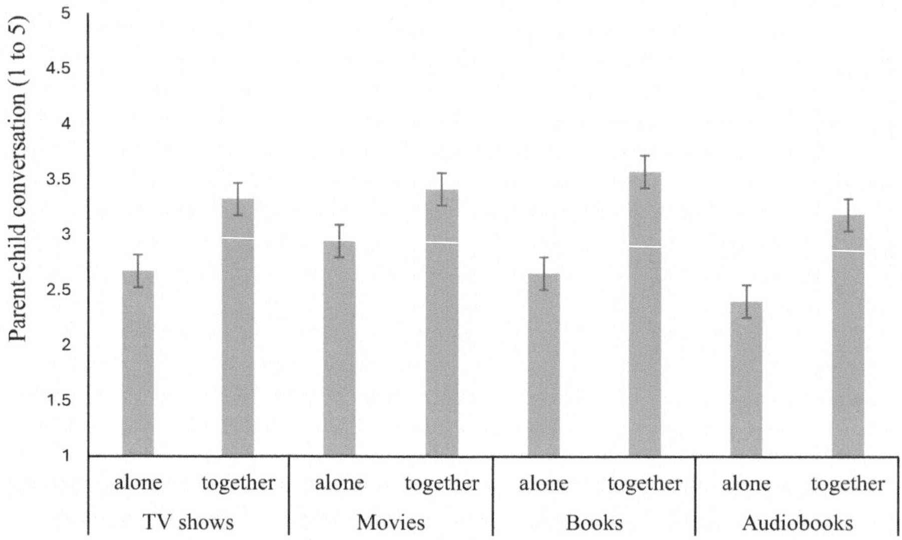

Fig. 2.2 Parent–child conversations about mental states during or after media exposure for the different media types and contexts for users only. *Note.* The figure depicts mean values and standard errors of the means

Compared to the whole sample, the differences between media types were less pronounced in the subsample of "users" only. Again, *parent–child conversations* about mental states occurred most frequently when parents and children engaged in book reading together (*books* together vs. other media types used together: *TV shows* together: $t(47) = 3.97$, $p < .001$, $d = 0.57$, 95% CI for d [0.27, 0.88]; *Movies* together: $t(39) = 2.49$, $p = .017$, $d = 0.39$, 95% CI for d [0.07, 0.71]; *Audiobooks* together: $t(24) = 2.89$, $p = .008$, $d = 0.58$, 95% CI for d [0.15, 1.00]).

Discussion

Summary and Interpretation

In the present study, we examined preschool children's *media use* concerning (a) the use of different types of media (*books, audiobooks, movies, TV shows*), (b) the context of *media use* (alone, together with the parents), and (c) *parent–child conversations* about mental states during *media use*. To do so, we conducted a questionnaire study with preschool children's parents.

Concerning children's *media use*, the results show that *books*, especially read together with the parents, were the medium most often used by children. *TV shows* came in second regarding their usage frequency. Compared to *books*, they were more frequently consumed by children alone. Overall, *movies* and *audiobooks* were less frequently used than *books* and *TV shows*. This resulted mainly from the observation that *audiobooks* were only rarely listened to by parents and their children together and *movies* were only seldom watched by children alone. Concerning the daily duration of *media use*, *TV shows*, when watched by children alone, were the medium that was used for the longest amount of time: almost half an hour on an average day. This is about the same amount of time as one episode of a TV show, including commercial breaks. Reading *books*, particularly by parents and children together, followed in daily duration.

By and large, these findings agree with the most recent *miniKim-study* (Medienpädagogischer Forschungsverbund Südwest, 2023), which found that children are exposed to a variety of different media types in their daily lives but that reading *books* is still the most common activity in many families. The *miniKim-study* also reported, comparable to our findings, that while parents and children typically read *books* together, *audiobooks* were listened to most frequently by children alone. Unfortunately, the *miniKIM-study 2023* did not differentiate between *TV shows* and *movies*, which ranged between *books* and *audiobooks*, limiting the comparability to our present results. Our finding that *audiobooks* and TV series were often used by children on their own also agrees with the notion that these types of media might be employed easily to allow parents to engage in other activities (e.g., cooking, cleaning) while their child is occupied. In their recent review on the effects of children's TV exposure, Kostyrka-Allchorne et al. (2017, p. 53) discuss this usage of TV as a "digital babysitter."

With regard to *parent–child conversations* about mental states, it was not surprising that those interactions mostly occurred when media types were used by children and parents together rather than when children consumed media on their own, with effect sizes ranging from small (*TV shows*) to medium (*movies*) and large (*books*). As expected, *parent–child conversations* occurred most frequently during shared reading of *books*. When only the "users" of each media type and context were analyzed, the differences between the different types of media became somewhat smaller, with effect sizes ranging from medium (*audiobooks*) to large (*TV shows*, *movies*, *books*). However, the higher frequency of *parent–child conversations* about mental states during shared *book* reading compared to joint consumption of *TV shows*, films, and *audiobooks*—with effect sizes once again ranging from medium (*TV shows*, *movies*) to large (*audiobooks*)—persisted even when only the "users" of each media type and context were considered—with effect sizes ranging from small (*movies*) to medium (*TV shows*, *audiobooks*). This also agrees with previous experimental (Lavigne et al., 2015; Nathanson & Rasmussen, 2011) and correlational studies (Tanimura et al., 2007) that found the quality and quantity of parental language to be reduced during TV consumption compared to free play and book reading. It also seems reasonable, as shared reading is probably the only form of media exposure where parents are in some way "forced" to focus on the content of the book because they either have to read the text aloud or make up a story fitting the images depicted in a picture book. Furthermore, many children's *books* are particularly rich regarding mental-state content (Cassidy et al., 1998; Dyer et al., 2000; Farkas et al., 2020), and it is much more comfortable to interrupt the reading process in order to take up these mental-state contents than it is to pause a running *TV show, movie, or audiobook*. Therefore, *books* appear to be a very valuable format in which stories for children can be presented. Of course, it is also possible that *books*, *audiobooks*, *TV shows*, and *movies* simply differ regarding mental-state content, although from a theoretical level, these media types should contain similar topics (Mar, 2018; Mar & Oatley, 2008). Unfortunately, to our knowledge, no such analyses comparing the content of different types of children's media have been conducted so far.

Although the SPaCEN framework (Mar, 2018) does not propose differential effects of different media types on recipients' social cognition, previous correlational research supports especially a positive association between exposure to children's *books* and children's social-cognitive development (Adrian et al., 2005; Lenhart & Richter, 2024; Mar et al., 2010). The associations for other types of media are either not well researched (e.g., *audiobooks*) or decidedly mixed (e.g., *TV shows* and *movies*) (for a recent discussion, see Lenhart & Richter, 2024). Given that we found that book reading was mostly a joint activity for parents and their children and that it stimulated most mental state talk, the association between book exposure and social-cognitive development seems likely. As those other media types were more often (than *books*) consumed alone and stimulated less *parent–child conversations* about mental states, we would expect less pronounced associations for those types of media. Interestingly, the differences in mental state talk seemed to be mostly driven by the differences in the context of *media use*. If the other types of media were used together by parents and their children, the differences in mental-state talk frequency were less pronounced. This trend was most strongly observable for *audiobooks*, where the differences to other types of media were much smaller when only the "users" were compared (see Fig. 2.2). Accordingly, those other media types might profit from increasing the time that the media types are used jointly by parents and children. However, this is only a tentative suggestion because as pointed out above for potential differences in content, the media types might also differ in other aspects relevant for beneficial media effects on children's social-cognitive development.

Limitations and Directions for Future Research

It is important to view the results and conclusions of this study with a certain amount of caution. One limiting factor of the present study is that it only used a relatively small sample, particularly when looking only at the "users." Furthermore, the investigated sample was a convenience sample, which is not representative for *media use* in the entirety of German preschoolers, especially regarding the representation of migration background and parents' educational background. Future research should aim to gather a larger, more diverse sample in order to enable a differentiated analysis of media content and accompanying parent–child talk.

Another limitation of the present study is the way data regarding children's media usage was collected. Different from Mar et al. (2010), who obtained data by using checklists, this study asked parents to provide an estimation of the minutes their children use the different media types every day. This proved to be not ideal as the manner in which parents answered this part of the questionnaire varied greatly in quality, with a substantial number of answers having to be substituted by approximations or having to be coded as missing because they could not be interpreted. In addition, both children's *media use* as well as the content and amount of parental discussions during media usage were assessed as self-report data in the form of a questionnaire from the parents' point of view only. Since the data were reported by parents themselves, it is also possible that parents might have overreported mental-state discussions during media usage due to perceived social desirability. Future research should use a less demanding measure of media duration, such as providing categories of use (e.g., "not at all," "0–30 minutes," or "30–60 minutes"), and the self-report data should be backed up by observational data on *media use* and *parent–child conversations*.

Finally, children's media usage has only been investigated with regard to the overall time spent with different types of media. Another factor that is highly relevant, given that only stories comprising mental-state content may foster social cognition (Mar, 2018), might be the precise content of *media used* by children. Accordingly, future research should not only focus on the amount of time children spend using certain media types but could also investigate media exposure with regard to mental-state themes. These mental-state themes included in the *books* as well as originating in accompanying parent–child discussion should be coded in a differentiated manner, for instance, separating desires, cognitions, emotions, physiological states and so on (e.g., Farkas et al., 2020), and related to specific aspects of children's social-cognitive development (e.g., emotion recognition, false belief understanding).

Conclusion

Summarizing the main results of the present study, we found that using media together, in particular by sharing *books*, was associated with the richest *parent–child conversations* about mental-state themes. Taken together with the finding that, in almost all families, parents and children read *books* together, this highlights the potential but also the practical role of shared book reading as a unique opportunity to talk about mental states. However, it has to be noted that across all media types and contexts, parental mediation of media content occurred on average only *rarely* to *sometimes*, indicating that parent–child discussions accompanying children's media exposure are not common in all situations and families. Aram et al. (2013) proposed that concrete instruction and guidance for parents might be necessary and important to encourage the inclusion of mental-state themes during shared reading. Schapira and Aram (2019) offer very valuable insights regarding what parents can do during shared reading in order to foster social cognition. They propose that parents should be encouraged to frequently elaborate on a story's plot, discuss social-emotional content and characters' feelings, encourage children's own input, and actively involve them during discussions about mental states. Those techniques might also be adapted to other types of media. The findings of the present study support these suggestions and emphasize that parents might also need to be made aware of the (perhaps) unknown potential of other types of media for parent–child discussion and a more deliberate and interactive use of children's media.

References

Adrian, J. E., Clemente, R. A., & Villanueva, L. (2007). Mothers' use of cognitive state verbs in picture-book reading and the development of children's understanding of mind: A longitudinal study. *Child Development, 78*(4), 1052–1067. https://doi.org/10.1111/j.1467-8624.2007.01052.x

Adrian, J. E., Clemente, R. A., Villanueva, L., & Rieffe, C. (2005). Parent-child picture-book reading, mothers' mental state language and children's theory of mind. *Journal of Child Language, 32*(3), 673–686. https://doi.org/10.1017/S0305000905006963

Aram, D., Fine, Y., & Ziv, M. (2013). Enhancing parent-child shared book reading interactions: Promoting references to the book's plot and socio-cognitive themes. *Early Childhood Research Quarterly, 28*(1), 111–122. https://doi.org/10.1016/j.ecresq.2012.03.005

Cassidy, K. W., Ball, L. V., Rourke, M. T., Werner, R. S., Feeny, N., Chu, J. Y., Lutz, D. J., & Perkins, A. (1998). Theory of mind concepts in children's literature. *Applied Psycholinguistics, 19*(3), 463–470. https://doi.org/10.1017/S0142716400010274

Cates, C. B., & Nicolopoulou, A. (2019). The effects of bookreading with and without mental state themes on preschoolers' theory of mind. In E. Veneziano & A. Nicolopoulou (Eds.), *Narrative, literacy and other skills: Studies in intervention* (pp. 129–149). John Benjamins. https://doi.org/10.1075/sin.25.07cat

de Rosnay, M., & Hughes, C. (2010). Conversation and theory of mind: Do children talk their way to socio-cognitive understanding? *British Journal of Developmental Psychology, 24*(1), 7–37. https://doi.org/10.1348/026151005X82901

Dodell-Feder, D., & Tamir, D. I. (2018). Fiction reading has a small positive impact on social cognition: A meta-analysis. *Journal of Experimental Psychology: General, 147*(11), 1713–1727. https://doi.org/10.1037/xge0000395

Dore, R. A., Amendum, S. J., Golinkoff, R. M., & Hirsh-Pasek, K. (2018). Theory of mind: A hidden factor in reading comprehension? *Educational Psychology Review, 30*, 1067–1089. https://doi.org/10.1007/s10648-018-9443-9

Dyer, J. R., Shatz, M., & Wellman, H. M. (2000). Young children's storybooks as a source of mental state information. *Cognitive Development, 15*(1), 17–37. https://doi.org/10.1016/S0885-2014(00)00017-4

Dyer-Seymour, J. R., Shatz, M., Wellman, H. M., & Saito, M. T. (2004). Mental state expressions in US and Japanese children's books. *International Journal of Behavioral Development, 28*(6), 546–552. https://doi.org/10.1080/01650250444000261

Farkas, C., Santelices, M. P., Vallotton, C. D., Brophy-Herb, H. E., Iglesias, M., Sieverson, C., del Pilar Cuellar, M., & Álvarez, C. (2020). Children's storybooks as a source of mental state references: Comparison between books from Chile, Colombia, Scotland and USA. *Cognitive Development, 53*, 100845. https://doi.org/10.1016/j.cogdev.2019.100845

Grazzani, I., Ornaghi, V., & Brockmeier, J. (2016). Conversation on mental states at nursery: Promoting social cognition in early childhood. *European Journal of Developmental Psychology, 13*(5), 563–581. https://doi.org/10.1080/17405629.2015.1127803

Happé, F., Cook, J. L., & Bird, G. (2017). The structure of social cognition: In(ter)dependence of sociocognitive processes. *Annual Review of Psychology, 68*, 243–267. https://doi.org/10.1146/annurev-psych-010416-044046

Kidd, D. C., & Castano, E. (2013). Reading literary fiction improves theory of mind. *Science, 342*(6156), 377–380. https://doi.org/10.1126/science.1239918

Kostyrka-Allchorne, K., Cooper, N. R., & Simpson, A. (2017). The relationship between television exposure and children's cognition and behaviour: A systematic review. *Developmental Review, 44*, 19–58. https://doi.org/10.1016/j.dr.2016.12.002

Lavigne, H. J., Hanson, K. G., & Anderson, D. R. (2015). The influence of television coviewing on parent language directed at toddlers. *Journal of Applied Developmental Psychology, 36*, 1–10. https://doi.org/10.1016/j.appdev.2014.11.004

Lenhart, J., Lenhard, W., Vaahtoranta, E., & Suggate, S. (2019). The effects of questions during shared-reading: Do demand-level and placement really matter? *Early Childhood Research Quarterly, 47*, 49–61. https://doi.org/10.1016/j.ecresq.2018.10.006

Lenhart, J., & Richter, T. (2024). Media exposure and preschoolers' social-cognitive development. *British Journal of Developmental Psychology, 42*(2), 234–256. https://doi.org/10.1111/bjdp.12478

Lenhart, J., Suggate, S., Lenhard, W., & Vaahtoranta, E. (2020). Shared-reading in small groups: Examining the effects of question demand level and placement. *Cognitive Development, 55*, Article 100914. https://doi.org/10.1016/j.cogdev.2020.100914

Mar, R. A. (2018). Evaluating whether stories can promote social cognition: Introducing the social processes and content entrained by narrative (SPaCEN) framework. *Discourse Processes, 55*, 454–479. https://doi.org/10.1080/0163853X.2018.1448209

Mar, R. A., & Oatley, K. (2008). The function of fiction is the abstraction and simulation of social experience. *Perspectives on Psychological Science, 3*(3), 173–192. https://doi.org/10.1111/j.1745-6924.2008.00073.x

Mar, R. A., Tackett, J. L., & Moore, C. (2010). Exposure to media and theory-of-mind development in preschoolers. *Cognitive Development, 25*(1), 69–78. https://doi.org/10.1016/j.cogdev.2009.11.002

Medienpädagogischer Forschungsverbund Südwest. (2023). *miniKIM-Studie 2023. Kleinkinder und Medien. Basisuntersuchung zum Medienumgang 2- bis 5-Jähriger in Deutschland* [miniKIM-study 2023. Children and media. Basis investigation of 2- to 5-year-old children's media consumption in Germany]. https://www.mpfs.de/fileadmin/files/Studien/miniKIM/2023/miniKIM2023_web.pdf

Mumper, M. L., & Gerrig, R. J. (2017). Leisure reading and social cognition: A meta-analysis. *Psychology of Aesthetics, Creativity, and the Arts, 11*(1), 109–120. https://doi.org/10.1037/aca0000089

Nathanson, A. I., & Fries, P. T. (2014). Television exposure, sleep time, and neuropsychological function among preschoolers. *Media Psychology, 17*(3), 237–261. https://doi.org/10.1080/15213269.2014.915197

Nathanson, A. I., & Rasmussen, E. E. (2011). TV viewing compared to book reading and toy playing reduces responsive maternal communication with toddlers and preschoolers. *Human Communication Research, 37*(4), 465–487. https://doi.org/10.1111/j.1468-2958.2011.01413.x

Nathanson, A. I., Sharp, M. L., Aladé, F., Rasmussen, E. E., & Christy, K. (2013). The relation between television exposure and theory of mind among preschoolers. *Journal of Communication, 63*(6), 1088–1108. https://doi.org/10.1111/jcom.12062

Oatley, K. (1999). Meeting of minds: Dialogue, sympathy, and identification, in reading fiction. *Poetics, 26*(5-6), 439–454. https://doi.org/10.1016/S0304-422X(99)00011-X

Oatley, K. (2016). Fiction: Simulation of social worlds. *Trends in Cognitive Sciences, 20*(8), 618–628. https://doi.org/10.1016/j.tics.2016.06.002

Petermann, F., & Gust, N. (2016). *EMK 3-6: Inventar zur Erfassung emotionaler Kompetenzen bei Drei- bis Sechsjährigen*. Hogrefe.

Poulain, T., Ludwig, J., Hiemisch, A., Hilbert, A., & Kiess, W. (2019). Media use of mothers, media use of children, and parent-child interaction are related to behavioral difficulties and strengths of children. *International Journal of Environmental Research and Public Health, 16*(23), 4651. https://doi.org/10.3390/ijerph16234651

Schapira, R., & Aram, D. (2019). Shared book reading at home and preschoolers' socio-emotional competence. *Early Education and Development, 31*(6), 819–837. https://doi.org/10.1080/10409289.2019.1692624

Sénéchal, M., & LeFevre, J. (2003). Parental involvement in the development of children's reading skill: A five-year longitudinal study. *Child Development, 73*(2), 445–460. https://doi.org/10.1111/1467-8624.00417

Statistisches Bundesamt. (2022a). Allgemeine Schulausbildung: *Bevölkerung nach Alter und Geschlecht (bis 2019) [General school education: Population by age and gender (until 2019)].* https://www-genesis.destatis.de/genesis/online?sequenz=tabelleErgebnis&selectionname=12211-9012&transponieren=true#abreadcrumb

Statistisches Bundesamt. (2022b). *Bevölkerung in Privathaushalten 2021 nach Migrationshintergrund* [Population in private households in 2021 by migration background]. https://www.destatis.de/DE/Themen/Gesellschaft-Umwelt/Bevoelkerung/Migration-Integration/Tabellen/migrationshintergrund-alter.html

Symons, D. K., Peterson, C. C., Slaughter, V., Roche, J., & Doyle, E. (2010). Theory of mind and mental state discourse during book reading and story-telling tasks. *British Journal of Developmental Psychology, 23*(1), 81–102. https://doi.org/10.1348/026151004X21080

Tanimura, M., Okuma, K., & Kyoshima, K. (2007). Television viewing, reduced parental utterance, and delayed speech development in infants and young children. *Archives of Pediatrics and Adolescent Medicine, 161*(6), 618–619. https://doi.org/10.1001/archpedi.161.6.618-b

Taumoepeau, M., & Ruffman, T. (2006). Mother and infant talk about mental states relates to desire language and emotion understanding. *Child Development, 77*(2), 465–481. https://doi.org/10.1111/j.1467-8624.2006.00882.x

Taumoepeau, M., & Ruffman, T. (2008). Stepping stones to others' minds: Maternal talk relates to child mental state language and emotion understanding at 15, 24, and 33 months. *Child Development, 79*(2), 284–302. https://doi.org/10.1111/j.1467-8624.2007.01126.x

Tompkins, V. (2015). Improving low-income preschoolers' theory of mind: A training study. *Cognitive Development, 36*, 1–19. https://doi.org/10.1016/j.cogdev.2015.07.001

Wellman, H. M. (2002). Understanding the psychological world: Developing a theory of mind. In U. Goswami (Ed.), *Blackwell Handbook of Childhood Cognitive Development* (pp. 167–187). Blackwell. https://doi.org/10.1002/9780470996652.ch8

West, R. F., Stanovich, K. E., & Mitchell, H. R. (1993). Reading in the real world and its correlates. *Reading Research Quarterly, 28*(1), 34–50. https://psycnet.apa.org/doi/10.2307/747815

Wimmer, L., Currie, G., Friend, S., Wittwer, J., & Ferguson, H. J. (2024). Cognitive effects and correlates of reading fiction: Two preregistered multilevel meta-analyses. *Journal of Experimental Psychology: General, 153*(6), 1464–1488. https://doi.org/10.1037/xge0001583

Zunshine, L. (2006). *Why we read fiction: Theory of mind and the novel*. Ohio State University Press.

Katharina Deckert studied teaching at the University of Bamberg (Germany) and holds a teaching degree in Psychology and English. She currently works as a research assistant in the research project *Digitale Kulturen der Lehre entwickeln (DiKuLe)* and is a PhD student at the Chair of English Linguistics at the University of Bamberg (Germany). Her research focuses on using corpus literacy and artificial intelligence for error detection and correction in learner English at the university level.

Jan Lenhart studied Psychology (B.Sc. and M.Sc.) as well as History and Political and Social Studies (B.A.) at the University of Würzburg (Germany). He obtained a PhD in Psychology from the University of Würzburg. He currently works as a Professor of Educational Psychology at the University of Bamberg (Germany). His research focuses on early education and development, primarily on children's language and social-emotional development.

Chapter 3
The Character Matters: Exploring Adult–Child Discourse in Shared Reading of Books with Animal vs. Human Protagonists

Dorit Aram, Inbar Avman Wolff, Sigalit Aviram-Brill, Yeal Roth-Barkai, and Anat Zaidman Zait

Contents

In Western society, shared book reading (SBR) is part of early childhood daily routines at home and in educational settings (Aram & Aviram, 2009; Zucker et al., 2013). The richness of adult–child discourse during SBR has significance for early childhood development (e.g., Schapira & Aram, 2020). Furthermore, the nature of parent–child discourse during book reading relates to the book's characteristics (Schapira et al., 2021). Book reading distances the reader from the situation and facilitates discussion about the character's feelings, motivations, and behaviors. Many books for young children contain animal characters that are anthropomorphized. In these books, the animals talk and engage in "human-like"

D. Aram (✉)
Constantiner School of Education, Tel Aviv University, Tel Aviv, Israel
e-mail: dorita@tauex.tau.ac.il

I. Avman Wolff · A. Zaidman Zait
Tel Aviv University, Tel Aviv, Israel

S. Aviram-Brill
Tel Aviv University, Tel Aviv, Israel

Beit Berl College, Beit Berl, Israel

Y. Roth-Barkai
The Academic College Levinsky-Wingate, Tel Aviv, Israel

R. Schapira, D. Aram (eds.), *Shared Book Reading and Children's Social-Emotional Competence*, https://doi.org/10.1007/978-3-032-14688-5_3

activities (Larsen et al., 2018). A topic that has not yet been addressed in research is how the characters' nature (human vs. animal) relates to the style of adult–child discourse during book reading. This chapter presents two studies of SBR. Each study employed a comparative methodology wherein readers (preservice teachers and parents) presented children with two books: one featuring human characters and another featuring animal characters. This chapter focuses on the distinctions between character types (human versus animal), examining the contribution of books with different protagonists to the nature of the adult–child discourse.

The Importance of SBR Discourse

Reading books to children is integral to daily adult–child interactions in educational settings and at home (e.g., Bergman Deitcher et al., 2017; Håland et al., 2020; He & Bowman, 2021). Children's books present a variety of social situations from the child's world, where characters are motivated by mental states such as desires, emotions, intentions, and beliefs. During reading, adults engage in meaningful discourse with children about the story's events, characters' feelings, and relationships, helping children construct understanding and meaning from the narrative (e.g., Schapira & Aram, 2020).

High-quality discourse during SBR is characterized by elaborations, open-ended questions, prediction questions, referring to mental states, relating the story to the child's life, etc. Children learn most effectively from books when they are actively involved in the reading process, and those who experience rich verbal interaction during SBR tend to derive more pleasure and show increased interest in reading later in childhood (e.g., Blewitt & Langan, 2016).

Research has consistently shown that the quality of this discourse significantly impacts children's development. A meta-analysis of 16 studies involving 626 children demonstrated that interactive reading—engaging children in dialogue about the text—significantly enhanced vocabulary growth compared to traditional reading approaches (Mol et al., 2009). Rich discourse during SBR has a positive relationship with brain activation among preschool children, supporting development in areas such as language (Noble et al., 2019) and social-emotional understanding (e.g., Cates & Nicolopoulou, 2019; Schapira & Aram, 2020). Moreover, parents' conversations with their children about characters' thoughts, feelings, and intentions while reading books contribute to developing theory of mind, morality, and empathy (e.g., Aram et al., 2017).

Aspects of the Book That Influence SBR Discourse

The book itself can significantly influence the nature of adult–child discourse during shared reading (Moschovaki & Meadows, 2005; Nyhout & O'Neill, 2013). For instance, research has shown that wordless picture books elicit richer discourse compared to books with text (Smadja et al., 2019; Ziv et al., 2013, 2014). Similarly, informational books have been found to promote broader and more in-depth discussions than narrative books (Bergman Deitcher et al., 2019a; Lennox, 2013). Mothers elaborate more when the book's central theme is related to "negative" emotions (e.g., anger, sadness) compared to books surrounding "positive" emotions (e.g., love, happiness) (Schapira et al., 2021).

Even within the same genre, book structure and content variations can lead to differences in reading styles. For example, in alphabet books, mothers engaged in more expansive discourse when the books contained fewer words and illustrations per page. These books prompted parents to focus more on the writing system and narrative elements and to actively seek their children's reactions during reading. In contrast, "busy" books with dense illustrations encouraged greater attention to the visual content, with parents frequently referencing the illustrations (Bergman Deitcher et al., 2019b). Determining the influence of key properties of books on the nature of adult–child discourse is important. With this in mind, we focus in this chapter on an aspect of the book's character—*anthropomorphism*—specifically, being an animal or human.

Anthropomorphism: Human vs. Animal Main Characters

Anthropomorphism is an element in children's literature. This literary device attributes human characteristics—including cognitive processes, emotional experiences, motivations, and behavioral patterns—to non-human entities such as animals or objects (e.g., Severson & Lemm, 2016). This imaginative transformation allows young readers to engage with familiar human experiences through the lens of non-human characters.

Reading a book inherently creates a sense of *psychological distance*, allowing readers to step away from their immediate experiences and engage in discussions about the characters' emotions, motivations, and behaviors. This distancing effect enables children to adopt a more neutral perspective, reducing the influence of their current emotional or physiological state on their thought processes (Lee & Atance, 2016).

The bibliotherapy approach highlights the power of books to create emotional distance and elicit rich discourse that this distance can inspire (Dughi & Cotrău, 2014). This therapeutic process fosters self-growth, understanding, and healing, with its primary objectives being to share information, provide insight, encourage discussion of new emotions and values, and demonstrate that others face similar challenges and find solutions (Kanewischer, 2013). Children's literature can be used therapeutically to facilitate emotional growth and healing (Heath et al., 2005).

Within this framework, animals in children's literature play a crucial role in alleviating fears, bolstering self-confidence, and strengthening the parent–child bond (Cohen, 1990). In many children's books, the main characters are animals. Marriot (2002) studied 1074 modern picture books and found that animals were characters in 521 of the books (48.5%), and animal characters can serve as symbolic role models for children (Suvilehto, 2019). Books featuring animals as protagonists, rather than human characters, provide a means for children to indirectly engage with thoughts and emotions that may be troubling or difficult to confront.

A few studies explored the strength of human and animal characters in promoting children's prosocial behavior. Larsen et al. (2018) found that stories with human characters promote prosocial behavior in young children more effectively than stories with anthropomorphized animal characters. Likewise, Balci et al. (2024) found that reading storybooks with human characters increases children's costly sharing behavior (generosity) more than reading storybooks with anthropomorphized animal or fantasy characters. However, Russell and Cain (2022) experimentally demonstrated that animal characters can influence children's prosocial behavior similarly to human characters.

The present chapter examines the nature of adult–child discourse during the SBR of books addressing social situations. Two themes are explored: birthday party celebrations and sibling relationships. For each theme, two books are analyzed—one featuring human protagonists and the other featuring animal protagonists. The focus is on the adult–child discourse, particularly the adults' contributions beyond the story text, with a comparison of the discourse when the protagonist is a human versus an animal.

Study 1

Method

Participants

Participants included 40 pre-service special education teachers. All the participants were female and ranged in age from 23 to 44 ($M = 26.58$, $SD = 3.71$). In total, participants read two books (in random order) with 120 children (66 boys, 54 girls) in early elementary school ($M = 7.85$ years, $SD = 0.65$). Each pre-service teacher read to three children individually.

Shared Book Reading

The books were selected as having similar lengths (approximately 580 words), genres (both are narratives), and topics (the story was about a birthday party). However, one book's main characters were animals, while the characters of the second book were human. "Frog's Very Special Day" (Velthuijs, 2000) tells the story of a frog whose animal friends make him a surprise birthday party, and "A Special Girl" (Hellman, 1997) tells the story of a girl with a hearing disability who has a birthday party. All the SBR meetings were recorded, transcribed, and coded by a Ph.D. and two M.A. students in Education.

Coding of SBR Discourse

We coded the preservice teachers' extratextual utterances. The coding system was based on previous SBR studies (Levin & Aram, 2012). The unit of analysis was an utterance, which contains semantic information and is limited by intonation without focusing on grammatical or syntactic correctness (Berman & Lustigman, 2012). We counted pre-service teachers' elaborations, references to the child's life, general knowledge, print concepts, and vocabulary, as detailed below.

- Elaboration: Utterances beyond the written story, like explanations of concepts or situations, including examples and transfer to other contexts. For example, the girl in the story had a hearing aid, and the preservice teacher said, "You can turn off the devices, and then she does not hear anything."
- The child's life: Utterances that relate the story to the child's life. For example: "Have you ever had a surprise birthday party?" "Do you know anyone with a hearing aid?"
- General knowledge: References to general knowledge unrelated to the books' plots. For example: "Usually when there are clouds, the weather is cold."
- Print concepts: Utterances that refer to the name of the book, the name of the author/illustrator, page numbers, reading from right to left (Hebrew), distinguishing between illustrations and text, etc. For example, "Max Velthuijs is the author's name," and "The name of this book is A Special Girl."
- Vocabulary: Utterances that refer to and explain unfamiliar words. For example, "That is right. A recitation is like a song only without a melody."

The coders coded 15% of the transcripts to establish inter-rater reliability between the three coders. The level of agreement between raters was high, ranging between 98% and 100%.

Results

We examined how the book type (Animal vs. Human) predicted the discourse during SBR. Given that our measures consisted of count data with large standard deviations following a Poisson distribution and included repeated measurements, we utilized Generalized Estimation Equations (GEE) with a Negative Binomial Distribution (NBD) model for our analysis (e.g., Hanley et al., 2003; Hilbe, 2011). This nonlinear regression method was particularly suitable for handling our data structure. Table 3.1 presents the descriptive results and the GEEs comparing the two books.

Results revealed that the protagonist's nature (human versus animal) significantly influenced the discourse between preservice teachers and children during book reading sessions. When reading about a human protagonist (a girl), the discourse was richer than sessions featuring an animal protagonist (a frog). With the human protagonist, preservice teachers elaborated more, made more connections to

Table 3.1 Preservice teachers' SBR discourse when reading the two books (frog/girl)

Protagonist	Elaborations *M* (*SE*)		Child's life *M* (*SE*)		General knowledge *M* (*SE*)		Print concepts *M* (*SE*)		Vocabulary *M* (*SE*)	
Human	3.85 (1.30)		5.58 (2.15)		1.32 (.68)		2.31 (1.45)		1.45 (1.63)	
Animal	3.21 (1.13)		3.49 (1.41)		0.72 (.41)		1.71 (1.06)		1.224 (1.27)	
	Wald χ^2	**B**	**Wald χ^2**	**B**	**Wald χ^2**	**B**	**Wald χ^2**	**B**	**Wald χ^2**	**B**
	4.64*	.18	15.27***	.47	11.62**	.62	8.15**	.30	.59	.17

Note. N = 40
*p <.05; ** p <.1; *** p <.001

children's personal experiences, and drew broader connections to the world. Notably, they also related more to print concepts and vocabulary.

Study 2

Method

Participants

Participants were 54 pairs of parents (108 parents), including a mother and father living together and 2 of their children (43 boys and 65 girls). The parents' ages ranged from 27.5 to 45 (M = 37.72, SD = 3.30). Most of the parents held an academic diploma (84%). The siblings' ages ranged from 2½ to 7 (M = 4.76 years, SD = 6.11), with the older child between 5 and 7 years (M = 5.77 years, SD = 5.70) and the younger child between 2½ and 5 years (M = 3.66 years, SD = 6.72). Each parent was videotaped at home (on separate days) while reading a book to two of their children (one older and one younger).

Shared Book Reading

The two books have similar genres (narrative) and topics. They both focus on relationships between siblings and describe how they move from teasing, envy, and discomfort to help and collaboration. The book Ktana (Meserve, 2007) describes the relationship between two human sisters. The book Ginger (Voake, 1997) describes the relationship between two cats.

We developed a coding tool to assess parent–child interactions based on previous SBR research and its emotional dimensions (Ziv et al., 2014). These interactions were analyzed using the ATLAS software (Hwang, 2008). As in Study 1 described above, the unit of analysis was an utterance. We referred to general aspects of parent–child discourse and central themes in the discourse.

General Discourse

- Parents' input: We counted parents' extratextual utterances. For example: "Here is the little cat" or "Good relations are important."
- Children's input: We counted the children's utterances, such as "I feel happy too" or "Here is the parrot."
- Emotions: We counted parents' specific references to emotions, such as, "Are you jealous of your older sister too?" or "You can see that she is sad."

Thematic Analysis

We focused on categorizing the discourse content into specific themes raised during the SBR. The themes related to the plots and relationships between siblings are as follows:

- Comparisons between the characters within the books. For example, "What did the little girl succeed in that her older sister did not?"
- Relating the books' characters to the family siblings. For example, "The kitten is silly all day, just like you sometimes are silly too."
- Family position. For example, "Do you always follow Imri because he is your older brother?"

Two coders (Ph.D. and MA students) coded transcripts of 15% of the sample to establish inter-rater reliability. The level of agreement between raters ranged between 85% and 95%. Disagreements were resolved through discussion.

Results

We examined how the book type (Animal vs. Human) predicted the discourse during SBR. As in the first study, due to our count data following a Poisson distribution with large standard deviations and repeated measurements, we used Generalized Estimation Equations (GEE) with a Negative Binomial Distribution model to study the differences between the two books. Table 3.2 focuses on the general measures of the discourse and presents the comparisons between the books.

Results showed that the protagonist's nature (a child or an animal) is significant to the nature of the parent–child general discourse when reading the book. The discourse was richer when the protagonists were human—two sisters compared to the two cats. Both parents and children elaborated and talked more (beyond the text) when sharing the story about the two sisters. Also, parents referred more specifically to emotions when the protagonist was human.

We used Generalized Estimation Equations (GEE) with a Negative Binomial Distribution model to study the differences between the main themes in the two books. Table 3.3 presents the differential patterns of thematic references between the two books.

Table 3.2 Differences in SBR discourse during the reading of the two books (cats/girls)

	Number of utterances					
Protagonist	Parents *M* (*SE*)		Children *M* (*SE*)		Emotions *M* (*SE*)	
Human	41.02 (3.60)		34.86 (3.26)		7.95 (1.02)	
Animal	34.40 (2.80)		27.46 (2.68)		4.62 (0.68)	
	Wald χ^2	**B**	**Wald χ^2**	**B**	**Wald χ^2**	**B**
	4.57*	−.17	8.07**	−.24	11.19**	−.54

Note. N = 108
p* <.05; ** *p* <.01; * *p* <.001

Results showed that the protagonist's nature (a child or an animal) is significant to the themes raised during the SBR interactions. When telling the story of the two sisters, the parents elaborated and related to the two characters in the books. They related the plot to the children's lives by referring more specifically to emotions when the protagonist was human.

The discourse in the book about human characters (sisters) was richer than that in the book about animal characters (cats). While reading the book about human characters, parents expanded on the relationship between the two characters and their comparison more than in the book with animal characters. They also connected the book more to the children's lives (their siblings to whom they read the books). In the book about the two sisters, they talked about the similarities between the sisters in the story and the siblings in their family. Also, in the book about the two sisters, parents addressed the roles of older siblings compared to the younger siblings more than in the book about the two cat brothers.

Discussion

The studies presented in this chapter aimed to explore differences in adult–child discourse characteristics when reading books that depict social situations based on how the identity of the main characters—human vs. animal—influenced the discourse. Analysis of the discourse patterns during SBR revealed significant protagonist-dependent variations in educational and familial contexts. In the educational setting, when reading the book about the girl's birthday, pre-service teachers exhibited significantly higher frequencies of elaborative statements, world knowledge references, connections to student experiences, book-oriented utterances, and references to vocabulary compared to the book about the frog's birthday. This pattern of enhanced discourse complexity was paralleled in the home environment, where parent–child dyads exhibited increased verbal engagement during readings of narratives with human protagonists. When reading the book about the two sisters, parents and children talked more, and parents referred more to emotions. The thematic analysis of parental discourse revealed that during the book about the sisters, parents tended toward comparative character analysis, specifically emphasizing

Table 3.3 Themes discussed during the reading of the two books (cats/girls)

Protagonist	Comparing the book's characters *M* (*SE*)		Relating the books' characters to the siblings *M* (*SE*)		Family position (older/younger) *M* (*SE*)	
Human	1.51 (0.31)		3.57 (0.55)		2.05 (0.52)	
Animal	0.52 (0.17)		2.22 (0.38)		0.59 (0.16)	
	Wald χ^2	**B**	**Wald χ^2**	**B**	**Wald χ^2**	**B**
	8.37**	−1.07	3.89*	−.47	12.96***	−1.24

Note. $N = 108$

*$p < .05$; *** $p < .001$

sibling dynamics and familial hierarchies more than when reading the book about the cats. These findings suggest that protagonist characteristics are meaningful to adult–child discourse.

Reading a book creates *psychological distance*, facilitating discussions about characters' emotions, motivations, and behaviors (Oatley, 2016). While books inherently provide psychological distancing that encourages parent–child discourse more than other daily parent–child interactions (Clemens & Kegel, 2021), the degree and nature of this distancing appear to vary systematically across different narrative frameworks. Our chapter suggests that books addressing everyday childhood experiences—such as sibling relationships or birthday celebrations—featuring human protagonists may elicit richer discourse during shared reading than those with anthropomorphized animal characters, potentially due to achieving optimal *psychological distance*. For example, parents might discuss a book about sibling conflicts and collaboration with their own children (siblings), using the distancing provided by the book's fictional context to foster identification with the characters. Maybe animals provide too much distance so that the adults and the children relate less to them. This balance of distancing and relatability may explain why the discussions were richer with human characters.

The results of the two studies in our chapter might align with observed patterns wherein parents demonstrate enhanced elaborative discourse during informational text reading compared to narrative text engagement (Robertson & Reese, 2017). Books featuring child protagonists may occupy an intermediate position between purely fictional and informational texts in terms of perceived *psychological distance*. Conversely, narratives featuring anthropomorphized animals—such as cats' relationships or a frog's birthday celebration—may exceed optimal *psychological distance* thresholds, inhibiting rich adult–child discourse during shared reading experiences.

Additionally, children may be more drawn to books featuring human characters. Despite the common assumption that children are strongly attracted to fantasy worlds, many children exhibit significant interest in realistic stories. When presented with choices between factual and fictional narratives, children aged 4–7 demonstrated a significant preference for authentic accounts (Barnes et al., 2015). It may be that in the studies described in this chapter, children showed greater interest in books with human characters, which in turn enhanced adult–child discourse observed during readings featuring human protagonists.

Empirical evidence suggests that text characteristics significantly influence children's learning outcomes and transfer abilities, with realistic characters facilitating more explicit and direct learning (Strouse et al., 2018). Related research examining parent–child discourse in zoological settings revealed that while parents frequently anthropomorphized animals, children aged 3–8 rarely engaged in such anthropomorphization (Geerdts, 2016). Given the spectrum of animal representation in children's literature—ranging from realistic to fantastical—preschool-aged children may experience difficulty navigating the fantasy-reality distinction (McCrindle & Odendaal, 1994). While children readily engage in animal-themed play, human protagonists may facilitate more direct personal connections. This aligns with experimental findings demonstrating increased prosocial sharing behaviors among children aged 4–6 when exposed to narratives with human protagonists, contrasted with decreased sharing following exposure to animal protagonists (Larsen et al., 2018). The researchers hypothesized that animal characters may impede social skill acquisition through picture books, whereas human protagonists facilitate enhanced behavioral modeling and message implementation.

Regarding thematic analysis of parental discourse patterns, the findings suggest that parents expanded their discussions more when reading the book about sisters. They compared the two sisters, linked the storyline to their children's lives, and discussed family relationships. They leveraged the narrative framework to explore role differentiation and sibling positioning with their children. They connected the story to their own family dynamics. Research indicates that sibling relationships provide foundational experiences for emotional and social skill development (Pickering & Sanders, 2017). Children's literature that focuses on sibling relationships can prompt parents to initiate conversations on these topics and serve as a model for family interactions and the role of parents in these interactions. Human protagonists may reduce cognitive demands associated with text-to-life connections, allowing parents to draw more readily from familial experiences without requiring extensive imaginative bridging.

In conclusion, the empirical findings presented in this chapter expand our theoretical understanding of a daily context—shared book reading between adults and children. SBR constitutes a rich environmental affordance for quality adult–child interactions, facilitating discourse about life events and social situations while promoting multiple developmental domains. The quality of discourse during shared reading has been empirically linked to literacy acquisition, cognitive development, and social-emotional competencies.

This chapter's focal analysis of protagonist characteristics illuminates the differential patterns of adult–child discourse across varying character frameworks. The observed disparity in discourse richness between narratives featuring human versus animal protagonists provides interesting insights into the mediating role of character representation in shared reading interactions. These findings suggest the importance of raising awareness among educators and parents regarding the influence of protagonist characteristics on their discourse patterns with children. Specifically, the tendency toward reduced elaborative discourse during readings featuring anthropomorphized animals merits particular attention in professional development and parental guidance contexts. Enhanced awareness of these discourse patterns may facilitate more intentional and adult–child interactions across diverse literary genres and character frameworks. These findings underscore the continued importance of promoting evidence-based shared reading practices emphasizing rich, developmentally supportive discourse patterns across different narratives.

References

Aram, D., & Aviram, S. (2009). Mothers' Storybook Reading and Kindergartners' Socioemotional and Literacy Development. *Reading Psychology, 30*(2), 175–194. https://doi.org/10.1080/02702710802275348

Aram, D., Bergman Deitcher, D., Sabag-Shushan, T., & Ziv, M. (2017). Shared book reading interactions within families from low socioeconomic backgrounds and children's social understanding and prosocial behavior. *Journal of Cognitive Education and Psychology, 16*(2), 157–177. https://doi.org/10.1891/1945-8959.16.2.157

Balci, A. C., Kotaman, H., & Topuz İn, B. (2024). Impact of type of storybook character on children's costly sharing behavior. *European Journal of Developmental Psychology*. https://doi.org/10.1080/17405629.2024.2335105

Barnes, J. L., Bernstein, E., & Bloom, P. (2015). Fact or fiction? Children's preferences for real versus make-believe stories. *Imagination, Cognition and Personality*. https://doi.org/10.1177/0276236614568632

Bergman Deitcher, D., Johnson, H., & Aram, D. (2019a). Does book genre matter? Boys' and girls' word learning from narrative and informational books in the preschool years. *Journal of Research in Reading, 42*(3), 193–211. https://doi.org/10.1111/1467-9817.12266

Bergman Deitcher, D., Aram, D., & Goldberg, A. (2019b). Alphabet books: The nature of parents' shared reading between and across books. *Journal of Early Childhood Literacy, 42*(1), 193–211. https://doi.org/10.1177/1468798418814103

Bergman Deitcher, D., Aram, D., & Adar, G. (2017). Book selection for shared reading: Parents' considerations and researchers' views. *Journal of Early Childhood Literacy*, 1–25. https://doi.org/10.1177/1468798417718236

Blewitt, P., & Langan, R. J. (2016). Learning words during shared book reading: The role of extratextual talk designed to increase child engagement. *Journal of Experimental Child Psychology, 150*, 404–410. https://doi.org/10.1016/j.jecp.2016.06.009

Cates, C. B., & Nicolopoulou, A. (2019). The effects of book reading with and without mental state themes on preschoolers' theory of mind. In E. Veneziano & A. Nicolopoulou (Eds.), *Narrative, literacy and other skills: Studies in Intervention* (pp. 129–150). I John Benjamins. http://digital.casalini.it/9789027262912

Clemens, L. F., & Kegel, C. A. (2021). Unique contribution of shared book reading on adult-child language interaction. *Journal of Child Language, 48*(2), 373–386. https://doi.org/10.1017/S0305000920000331

Cohen, A. (1990). *Bibliotherapy*. Ach.

Dughi, T., & Cotrău, S. (2014). Child development through bibliotherapy. *Journal Plus Education, 10*(1), 239–250. https://www.uav.ro/jour/index.php/jpe/article/view/233

Geerdts, M. S. (2016). (Un)real animals: Anthropomorphism and early learning about animals. *Child Development Perspectives, 10*(1), 10–14. https://doi.org/10.1111/cdep.12153

Håland, A., Hoem, T. F., & McTigue, E. M. (2020). The quantity and quality of teachers' self-perceptions of read-aloud practices in NORWEGIAN first grade classrooms. *Early Childhood Education Journal*. https://doi.org/10.1007/s10643-020-01053-5

Hanley, J. A., Negassa, A., Edwardes, M. D., & Forrester, J. E. (2003). Statistical analysis of correlated data using generalized estimating equations: An orientation. *American Journal of Epidemiology, 157*, 364–375. https://doi.org/10.1093/aje/kwf215

Heath, M. A., Sheen, D., Leavy, D., Young, E., & Money, K. (2005). Bibliotherapy: A resource to facilitate emotional healing and growth. *School Psychology International, 26*(5), 563–580. https://doi.org/10.1177/0143034305060792

He, K., & Bowman, Y. Z. (2021). Association between teachers' shared book reading strategies and children's vocabulary development in rural China preschools. *Journal of Chinese Writing Systems, 5*(3), 185–193. https://doi.org/10.1177/25138502211025643

Hellman, A. (1997). (A special girl). *Yalda meyouchedet bmina.* Am-Oved. [Hebrew].

Hilbe, J. M. (2011). *Negative binomial regression* (2nd ed.). Cambridge University Press.

Hwang, S. (2008). Utilizing qualitative data analysis software: A review of Atlas.ti. *Social Science Computer Review, 26*(4), 519–527. https://doi.org/10.1177/0894439307312485

Kanewischer, E. W. (2013). Do you ever feel that way? A story and activities about families and feelings. *Journal of Creativity in Mental Health, 8*(1), 70–80. https://doi.org/10.1080/15401383.2013.763686

Larsen, N. E., Lee, K., & Ganea, P. A. (2018). Do storybooks with anthropomorphized animal characters promote prosocial behaviors in young children? *Developmental Science, 21*(3), e12590. https://doi.org/10.1111/desc.12590

Lee, W. S., & Atance, C. M. (2016). The effect of psychological distance on children's reasoning about future preferences. *PLoS One, 11*, 1–18. https://doi.org/10.1371/journal.pone.0164382

Lennox, S. (2013). Interactive read-alouds—an avenue for enhancing children's language for thinking and understanding: a review of recent research. *Early Childhood Education Journal, 41*, 381–389. https://doi.org/10.1007/s10643-013-0578-5

Levin, I., & Aram, D. (2012). Mother–child joint writing and storybook reading and their effects on kindergartners' literacy: An intervention study. *Reading and Writing, 25*, 217–249. https://doi.org/10.1007/s11145-010-9254-y

Lustigman, L. (2012). 4 HARSP: A developmental language profile for Hebrew. In M. Ball, D. Crystal, & P. Fletcher (Eds.), *Assessing grammar: The languages of LARSP* (pp. 43–76). Multilingual Matters. https://doi.org/10.21832/9781847696397-006

Marriott, S. (2002). Red in tooth and claw? Images of nature in modern picture books. *Children's Literature in Education, 33*, 175–183. https://doi.org/10.1023/A:1019677931406

Meserve, J. (2007). Kittle one (*Ktana*). Maariv. [Hebrew].

McCrindle, C. M., & Odendaal, J. S. (1994). Animals in books are used for preschool children. *Anthrozoös, 7*(2), 135–146. https://doi.org/10.2752/089279394787057561

Mol, S. E., Bus, A. G., & de Jong, M. T. (2009). Interactive book reading in early education: A tool to stimulate print knowledge as well as oral language. *Review of Educational Research, 79*(2), 979–1007. https://doi.org/10.3102/0034654309332561

Moschovaki, E., & Meadows, S. (2005). Young children's spontaneous participation during classroom book reading: Differences according to various types of books. *Early Childhood Research & Practice, 7*(1), n1. https://eric.ed.gov/?id=EJ1084884

Noble, C., Sala, G., Peter, M., Lingwood, J., Rowland, C., Gobet, F., & Pine, J. (2019). The impact of shared book reading on children's language skills: A meta-analysis. *Educational Research Review, 28*(October 2018), 100290. https://doi.org/10.1016/j.edurev.2019.100290

Nyhout, A., & O'Neill, D. K. (2013). Mothers' complex talk when sharing books with their toddlers: Book genre matters. *First Language, 33*(2), 115–131. https://doi.org/10.1177/0142723713479438

Oatley, K. (2016). Fiction: Simulation of social worlds. *Trends in Cognitive Sciences, 20(8), 618–628* https://doi.org/10.1016/j.tics.2016.06.002

Pickering, J. A., & Sanders, M. R. (2017). Integrating parents' views on sibling relationships to tailor an evidence-based parenting intervention for sibling conflict. *Family Process, 56*(1), 105–125. https://doi.org/10.1111/famp.12173

Robertson, S.-J. L., & Reese, E. (2017). The very hungry caterpillar turned into a butterfly: Children's and parents' enjoyment of different book genres. *Journal of Early Childhood Literacy, 17*(1), 3–25. https://doi.org/10.1177/1468798415598354

Russell, S. J., & Cain, K. (2022). The animals in moral tales: Does character realism influence children's prosocial response to stories? *Journal of Experimental Child Psychology, 219*, 105392. https://doi.org/10.1016/j.jecp.2022.105392

Schapira, R., & Aram, D. (2020). Shared book reading at home and preschoolers' socio-emotional competence. *Early Education and Development, 31*(6), 819–837. https://doi.org/10.1080/10409289.2019.1692624

Schapira, R., Bergman Deitcher, D., & Aram, D. (2021). Mothers' discourse during shared reading of books relating to 'positive' and 'negative' emotions in different genres. *Journal of Research in Reading*. https://doi.org/10.1111/1467-9817.12370

Severson, R. L., & Lemm, K. M. (2016). Kids see human too: Adapting an individual differences measure of anthropomorphism for a child sample. *Journal of Cognition and Development, 17*(1), 122–141. https://doi.org/10.1080/15248372.2014.989445

Smadja, M. L., Aram, D., & Ziv, M. (2019). The impact of variations in text presence in children's storybooks on preschool teachers' discourse. *Journal of Research in Childhood Education, 33*(2), 194–211. https://doi.org/10.1080/02568543.2019.1577774

Strouse, G. A., Nyhout, A., & Ganea, P. A. (2018). The role of book features in young children's transfer of information from picture books to real-world contexts. *Frontiers in Psychology, 9*, 299131. https://doi.org/10.3389/fpsyg.2018.00050

Suvilehto, P. (2019). A study of animal characters as representations of humans: The animality/bibliotherapy test. *Journal of Poetry Therapy, 32*, 108–195. https://doi.org/10.1080/08893675.2019.1583414

Velthuijs, M. (2000). *(Frog on a very special day) Tsfardea beyom meyuchad meod*. Zmora-Bitan. [Hebrew].

Voake, J. (1997). *Jinger*. Walker Books.

Ziv, M., Smadja, M. L., & Aram, D. (2013). Mothers' mental-state discourse with preschoolers during storybook reading and wordless storybook telling. *Early Childhood Research Quarterly, 28*(1), 177–186. https://doi.org/10.1016/j.ecresq.2012.05.005

Ziv, M., Smadja, M. L., & Aram, D. (2014). Mothers' and teachers' mental-state discourse with preschoolers during storybook reading. *Journal of Cognitive Education and Psychology, 13*(1), 103. https://doi.org/10.1891/1945-8959.13.1.103

Zucker, T. A., Cabell, S. Q., Justice, L. M., Pentimonti, J. M., & Kaderavek, J. N. (2013). The role of frequent, interactive prekindergarten shared reading in the longitudinal development of language and literacy skills. *Developmental Psychology, 49*(8), 1425–1439. https://doi.org/10.1037/a0030347

Dorit Aram is a Full Professor at Tel Aviv University, where she leads the Early Childhood Research Lab. Her research examines adult–child literacy interactions, including joint writing and shared book reading, and their contributions to children's early literacy and socio-emotional development. She also investigates the Parenting Pentagon Model, focusing on how positive parenting practices foster the well-being of both parents and young children.

Inbar Avman Wolff is an Educational Counselor specializing in Early Education. Her master's thesis focused on parental discourse in relation to storybook protagonists. Currently, she is pursuing a second M.A. in Educational Psychology, where her research examines the associations between parenting style and children's sleep quality.

Sigalit Aviram-Brill is a researcher, lecturer, and pedagogical instructor in the Early Childhood Education Department at Beit Berl College. Her research focuses on family dynamics, with a particular interest in the parenting of siblings in early childhood and parent–sibling shared book reading.

Yeal Roth-Barkai is a researcher, lecturer, and pedagogical instructor in the Special Education Department at the Academic College Levinsky-Wingate. Her research focuses on preservice teachers' experiences.

Anat Zaidman Zait is an Associate Professor in the Department of Educational Counseling and Special Education at Tel Aviv University, Israel. Her research focuses on stress and coping processes among children with disabilities and their families, the determinants of parenting, and parents' well-being and health.

Chapter 4
"What a Naughty Little Girl!" A Cross-Cultural Comparison of Emotion Talk During Booksharing in Costa Rican and German Mother–Child Dyads

Ana M. Carmiol and Lisa Schröder

Contents

Throughout childhood and adolescence, individuals develop their emotional competence, defined as "the ability to purposefully and fully experience and express a variety of emotions, regulate emotional expressiveness and experience when

Authors' Note: We would like to thank the participating mothers and children. This research was supported by a grant from Vicerrectoría de Investigación, Universidad de Costa Rica (N° C4774) to Ana M. Carmiol and by a grant from the Kompetenzzentrum frühe Bildung in Stendal to Lisa Schröder.

A. M. Carmiol (✉)
Universidad de Costa Rica, San José, Costa Rica
e-mail: ana.carmiol@ucr.ac.cr

L. Schröder
University of Applied Sciences Magdeburg-Stendal, Magdeburg, Germany

University of Applied Sciences and Arts Bielefeld, Bielefeld, Germany
e-mail: lisa.schroeder@hsbi.de

R. Schapira, D. Aram (eds.), *Shared Book Reading and Children's Social-Emotional Competence*, https://doi.org/10.1007/978-3-032-14688-5_4

necessary, and understand the emotions of self and others" (Denham, 2019, p. 493). Parent–child conversation about emotions has been identified as a key socialization behavior for emotional competence, with implications for children's experience of their own emotions (Brumariu & Kerns, 2015), emotion knowledge (Dunn et al., 1991), and emotion regulation (Garner et al., 2008). From a social-interactionist perspective, children's active participation in conversations with more culturally and developmentally advanced individuals is essential, as such cooperative exchanges are gradually internalized and form the foundation for understanding, expressing, and regulating emotions (Ratner, 2000; Vygotsky & Cole, 1978).

During emotion-related discussions, caregivers may choose to emphasize different aspects of emotional experiences. They might simply label an emotion, explain its causes and consequences, or describe its associated behaviors. These preferences vary based on several factors, including child and parent characteristics, the conversational setting, and the cultural context (N. Eisenberg et al., 1998a). The present study examines mother–child conversations during booksharing in two cultural contexts: *Costa Rica* and *Germany*. We aim to explore cultural differences in the emotional terms that mothers and children use while reading together a children's book.

Emotions and Culture

Parental emotion socialization refers to caregivers' actions that (a) impact how a child learns about, experiences, expresses, and regulates emotions and related behaviors, and (b) are expected to shape the child's emotional development, learning processes, and emotional behaviors in a way that reflects the caregivers' values, beliefs, and goals about emotions, and their role in individual functioning and social adaptation (N. Eisenberg et al., 1998b). By learning to understand, express, and regulate emotions, children are socialized into culturally valued emotional behaviors, which contribute to their social competence within their communities (Keller, 2019). Previous findings indicate that there are biologically innate nonverbal displays for specific emotions, providing a universal repertoire of expressions (Tracy & Matsumoto, 2008). However, cultural norms direct when it is appropriate to express particular emotions and to what extent, reflecting distinctive patterns of emotional expression (Morelen & Thomassin, 2013). Thus, while the foundation for emotional expression is universal, the ecocultural environment shapes emotional responses to align with culturally valued behaviors (Keller & Kärtner, 2013). These culture-specific patterns have evolved as adaptive strategies to different demands of specific eco-social contexts (Keller, 2019).

Three distinct types of eco-social contexts, linked to specific cultural models, have been theorized and empirically studied for their role in shaping children's everyday experiences and developmental outcomes (Gernhardt et al., 2013; Keller, 2007; Keller & Otto, 2009; Schröder et al., 2013a, 2013b). These cultural models are understood to have evolved as adaptive strategies, providing meaningful responses to the unique circumstances and challenges of their respective eco-social environment: Western, urban, middle-class contexts and non-Western, rural, subsistence-based contexts have been described as representing two prototypes. In urban, Western, middle-class settings, socialization strategies often emphasize psychological autonomy, fostering independence and self-reflection; hence, this cultural model is described as *psychologically autonomous*. Conversely, rural, subsistence-based societies emphasize hierarchical relatedness, stressing collective responsibilities and interdependence within social roles; thus, this cultural model is termed *hierarchical-related*. Urban, middle-class settings outside the West represent a third cultural model, promoting values of independence and assertiveness alongside strong interpersonal connections and social responsibilities. This model has been referred to as *autonomous-related* (Kağitçibaşi, 2007). Although the two prototypical contexts express cultural values similarly across settings, the third context shows substantial variation in the expression of psychological autonomy and hierarchical relatedness, and it has been observed in contexts such as middle-class families of San José, *Costa Rica*, Delhi, India, and urban Nso, Cameroon (Keller, 2007). These contexts and their related cultural models are the foundation for different developmental pathways in children, including parental emotion socialization and emotional development.

Cross-Cultural Differences in Parent–Child Emotion Talk

Parent–child *emotion talk* gives insight into caregivers' culture-specific socialization goals. Previous findings indicate that compared to Chinese parents, Euro--American, middle-class parents tend to engage in more extensive *emotion talk* with their preschoolers, where parents elaborate on emotions, describe emotional causes, and validate the child's feelings (Wang, 2001; Wang & Fivush, 2005). This frequent discussion of emotions aligns with the emphasis on self-expression of internal attributes, where emotions serve as a prominent form of such expression (Markus & Kitayama, 1991). It also reflects an understanding and awareness of emotions that is consistent with the psychologically autonomous cultural model (Keller & Kärtner, 2013). In contrast, middle-class Chinese parents, representing an autonomous--related context, often emphasize teaching emotional restraint. Their discussions about emotions typically focus on the importance of self-control and the social appropriateness of emotional expressions (Wang, 2021). This approach places less emphasis on individual internal attributes and personal experiences, instead prioritizing public behaviors that support social harmony (Markus & Kitayama, 1991).

Cross-cultural evidence about *emotion talk* in Latin American, urban, middle--class families remains sparse. Eisenberg (1999) found that middle-class Mexican--American dyads talked more about emotions than Anglo-American dyads. Regardless of socioeconomic status, Mexican-American mothers talked proportionally less about their children's emotions and more about mothers' and others' emotions than did Anglo-American mothers, and Anglo-American mothers used more explanatory *emotion talk*, often referencing emotional causes, than Mexican-American mothers.

In Latin American settings, discussions about emotions with children in everyday situations are influenced by distinct cultural values such as *familismo*. Familismo encompasses prioritizing the family over the individual, maintaining strong emotional and physical connections within the family group, embracing reciprocity, and upholding familial honor (Calzada et al., 2013; Cortes Barragan & Meltzoff, 2025; Gibbons, 2024; Steidel & Contreras, 2003). Within this cultural framework, personal qualities such as *simpatía*—a highly valued relational style (Holloway et al., 2009)—and *respeto*, which emphasizes children's deference, affection, and honor toward adult authority figures (Zayas & Solari, 1994) as well as proper demeanor (Harwood et al., 2002), are regarded as crucial. These attributes likely shape caregivers' use of *emotion talk*, not primarily to encourage individual emotional expression but rather to foster understanding of others' emotions and support relational harmony.

By contrast, in German middle-class families, socialization practices emphasize psychological autonomy, individuality, and emotional expressiveness as central to fostering an independent self-concept (Friedlmeier et al., 2008; Keller & Kärtner, 2013; Keller & Otto, 2009). Within this cultural model, emotion regulation strategies support the expression of positive emotions as affirmations of individuality, and even the expression of negative emotions is legitimized as a valid personal experience (Keller & Otto, 2009). Emotions are treated as ego-focused phenomena, with emotional competence defined by the ability to recognize, express, and regulate one's own feelings independently, rather than adjusting them to preserve interpersonal harmony (Friedlmeier et al., 2011). In contrast to the relational emphasis in many Latin American cultures, German middle-class contexts encourage emotional expression as a means of reinforcing personal agency and choice in everyday life. In this view, making choices is seen as foundational to the development of self--sufficiency and autonomy (Iyengar & Lepper, 1999; Keller, 2007).

Recently, Carmiol and Schröder (2019) compared middle-class mother–child *emotion talk* during reminiscing and booksharing in two cultural contexts: *Germany*, a context of psychological autonomy, and San José, *Costa Rica*, an autonomous--related context. Similar to Eisenberg's (1999) findings, *Costa Rican* mothers and children engaged in more frequent *emotion talk* across conversational situations than their German counterparts, and *Costa Rican* mothers were more likely to talk about others' emotions than German mothers. Contrary to Eisenberg's findings, their results showed no significant differences in explanatory *emotion talk* across cultural contexts, as the mention of emotional causes and consequences was similar between groups. However, this study focused on overall emotional language and did not differentiate among specific emotional terms. Providing a more detailed perspective, with an in-depth analysis of the various emotional terms used, could offer better insights into differences in emotional language associated with different cultural models.

Emotion Talk During Booksharing

Across cultural contexts, *emotion talk* takes place within various everyday situations, which serve as important learning environments for children. Some of these everyday situations include booksharing (Chan et al., 2023; Perez-Rivera & Dunsmore, 2011; Ruba et al., 2022), play (Cervantes, 2002), conversations about past, personal experiences (Laible, 2004; Melzi & Fernández, 2004), car rides (A. R. Eisenberg, 1999), and regular interactions (Dunn et al., 1991; Lagattuta & Wellman, 2002). Booksharing is particularly valuable for emotion socialization, especially in middle-class contexts.

Booksharing provides children with exposure to a rich and diverse vocabulary. Research has shown that the text in picture books contains a greater variety of unique words than those used in natural conversations between adults and children (Dawson et al., 2021). Observational studies of daily activities revealed that booksharing significantly increases both the quantity and diversity of words directed at children, surpassing levels observed during activities such as grooming, mealtime, play, and reminiscing (Hoff et al., 2024; Soderstrom & Wittebolle, 2013).

Booksharing not only supports language and literacy development (De Bondt et al., 2020; Dowdall et al., 2020) but also provides a structured context for discussing emotions (Aram et al., 2013; Ziv et al., 2013). Parents may describe the emotions of story characters, ask questions about these emotions, and relate them to the child's experiences. Studies show that booksharing enables children to gain insight into complex social concepts, such as empathy, emotional regulation, and their understanding of mind, by engaging with the characters' feelings, intentions, and social interactions. Parents' emotional discourse during shared book reading, including elaborating on characters' motivations and emotions, directly enhances children's understanding of emotions and social cues. For example, Schapira and Aram (2020) found that parental references to emotions during booksharing were linked to children's prosocial attitudes and social coherence, which are critical for social competence. Experimental evidence also indicates the positive effects of *emotion talk* during booksharing on children's socioemotional competence, including emotional expression, emotional knowledge, and their ability to connect thoughts and emotions (Bergman Deitcher et al., 2021; Voltmer & von Salisch, 2022).

Present Study

In a previous cross-cultural study on *emotion talk*, our results showed that *Costa Rican* mothers and children tended to produce more emotion references than their German counterparts while sharing a book and talking about a past, personal event (Carmiol & Schröder, 2019). However, we found no statistically significant differences in the use of explanatory *emotion talk*, which refers to the mentioning of causes and consequences of emotions, instead of only referring to attributions.

While analyzing the total amount and complexity of *emotion talk* is crucial for understanding this key socialization behavior, other aspects of how parents discuss emotions may also play a significant role in the development of children's socio-emotional abilities. These aspects, which could differ across cultural contexts, extend beyond attributions, causes, and consequences of emotions. For instance, parents may refer to emotional states, discuss facial expressions (e.g., crying, yelling), explore emotional evaluative attitudes (e.g., like, hate, fun, boring), or make moral appraisals (e.g., to misbehave, to be good/bad). Examining these specific emotional terms could provide a more nuanced understanding of how caregivers foster socioemotional skills in their children. Additionally, such an approach could uncover cultural variations in *emotion talk* that remain unexplored in existing research comparing cultural contexts.

The present study aims to investigate whether these more specific aspects of *emotion talk* reveal *cross-cultural differences* between an autonomous-related context and a psychologically autonomous one. The research question guiding this work is: Do mothers and children from an autonomous-related context in *Costa Rica*, and a psychologically autonomous cultural context in *Germany*, differ in their use of four distinct emotional terms—emotional states, emotional behaviors, evaluative references, and moral appraisals—during booksharing conversations?

Method

Participants

Fifty-two *Costa Rican* and German preschoolers and their mothers participated. The *Costa Rican* subsample included 26 monolingual, Spanish-speaking dyads from a large metropolitan area of *Costa Rica* (18 girls, M_{age} = 4 years and 9 months). The German subsample included 26 monolingual, German-speaking dyads from households located in a Western metropolitan city (18 girls, M_{age} = 4 years and 9 months). Table 4.1 shows that maternal education was middle to high in both contexts.

Dyads in both cultural contexts were matched according to child gender, child's age in months, and maternal education. *Costa Rican* children of the same sex with the closest age in months and maternal years of education were drawn from a bigger

Table 4.1 Descriptive statistics of the sociodemographic variables as a function of cultural group *(N = 52)*

	Costa Rican subsample (*n* = 26)		German subsample (*n* = 26)	
Variables	M (SD)	Range	M (SD)	Range
Maternal education (in years)	11.54 (2.14)	9–17	11.92 (1.65)	10–17
Child's age (in months)	56.77 (2.50)	53–62	57.46 (5.62)	49–68
Percentage of girls (freq.)	69.23 (18)		69.23 (18)	

sample in order to match, as much as possible, the German sample. No significant differences were observed between the two samples in child gender ($\chi^2 = 0.00$, $p = .62$), child's age (t (50) = −0.57, $p = .57$), or maternal education (t (50) = 0.73, $p = .47$).

Procedure and Materials

Data were collected during 2015 in both cultural contexts. Participants were recruited through preschools. After reading and signing the consent form with an experimenter, mother and child completed a series of different tasks, but the focus of this study is only on mother–child booksharing conversations. In *Costa Rica*, a researcher met individually with children at preschool and visited their households to meet with each dyad. *Booksharing* conversations and sociodemographic information were collected during the home visit. In *Germany*, all dyads completed all tasks in preschools.

Mothers were provided with the Spanish or German versions of the children's book *Shopping with mom* (Mayer, 1998) to read with their child. This selection was based on the book's unfamiliarity to both populations, while covering a relatable theme (i.e., grocery shopping) for both cultural contexts. The book includes 24 color illustrations depicting a family's shopping experience, following a mother and her three children through a grocery store. The graphic presentations and the text in the book call for different emotions, such as happiness, anger, fear, and worry. For example, one scene shows the younger sister throwing a tantrum in the candy aisle after being told they won't be buying sweets. Another depicts a worried Little Critter frantically searching for his sister after she wanders off in the supermarket. A final scene shows the family enjoying ice cream together, their smiling faces suggesting relief and a sense of togetherness after a hectic outing. All mothers were instructed to interact with their child as they normally do while engaging in booksharing. Dyads were left alone in the room to complete the task, and no time restriction was placed on the interactions. Conversations were audiotaped and subsequently transcribed verbatim.

Coding

Coding of the booksharing conversations was conducted with an adapted version of coding systems previously used to classify mothers' and children's *emotion talk* during conversational contexts such as reminiscing and booksharing (Doan & Wang, 2010; Goodvin & Romdall, 2013; Lagattuta & Wellman, 2002; Nolivos & Leyva, 2013; Sáenz et al., 2025). Only extra-textual talk, different from the literal reading of the text, was coded. Mother and child propositions were coded. A propositional unit was defined as an utterance that contains a subject (typically a noun or pronoun) and a predicate (typically a verb), expressing a single idea or meaning. For example, "She's shouting" and "Was she a good girl?" When a sentence included conjunctions such as *but*, *because*, *when*, *where*, or *even*, the entire utterance was considered a single proposition. In contrast, utterances connected by *and* were coded as two separate propositions (e.g., "She is shouting *and* crying"). In addition, responses such as *yes* or *no* were interpreted as implicitly including the content of the preceding proposition. For example, in the exchange: Mother: "Was she being a good girl?" Child: "Yes", the child's response was coded as "Yes, she was being a good girl."

All propositions in transcripts were first classified as *off topic* or *on topic*. Off--topic talk included propositions unrelated to the content of the book, such as personal or behavioral comments (e.g., "Would you like to sit on my lap?") and general remarks about the activity of reading (e.g., "Let's turn the page"). On-topic talk was coded according to the five following types: *factual talk,* or descriptions of characters or events (e.g., "She's got the red ribbon in her hair"); *mental-state talk* (e.g., "I think she is too big for the ride"); *associative talk*, which connects the content of the book to either personal experiences (e.g., "You dropped an ice-cream cone the other day at grandma's") or general world knowledge (e.g., "Plums are similar to apples, but plums are smaller"); *conversational strategies* aimed at maintaining the flow of the conversation (e.g., "What else?"); and *emotion talk.*

Emotion talk included propositions involving the use of the following terms: *emotional states* (e.g., angry, ashamed, happy, sad; e.g., "The man at the supermarket is angry"), *emotion-related behaviors* (e.g., to cry, to hit, to smile, to scold; e.g., "She's shouting"), *emotional-evaluative language*, which expressed likes or dislikes (e.g., to like, to prefer, to enjoy; e.g., "It was a nice ride, wasn't it?"); and *moral appraisals*, which explicitly framed a behavior or character in normative terms (e.g., to misbehave, to be good/bad; e.g., "She misbehaved"). Propositions including both associative and *emotion talk* (e.g., Mother: "Does it always have to be like this when children go to the supermarket?" Child: "No, because mom scolds you"), or propositions including mental-state and *emotion talk* (e.g., "Do you know why he got angry?"), were coded as *emotion talk*, as this category was prioritized. When a proposition contained more than one emotional term, whether from the same category (e.g., Mother: "He was laughing when the mom scolded her") or from different categories, only one term was coded. To ensure consistency, we applied a predetermined prioritization hierarchy in cases where a proposition included two or more emotional terms belonging to different categories: emotional states were prioritized over emotional behaviors, followed by emotional evaluations, and finally moral appraisals. Such cases were extremely rare, with only the instance mentioned above occurring during the reliability coding process.

For reliability, transcripts were randomly selected and first translated to English by Spanish–English and German–English bilingual research assistants. Half of the transcripts were *Costa Rican*, and the other half were German. Authors independently coded 15% ($n = 8$) of booksharing transcripts. Cohen's kappa indexes showed excellent levels of agreement for the type of talk (Cohen's $\kappa = .87$, SE = 0.03, 85% CI = 0.81–0.92) and emotional terms (Cohen's $\kappa = .81$, SE = 0.03, 85% CI

= 0.75–0.87). Disagreements were discussed and resolved before the first author coded the remaining *Costa Rican* transcripts and the second author coded the remaining German transcripts.

Results

Preliminary Analyses

The participating mothers produced 57.54 on-topic propositions, while the children produced 24.39 propositions during the book-reading activity. *Costa Rican* mothers produced more on-topic propositions (M = 60.69) than German mothers (M = 54.39). Similarly, *Costa Rican* children (M = 25.12) produced more on-topic propositions than their German counterparts (M = 23.65) (see Table 4.2), but these differences were not statistically significant ($ps \geq .38$). Within and across contexts, mothers' and children's on-topic propositions primarily referred to factual talk, while other types of talk were less frequent. Additionally, the frequency of on-topic talk, including *emotion talk*, varied substantially within both samples. To account for this variability, the frequency of each emotional term was divided by the total number of on-topic propositions the speaker produced, such that the combined proportions of the four specific emotional terms equaled the total proportion of *emotion talk*. Table 4.2 presents descriptive statistics for the proportions of total *emotion talk* and each of the four specific emotional terms, by speaker, cultural context, and for the entire sample. Most variables for mothers and children were not normally distributed; therefore, nonparametric statistics were used. All analyses were conducted using JASP version 0.19.1 (JASP Team, 2024).

Main Analyses

Cross-cultural differences in emotional terms used In order to explore differences in *emotion talk* between *Costa Rican* and German mother–child dyads, we conducted independent samples Mann–Whitney tests for mothers and children, with cultural context as the between-subjects factor. As a first step, *emotion talk*, understood as the total proportion of propositions including emotional terms, was compared between the cultural contexts. Results indicated that *Costa Rican* mothers produced a significantly greater proportion of propositions including emotional terms than German mothers, $U = 460.50$, $p = .025$. Both groups showed similar proportions of emotional states, emotional behaviors, and emotional-evaluative references, with no significant differences. There was a trend for *Costa Rican* mothers producing a higher proportion of moral appraisals than German mothers; however, this difference was marginally significant, $U = 426.50$, $p = .095$.

Table 4.2 Means (standard deviations) and medians for all emotional terms for all sample and for each sample, for mothers and children

	All sample (*N* = 52)				Costa Rica (*N* = 26)				Germany (*N* = 26)			
	Mothers		Children		Mothers		Children		Mothers		Children	
Variable	*M* (*SD*)	*Mdn*	*M* (*SD*)	*Mdn*	*M* (*SD*)	*Mdn*	*M* (*SD*)	*Mdn*	*M* (*SD*)	*Mdn*	*M* (*SD*)	*Mdn*
On-topic talk (freq.)	57.54 (46.94)	49.00	24.39 (19.81)	21.00	60.69 (60.41)	30.00	25.12 (21.32)	19.00	54.39 (28.71)	53.50	23.65 (18.58)	22.00
Factual talk	29.64 (25.14)	22.50	14.98 (12.92)	13.00	28.65 (30.13)	17.50	15.42 (14.79)	11.00	30.62 (19.48)	29.50	14.54 (11.01)	13.50
Mental-state talk	3.77 (4.12)	3.00	1.48 (2.06)	1.00	3.35 (5.18)	1.00	1.23 (2.27)	0.00	4.19 (2.71)	4.00	1.73 (1.85)	1.00
Associative talk	7.98 (9.07)	4.50	3.44 (4.49)	1.5	7.65 (10.05)	1.50	2.86 (3.80)	1.00	8.31 (8.16)	6.50	4.00 (5.03)	2.00
Conv strategies	8.12 (9.83)	6.00	1.23 (2.25)	0.00	10.62 (13.12)	6.50	1.31 (2.17)	0.00	5.62 (3.48)	5.50	1.15 (2.36)	0.00
Emotion talk	8.04 (8.94)	5.00	3.25 (3.35)	3.00	10.42 (11.73)	5.50	4.27 (3.96)	4.00	5.65 (3.71)	4.50	2.23 (2.25)	2.00
Emotion talk (%)	0.19 (0.11)	0.16	0.16 (0.12)	0.14	0.22 (0.12)	0.21	0.20 (0.13)	0.19	0.15 (0.08)	0.15	0.12 (0.09)	0.13
Emotional states	0.08 (0.06)	0.070	0.07 (0.08)	0.04	0.08 (0.06)	0.08	0.09 (0.09)	0.05	0.07 (0.06)	0.07	0.05 (0.06)	0.01
Emotional behav	0.03 (0.04)	0.020	0.02 (0.03)	0.00	0.03 (0.04)	0.01	0.02 (0.03)	0.00	0.03 (0.04)	0.03	0.03 (0.04)	0.00
Emotional-eval ref	0.03 (0.04)	0.00	0.03 (0.06)	0.00	0.03 (0.05)	0.01	0.03 (0.07)	0.00	0.02 (0.03)	0.00	0.03 (0.05)	0.00
Moral appraisals	0.05 (0.08)	0.02	0.04 (0.08)	0.00	0.08 (0.10)	0.04	0.07 (0.10)	0.00	0.03 (0.04)	0.02	0.02 (0.05)	0.00

Notes. Descriptive statistics for total on-topic talk and all types of on-topic talk are presented as frequencies. Descriptive statistics for emotional terms are presented as proportions. *Conv* conversational. *Behav* behaviors. *Eval* evaluative. *Ref* references

Costa Rican children also produced a significantly higher proportion of propositions including emotional terms than German children, $U = 463.00$, $p = .022$. Similar to mothers, the two groups of children exhibited comparable proportions of emotional states, emotional behaviors, and emotional-evaluative references, with no significant differences. Nonetheless, *Costa Rican* children produced a significantly higher proportion of propositions including moral appraisals than German children, $U = 446.00$, $p = .016$.

As shown in Table 4.2, all four emotional terms were used in low proportions. However, significant differences in their use were observed within cultural contexts. Repeated-measures nonparametric analyses using the Friedman test revealed differences in the proportions of the four emotional terms used by both *Costa Rican* mothers (χ^2_F (3) = 19.72, $p < .001$, Kendall's $W = 0.25$) and German mothers (χ^2_F (3) = 11.81, $p = .008$, Kendall's $W = 0.15$). Conover's post hoc comparisons showed that *Costa Rican* mothers used emotional state terms significantly more than emotional behavior and emotional evaluation terms (*ps* < .001), but not more than moral appraisals ($p = .16$). Additionally, this group of mothers used moral appraisals significantly more than emotional behaviors ($p = .006$) and emotional evaluations ($p = .011$). In the German context, mothers referred to emotional states significantly more than to emotional behaviors ($p = .029$), emotional evaluations ($p < .001$), and moral appraisals ($p = .009$).

Results also revealed differences in children's use of the four emotional terms in the *Costa Rican* context (χ^2_F (3) = 13.40, $p = .004$, Kendall's $W = 0.17$) and in the German context (χ^2_F (3) = 8.12, $p = .044$, Kendall's $W = 0.10$). Conover's post hoc comparisons showed that *Costa Rican* children referred to emotional states significantly more than to emotional behaviors ($p < .001$), emotional evaluations ($p = .001$), and moral appraisals ($p = .040$). German children referred to moral appraisals significantly less than to emotional states ($p = .005$). They also referred to moral appraisals less than to emotional behaviors and emotional evaluations, but these differences were marginally significant (*ps* = .069 and.080, respectively).

Relations Between Maternal and Child Emotion Talk To examine associations between maternal and children's proportional use of the different emotional terms, we conducted a series of correlations within each cultural context. As shown in Table 4.3, strong, positive correlations (all *rs* > .37) were observed between maternal and children's use of emotional terms in both cultural contexts, indicating that children tended to mirror their mothers' *emotion talk*. In the *Costa Rican* context, significant correlations were found for emotional states, emotional-evaluative references, and moral appraisals. Maternal and children's use of emotional behaviors was also positively correlated but reached only marginal significance ($p = .065$). In the German context, a positive, significant correlation was observed between mothers' and children's use of all four different emotional terms.

Table 4.3 further highlights negative correlations in the German context between maternal use of emotional behaviors and both maternal and children's use of moral appraisals. Conversely, in the *Costa Rican* context, maternal use of emotional

Table 4.3 Spearman's rho correlations of mothers and children's use of emotional terms during booksharing, Costa Rica and Germany

	(1)	(2)	(3)	(4)	(5)	(6)	(7)	(8)
(1) Mothers, emotional states		−0.01	−0.02	−0.18	0.39*	−0.31	−0.11	0.09
(2) Mothers, emotional behaviors	−0.14		−0.31	−0.52**	0.21	0.41*	−0.08	−0.45*
(3) Mothers, emotional-evaluative ref	−0.20	0.07		0.23	0.02	−0.04	0.53**	0.17
(4) Mothers, moral appraisals	−0.02	0.34†	−0.05		−0.28	0.06	0.06	0.49*
(5) Children, emotional states	0.56**	0.04	−0.19	−0.29		0.19	0.20	−0.09
(6) Children, emotional behaviors	0.10	0.37†	0.09	−0.07	0.35†		0.15	−0.22
(7) Children, emotional-evaluative ref	−0.15	−0.04	0.60**	−0.02	0.01	0.13		−0.12
(8) Children, moral appraisals	0.03	0.38†	0.12	0.83***	−0.26	−0.01	0.20	

Notes. Correlations within the Costa Rican sample are presented below the diagonal. Correlations within the German sample are presented above the diagonal.
ref references
†p <.10, *p <.05, **p <.01, ***p <.001, two-tailed

behaviors was positively associated with children's use of moral appraisals, though this relationship was marginally significant ($p = .055$).

Finally, a good portion of correlations among the four emotional terms within mothers and children in each cultural context were low, supporting our decision to analyze these terms separately. In *Costa Rica*, marginally significant, positive correlations were found between maternal emotional behaviors and maternal moral appraisals ($p = .092$) as well as between children's emotional states and emotional behaviors ($p = .081$).

Discussion

The present study examined the different kinds of emotional terms mothers and children spontaneously used during booksharing in two cultural contexts. Based on the ecocultural model (Keller, 2007), the investigated contexts can be assumed to represent the cultural model of autonomy relatedness (urban, educated *Costa Rican* families) and the cultural model of psychological autonomy (urban, educated German families); contexts that have been shown to vary concerning children's emotion socialization and development.

Regarding the similarities between the groups, it is important to note that *emotion talk* was relatively infrequent in both groups, especially when compared to other types of conversation, such as factual statements or descriptions of characters and events in the book. This limited use is consistent with findings from previous studies conducted in the same cultural contexts but in different conversational settings, such as reminiscing (Sáenz et al., 2025; Tõugu et al., 2023, 2025). It also aligns with evidence from booksharing studies conducted in other cultural contexts (Doan & Wang, 2010). Despite the relatively low proportion of *emotion talk* overall, our results revealed significant differences. In particular, *Costa Rican* dyads referenced emotions in greater proportion than their German counterparts during booksharing, a finding that supports our previous work (Carmiol & Schröder, 2019).

The focus of our current research was to better understand where differences occur, aiming to gain deeper insights into culture-specific emotion socialization. When examining various emotional terms, we found that *Costa Rican* and German dyads discussed emotional states, emotional behaviors, and emotional-evaluative references with similar proportions. Notably, the two groups differed in their use of moral appraisals: *Costa Rican* mothers showed a marginally higher proportion of moral appraisals than German mothers, and *Costa Rican* children exhibited a higher proportion of moral appraisals compared to their German counterparts.

This pattern conforms with the underlying cultural models: In both samples, mothers used the context of booksharing to discuss the internal emotional states of individuals similarly, reflecting the value placed on psychological autonomy. However, only in the *Costa Rican* sample did mothers also use booksharing interactions to refer to moral appraisals (8%) as frequently as they mentioned emotional states (8%). They also used moral appraisals significantly more than emotional behaviors and emotional-evaluative terms. In the German sample, moral appraisals were mentioned significantly less often by mothers (3%) compared to emotional states (7%), which was the most frequently used emotional term in this group. Moreover, the proportion of moral appraisals did not vary significantly from the proportions of emotional behaviors and emotional evaluations.

A similar pattern was observed in children. Although emotional state terms were the most frequently used by children in both groups (9% in *Costa Rica*, 5% in *Germany*), only in the German sample was the proportion of moral appraisals (2%) marginally lower than that of emotional behaviors (3%) and emotional evaluations (3%), making moral appraisals the least common emotional term used in this group. Our results do not allow us to draw conclusions about children's independent role in shaping *emotion talk*, as such an analysis would require examining which speaker initiates the use of each emotional term (e.g., Benga et al., 2005). However, it is clear that, much like adults, children in these two distinct cultural contexts engage in *emotion talk* in systematically different ways. Children's participation may downplay or emphasize specific emotional themes, shaping the course of the interaction. Their contributions, whether reinforcing their mothers' moral appraisals or introducing new ones (such as in Example 44 below), reflect specific cultural values and influence how emotions are discussed in the context of booksharing.

Our findings suggest that *Costa Rican* but not German mothers used *emotion talk* during booksharing to teach their children about appropriate social behavior, highlighting the importance of the relatedness component of their cultural model. The emphasis on proper demeanor is deeply rooted in the cultural value of familismo, particularly the principle of upholding familial honor (Steidel & Contreras, 2003). This principle posits that each family member represents the larger family unit, making it essential for individuals to act honorably to benefit the family as a whole. For children, this includes demonstrating respect and exhibiting good social behavior. This finding aligns with results from a previous interview study by Calzada et al. (2013), where a Mexican-American mother explained the following principle as part of her parenting approach: "When you do something great, you make me look great. When you mess up, you make me look bad" (p. 1705).

The following excerpt from a *Costa Rican* dyad's transcript illustrates how moral appraisals were incorporated into their conversation, followed by explicit lessons directed at the child on how to behave when a sibling is being scolded by an adult. The noncursive text represents the extra-textual talk, while the propositions containing the moral appraisals are underlined:

Example 1:

Mother: *My little sister said, "I want candy."*
Mother: *Mom said, "I told you, no candy today. Would you like to go to time out instead?"*
Child: No.
Mother: Uh-huh, right?
Mother: *"No," said the girl.*
Mother: But the thing is, the mom has to get mad so that she obeys.

Mother: And look, the brother was laughing. He is being rude.
Mother: He was laughing when the mom scolded her.
Mother: Was that cute or was that ugly?
Child: Ugly.
Mother: No, one shouldn't laugh or make funny faces like that, right?
Mother: One should, you know, stay quiet.
Child: Uh-huh.

In this example, the mother evaluated the behavior of one of the book's characters and, through a closed-ended question, prompted the child to assess this behavior as either positive or negative. After the child makes their judgment, the mother offers explicit guidance on how to respond appropriately in similar situations. She emphasized the importance of regulating emotional expressions, such as laughter, likely to prevent further conflict, maintain harmony, and show respect. This interaction demonstrates how the mother uses the narrative context to teach social norms and emotional regulation, reinforcing culturally appropriate behaviors.

In contrast, in the following German example, the mother transforms the situation in the book into a scenario from the child's own life, without emphasizing proper behavior or offering general teaching moments.

Example 2:

Mother: *My little sister said, "I want candy."*
Mother: *Mom said, "I told you, no candy today. Would you like to go to time out instead?"*
Mother: That sounds familiar to me.
Child: Uh-huh.
Mother: Uh-huh, yes.
Child: Like me?
Mother: Yes.
Child: Eating candy.
Mother: Exactly.

In another scene from the book, one of the characters misbehaves by pulling a paper towel roll from the bottom of a pile at the supermarket, creating a mess and causing discomfort for the store manager. In this instance, another German mother similarly connects the situation in the book to her child's own life, describing what she would have done. However, she does not offer moral appraisals to evaluate the character's actions.

Example 3:

Mother: *Mom wanted paper towels. My little sister pulled out a roll from the bottom of the pile.*
Mother: *Everything fell down.*
Child: There's the mouse.
Mother: *The man who owned the store didn't look too happy.*
Mother: Oh dear... I think he's scolding them.
Child: Me too.

Child: And she's happy.
Mother: Yes, the baby is happy. That's right.
Mother: But I think I would be scolding you as well if you would put the paper towels all over the supermarket.

In contrast, a *Costa Rican* dyad's discussion of the same scene includes a moral appraisal, with the child being the first to judge the character's actions using the term *malcriado* (translated as "naughty"), followed by the mother's response. As previous research has shown, malcriado is used in Latin American communities to describe someone who is rebellious, disobedient, disrespectful, or unwilling to follow instructions and heed the guidance of elders (Zucker & Howes, 2009). This term contrasts with *educado*, which refers to children who are attuned to social relationships and respectfully attentive to the teachings, directions, and advice of adults:

Example 4:

Mother: *Mom wanted paper towels. My little sister pulled out a roll from the bottom of the pile.*
Mother: Where did the girl get the towels from?
Child: From there.
Mother: From there.
Child: There, it was holding those.
Mother: Yes, the bottom ones, and she took the ones at the bottom that were holding up the ones on top.
Mother: And what do you think it happened?
Child: Then, then it made a mess.
Mother: It made a mess. They all fell.
Mother: *Everything fell down. The man who owned the store didn't look too happy.*
Mother: See?
Mother: Why was the store owner angry?
Child: Because… because she made a mess. The towel tower got ruined.
Mother: Oh no, what a girl!
Child: <u>What a naughty little girl!</u>
Mother: <u>What a naughty little girl!</u>

It is crucial to interpret our findings within the context of the interactional setting from which they emerge. During booksharing, the emotions of others are more readily observable, and prior research indicates that mothers in Latin American communities tend to focus on discussing others' emotions more frequently than mothers from psychologically autonomous contexts, such as *Germany* and Anglo-American settings (Carmiol & Schröder, 2019; Eisenberg, 1999). Moreover, the book used in the current study may have been more engaging for *Costa Rican* mothers than for German mothers, partly due to its topic, which featured multiple episodes of misbehavior that may have resonated more strongly with *Costa Rican* cultural values. Previous studies have shown that emotion words are used differently in children's books produced across cultural contexts (Farkas et al., 2020;

Grady et al., 2019). Therefore, future research should examine *cross-cultural differences* in *emotion talk* using a variety of children's books, including those with themes that are culturally relevant and resonant for the different populations under study. It could also explore other interactional contexts across the investigated settings, such as reminiscing about events with varying emotional valence, engaging in play, or navigating everyday interactions.

The findings of this study must also be considered alongside its limitations. Although our results advance the field by examining and comparing phenomena in two cultural contexts that are still rather seldom compared, the small sample sizes used in this research and the marginal significance of some findings are notable constraints. Future research should aim to include larger sample sizes. Second, our study gathered booksharing conversations in different settings for each cultural context: German dyads participated in conversations within a preschool environment, while *Costa Rican* dyads completed theirs at home. This presents a methodological limitation. Nonetheless, maternal conversational styles have been shown to reflect core cultural values in cross-cultural studies (Schröder et al., 2013a; Wang, 2007), and the underlying norms and values are expected to remain consistent regardless of the setting where interactions occur. Third, this study employed a cross-sectional design. Longitudinal research is needed to determine whether early differences in *emotion talk*, such as those observed here, predict later socioemotional outcomes, including emotional understanding, regulation, and moral reasoning. Expanding cross-cultural research to explore these effects is particularly important for early childhood education, where classrooms are becoming increasingly culturally diverse. Gaining insight into how families from different cultural backgrounds engage in *emotion talk*—and how this shapes early emotional competence—can help educators better interpret children's emotional expressions and behaviors and interact with them in more culturally responsive and supportive ways.

Overall, our findings highlight booksharing as a meaningful context for examining cross-cultural variations in mother–child *emotion talk*, even though this specific interaction context is culture-specific itself, as literacy-related interactions are especially relevant in family contexts where formal education is highly valued.

References

Aram, D., Fine, Y., & Ziv, M. (2013). Enhancing parent–child shared book reading interactions: Promoting references to the book's plot and socio-cognitive themes. *Early Childhood Research Quarterly, 28*(1), 111–122. https://doi.org/10.1016/j.ecresq.2012.03.005

Benga, O., Petra, L., & Inca, I. (2005). A dynamic approach to the co-construction of autobiographical memory: Insights from dyadic conversations about the past. *Proceedings of the Annual Meeting of the Cognitive Science Society, 27*(27) https://escholarship.org/uc/item/5pf069wj

Bergman Deitcher, D., Aram, D., Khalaily-Shahadi, M., & Dwairy, M. (2021). Promoting preschoolers' mental-emotional conceptualization and social understanding: A shared book-reading study. *Early Education and Development, 32*(4), 501–515. https://doi.org/10.1080/10409289.2020.1772662

Brumariu, L. E., & Kerns, K. A. (2015). Mother–child emotion communication and childhood anxiety symptoms. *Cognition and Emotion, 29*(3), 416–431. https://doi.org/10.1080/02699931.2014.917070

Calzada, E. J., Tamis-LeMonda, C. S., & Yoshikawa, H. (2013). Familismo in Mexican and Dominican families from low-income, urban communities. *Journal of Family Issues, 34*(12), 1696–1724. https://doi.org/10.1177/0192513X12460218

Carmiol, A. M., & Schröder, L. (2019). Emotion talk during mother–child reminiscing and book sharing and children's socioemotional competence: Evidence from Costa Rica and Germany. *Culture and Brain, 7*(2), 1–22. https://doi.org/10.1007/s40167-019-00078-x

Cervantes, C. A. (2002). Explanatory emotion talk in Mexican immigrant and Mexican American families. *Hispanic Journal of Behavioral Sciences, 24*(2), 138–163. https://doi.org/10.1177/0739986302024002003

Chan, M., Teng, D., Teng, Y.-P. T., & Zhou, Q. (2023). Parent emotion talk with preschoolers from low-income Mexican American and Chinese American families: Links to sociocultural factors. *Social Development, 32*(2), 481–500. https://doi.org/10.1111/sode.12656

Cortes Barragan, R., & Meltzoff, A. N. (2025). The socialization of cultural values and the development of Latin American prosociality. *Child Development Perspectives*, Advance online publication. https://doi.org/10.1111/cdep.12545

Dawson, N., Hsiao, Y., Banerji, N., Tan, A. W. M., & Nation, K. (2021). Features of lexical richness in children's books: Comparisons with child-directed speech. *Language Development Research*. https://ora.ox.ac.uk/objects/uuid:869403f5-9f11-465b-94bd-0a323b1dd8a9

De Bondt, M., Willenberg, I. A., & Bus, A. G. (2020). Do book giveaway programs promote the home literacy environment and children's literacy-telated behavior and skills? *Review of Educational Research, 90*(3), 349–375. https://doi.org/10.3102/0034654320922140

Denham, S. A. (2019). Emotional competence during childhood and adolescence. In V. LoBue, K. Pérez-Edgar, & K. A. Buss (Eds.), *Handbook of emotional development* (pp. 493–541). Springer International. https://doi.org/10.1007/978-3-030-17332-6_20

Doan, S. N., & Wang, Q. (2010). Maternal Discussions of mental states and behaviors: Relations to emotion situation knowledge in European American and Immigrant Chinese children. *Child Development, 81*(5), 1490–1503. https://doi.org/10.1111/j.1467-8624.2010.01487.x

Dowdall, N., Melendez-Torres, G., Murray, L., Gardner, F., Hartford, L., & Cooper, P. J. (2020). Shared picture book reading interventions for child language development: A systematic review and meta-analysis. *Child Development, 91*(2), e383–e399. https://doi.org/10.1111/cdev.13225

Dunn, J., Brown, J., & Beardsall, L. (1991). Family talk about feeling states and children's later understanding of others' emotions. *Developmental Psychology, 27*(3), 448.

Eisenberg, A. R. (1999). Emotion talk among Mexican American and Anglo American mothers and children from two social classes. *Merrill-Palmer Quarterly (1982-)*, 267–284. https://www.jstor.org/stable/23093678

Eisenberg, N., Cumberland, A., & Spinrad, T. L. (1998a). Parental socialization of emotion. *Psychological Inquiry, 9*(4), 241–273. https://doi.org/10.1207/s15327965pli0904_1

Eisenberg, N., Spinrad, T. L., & Cumberland, A. (1998b). The socialization of emotion: Reply to Commentaries. *Psychological Inquiry, 9*(4), 317–333. https://doi.org/10.1207/s15327965pli0904_17

Farkas, C., Gerber, D., Mata, C., & Santelices, M. P. (2020). Are children from different countries exposed to diverse emotions in storybooks? Comparative study between Chile and the United States. *Social Development, 29*(4), 1134–1154. https://doi.org/10.1111/sode.12443

Friedlmeier, W., Corapci, F., & Cole, P. M. (2011). Emotion socialization in cross-cultural perspective. *Social and Personality Psychology Compass, 5*(7), 410–427. https://doi.org/10.1111/j.1751-9004.2011.00362.x

Friedlmeier, W., Schiifermeier, E., Vasconcellos, V., & Trommsdorff, G. (2008). Self-construal and cultural orientation as predictors for developmental goals: A comparison between Brazilian and German caregivers. *European Journal of Developmental Psychology, 5*(1), 39–67. https://doi.org/10.1080/17405620600751085

Garner, P. W., Dunsmore, J. C., & Southam-Gerrow, M. (2008). Mother–child conversations about emotions: Linkages to child aggression and prosocial behavior. *Social Development, 17*(2), 259–277. https://doi.org/10.1111/j.1467-9507.2007.00424.x

Gernhardt, A., Rübeling, H., & Keller, H. (2013). "This is my family": Differences in children's family drawings across cultures. *Journal of Cross-Cultural Psychology, 44*(7), 1166–1183. https://doi.org/10.1177/0022022113478658

Gibbons, J. L. (2024). Enriching developmental science from the Global South: Contributions from Latin America. *American Psychologist, 79*(5), 735–747. https://doi.org/10.1037/amp0001367

Goodvin, R., & Romdall, L. (2013). Associations of mother–child reminiscing about negative past events, coping, and self-concept in early childhood. *Infant and Child Development, 22*(4), 383–400. https://doi.org/10.1002/icd.1797

Grady, J. S., Her, M., Moreno, G., Perez, C., & Yelinek, J. (2019). Emotions in storybooks: A comparison of storybooks that represent ethnic and racial groups in the United States. *Psychology of Popular Media Culture, 8*(3), 207–217. https://doi.org/10.1037/ppm0000185

Harwood, R., Leyendecker, B., Carlson, V., Asencio, M., & Miller, A. (2002). Parenting among Latino families in the US. In *Handbook of parenting* (4th ed., pp. 21–46). Erlbaum Mahwah.

Hoff, E., Trecca, F., Højen, A., Laursen, B., & Bleses, D. (2024). Context and education affect the quality of parents' speech to children. *Journal of Applied Developmental Psychology, 91*, 101632. https://doi.org/10.1016/j.appdev.2024.101632

Holloway, R. A., Waldrip, A. M., & Ickes, W. (2009). Evidence that a simpático self-schema accounts for differences in the self-concepts and social behavior of Latinos versus Whites (and Blacks). *Journal of Personality and Social Psychology, 96*(5), 1012.

Iyengar, S. S., & Lepper, M. R. (1999). Rethinking the value of choice: A cultural perspective on intrinsic motivation. *Journal of Personality and Social Psychology, 76*(3), 349.

JASP Team. (2024). *JASP* (Version 0.19.1) [Computer software]. https://jasp-stats.org/

Kağitçibaşi, Ç. (2007). *Family, self, and human development across cultures: Theories and applications* (2nd ed.). Lawrence Erlbaum Associates.

Keller, H. (2007). *Cultures of infancy*. Lawrence Erlbaum Associates. https://doi.org/10.4324/9781003284079

Keller, H. (2019). The role of emotions in socialization processes across cultures: Implications for theory and practice. In D. Matsumoto & H. C. Hwang (Eds.), *The handbook of culture and psychology* (pp. 209–232). Oxford University Press. https://doi.org/10.1093/oso/9780190679743.003.0008

Keller, H., & Kärtner, J. (2013). The cultural solution of universal developmental tasks. *Advances in Culture and Psychology, 3*, 63–116. https://doi.org/10.1093/acprof:oso/9780199930449.001.0001

Keller, H., & Otto, H. (2009). The cultural socialization of emotion regulation during infancy. *Journal of Cross-Cultural Psychology, 40*(6), 996–1011. https://doi.org/10.1177/0022022109348576

Lagattuta, K. H., & Wellman, H. M. (2002). Differences in early parent-child conversations about negative versus positive emotions: Implications for the development of psychological understanding. *Developmental Psychology, 38*(4), 564–580. https://doi.org/10.1037/0012-1649.38.4.564

Laible, D. J. (2004). Mother-child discourse surrounding a child's past behavior at 30 months: Links to emotional understanding and early conscience development at 36 months. *Merrill-Palmer Quarterly, 50*(2), 159–180. https://doi.org/10.1353/mpq.2004.0013

Markus, H. R., & Kitayama, S. (1991). Culture and the self: Implications for cognition, emotion, and motivation. *Psychological Review, 98*(2), 224–253. https://doi.org/10.1037/0033-295X.98.2.224

Mayer, M. (1998). *Just shopping with mom*. Random House Books for Young Readers.

Melzi, G., & Fernández, C. (2004). Talking about past emotions: Conversations between Peruvian mothers and their preschool children. *Sex Roles, 50*(9), 641–657. https://doi.org/10.1023/B:SERS.0000027567.55262.10

Morelen, D., & Thomassin, K. (2013). Emotion socialization and ethnicity: An examination of practices and outcomes in African American, Asian American, and Latin American Families. *The Yale Journal of Biology and Medicine, 86*(2), 168.

Nolivos, V., & Leyva, D. (2013). Fun and frustrations: Low-income Chilean parents reminiscing with their children about past emotional experiences. *Actualidades En Psicología, 27*(115), 31–48. https://doi.org/10.15517/ap.v27i115.9278

Perez-Rivera, M. B., & Dunsmore, J. C. (2011). Mothers' acculturation and beliefs about emotions, mother–child emotion discourse, and children's emotion understanding in Latino Families. *Early Education and Development, 22*(2), 324–354. https://doi.org/10.1080/10409281003702000

Ratner, C. (2000). A cultural-psychological analysis of emotions. *Culture & Psychology, 6*(1), 5–39. https://doi.org/10.1177/1354067X0061001

Ruba, A. L., Kalia, V., & Wilbourn, M. P. (2022). Happy, sad, or yucky? Parental emotion talk with infants in a book-sharing task. *Infancy, 27*(2), 277–290. https://doi.org/10.1111/infa.12448

Sáenz, N., Ríos, M., Salazar, K., & Carmiol, A. M. (2025). Emotion talk during reminiscing: A comparative study between mother-son and mother-daughter dyads from two different educational backgrounds in Costa Rica. In M. Rosabal-Coto & J. Tapia-Balladares (Eds.), *Family and contexts of development: Challenges in Latin America*. Oxford University Press. https://doi.org/10.1093/oso/9780197675144.003.0008

Schapira, R., & Aram, D. (2020). Shared book reading at home and preschoolers' socio-emotional competence. *Early Education and Development, 31*(6), 819–837. https://doi.org/10.1080/10409289.2019.1692624

Schröder, L., Keller, H., Kärtner, J., Kleis, A., Abels, M., Yovsi, R. D., Chaudhary, N., Jensen, H., & Papaligoura, Z. (2013a). Early reminiscing in cultural contexts: Cultural models, maternal reminiscing styles, and children's memories. *Journal of Cognition and Development, 14*(1), 10–34. https://doi.org/10.1080/15248372.2011.638690

Schröder, L., Keller, H., & Kleis, A. (2013b). Parent-child conversations in three urban middle-class contexts: Mothers and fathers reminisce with their daughters and sons in Costa Rica, Mexico, and Germany. *Actualidades En Psicología, 27*(115), 49–73. https://doi.org/10.15517/ap.v27i115.9885

Soderstrom, M., & Wittebolle, K. (2013). When do caregivers talk? The influences of activity and rime of day on caregiver speech and child vocalizations in two childcare environments. *PLoS One, 8*(11), e80646. https://doi.org/10.1371/journal.pone.0080646

Steidel, A. G. L., & Contreras, J. M. (2003). A new familism scale for use with Latino populations. *Hispanic Journal of Behavioral Sciences, 25*(3), 312–330. https://doi.org/10.1177/0739986303256912

Tõugu, P., Schröder, L., & Tulviste, T. (2025). Children's mental health and parent-child elaborative reminiscing during the COVID-19 pandemic: Insights from Estonian and German middle-class families. *Developmental Psychology*. https://doi.org/10.1037/dev0001975

Tõugu, P., Tulviste, T., & Schröder, L. (2023). Making sense of the pandemic: Parent-child conversations in two cultural contexts. *PLoS One, 18*(1), e0280781. https://doi.org/10.1371/journal.pone.0280781

Tracy, J. L., & Matsumoto, D. (2008). The spontaneous expression of pride and shame: Evidence for biologically innate nonverbal displays. *Proceedings of the National Academy of Sciences, 105*(33), 11655–11660. https://doi.org/10.1073/pnas.0802686105

Voltmer, K., & von Salisch, M. (2022). The feeling thinking talking intervention with teachers advances young children's emotion knowledge. *Social Development, 31*(3), 846–861. https://doi.org/10.1111/sode.12586

Vygotsky, L. S., & Cole, M. (1978). *Mind in society: Development of higher psychological processes*. Harvard University Press.

Wang, Q. (2001). "Did you have fun?": American and Chinese mother–child conversations about shared emotional experiences. *Cognitive Development, 16*(2), 693–715. https://doi.org/10.1016/S0885-2014(01)00055-7

Wang, Q. (2021). Emotion socialization in cultural context: Lessons from Asian-heritage families. *Social Development, 32*(2), 517–526. https://doi.org/10.1111/sode.12658

Wang, Q., & Fivush, R. (2005). Mother–child conversations of emotionally salient events: Exploring the functions of emotional reminiscing in European-American and Chinese families. *Social Development, 14*(3), 473–495. https://doi.org/10.1111/j.1467-9507.2005.00312.x

Zayas, L. H., & Solari, F. (1994). Early childhood socialization in Hispanic families: Context, culture, and practice implications. *Professional Psychology: Research and Practice, 25*(3), 200–206. https://doi.org/10.1037/0735-7028.25.3.200

Ziv, M., Smadja, M.-L., & Aram, D. (2013). Mothers' mental-state discourse with preschoolers during storybook reading and wordless storybook telling. *Early Childhood Research Quarterly, 28*(1), 177–186. https://doi.org/10.1016/j.ecresq.2012.05.005

Zucker, E., & Howes, C. (2009). Respectful relationships: Socialization goals and practices among Mexican mothers. *Infant Mental Health Journal, 30*(5), 501–522. https://doi.org/10.1002/imhj.2022

Wang, Q. (2007). "Remember when you got the big, big bulldozer?" Mother–child reminiscing over time and across cultures. *Social Cognition, 25*(4), 455-471. https://doi.org/10.1521/soco.2007.25.4.455

Ana M. Carmiol is a professor in the Escuela de Psicología and a researcher at the Instituto de Investigaciones Psicológicas of the Universidad de Costa Rica. She specializes in developmental psychology and research methods, with her teaching and research focusing on language and literacy development during infancy and early childhood. Her work investigates how the quality of the home environment, including caregiver–child interactions, influences children's developmental outcomes in Costa Rica.

Lisa Schröder conducted this study while serving as a professor in the Department of Applied Human Sciences at the University of Applied Sciences Magdeburg-Stendal. Since the beginning of 2025, she has been a professor in the Department of Social Work at the University of Applied Sciences and Arts Bielefeld. She specializes in developmental psychology and pedagogy, focusing on early childhood education and care (ECEC), and teaches courses on these topics as well as research methodologies. Her research explores *cross-cultural differences* in child socialization and development, emphasizing their implications for fostering culturally sensitive approaches in ECEC.

Chapter 5
The Relation Between Parent–Child Shared Book Reading and Children's Socioemotional Competence: A Correlational Meta-Analysis

Carmen López-Escribano

Contents

Introduction

Shared book reading (SBR) is a widely used practice that involves adults reading books with children in an interactive manner. Rather than simply reading the text aloud, adults use a scaffolding instructional approach, incorporating strategies such as oral language prompts, open-ended questions that extend beyond the content of the book, elaborations of children's utterances, evaluation of children's responses, and praise for participation (Noble et al., 2019; Towson et al., 2016).

Shared book reading activities occur in various settings, including community centers, preschools, and homes, often in small groups or one-to-one sessions (Dowdall et al., 2020). This approach is popular due to its accessibility, requiring only books that are available through public libraries. Additionally, repeated

C. López-Escribano (✉)
Complutense University of Madrid, Madrid, Spain
e-mail: carmenle@edu.ucm.es

R. Schapira, D. Aram (eds.), *Shared Book Reading and Children's Social-Emotional Competence*, https://doi.org/10.1007/978-3-032-14688-5_5

readings of the same book can enhance children's learning, as parents often engage in discussions about the story even after the reading session (Koskinen et al., 2000).

For nearly four decades, following the seminal work of Ninio and Bruner (1978), and framed within Vygotsky's (1978) theory of the zone of proximal development, researchers have investigated the impact of SBR on child development (Denham et al., 2007; Dowdall et al., 2020; Grøver et al., 2020; Harris et al., 1987; Lonigan et al., 2008; Mol & Bus, 2011; Xie et al., 2018). Through adult guidance, children expand their knowledge and skills, including cognitive, language, and socioemotional learning.

Early childhood is a critical period for socioemotional learning (SEL) (Denham, 2006; Durlak et al., 2011; Ziv et al., 2013) encompassing the development of emotional regulation, social competence, and understanding of emotions. During the preschool years, children start recognizing the antecedents of emotional states and can identify both individual emotions and the situations that trigger them (Denham, 2006; Denham et al., 2007, 2015). Parent–child conversations about emotions play a pivotal role in shaping socioemotional skills, which are essential for psychosocial well-being, behavioral regulation, and academic success (Dunn et al., 1991). Particularly in the realm of socioemotional learning (SEL), shared book reading fosters children's understanding of emotions by providing structured opportunities for discussion and reflection.

Research suggests that during SBR, parents and caregivers help children interpret emotional states, describe social situations, and discuss characters' thoughts and feelings, thereby enhancing children's emotional intelligence and social skills (Symons et al., 2005). The frequency, style, and elaboration of SBR have been associated with a range of socioemotional outcomes including children's understanding of mental states and behaviors (Adrian et al., 2005; Doan & Wang, 2010; Symons et al., 2005; Venkadasalam et al., 2022; Wang et al., 2023; Yurdakul et al., 2023), empathy skills (Aram & Shapira, 2012; Xu, 2024), socioemotional understanding and prosocial behavior (Aram et al., 2017; Bierman et al., 2015; Curenton & Craig, 2011; Denham, 2006; Laible, 2004; Laible & Song, 2006; Schapira & Aram, 2020; Wellman et al., 2003; Ziv et al., 2013), socioemotional adjustment and development (Aram & Aviram, 2009), and affective attribution in moral reasoning (Chou et al., 2021). In this context, morality refer to a set of personal or social standards that guide good behavior and character (Tappan, 2006).

Research on shared book reading has been conducted in various settings, ranging from naturalistic observations to structured interventions, and findings indicate that cultural contexts influence the way parents engage in book reading and how children develop emotional understanding (Doan & Wang, 2010). For instance, Western cultures emphasize individual expression during storytelling, whereas East Asian cultures focus more on behavioral guidance and socialization (Wang et al., 2000; Chou et al., 2021). Despite these variations, most research on SBR and socio**emotional development** has been conducted in Western contexts, leaving gaps in cross-cultural understanding (Yang & Wang, 2019).

While SBR's role in language and literacy development is well documented (e.g., Denham et al., 2007; Dowdall et al., 2020; Harris et al., 1987; Lonigan et al.,

2008; Mol & Bus, 2011; Noble et al., 2019), fewer studies have systematically examined its influence on socioemotional competence. Two meta-analyses examined the socioemotional effects of adult–child book reading (Grøver et al., 2020; Xie et al., 2018).

Grøver et al. (2020) conducted a qualitative systematic review, identifying 9 correlational studies, 3 single-group design studies, and 11 experimental or quasi-experimental studies on the effects of book-reading on SEL outcomes. Despite variations in how SEL outcomes were conceptualized and assessed, most experimental studies in the review suggested that SBR positively influences children's social and emotional understanding. Additionally, all three single-group intervention studies designed to support SEL skills found significant effects. However, the correlational studies yielded mixed findings regarding the relationship between book reading and children's socioemotional understanding. It is important to consider that this is a qualitative systematic review.

Xie et al. (2018) examined the effects of SBR interventions on children's and parent's psychosocial functioning. Their **meta-analysis** included 19 randomized controlled trials, considering variables such as socioemotional adjustment, behavioral problems, reading interest, and quality of life. Results indicated that SBR had a small but significant positive effect on both children's and parents' psychosocial functioning.

While experimental and intervention-based studies generally report positive effects of SBR on SEL, the correlational studies, qualitatively analyzed by Grøver et al. (2020), yield less consistent findings. Moreover, existing meta-analyses have not quantitatively synthesized the relationship between SBR and socioemotional competence across different contexts. To address this gap and given the growing recognition of the importance of early socio**emotional development**, the present **meta-analysis** aims to systematically examine studies investigating the association between parent–child SBR (both in quantity and quality) and children's socioemotional competence. Additionally, it seeks to determine whether cultural background moderates this relationship. A correlational **meta-analysis** can help identify patterns, potential moderators (such as cultural background), and gaps in the literature, ultimately strengthening the understanding of how SBR contributes to children's socio**emotional development**.

Method

Literature Search and Study Selection

A detailed search for published studies relevant to this **meta-analysis** was undertaken during June and July 2024. Comprehensive searches of ERIC, Scopus, Medline, ISI Web of Science (ISI WOS), and ProQuest databases were conducted using the following string: *(dialogic reading OR shared book reading OR storybook* *reading) AND (kindergarten OR preschool) AND (social OR emotional OR attitudes OR empathy OR awareness OR theory of mind).* Additionally, we examined previous reviews of this topic (Grøver et al., 2020; Xie et al., 2018), and other references were added in the selected studies.

Studies were included if they met the following criteria: 1) sampled kindergartens or **preschoolers** aged 7 years or younger; 2) assessed the quality or quantity of parent–child shared book reading and reported its relationship to any socioemotional construct and provided the necessary data to calculate an effect size estimate; 3) examined parent–child or caretaker–child reading at home; and 4) articles published in scientific journals between 2000 and July 2024 (when the search ended). Studies were excluded if they were published in a language other than English or Spanish and/or if the population, aims, methodology, instruments, and outcomes were not clearly defined. All search results were exported to Medline, and duplicates were removed. These selection criteria resulted in a final sample of 13 articles with a total of 14 outcomes, as one of the articles analyzed two different samples and provided two separate outcomes. Figure 5.1 is a PRISMA chart that shows the search and flow of studies through the review.

Data Extraction

The author coded the 13 eligible studies, and 2 weeks later, the 13 studies were coded again by the author. Any discrepancies between the two times the studies were coded were resolved by rechecking the given paper. A coding template was developed to extract the relevant data from studies included in the **meta-analysis**. The following information was extracted from each study: author/s (year of the study), number of participants, percentage of girls participating in the study, mean age in years and standard deviation in months, socioeconomic status (SES), time frame of the shared book reading activities, parents' shared book reading assessments, and children's socioemotional measures.

All the studies included in this **meta-analysis** (Adrian et al., 2005; Aram & Aviram, 2009; Aram & Shapira, 2012; Aram et al., 2017; Bierman et al., 2015; Chou et al., 2021; Curenton & Craig, 2011; Doan & Wang, 2010; Laible, 2004; Laible & Song, 2006; Schapira & Aram, 2020; Symons et al., 2005; Venkadasalam et al., 2022) evaluated and reported more than one relationship between one aspect of parent's shared-book reading and children's language, vocabulary, and socioemotional assessments. Given that each study could only contribute one effect size to the **meta-analysis** (Quintana, 2015), we selected the correlations most closely related to parents' shared-book reading and children's socioemotional understanding. When multiple correlations related to parents' shared book reading and children's socioemotional outcomes were presented in the same study, each outcome was assigned a number, and one was randomly selected. Effect sizes were calculated for the total of the 14 eligible outcomes, resulting in a total of 14 independent effect sizes for analyses from 1410 participants.

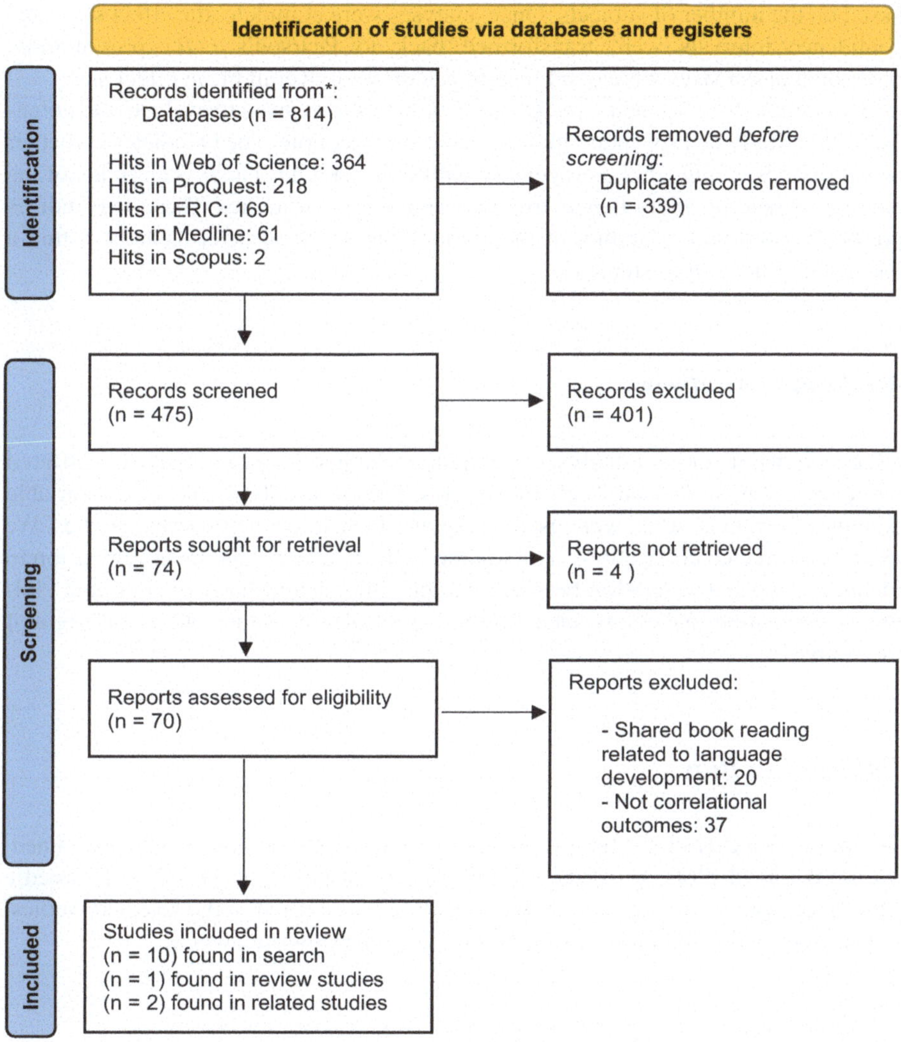

Fig. 5.1 PRISMA 2020 flow diagram. From: Page MJ, McKenzie JE, Bossuyt PM, Boutron I, Hoffmann TC, Mulrow CD, et al. The PRISMA 2020 statement: an updated guideline for reporting systematic reviews. BMJ 2021; 372: n71. doi: https://doi.org/10.1136/bmj.n71

Meta-Analysis

In the present **meta-analysis**, we used a random-effects model to account for expected between-study variability. The Pearson correlation coefficient, *r*, was used as the indicator of effect size (range = −1.0 to +1.0; Rosenthal, 1991). Once study characteristics were coded and effect sizes were extracted, a Fisher's *r*-to-z (Fisher, 1921) was performed. For this transformed correlation, a standard error is estimated based on the number of subjects. Once analyses were complete, the effect sizes and confidence intervals were transformed back to Pearson's r for presentation. Individual effect sizes were combined to calculate an overall mean effect size.

To examine heterogeneity, the Q and I^2 statistics were used to evaluate the potential within-study heterogeneity in the present study sample. The Q indicates whether or not there is significant heterogeneity within the sample. The I^2 is an index of the amount of heterogeneity that is true between-study variability. These two indices provide a good understanding of the amount and scope of heterogeneity within a particular collection of studies.

Moderator Analysis

We conducted moderator analyses to examine whether the mean effect size differed based on within-study sample characteristics. The effects of the categorical variable country of origin of study were used to explain the heterogeneity across studies. We used the corrected correlations (r) with fixed effects models and meta-regression to identify whether the relation between parent–child shared book reading and children's socioemotional competence differed as a function of the country of origin of the study.

Publication Bias

In order to detect retrieval bias, funnel plots for fixed-effect models were examined. We used funnel plots, trim and fill analyses as proposed by Duval and Tweedie (2000) to explore whether potential publication bias existed in the selected studies. All analyses were conducted using *Meta-Essentials* (Suurmond et al., 2017).

Results

Study Characteristics

Fourteen non-overlapping samples were identified and included in the present meta-analyses. The study selection process is presented in Fig. 5.1. The characteristics of all studies are displayed in Table 5.1. The total number of participants was 1410 (range 33–656). The majority of participants came from two Canadian studies ($N = 707$), five USA studies (one of them with two outcomes) ($N = 361$), followed by four studies from Israel ($N = 229$), one study from Taiwan ($N = 79$), and one study from Spain ($N = 34$). Mean age of children was 4.49 years (SD = 5.83 months),

Table 5.1 Study characteristics and effect sizes included in meta-analysis

Study and location	*N*	Girls	Age M yrs. (SD) mos	Dyads	SES	Time frame	a) Mothers'/fathers' shared-book-reading assessment b) Children's socioemotional measures	*r*
Adrian et al. (2005) Spain	34	44%	4.10 (5.83)	Mother/child	Mixed	4 sessions 4 stories	a) Mental state terms during reading (Coded according to Bretherton & Beeghly, 1982) b) False belief task (The 'unexpected transfer task' (Wimmer & Perner, 1983))	0.38*
Aram and Aviram (2009) Israel	40	45%	5.9 (4.39)	Mother/child	Middle	1 session (30 min)	a) Frequency of storybook reading (Mothers' Recognition of children literature, according to Stainthorp, 1997) b) Socioemotional adjustment (The 'teacher–child rating scale' (Hightower et al., 1986))	0.35*
Aram and Shapira (2012) Israel	78	60%	4.56 (5.70)	Mother/child	Mixed	1 session	a) Mental-emotional discourse (Open/closed questions & expansions related to the mental and emotional realm coded during reading) b) Empathy (Empathy assessment tool by Strayer & Roberts, 2004)	0.22*
Aram et al. (2017) Israel	61	49%	5.8 (7.39)	Mother/child	Low	2 sessions (30–40 min)	a) Socioemotional utterances (Statements related to emotions coded during reading) b) Social behavior (Sharing game by Levin & Bekerman-Greenberg, 1980)	0.25*

(continued)

Table 5.1 (continued)

Study and location	*N*	Girls	Age M yrs. (SD) mos	Dyads	SES	Time frame	a) Mothers'/fathers' shared-book-reading assessment b) Children's socioemotional measures	*r*
Bierman et al. (2015) USA	95	44%	4.45 (0.29)	Parent/child (mainly mothers 89%)	Low	Ten weeks of daily sessions	a) Quality of dialogic reading (Parents described the degree of interactively reading from the participation subscale of the Reading Belief Inventory by DeBaryshe & Binder, 1994) b) Socioemotional adjustment (School readiness questionnaire by Bierman et al., 2008)	0.01
Chou et al. (2021) Taiwan	79	49%	4.45 4.62 (age range 49–73 months)	Parent/child (mainly mothers 92%)	Mixed	2 sessions	a) Parents' explanation of moral judgment (The coding scheme used was adapted according to the moral narrative coding scheme by Malti and Latzko (2010)) b) Moral evaluation of the child (Moral reasoning task that contains two short moral violation stories: stealing and not sharing (adapted by Chou, 2014))	0.27*
Curenton and Craig (2011) USA	33	45%	4.41 (7.96)	Mother/child	Mixed	1 session	a) Frequency of shared reading (Mothers were asked to report frequency of shared reading in a typical week, 1 = not at all to 4 = 4 or more times) b) Children's prosocial skills (Social skills rating system by Gresham & Elliott, 1990)	0.38*
Doan and Wang (2010) USA	71[a]	48%	2.95 (age range 30–42 months)	Mother/child	Middle	1 session	a) Mental states focus (Mothers' mental state language was coded following Ruffman et al. (2002)) b) Emotional situation knowledge (ESK) (Children's ESK was assessed using an emotion production task by Harris et al. (1987))	0.24*

Doan and Wang (2010) USA	60[b]	50%	2.91 (age range 30–43 months)	Mother/child	Middle	1 session	a) Mental states focus (Mothers' mental state language was coded following Ruffman et al. (2002)) b) Emotional situation knowledge (Children's ESK was assessed using an emotion production task by Harris et al. (1987))	0.11
Laible (2004) USA	51	55%	4.07 (9.47)	Mother/child	N/S	2 sessions	a) Maternal elaboration during the storybook (Quality of discourse (see Fivush & Fromhoff, 1988; Laible & Thompson, 1998)) b) Prosocial behavior (Child's behavior scale (Ladd & Profilet, 1996))	0.09
Laible and Song (2006) USA	51	51%	4.4 (8.69)	Mother/child	N/S	1 session	a) Maternal elaboration during the storybook (From the transcripts, all references to emotions were identified and coded (Dunn & Munn, 1987; Kuebli et al., 1995)) b) Emotional understanding (Perspective-taking task (Denham, 1986))	0.10
Schapira and Aram (2020) Israel	50	48%	4.63 (4.53)	Parent/child (mainly mothers 88%)	Mixed	3 sessions	a) Parents' socioemotional utterances (Parents' pieces of verbal outputs that were categorized as either general or socioemotional content (Levin & Aram, 2012)) b) Prosocial attitude (MacArthur Story Stem Battery (MSSB) (Oppenheim et al., 1997))	0.32*

(continued)

Table 5.1 (continued)

Study and location	N	Girls	Age M yrs. (SD) mos	Dyads	SES	Time frame	a) Mothers'/fathers' shared-book-reading assessment b) Children's socioemotional measures	r
Symons et al. (2005) Canada	51	69%	5.68 (6.27)	Parent/child (mainly mothers 90%)	Mixed	1 session	a) Parents' on-task elaboration (Elaboration of the text by parents was transcribed (Golinkoff & Ames, 1979)) b) Child mentalistic (A ToM aggregate score resulting from the average of three types of tasks (see Fahie & Symons, 2003))	0.66**
Venkadasalam et al. (2022) Canada	656	N/R	5.16 (0.50)	Mother/child	Mixed	2 sessions	a) Maternal input during shared reading (Systematic assessment of book reading (Pentimoni et al., 2012)) b) Theory of mind (Children's ToM was measured using an adaptation of Wellman and Liu (2004))	0.16*

*$p < 0.05$; **$p < 0.01$
N/S = Not specified
[a] European American mother–child pairs
[b] Chinese immigrant mother–child pairs

and the percentage of girls in the total studies where this data was reported ranged from 44% to 69% (M = 49, SD = 6.65). Out of the 13 selected studies, two of them examined SBR frequency, while 11 analyzed the quality of parents' discourse while sharing a book with their child (see Table 5.1).

Overall Correlation Between Parent–Child Shared Book Reading and Children's Social Competence

Figure 5.2 shows the forest plot with effect sizes and confidence intervals for the 13 studies (k = 13) and each study outcome (n = 14), in addition to the pooled result, calculated with the random effects weights. The average corrected correlation between parent–child shared book reading and children's social competence was significant ($r = 0.24$ [95% CI = 0.14, 0.34], $Z = 4.95$, $p < 0.01$). That is, higher levels of social competence were significantly associated with higher levels of quality and quantity of parent–child shared book reading. While this association is statistically significant, the effect size is relatively small, suggesting that other factors may influence socio**emotional development**. There was a significant moderate mean effect size in the observed studies ($Q = 27.69$, $p = 0.01$; $I^2 = 53.05$).

Study name	Stadistics for each study				
	Correlation	Lower limit	Upper limit	Z-Value	p-Value
Adrian et al. (2005)	0.38	0.03	0.64	2.23	0.01
Aram & Aviram (2009)	0.35	0.03	0.60	2.22	0.01
Aram & Shapira (2012)	0.22	-0.01	0.42	1.94	0.03
Aram et al. (2017)	0.25	-0.01	0.48	1.95	0.03
Bierman et al. (2015)	0.01	-0.19	0.21	0.10	0.46
Chou et al. (2021)	0.27	0.05	0.47	2.41	0.00
Curenton & Craig (2011)	0.38	0.03	0.65	2.19	0.01
Doang & Wang (2010)	0.24	0.00	0.45	2.02	0.02
Doang & Wang (2010)	0.11	-0.15	0.36	0.83	0.20
Laible (2006)	0.09	-0.20	0.36	0.63	0.27
Laible & Song (2006)	0.10	-0.19	0.37	0.70	0.24
Schapira & Aram (2019)	0.32	0.04	0.55	2.27	0.01
Symons et al. (2005)	0.66	0.46	0.79	5.49	0.00
Venkadasalan et al (2022)	0.16	0.08	0.23	4.12	0.00

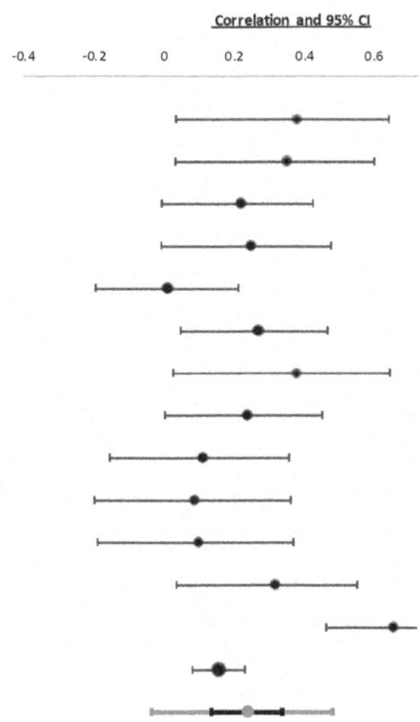

Fig. 5.2 Forest plot showing effect size with confidence interval, z-value, and p-value for the correlation between parent–child shared book reading and children's social competence for each study, and the overall correlation (black dot) across studies

Moderator Analysis

Due to the moderate heterogeneity of the overall effect sizes in the relation between parent–child shared book reading and children's social competence, a moderator analysis was conducted. The country of origin of study was considered as a categorical moderator, provided it had at least four studies. However, only two studies from Canada, one from Spain, and one from Taiwan were available, so these countries could not be included in between-country comparisons. Analyses were performed using studies from the USA ($k = 5$) and Israel ($k = 4$). The weighted effect size for the relation between parent–child shared book reading and children's social competence was $r = 0.22$ (95% CI [0.06, 0.36], $p = 0.4$). The between-level Q appeared not significant ($Q = 2.57$, $p = 0.10$), suggesting that the correlation between parent–child shared book reading and children's social competence was not significant by the country of origin analyzed.

Publication Bias

Figure 5.3 presents a funnel plot of the effect sizes observed in the included 14 outcomes of 13 studies. Egger's regression intercept indicated no evidence for publication bias in the identified studies (95% CI, −0.27, 2.80) (t test = 1.77; $p = 0.10$).

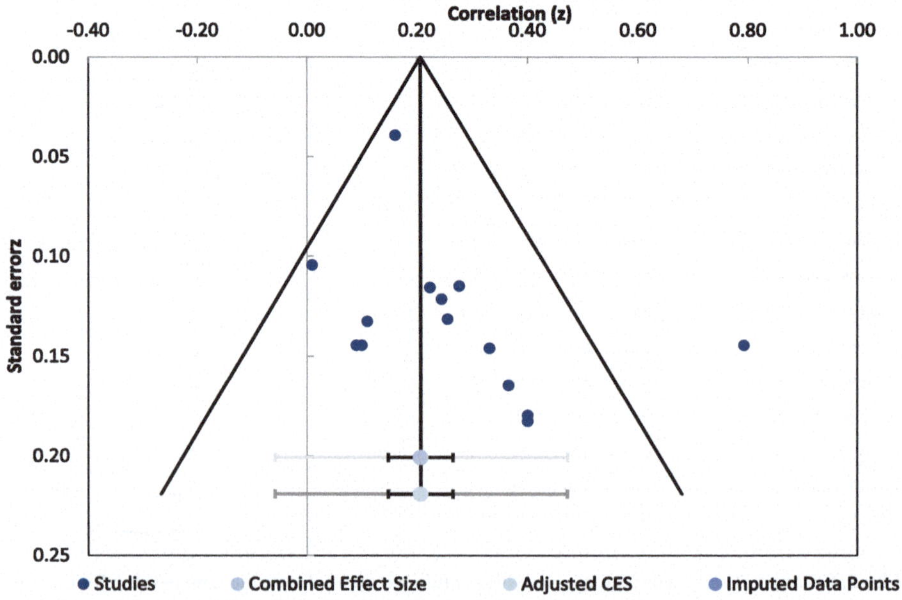

Fig. 5.3 Funnel plot of standard error by Fisher's Z of the 13 outcomes included

Discussion

To our knowledge, this is the first meta-analytic correlational review of parent–child shared book reading related to children's socioemotional competence.

The aims of the study were (1) to review and systematically examine studies testing the correlation between parent–child shared book reading and children's socioemotional competence and (2) to explore whether the participants' origin and culture moderate this association.

Even though the length and dosage of SBR activities of the review studies were small, **meta-analysis** revealed that parent–child shared book reading is associated with children's socioemotional competence with a small-to-moderate effect size. SBR might positively impact children's moral judgment, prosocial skills, emotional knowledge, and children's mentalistic or theory of mind (see Table 5.1). These findings have both theoretical and practical implications and offer a strong justification for initiating more systematic research about the relationship between shared book reading and children's socioemotional competence in different contexts and cultures.

Shared book reading is a low-cost and simple adapted approach for any parent–child dyad, no matter what the circumstances. In fact, shared book reading is considered one of the most frequent activities within the family context (López-Escribano et al., 2021). A large number of family interventions have traditionally focused on behavioral problems of children instead of the interactions between parents and children. However, the individual focus approach has limited long-term efficacy and more and more psychologists recommend the importance of relationship-focused interventions (Xie et al., 2018). Since young children's learning primarily occurs in dyadic interaction with knowledgeable caregivers, engaging in dialogic parent–child communication through SBR at an early age effectively promotes communication and socio**emotional development** (Loredana et al., 2024). In our review, we identified that only a limited number of the reported SBR activities involved fathers. Given the importance of father–child interaction in the development of children, future SBR activities should be designed to attract the participation of fathers.

We conducted one exploratory single-predictor moderator analysis. We were interested in examining whether the mean effect size differed based on participant origin and culture. The results indicated that the country of origin was not a significant predictor of the effect size. Both countries included in the exploratory single-predictor moderator analysis (USA and Israel) are considered to be of Western culture. Besides, the number of studies in the analysis was quite limited. Both facts could explain why the country of origin was not a significant predictor of the association between parent–child shared book reading and children's socioemotional competence. Nevertheless, growing evidence suggests that the sociocultural context shapes children's **emotional development** (see Savina & Wan, 2017). Consequently, SBR programs to develop children's psychosocial skills should take into consideration the sociocultural background using storybooks with characters and issues relevant to the culture and the community they are directed to. More research on SBR and socio**emotional development** across different countries and cultures is scarce and urgently needed.

Limitations

Several limitations of this study should be considered. First, although we attempted to identify all eligible studies using different search methods, it is likely that some studies were not captured by our search strategy. Second, there are a limited number of studies reporting the correlation between the parent–child shared book reading and children's socioemotional competence that met the selected criteria. Due to the scarcity of studies on this topic, the limited sample size may introduce bias in the results. Third, in the included studies, we identified a range of socioemotional outcomes (children's moral judgment, prosocial skills, emotional knowledge, and theory of mind) and different parents' inputs during shared reading (different frequency and type of parents' explanations). To make sense of these different measures, we treated all of them as personal social competence in children and the use of reading strategies as an important parental competence. The goal of this study was to explore the pattern of relationship between children's socioemotional competence and parent–child SBR activities by assessing the psychosocial effectiveness of SBR. Fourth, correlational studies suggest a relationship between shared book reading and children's socioemotional competence, though more intervention studies are needed to confirm causality. Fifth, as parent-reported data may be influenced by social desirability bias, future studies should incorporate observational measures to validate findings. Finally, it is possible that the nonsignificant moderating effects of country of origin would reach significance if a larger number of studies from diverse countries had been available for analysis. Moreover, the methodological quality of the studies was not assessed beyond ensuring that they met the inclusion criteria for this **meta-analysis**. Only peer-reviewed journal articles were included, and they were deemed satisfactory for inclusion based on the adequacy and clarity of their population, aims, methodology, instruments, and outcomes.

Conclusion

While considering study limitations, this paper extends the literature in several ways. We add to the existing systematic reviews by estimating a significant association between parent–child shared book reading and children's socioemotional competence. A cumulative body of research has described co-occurrence, correlation, and prediction of parent–child shared book reading and children's socioemotional competence (Grøver et al., 2020; Xie et al., 2018). Given the importance of socioemotional learning skills to children's life outcomes, this area of research warrants further investigation. Future studies should explore potential moderators of the explicit relations between parent–child shared book reading and children's socio-emotional competence, such as age, cultural influences, discourse style, genres, and content of books, while also refining measurement approaches and ensuring construct validity to gain a more comprehensive understanding of the impact of shared book reading on children's socio**emotional development**. Then, probing results in intervention with the goal of improving social, emotional, and educational outcomes for children.

The results of the moderator analyses indicated that country of origin was not a significant predictor of the effect size. Nevertheless, child **emotional development** and learning are shaped by cultural values and practices. Therefore, SBR psychosocial intervention should be sensitive to the different contexts and cultures that guide children's socio**emotional development** and behavior.

This study may also provide important implications for families, for teachers, and for students of early childhood education. Different shared book reading strategies should be included in the curriculum of teachers so that they know how to share a book with children and are able to show families the best way to perform this task at home with their children. In this way, our faculty has established a reading lab with children's literature, enabling future teachers to become familiar with print-based, manipulative books, which are ideal resources for teaching reading to young children. This initiative also aims to counteract the excessive use of technological devices in early childhood education. Additionally, future teachers can learn and practice shared book reading strategies.

References

Adrian, J. E., Clemente, R. A., Villanueva, L., & Rieffe, C. (2005). Parent-child picture-book reading, mothers' mental state language and children's theory of mind. *Journal of Child Language, 32*(3), 673–686. https://doi.org/10.1017/S0305000905006963

Aram, D., & Aviram, S. (2009). Mothers' storybook reading and kindergartners' socio-emotional and literacy development. *Reading Psychology, 30*(2), 175–194. https://doi.org/10.1080/02702710802275348

Aram, D., Bergman Deitcher, D., Sabag Shoshan, T., & Ziv, M. (2017). Shared book reading interactions within families from low socioeconomic backgrounds and children's social understanding and prosocial behavior. *Journal of Cognitive Education and Psychology, 16*(2), 157–177. https://doi.org/10.1891/1945-8959.16.2.157

Aram, D., & Shapira, R. (2012). Parent-child shared book reading and children's language, literacy, and empathy development. *Rivista Italiana di Educazione Familiare, 2*, 55–65. https://core.ac.uk/download/pdf/228546676.pdf

Bierman, K. L., Domitrovich, C. E., Nix, R. L., Gest, S. D., Welsh, J. A., Greenberg, M. T., & Gill, S. (2008). Promoting academic and social-emotional school readiness: The Head Start REDI program. *Child Development, 79*, 1802–1817. https://doi.org/10.1111/j.1467-8624.2008.01227.x

Bierman, K. L., Welsh, J. A., Heinrichs, B. S., Nix, R. L., & Mathis, E. T. (2015). Helping Head Start parents promote their children's kindergarten adjustment: The REDI parent program. *Child Development, 86*(6), 1877–1891. https://doi.org/10.1111/cdev.12448

Bretherton, I., & Beeghly, M. (1982). Talking about internal states: The acquisition of an explicit theory of mind. *Developmental Psychology, 18*(6), 906–921. https://doi.org/10.1037/0012-1649.18.6.906

Chou, Y. J. (2014). Young children's justifications of emotion attributions of moral events. *Bulletin of Educational Psychology, 45*(2), 475–496. https://doi.org/10.6251/BEP.20130730

Chou, Y.-J., Hu, B.-Y., & Roberts, S. K. (2021). Features of Taiwanese parents' moral discourse in shared storybook reading: Exploring associations related to preschoolers' cognitive and affective moral attribution. *Early Childhood Education Journal, 49*(6), 1007–1019. https://doi.org/10.1007/s10643-020-01110-z

Curenton, S. M., & Craig, M. J. (2011). Shared-reading versus oral storytelling: Associations with preschoolers' prosocial skills and problem behaviours. *Early Child Development and Care, 181*(1), 123–146. https://doi.org/10.1080/03004430903292208

DeBaryshe, B. D., & Binder, J. C. (1994). Development of an instrument for measuring parental beliefs about reading aloud to young children. *Perceptual and Motor Skills, 78*, 1303–1311. https://doi.org/10.2466/pms.1994.78.3c.1303

Denham, S. A. (1986). Social cognition, prosocial behavior, and emotion in preschoolers: Contextual validation. *Child Development, 57*(1), 194–201. https://doi.org/10.2307/1130651

Denham, S. A. (2006). Social-emotional competence as support for school readiness: What is it and how do we assess it? *Early Education and Development, 17*(1), 57–89. https://doi.org/10.1207/s15566935eed1701_4

Denham, S. A., Bassett, H. H., Brown, C., Way, E., & Steed, J. (2015). "I know how you feel": Preschoolers' emotion knowledge contributes to early school success. *Journal of Early Childhood Research, 13*(3), 252–262. https://doi.org/10.1177/1476718X13497354

Denham, S. A., Bassett, H. H., & Wyatt, T. (2007). The socialization of emotional competence. In J. Grusec & P. D. Hastings (Eds.), *Handbook of socialization: Theory and research* (pp. 614–637). Guilford Press.

Doan, S. N., & Wang, Q. (2010). Maternal discussions of mental states and behaviors: Relations to emotion situation knowledge in European American and Immigrant Chinese Children. *Child Development, 81*(5), 1490–1503. https://doi.org/10.1111/j.1467-8624.2010.01487.x

Dowdall, N., Melendez-Torres, G. J., Murray, L., Gardner, F., Hartford, L., & Cooper, P. J. (2020). Shared picture book reading interventions for child language development: A systematic review and meta-analysis. *Child Development, 91*(2), e383–e399. https://doi.org/10.1111/cdev.13225

Dunn, J., Brown, J., Slomkowski, C., Tesla, C., & Youngblade, L. (1991). Young children's understanding of other people's feelings and beliefs: Individual differences and their antecedents. *Child Development, 62*, 1352–1366. https://doi.org/10.2307/1130811

Dunn, J., & Munn, P. (1987). Development of justification in disputes with mother and sibling. *Developmental Psychology, 23*(6), 791–798. https://doi.org/10.1037/0012-1649.23.6.791

Durlak, J. A., Weissberg, R. P., Dymnicki, A. B., Taylor, R. D., & Schellinger, K. B. (2011). The impact of enhancing students' social and emotional learning: A meta-analysis of schoolbased universal interventions. *Child Development, 82*, 405–432. https://doi.org/10.1111/j.1467-8624.2010.01564.x

Duval, S., & Tweedie, R. (2000). A nonparametric "trim and fill" method of accounting for publication bias in meta-analysis. *Journal of the American Statistical Association, 95*(449), 89–98. https://doi.org/10.1080/01621459.2000.10473905

Fahie, C. M., & Symons, D. K. (2003). Executive functioning and theory of mind in children clinically referred for attention and behavior problems. *Journal of Applied Developmental Psychology, 24*(1), 51–73. https://doi.org/10.1016/S0193-3973(03)00024-8

Fisher, R. A. (1921). On the "probable error" of a coefficient of correlation deduced from a small sample. *Metron, 1*, 3–32. hdl.handle.net/2440/15169

Fivush, R., & Fromhoff, F. A. (1988). Style and structure in mother-child conversations about the past. *Discourse Processes, 11*(3), 337–355. https://doi.org/10.1080/01638538809544707

Golinkoff, R. M., & Ames, G. J. (1979). A comparison of fathers' and mothers' speech with their young children. *Child Development, 50*, 28–32.

Gresham, F., & Elliott, S. (1990). *Social skills rating system*. American Guidance Service.

Grøver, V., Rydland, V., Gustafsson, J.-E., & Snow, C. E. (2020). Shared book reading in preschool supports Bilingual children's second-language learning: A cluster-randomized trial. *Child Development, 91*(6), 2192–2210. https://doi.org/10.1111/cdev.13348

Harris, P. L., Olthof, T., Terwogt, M. M., & Hardman, C. E. (1987). Children's knowledge of the situations that provoke emotion. *International Journal of Behavioral Development, 10*(3), 319–343. https://doi.org/10.1177/016502548701000304

Hightower, A. D., Work, W. C., Cowen, E. L., Lotyczewski, B. S., Spinell, A. P., Guare, J. C., et al. (1986). The teacher-child rating scale: A brief objective measure of elementary children's school problem behaviors and competencies. *School Psychology Review, 15*, 393–409. https://doi.org/10.1080/02796015.1986.12085242

Koskinen, P. S., Blum, I. H., Bisson, S. A., Phillips, S. M., Creamer, T. S., & Baker, T. K. (2000). Book access, shared reading, and audio models: The effects of supporting the literacy learning of linguistically diverse students in school and at home. *Journal of Educational Psychology, 92*(1), 23–36. https://doi.org/10.1037/0022-0663.92.1.23

Kuebli, J., Butler, S., & Fivush, R. (1995). Mother-child talk about past emotions: Relations of maternal language and child gender over time. *Cognition and Emotion, 9*(2–3), 265–283. https://doi.org/10.1080/02699939508409011

Ladd, G. W., & Profilet, S. M. (1996). The child behavior scale: A teacher-report measure of young children's aggressive, withdrawn, and prosocial behaviors. *Developmental Psychology, 32*(6), 1008–1024. https://doi.org/10.1037/0012-1649.32.6.1008

Laible, D., & Song, J. (2006). Constructing emotional and relational understanding: The role of affect and mother-child discourse. *Merrill-Palmer Quarterly-Journal Of Developmental Psychology, 52*(1), 44–69. https://doi.org/10.1353/mpq.2006.0006

Laible, D. (2004). Mother-child discourse in two contexts: Links with child temperament, attachment security, and socioemotional competence. *Developmental Psychology, 40*(6), 979–992. https://doi.org/10.1037/0012-1649.40.6.979

Laible, D., & Thompson, R. (1998). Attachment and emotional understanding in preschool children. *Developmental Psychology, 34*:1038–1045. https://doi.org/10.1037/0012-1649.34.5.1038

Levin, I., & Aram, D. (2012). Mother–child joint writing and storybook reading and their effects on kindergartners' literacy: An intervention study. *Reading and Writing, 25*, 217–249. https://doi.org/10.1007/s11145-010-9254-y

Levin, I., & Bekerman-Greenberg, R. (1980). Moral judgment and moral behavior in sharing: A developmental analysis. *Israeli Journal of Psychology & Counseling in Education, 11*, 24–34. https://psycnet.apa.org/record/1981-10232-001

Lonigan, C. J., Shanahan, T., & Cunningham, A. (2008). Impact of shared-reading interventions on young children's early literacy skills. In *Developing early literacy: Report of the National Early Literacy Panel* (pp. 153–171). National Institute for Literacy.

López-Escribano, C., Escudero, A., & Pérez-López, R. (2021). An exploratory study about patterns of parental home literacy activities during the COVID-19 confinement among Spanish families. *Early Education and Development, 32*(6), 812–829. https://doi.org/10.1080/10409289.2021.1916184

Loredana, C., Alice, T., Lynne, M., Peter, C., Stefano, C., & Mauro, B. (2024). Early parent-child intervention with Dialogic Book-Sharing: Effects on child communicative and socio-emotional development and on parenting. Study protocol for a multicentre randomised controlled trial in Italy. *Trials, 25*(1), 1–12. https://doi.org/10.1186/s13063-024-08232-4

Malti, T., & Latzko, B. (2010). Children's moral emotions and moral cognition: Towards an integrative perspective. In B. Latzko & T. Malti (Eds.), *Children's moral emotions and moral cognition: Developmental and educational perspectives* (Vol. 129, pp. 1–10). New Directions for Child and Adolescent Development. https://doi.org/10.1002/cd.272

Mol, S. E., & Bus, A. G. (2011). To read or not to read: A meta-analysis of print exposure from infancy to early adulthood. *Psychological Bulletin, 137*(2), 267–296. https://doi.org/10.1037/a0021890

Ninio, A., & Bruner, J. (1978). The achievement and antecedents of labelling. *Journal of Child Language, 5*(1), 1–15. https://doi.org/10.1017/S0305000900001896

Noble, C., Sala, G., Lowe, M., Lingwood, J., Rowland, C. F., Gobet, F., & Pine, J. (2019). The impact of shared book reading on children's language skills: A meta-analysis. *Educational Research Review, 28*, 1–10. https://doi.org/10.1016/j.edurev.2019.100290

Oppenheim, D., Nir, A., Warren, S., & Emde, R. N. (1997). Emotion regulation in mother–child narrative co-construction: Associations with children's narratives and adaptation. *Developmental Psychology, 33*(2), 284–294. https://doi.org/10.1037/0012-1649.33.2.284

Pentimonti, J. M., Zucker, T. A., Justice, L. M., Petscher, Y., Piasta, S. B., & Kaderavek, J. N. (2012). A standardized tool for assessing the quality of classroom-based shared reading: Systematic assessment of book reading (SABR). *Early Childhood Research Quarterly, 27*(3), 512–528. https://doi.org/10.1016/j.ecresq.2011.12.007

Quintana, D. S. (2015). From pre-registration to publication: A non-technical primer for conducting a meta-analysis to synthesize correlational data. *Frontiers in Psychology, 6*, 1554. https://doi.org/10.3389/fpsyg.2015.01549

Rosenthal, R. (1991). *Meta-analytic procedures for social research*. Sage Publications, Inc. https://doi.org/10.4135/9781412984997

Ruffman, T., Slade, L., & Crowe, E. (2002). The relation between children's and mothers' mental state language and theory-of-mind understanding. *Child Development, 73*(3), 734–751. https://doi.org/10.1111/1467-8624.00435

Savina, E., & Wan, K. P. (2017). Cultural pathways to socio-emotional development and learning. *Journal of Relationships Research, 8, E19*. https://doi.org/10.1017/jrr.2017.19

Schapira, R., & Aram, D. (2020). Shared book reading at home and preschoolers' socio-emotional competence. *Early Education and Development, 31*(6), 819–837. https://doi.org/10.1080/10409289.2019.1692624

Stainthorp, R. (1997). A children's author recognition test: A useful tool in reading research. *Journal of Research in Reading, 20*, 148–158. https://doi.org/10.1111/1467-9817.00027

Strayer, J., & Roberts, W. L. (2004). *The empathy continuum scoring manual*. Simon Fraser University.

Suurmond, R., van Rhee, H., & Hak, T. (2017). Introduction, comparison and validation of meta-essentials: A free and simple tool for meta-analysis. *Research Synthesis Methods, 8*(4), 537–553. https://doi.org/10.1002/jrsm.1260

Symons, D. K., Peterson, C. C., Slaughter, V., Roche, J., & Doyle, E. (2005). Theory of mind and mental state discourse during book reading and story-telling tasks. *British Journal of Developmental Psychology, 23*(1), 81–102. https://doi.org/10.1348/026151004X21080

Tappan, M. B. (2006). Mediated moralities: Sociocultural approaches to moral development. In M. Killen & J. Smetana (Eds.), *Handbook of moral development* (pp. 351–374). Erlbaum.

Towson, J. A., Gallagher, P. A., & Bingham, G. E. (2016). Dialogic reading: Language and pre-literacy outcomes for young children with disabilities. *Journal of Early Intervention, 38*(4), 230–246. https://doi.org/10.1177/1053815116668643

Venkadasalam, V. P., Jenkins, J. M., Ganea, P. A., & Wade, M. (2022). Linking early maternal input during shared reading to later theory of mind through receptive language and executive function: A within- and between-family design. *Journal of Experimental Child Psychology, 223*, 105469. https://doi.org/10.1016/j.jecp.2022.105469

Vygotsky, L. (1978). *Mind in society*. Harvard University Press.

Wang, J., Wu, Y., Wu, J., Gong, Y., Dong, Y., Li, L., & Fang, H. (2023). Enhancing 3–4-year-old rural Chinese children's theory of mind: A randomized control trial to evaluate a parent-involved school-based dialogic reading intervention programme. *Early Child Development and Care, 193*(15–16), 1543–1557. https://doi.org/10.1080/03004430.2023.2264524

Wang, Q., Leichtman, M. D., & Davies, K. I. (2000). Sharing memories and telling stories: American and Chinese mothers and their 3-year-olds. *Memory, 8*(3), 159–177. https://doi.org/10.1080/096582100387588

Wellman, H. M., & Liu, D. (2004). Scaling of theory-of-mind tasks. *Child Development, 75*, 523–541. https://doi.org/10.1111/j.1467-8624.2004.00691.x

Wellman, H. M., Phillips, A. T., & Rodriguez, T. (2003). Young children's understanding of perception, desire, and emotion. *Child Development, 71*(4), 895–912. https://doi.org/10.1111/1467-8624.00198

Wimmer, H., & Perner, J. (1983). Beliefs about beliefs: Representations and constraining function of wrong beliefs in young children's understanding of deception. *Cognition, 13*, 103–128. https://doi.org/10.1016/0010-0277(83)90004-5

Xie, Q. W., Chan, C. H. Y., Ji, Q., & Chan, C. L. W. (2018). Psychosocial effects of parent-child book reading interventions: A meta-analysis. *Pediatrics, 141*(4), e20172675. https://doi.org/10.1542/peds.2017-2675

Xu, J. (2024). Developing emotional intelligence in children through dialogic reading, self-made books, and visible thinking routines. *Early Childhood Education Journal, 52*(7), 1693–1705. https://doi.org/10.1007/s10643-023-01520-9

Yang, Y., & Wang, Q. (2019). Culture in emotional development. In V. Lobue, K. Pérez-Edgar, & K. A. Bus (Eds.), *Handbook of emotional development* (pp. 569–593). Springer.

Yurdakul, Y., Beyazit, U., & Ayhan, A. B. (2023). The effect of dialogic book reading on preschool children's perspective taking skills. *Early Childhood Education Journal, 2*, 49–62. https://doi.org/10.1007/s10643-023-01567-8

Ziv, M., Smadja, M. L., & Aram, D. (2013). Mothers' mental-state discourse with preschoolers during storybook reading and wordless storybook telling. *Early Childhood Research Quarterly, 28*(1), 177–186. https://doi.org/10.1016/j.ecresq

Carmen López-Escribano (PhD) is an Associate Professor and head of the Department of Research and Psychology in Education at Complutense University of Madrid. She is a Fulbright fellow and a former visiting scholar at Harvard Graduate School of Education. Her research focuses on the assessment and intervention of reading and writing, with a particular emphasis on learning difficulties and special educational needs. Currently, she contributes to two international research projects, including one with Save the Children aimed at supporting children's learning and well-being in vulnerable contexts.

Chapter 6
Working with Stories: A Bibliotherapeutic Perspective

Inbar Sofri and Yair Ziv

Contents

In the current chapter, we look at **storytelling** from the point of view of **Bibliotherapy**—a therapeutic method that relies on reading and writing processes to help therapy clients (here we will focus mainly on young children) gain a deeper understanding of themselves and others, and to advance their well-being. We will introduce three constructs describing mental processes that occur while listening to a story and stem from bibliotherapeutic literature: identification, echoing, and insight. We will also introduce a new research and evaluation tool (The Story Processing Assessment; SPA), which aims to assess these mental processes in young children when they listen to a story, and discuss different ways in which this tool can be useful in the clinic.

Bibliotherapy

Bibliotherapy is a therapeutic method that utilizes guided reading and writing processes for better understanding children's emotions, thoughts, interactions, communication patterns, and coping strategies (Cohen, 1990; Kobovi, 1992; Lucas &

I. Sofri (✉) · Y. Ziv
University of Haifa, Haifa, Israel
e-mail: inbarsofri@gmail.com; yziv@edu.haifa.ac.il

R. Schapira, D. Aram (eds.), *Shared Book Reading and Children's Social-Emotional Competence*, https://doi.org/10.1007/978-3-032-14688-5_6

Soares, 2013; Sharma, 2022; Wang et al., 2022; Yamashita, 2023; Zoran, 2009). The term itself, "**bibliotherapy**," refers to a therapy that combines the therapist's preferred psychotherapeutic approach with literature (Rottenberg, 2022). In **bibliotherapy**, reading and writing processes are mediated by the bibliotherapist, and the action of mediation is used for therapeutic purposes (Zoran, 2009).

Communication through text is a form of indirect communication that allows participants to choose the pace and depth of their reaction, while keeping a certain distance from the events that occur in the text (Cook et al., 2006). There is a certain ambiguity in most texts, and it is that quality that makes the readers use their personal experience to fill in the gaps (Iser, 1974). Therefore, **bibliotherapy** is considered a gentle, non-threatening way to help therapy clients unravel their personal story and to support and enhance their well-being (Lucas & Soares, 2013; Sharma, 2022; Wang et al., 2022; Yamashita, 2023). Bibliotherapists can use existing texts and bring them to sessions, or, in other cases, invite their clients to bring texts or their own writings to therapy, including journals, poems, stories, and dreams.

A central tenet of **Bibliotherapy** is that it relies on, and encourages, certain processes that typically naturally occur while reading or listening to stories: 1) identification: the readers identify with a character in the text (usually, the main character). 2) Projection: The reader projects certain aspects of their inner world onto the character and vice versa. 3) Catharsis: The previous stages enable the readers to release built-up tension and deal with repressed emotions, thus creating a cathartic effect. 4) Insight: The process results in gaining new insights into the subject or emotional theme at hand (Cohen, 1990; Zaccaria et al., 1978).

Kobovi (1992) elaborated on these processes and suggested ways to work with texts and ask questions that encourage the mental processes that take place while encountering a text. Kobovi defined those processes as "identification" (identify with the main character in the text), "echoing" (connect the events in the story to the reader's inner world), and "detachment" (distance oneself from the story to gain insight from the story). Here, we will refer to the term "detachment" as "insight" to emphasize the positive nature of this process.

During therapy, the client's ability to experience the steps of identification–echoing–insight can provide valuable information to the therapist and serve as a therapeutic guide. With young children, who may find it difficult to put their feelings into words, this process may help with their overall ability to reflect and to regulate their emotions (Torre & Lieberman, 2018).

Storytelling and story completion procedures are sometimes used to explore young children's inner worlds (Adler & Oppenheim, 2014, 2023; Bretherton & Oppenheim, 2003; Koren-Karie et al., 2003; Oppenheim et al., 2007), and the bibliotherapeutic process can add its unique features to this exploration and provide new ways to set therapeutic goals, to assess progress in therapy and to facilitate conversation on emotional topics. Within this context, the next section describes a new assessment tool that uses a **storytelling** procedure to tap young children's identification–echoing–insight processes.

The Story Processing Assessment (SPA)

The Story Processing Assessment (SPA) is a new research and assessment measure developed to capture the identification–echoing–insight processes that occur during a **storytelling** procedure. It was tailored specifically for preschool and kindergarten children, but it could be adapted for other ages by using an age-appropriate story to stimulate these processes.

During the procedure, the interviewer reads a selected story to the child and asks open-ended questions at specific points that are later coded to represent the level of identification, echoing, and insight provided by the children in their responses.

Choosing a Text

While every story can be used to guide the process of identification–echoing–insight, bibliotherapists invest time and effort in choosing the appropriate text for their clients. When using the procedure with young children, it is important to choose a story that children can relate to, that is relevant to their lives, and that includes different social and emotional aspects. Moreover, in preschool ages, there is a preference to text with fictional non-human characters since they usually have more distinct traits, which allow children to identify with them more easily. Also, between the ages of four and seven, children are entering the world of imagination. Stories with magical content in which miracles can happen excite them and give them an emotional outlet while dealing with reality (Cohen, 1990).

For the SPA procedure that was validated (Sofri et al., 2023; Sofri & Ziv, 2024), the Hebrew version of the story "Two wheels for Grover" (Elliott & Mathieu, 1984) was selected. The story, with fictional characters (Muppets), addresses a familiar situation for preschoolers and kindergartners: Grover does not know how to ride a bike and is too ashamed and embarrassed to tell anyone. His cousin Rosie offers him the chance to ride the bike with her every day, and every day, Grover makes different excuses as to why he cannot ride. Eventually, he talks to his older cousin and tells him the truth. His cousin helps him to learn how to ride.

A central theme in the story is the feeling of shame Grover experiences from not knowing a certain skill (riding a bike). This is in accordance with how shame is experienced in young children who tend to compare their own and others' performances. A child can compare his performance to others in different situations and may judge and decide that he lacks a valued trait (Mascolo & Fischer, 1995). The story contains a variety of emotions and themes that children can relate to and can target the process of identification–echoing–insight.

The Interview

The story is read to the child by a trained interviewer unfamiliar to the child, to account for the reader's influence on child responses (Kobovi, 1992). Questions are asked during and after the story, and responses are scored on a 0 to 3 scale, with a higher score indicating greater quality of responses. Identification questions measure how well the child can recognize the character's motives, thoughts, and feelings: (1) Why didn't Grover want Rosie to know he does not know how to ride a bike? (2) Why did Grover tell Rosie his leg hurt so he could not ride the bike? and (3) How did Grover feel when Rosie asked him every day to ride the bike with her? The echoing questions examine the child's ability to use personal experience and inner world to understand the story: (1) [after stopping in specific points of the story] "Tell me about a time in which you felt ashamed." (2) "What do you think would happen next?" The stopping points in the current story were: (a) after Grover gives excuses as to why he could not ride the bike, and (b) when he expresses fear of falling off the bike.

Finally, the insight questions assess the child's ability to draw insight from the story, understand the larger context, and recognize different points of view: (1) What advice can you give Grover to help him when Rosie asks him to ride the bike with her? (2) Do you think Grover has a good reason not to tell Rosie he could not ride the bike? If so, what is the reason? and (3) What did Rosie think when Grover told her he could not come with her to ride the bike because his hand hurt?

After the interview, the interviewer reads the child's answers and codes the answers, generating the three different scales of identification, echoing, and insight. The three questions for each scale are examined together to yield a single general score. There are also specific instructions for coding. For example, in order to get a score of "3" for identification, the child needs to refer to more than one aspect of the character's inner world and to show an understanding of the character's inner motives, thoughts, and feelings. For specific administration, coding, and scoring instructions, refer to Appendices A, B, and C.

The data were coded by the first author, with 20% of the cases coded by a second coder trained by the first author. Interrater reliability was calculated using Intraclass Correlation Coefficient (ICC) and was found adequate: identification = 0.65 ($p < 0.001$); echoing = 0.91 ($p < 0.001$); insight = 0.70 ($p < 0.001$). Disagreements were resolved in a consensus meeting between coders.

Learning About Children's Developmental Trajectory and Mental States from Their Story Processing Patterns

From a developmental perspective, we can learn quite a lot from the way children process information about mental states. **Storytelling** is a wonderful way to explore such capacities, as it is likely one of the more naturally occurring situations in children's lives, especially in the Western world. To accurately and competently process mental aspects in a specific story, children need to acquire several important developmental skills. For example, understanding the content of the story, knowing how to answer open-ended questions, and, perhaps most importantly, understanding and focusing on characters' inner motives and their different emotions and perspectives. In the next two sub-sections, we focus on the ways in which children's story processing tendencies can inform us about their socioemotional capacities and their readiness for school.

Story Processing Assessment (SPA) and Social-Emotional Capacities

The exploration of children's social-emotional capacities using bibliotherapeutic methods through identification–echoing–insight processes can shed light on the different ways in which children think and reflect on socio-emotional situations. The development of children's social and emotional skills is rooted and shaped within their first meaningful relationship with their caregiver. The parent–child relationship and social relationships in general are major contributors to molding different types of emotions, especially social emotions such as guilt or shame (Barret, 1995; Gross & Hansen, 2000; Menesini & Camodeca, 2008). The parent–child relationship is a crucial factor in shaping the ways children express and regulate their emotions (Ainsworth, 1979; Bretherton, 1992, 2013; Southam-Gerow & Kendall, 2002; Steele et al., 2008). The link between the parent–child relationship quality and children's ability to regulate and understand their emotions has been well-established (Bocknek et al., 2009; Braungart & Stifter, 1991; Ontai & Thompson, 2002; Southam-Gerow & Kendall, 2002; Waters et al., 2010; Zimmermann, 1999) already in early infancy (Braungart-Rieker et al., 2001) and in the preschool years (Mathis & Bierman, 2012).

An important milestone of emotion regulation is Reflective Functioning (RF) (Cole et al., 1994; Finn et al., 2019), which is defined as the "the capacity of the Self to recognize and to reflect upon one's own mental experience, including feelings, thoughts, desires and beliefs, being able to construct representations of one's own psychic life as well as being aware of the interpersonal implications of the mental states" (Camoirano, 2017, p. 2). In other words, reflective functioning refers to the ability to understand and articulate one's own intentions and emotions, as well as those of others.

Therefore, parent–child relationship is a major factor in the development of social-emotional capacities such as emotion regulation and reflectivity. In this context, **bibliotherapy** is not simply an encounter with text; it is a guided process that allows for **reflecting** on the reading (Lucas & Soares, 2013). The Story Processing Assessment (SPA) requires children to recognize characters' inner motives, thoughts, feelings, and behaviors. Moreover, children are asked to connect the emotional experience from the story to their own lives by giving a personal example of a time when they felt like the character. Children are also asked to give advice to the character and to try and examine situations in the story from different perspectives. This process of recognizing, understanding, and verbalizing one's own and others' (in this case, characters from the story) motives helps facilitate a better understanding of specific connections between those skills and the parent–child relationship.

The Story Processing Assessment (SPA) can help gain knowledge of children's emotional reflectivity skills and provide a better understanding of the specific connections between those skills and the parent–child relationship. Initial results found positive connections between the mother–child relationship and the child's identification and echoing scores. It was found that high maternal emotional availability and high child responsiveness toward the mother are associated with higher child emotional reflectivity (as measured by the child's SPA scores), which in turn is linked to more prosocial behaviors (Sofri et al., 2024). These results provide support for the use of bibliotherapeutic approaches and book-reading practices in early intervention.

The exploration of children's emotional capacities using bibliotherapeutic methods can shed light on the different ways in which children think and reflect on socio-emotional situations. Recognizing, understanding, and verbalizing one's own and others' (in this case, characters from the story) motives and emotions can be used to foster reflectivity skills in both early intervention and early education efforts. In terms of book-reading, there is strong empirical evidence that **storytelling** in kindergarten is linked to improved social skills (Aram et al., 2017; Schapira & Aram, 2020). Thus, fostering reading situations in which children are asked questions that encourage them to think and reflect about the different perspectives of characters, their motives, and emotions can help their social skills while encountering the need to reflect on other children's emotions and motives in day-to-day situations. In early intervention programs, shared reading and story completion procedures were previously used to explore children's inner worlds (Bretherton & Oppenheim, 2003; Koren-Karie et al., 2003; Oppenheim et al., 2007; Adler & Oppenheim, 2023). SPA can contribute and add to such explorations by emphasizing identification–echoing–insight processes during shared reading situations and can help foster early relationships and enhance reflectivity and socio-emotional skills.

Story Processing Assessment (SPA) and School Readiness

School readiness is defined as "the state of a child's competencies at the time of school entry that are important for later success" (Snow, 2006, p. 9). There are many different contributors to it, including children's socio-emotional and academic abilities, their home environment, the parent–child relationship, and the kindergarten environment (Blair & Raver, 2015; Duncan et al., 2007; Grismmer et al., 2010; Linder et al., 2013). Children's abilities at school entry predict their later success, especially in literacy and math (Duncan et al., 2007; Snow, 2006), but also their social skills (Pianta & McCoy, 1997).

Children's ability to recognize and identify emotions, their emotional knowledge, and emotional regulation skills are all important factors contributing to different aspects of children's adjustment to school (Bierman et al., 2008; Harrington et al., 2020; Raver, 2002). Verbal abilities, approaches toward learning, and social skills during these early years are considered major indicators for school success (Agostin & Bain, 1997; Bredekamp, 2005; Bierman et al., 2008; Denham et al., 2012; Fantuzzo et al., 2007; Stacks & Oshio, 2009; Welsh et al., 2010; Ziv, 2013).

Approaches Toward Learning (ATL) can be defined as "effortful and goal-oriented mechanisms by which children go about classroom learning processes" (McDermott et al., 2018, p. 1206). ATL is important for **school readiness** both cognitively and socially (Chen & McNamee, 2011; Fantuzzo et al., 2007; Li-Grining et al., 2010; McWayne et al., 2004). Persistence, for example, was found to relate to language and math skills (Mokrova et al., 2013). Additionally, children who demonstrated better ATL skills, such as initiative, motivation, attention, and persistence, also showed more positive interactions in peer play (Coolahan et al., 2000; Fantuzzo et al., 2004), while poor ATL skills were linked to social and academic difficulties (Bultosky-Shearer et al., 2011).

School readiness indicators have multiple and different connections among them. For example, verbal abilities contribute to children's social development (Choe et al., 2013; Denham & Brown, 2010; Gremillion & Martel, 2014; Meyer et al., 2006; Pianta & McCoy, 1997). When children are interviewed during a **storytelling** procedure, verbal abilities can affect their understanding of the story and also their ability to answer open-ended questions regarding the story. The other direction of associations is also plausible, as **storytelling** is likely to contribute to both verbal and social skills. Indeed, previous research provides evidence for a link between **storytelling** and improved verbal (As, 2016; Morrow et al., 1990; Wasik & Bond, 2001; Yazici & Bolay, 2017) and social (Aram et al., 2017; Schapira & Aram, 2020) skills in kindergarten.

In our own research using the Story Processing Assessment (SPA), we recently found evidence that both identification and insight are positively correlated with verbal abilities. Moreover, insight was correlated with approaches toward learning (motivation, persistence) and mediated the relationship between verbal abilities and approaches toward learning (Sofri et al., 2023). Insight, the ability to view the situation in the story from a more distant and broader perspective, contains both emotional and cognitive abilities, and this combination can be crucial for children's approaches toward learning.

Furthermore, echoing and insight were both found to negatively correlate with hyperactivity. Insight was also found to mediate the relationship between verbal abilities and hyperactivity (Sofri et al., 2023)—a core component in the diagnosis of ADHD. Students with a diagnosis of ADHD demonstrate more behavioral problems, social problems, and difficulties in school functioning (DuPaul et al., 2001; Spira & Fischel, 2005). Thus, the reason hyperactive children may find it difficult to answer SPA questions adaptively could be related to their challenges in pausing to look at the bigger picture and examining a situation from multiple perspectives. This might relate to other situations in their day-to-day lives, for example, to stop and think before reacting to social situations in class.

Overall, SPA can be used by educators to both assess children's different abilities according to their reactions to a chosen text and to foster verbal, cognitive, and emotional skills.

Clinical Work with Story Processing Assessment

SPA is rooted in the bibliotherapeutic field and can be used by therapists to assist in their clinical work. The questions related to identification require children to relate and try to understand characters' inner motives, thoughts, and feelings. Answers to these questions can provide valuable insights into children's fears and insecurities. For example, children who think that Grover did not tell Rosie he could not ride the bike because he felt ashamed and did not want her to be mad at him might link failure to anger in their everyday lives. In the safer environment of the clinic, children with those types of tendencies could explore and experience failure in a safe space with an appropriate response.

Echoing, the ability to connect the events in the story to the children's own personal lives and give an example of an event in which they also felt similar to the character in the story, can help clinicians understand children's ability to understand, reflect, and talk about their own feelings. For example, children who answer "I don't know" or are unable to give an example from their personal lives might find it hard to talk and reflect about their feelings in general. Therapists can use this as valuable information to help children express their feelings in a variety of ways, such as art, writing, imaginary play, and other means that can be used following a certain text (Pardeck, 1998).

Insight questions require children to think more broadly about the situation in the story and from multiple perspectives. They are asked to think of possible advice they can share with the character in order to examine what kind of insight they gain from the story. This can provide insight into children's various coping strategies. For example, a child might focus on the emotional aspects of their advice to Grover, such as "Grover needs to tell Rosie he is ashamed" or focus on the technical aspect: "Rosie can hold the handles for him." In the clinical setting, this can help therapists understand what kind of responses can help a certain child feel more secure, and they can relate this information to the children's caretakers.

The use of validated assessments such as the Story Processing Assessment (SPA) can also assist therapists in setting therapeutic goals and gaining a better understanding of children's inner worlds, their coping mechanisms, fears, insecurities, and strengths. In a recent article, clinical work with the SPA, including different case examples and how they might be related to other developmental aspects, is being discussed (Sofri & Ziv, 2024).

Since **storytelling** is a common occurrence in educational environments, especially in kindergarten and early elementary school, SPA can be used by educators with relative ease. Educators can learn about the processes highlighted in the SPA (identification, echoing, insight) that readers go through while listening to stories, and encourage those processes by asking questions about the character's motives and feelings, asking examples from the student's inner worlds or everyday lives, and encourage them to look at multiple perspectives and offer different solutions to the situations that occur in the stories. Educators can pick stories while taking into account emotional and social themes they want to emphasize and work through the stories about children's reflectivity skills.

Educators can also identify children who struggle more with those processes and try to better understand the reason: Does the child struggle to articulate herself in front of the teacher and friends? Does the child struggle to answer questions about the story both in front of the class and in one-on-one time with a teacher or teacher assistant? Is there a specific difficulty (e.g., the child can identify motives and feelings of the characters but fails to find connections to her inner world)? This can give educators a better understanding of children's strengths and difficulties and offer a variety of work directions. Moreover, SPA assessment can be used at different times of the year to assess progress both in therapy and in educational environments.

At home, parents can gain from knowledge about the variety of processes children go through while listening to a story and can ask questions during a shared reading situation with their child in order to learn about their children's inner worlds and to communicate with their children in a different, creative way. There is a need to learn the processes deeply and use them in accordance with the child's needs, not to ask too many questions in order to keep the shared reading situation an experience filled with fun and pleasure.

With all that said, these recommendations should be viewed with caution. Whereas both educators and parents can certainly gain knowledge about children's strengths and difficulties through an introduction to the SPA and its driving theory, these recommendations do not suggest that such knowledge should replace professional intervention when needed.

The SPA measure offers a creative and approachable way to better understand children's inner world and the ways in which they think about and reflect on certain situations. The chapter presented results from the first studies that used and validated the measure. In the future, more studies can examine the measure with different age groups and more diverse populations, and continue exploring the relationships among texts, storytelling, and children's inner worlds.

Summary

Our main purpose was to show how **storytelling** could benefit children from the clinical perspective of **bibliotherapy**. The Story Processing Assessment, a new assessment and evaluation tool introduced here, was developed to recognize and assess children's responses to a story using bibliotherapeutic principles. Children usually find it difficult to talk at length about their emotions, and the SPA offers a useful way to assess different emotional abilities and how they relate to other important areas in children's lives. SPA can aid therapists in the initial intake and in setting therapeutic goals. The procedure also allows tracking the progress of therapy by administering it at different time points. Through children's answers related to *identification*, *echoing*, and *insight*, therapists can recognize central issues that children are dealing with and consequently choose treatment directions and work methods accordingly. The ways in which children approach a story can correspond with the ways in which they approach other aspects in their lives, such as their ATL, social situations, and even their own emotions. The exploration of these connections can lead to interesting directions in working with children.

Appendix 1

General Instructions for the Interviewer

There is a need to form a rapport with the child and make sure the child feels comfortable before the beginning of the formal interview. Connect with the child by having a short conversation and asking questions regarding his hobbies, games he likes to play, etc.

During the interview, give the child positive reassurance and remind the child that there are no right or wrong answers. If the child hesitates, remind him that we are interested in his opinion: "We want your opinion, there is no right or wrong answers"/"What do you think?"/"Do you have an idea?" Give the child compliments regarding his effort and concentration, but do not use words like "good" or "great." Instead, use more general compliments like "I see you're trying very hard." If the child seems troubled by some of the questions, stop the interview for a few minutes, give the child positive feedback regarding his behavior and effort, and talk about another subject for a few moments. If the child is still troubled, the interview should be stopped. If the child does not respond to a question, wait a few moments and repeat the question. If the answer is too short, ask if there is anything else he wants to add. Throughout the interview, make sure to give the child positive feedback and do not use your own ideas to help the child answer the questions. It is possible to ask informative questions and follow-up questions that are detailed in the answer sheet.

Appendix 2

Coding Sheet

Child's name: _________ Gender: F/M agrees to participate: Yes/No
date of birth________

"Now we'll read a story together and discuss it a little bit"

Story: Two wheels for Grover

A1: So far, we read that Grover arrived at the village, and Rosie asked him to ride the bike together. Grover does not know how to ride a bike. Grover does not want Rosie to find out that he does not know how to ride. He thinks to himself that he does not know how to ride, and he is afraid to fall "What doesn't Grover want Rosie to know?" (If the child does not understand, clarify that Grover didn't want Rosie to know that he can't ride a bike, and ask again to make sure the child understands.) "Why didn't Grover want Rosie to know he can't ride a bike?" (Clarification question: Why didn't he want Rosie to know that? What do you think?)	____________________ ____________________ ____________________ ____________________ ______________
A.2. Now we read that Grover, who does not know how to ride a bike, tells Rosie that his mother does not allow him to ride the bike. Rosie tells him they called the mother, and she does allow Grover to ride the bike. After that, Grover says to Rosie that his leg hurts and he can't ride the bike today. "Why does Grover say his leg hurts?" (A longer answer can be encouraged by asking: ""and what else?")	____________________ ____________________ ____________________ ____________________ ____________
A.3. We read that Grover played with Rosie and Frank every day in all sorts of games, and every day Rosie asked Grover to come ride the bike with her, but Grover tells her every time that his hand hurts or that he ate too much or that he doesn't feel like riding "How did Grover feel when Rosie asked him to ride with her every day?" (A longer answer can be encouraged by asking: ""and what else?" If the child replies, then it's possible to ask: ""why do you think he felt that way?")	____________________ ____________________ ____________________ ____________________ _________

B.1. "Tell me about a time in which you felt ashamed" Can be added: "Like Grover was ashamed and didn't want to tell Rosie he doesn't know how to ride" Follow-up questions: "When did that happen?" "Did you not want others to know about it?" "How does it feel to be ashamed?"	______________________________ ______________________________ ______________________________ ______________________________ ______________________________ _______________
B.2. We now read that Grover tells Frank that he doesn't know how to ride a bike. Frank tells Grover that he will teach him to ride "What will happen next?"	______________________________ ______________________________ ______________________________ ______________________________ ______________________________ ______________________________ ________
C.1. Do you remember we read that every day Rosie would ask Grover to ride with her, and every day Grover would say he doesn't want to ride and that his leg hurts? "Which advice can you give Grover to help him when Rosie asks him if he can come and ride with her?"	______________________________ ______________________________ ______________________________ ______________________________ __________
C.2. Do you remember that Grover didn't want to tell Rosie he can't ride a bike? "In your opinion, does Grover have a good reason not to tell her he can't ride with her? What is the reason?"	______________________________ ______________________________ ______________________________ ______________
C.3. Do you remember that time when Grover told Rosie he can't ride with her because his hand hurts? "What did Rosie think when Grover told her he can't ride with her because his hand hurts?"	______________________________ ______________________________ ______________________________ ______________________________ ______

Appendix 3

Coding Instructions

Identification

0	The child does not refer to the emotions, thoughts, or motives of the character
1	The child refers to emotions/thoughts/motives, but they do not match the character's inner world and feelings

1.5	This score can be given if, in general, the answers do not match the character's inner world, but there is one example that reflects an understanding of the character's thoughts or motives
2	The child refers to one or two aspects of the character's inner world: an emotion, a thought, or a motive
2.5	The answers reflect the character's inner world besides one answer, or all of the answers reflect the character's inner world; however, the answers are sparse
3	The child refers to more than one aspect of the character's inner world and shows understanding of the internal motives, thoughts, and feelings of the character

Echoing

0	The child does not give an example from personal experience and does not fill in gaps in the story when asked
1	The child can fill in gaps in the story but does not give a personal example
1.5	The child fills in the gaps in the story and gives a personal example, but the example is unrelated to the theme of the story
2	The child fills in the gaps in the story when asked and gives a personal example, but the answers are very short and limited
2.5	This score is given considering the richness of the answer
3	The child fills in gaps in the story when asked and connects a personal experience to the story

Insight

0	The child does not know how to answer the insight questions or gives non-insightful answers (answers that do not reflect an ability to look at things from more than one perspective and do not reflect an ability to think about the bigger picture and have new insights)
1	The child answers the insight questions, but the answers are not suited to the story and the plot line
1.5	Only one full answer
2	The child answers the insight questions in a short and limited fashion
2.5	Adequate answers except one answer that is not in line with the story
3	The child answers the insight questions and shows an ability to think about the bigger picture and to share insights

References

Adler, S. Y., & Oppenheim, D. (2014). Story completion play narrative methods for preschool children. In *Handbook of research methods in early childhood education* (Vol. 1, pp. 323–381).

Adler, S. Y., & Oppenheim, D. (2023). The contribution of mother-father-child interactions to children's emotion narratives. *Social Development, 32*(1), 299–314. https://doi.org/10.1111/sode.12642

Agostin, T. M., & Bain, S. K. (1997). Predicting early school success with developmental and social skills screeners. *Psychology in the Schools, 34*(3), 219–228. https://doi.org/10.1002/(SICI)1520-6807(199707)34:3<219::AID-PITS4>3.0.CO;2-J

Ainsworth, M. S. (1979). Infant–mother attachment. *American Psychologist, 34*(10), 932. https://doi.org/10.1037/0003-066X.34.10.932

Aram, D., Deitcher, D. B., Shoshan, T. S., & Ziv, M. (2017). Shared book reading interactions within families from low socioeconomic backgrounds and children's social understanding and prosocial behavior. *Journal of Cognitive Education and Psychology, 16*(2), 157–177. https://doi.org/10.1891/1945-8959.16.2.157

As, A. B. (2016). Storytelling to improve speaking skills. *English Education Journal, 7*(2), 194–205.

Barret, K. C. (1995). A functionalist approach to shame and guilt. In K. W. Fischer & J. P. Tangney (Eds.), *Self-conscious emotions: The psychology of shame, guilt, embarrassment, and pride* (pp. 25-63). New York: Guilford Press.

Bierman, K. L., Domitrovich, C. E., Nix, R. L., Gest, S. D., Welsh, J. A., Greenberg, M. T., et al. (2008). Promoting academic and social-emotional school readiness: The Head Start REDI program. *Child Development, 79*(6), 1802–1817. https://doi.org/10.1111/j.1467-8624.2008.01227.x

Blair, C., & Raver, C. C. (2015). School readiness and self-regulation: A developmental psychobiological approach. *Annual Review of Psychology, 66*, 711. https://doi.org/10.1146/annurev-psych-010814-015221

Bocknek, E. L., Brophy-Herb, H. E., & Banerjee, M. (2009). Effects of parental supportiveness on toddlers' emotion regulation over the first three years of life in a low-income African American sample. *Infant Mental Health Journal: Official Publication of The World Association for Infant Mental Health, 30*(5), 452–476. https://doi.org/10.1002/imhj.20224

Braungart, J. M., & Stifter, C. A. (1991). Regulation of negative reactivity during the strange situation: Temperament and attachment in 12-month-old infants. *Infant Behavior and Development, 14*(3), 349–364.

Braungart-Rieker, J. M., Garwood, M. M., Powers, B. P., & Wang, X. (2001). Parental sensitivity, infant affect, and affect regulation: Predictors of later attachment. *Child Development, 72*(1), 252–270. https://doi.org/10.1111/1467-8624.00277

Bredekamp, S. (2005). Play and school readiness. *Educational Perspectives, 38*(1), 18–26.

Bretherton, I. (1992). The origins of attachment theory: John Bowlby and Mary Ainsworth. *Developmental Psychology, 28*(5), 759. https://doi.org/10.1037/0012-1649.28.5.759

Bretherton, I. (2013). Revisiting Mary Ainsworth's conceptualization and assessments of maternal sensitivity-insensitivity. *Attachment & Human Development, 15*(5–6), 460–484. https://doi.org/10.1080/14616734.2013.835128

Bretherton, I., & Oppenheim, D. (2003). The MacArthur Story Stem Battery: Development, administration, reliability, validity, and reflections about meaning. In *Revealing the inner worlds of young children: The MacArthur Story Stem Battery and parent-child narratives* (Vol. 55, p. 80).

Bulotsky-Shearer, R. J., Fernandez, V., Dominguez, X., & Rouse, H. L. (2011). Behavior problems in learning activities and social interactions in Head Start classrooms and early reading, mathematics, and approaches to learning. *School Psychology Review, 40*(1), 39–56. https://doi.org/10.1080/02796015.2011.12087727

Camoirano, A. (2017). Mentalizing makes parenting work: A review about parental reflective functioning and clinical interventions to improve it. *Frontiers in Psychology, 8*, 14.

Chen, J. Q., & McNamee, G. D. (2011). Positive approaches to learning in the context of preschool classroom activities. *Early Childhood Education Journal, 39*(1), 71–78. https://doi.org/10.1007/s10643-010-0441-x

Choe, D. E., Lane, J. D., Grabell, A. S., & Olson, S. L. (2013). Developmental precursors of young school age children's hostile attribution bias. *Developmental Psychology, 49*(12), 2245. https://doi.org/10.1037/a0032293

Cohen, A. (1990). *Story of the psyche (in Hebrew)*. Ach Publication.

Cole, P. M., Michel, M. K., & Teti, L. O. D. (1994). The development of emotion regulation and dysregulation: A clinical perspective. *Monographs of the Society for Research in Child Development*, 73–100. https://doi.org/10.1111/j.1540-5834.1994.tb01278.x

Cook, K. E., Earles-Vollrath, T., & Ganz, J. B. (2006). Bibliotherapy. *Intervention in School and Clinic, 42*(2), 91–100.

Coolahan, K., Fantuzzo, J., Mendez, J., & McDermott, P. (2000). Preschool peer interactions and readiness to learn: Relationships between classroom peer play and learning behaviors and conduct. *Journal of Educational Psychology, 92*(3), 458. https://doi.org/10.1037/0022-0663.92.3.458

Denham, S. A., Bassett, H., Mincic, M., Kalb, S., Way, E., Wyatt, T., & Segal, Y. (2012). Social emotional learning profiles of preschoolers' early school success: A person-centered approach. *Learning and Individual Differences, 22*(2), 178–189. https://doi.org/10.1016/j.lindif.2011.05.001

Denham, S. A., & Brown, C. (2010). "Plays nice with others": Social–emotional learning and academic success. *Early Education and Development, 21*(5), 652–680. https://doi.org/10.1080/10409289.2010.497450

Duncan, G. J., Dowsett, C. J., Claessens, A., Magnuson, K., Huston, A. C., Klebanov, P., et al. (2007). School readiness and later achievement. *Developmental Psychology, 43*(6), 1428. https://doi.org/10.1037/0012-1649.43.6.1428

DuPaul, G. J., McGoey, K. E., Eckert, T. L., & VanBrakle, J. (2001). Preschool children with attention deficit/hyperactivity disorder: Impairments in behavioral, social, and school functioning. *Journal of the American Academy of Child & Adolescent Psychiatry, 40*(5), 508–515.

Elliott, D., & Mathieu, J. (1984). Two wheels for Grover. Random house children's books.

Fantuzzo, J., Bulotsky-Shearer, R., McDermott, P. A., McWayne, C., Frye, D., & Perlman, S. (2007). Investigation of dimensions of social-emotional classroom behavior and school readiness for low-income urban preschool children. *School Psychology Review, 36*(1), 44–62. https://doi.org/10.1080/02796015.2007.12087951

Fantuzzo, J., Perry, M. A., & McDermott, P. (2004). Preschool approaches to learning and their relationship to other relevant classroom competencies for low-income children. *School Psychology Quarterly, 19*(3), 212. https://doi.org/10.1521/scpq.19.3.212.40276

Finn, M. T., Smith, C. L., McKernan, L. C., & Nash, M. R. (2019). Moving and reflective functioning under stress. *Psychodynamic Psychiatry, 47*(2), 197–121.

Gremillion, M. L., & Martel, M. M. (2014). Merely misunderstood? Receptive, expressive, and pragmatic language in young children with disruptive behavior disorders. *Journal of Clinical Child & Adolescent Psychology, 43*(5), 765–776. https://doi.org/10.1080/15374416.2013.822306

Grissmer, D., Grimm, K. J., Aiyer, S. M., Murrah, W. M., & Steele, J. S. (2010). Fine motor skills and early comprehension of the world: Two new school readiness indicators. *Developmental Psychology, 46*(5), 1008. https://doi.org/10.1037/a0020104.supp

Gross, C. A., & Hansen, N. E. (2000). Clarifying the experience of shame: The role of attachment style, gender, and investment in relatedness. *Personality and Individual Differences, 28*(5), 897–907.

Harrington, E. M., Trevino, S. D., Lopez, S., & Giuliani, N. R. (2020). Emotion regulation in early childhood: Implications for socioemotional and academic components of school readiness. *Emotion, 20*(1), 48. https://doi.org/10.1037/emo0000667

Iser, W. (1974). *The implied reader: Patterns of communication in prose fiction from Bunyan to Beckett*. Johns Hopkins UP.

Kobovi, D. (1992). *Bibliotherapy: Literature, education and mental health (in Hebrew)*. Magnes.
Koren-Karie, N., Oppenheim, D., Haimovich, Z., & Etzion-Carasso, A. (2003). Dialogues of seven-year-olds withtheir mothers about emotional events: Development of atypology. In R. N. Emde, D. P. Wolf, & D. Oppenheim (Eds.), *Revealing the inner worlds of young children: TheMacArthur story stem battery and parent–child narratives* (pp. 338–354). Oxford University Press.
Li-Grining, C. P., Votruba-Drzal, E., Maldonado-Carreño, C., & Haas, K. (2010). Children's early approaches to learning and academic trajectories through fifth grade. *Developmental Psychology, 46*(5), 1062. https://doi.org/10.1037/a0020066
Linder, S. M., Ramey, M. D., & Zambak, S. (2013). Predictors of school readiness in literacy and mathematics: A selective review of the literature. *Early Childhood Research & Practice, 15*(1), n1.
Lucas, C. V., & Soares, L. (2013). Bibliotherapy: A tool to promote children's psychological well-being. *Journal of Poetry Therapy, 26*(3), 137–147. https://doi.org/10.1080/08893675.2013.823310
Mathis, E., & Bierman, K. (2012). Child emotion regulation and attentional control in pre--kindergarten: Associations with parental stress, parenting practices, and parent-child interaction quality. *Society for Research on Educational Effectiveness*.
Mascolo, M. F. & Fischer, K. W. (1995). Developmental transformations in appraisals for pride, shame and guilt. In J. P. Tangney & K. W. Fischer (Eds.), *Self conscious emotions: The psychology of shame, guilt, embarrassment, and pride* (pp. 64-113). New York: Guilford Press.
McDermott, P. A., Rovine, M. J., Reyes, R. S., Chao, J. L., Scruggs, R., Buek, K., & Fantuzzo, J. W. (2018). Trajectories of early education learning behaviors among children at risk: A growth mixture modeling approach. *Psychology in the Schools, 55*(10), 1205–1223. https://doi.org/10.1002/pits.22145
McWayne, C. M., Fantuzzo, J. W., & McDermott, P. A. (2004). Preschool competency in context: An investigation of the unique contribution of child competencies to early academic success. *Developmental Psychology, 40*(4), 633. https://doi.org/10.1037/0012-1649.40.4.633
Menesini, E., & Camodeca, M. (2008). Shame and guilt as behaviour regulators: Relationships with bullying, victimization and prosocial behaviour. *British Journal of Developmental Psychology, 26*(2), 183–196.
Meyer, J. A., Mundy, P. C., Van Hecke, A. V., & Durocher, J. S. (2006). Social attribution processes and comorbid psychiatric symptoms in children with Asperger syndrome. *Autism, 10*(4), 383–402. https://doi.org/10.1177/1362361306064435
Mokrova, I. L., O'Brien, M., Calkins, S. D., Leerkes, E. M., & Marcovitch, S. (2013). The role of persistence at preschool age in academic skills at kindergarten. *European Journal of Psychology of Education, 28*(4), 1495–1503. https://doi.org/10.1007/s10212-013-0177-2
Morrow, L. M., O'connor, E. M., & Smith, J. K. (1990). Effects of a story reading program on the literacy development of at-risk kindergarten children. *Journal of Reading Behavior, 22*(3), 255–275. https://doi.org/10.1080/10862969009547710
Ontai, L. L., & Thompson, R. A. (2002). Patterns of attachment and maternal discourse effects on children's emotion understanding from 3 to 5 years of age. *Social Development, 11*(4), 433–450. https://doi.org/10.1111/1467-9507.00209
Oppenheim, D., Koren-Karie, N., & Sagi-Schwartz, A. (2007). Emotion dialogues between mothers and children at 4.5 and 7.5 years: Relations with children's attachment at 1 year. *Child Development, 78*(1), 38–52. https://doi.org/10.1111/j.1467-8624.2007.00984.x
Pianta, R. C., & McCoy, S. J. (1997). The first day of school: The predictive validity of early school screening. *Journal of Applied Developmental Psychology, 18*(1), 1–22. https://doi.org/10.1016/S0193-3973(97)90011-3
Pardeck, J. T. (1998). *Using books in clinical social work practice: A guide to bibliotherapy*. Haworth Press. https://doi.org/10.4324/9781315821719

Raver, C. C. (2002). Emotions matter: Making the case for the role of young children's emotional development for early school readiness. Social policy report. *Society for Research in Child Development, 16*(3).

Rottenberg, B. (2022). Bibliotherapy as an integrative psychotherapeutic channel. *Journal of Poetry Therapy, 35*(1), 27–41.

Schapira, R., & Aram, D. (2020). Shared book reading at home and preschoolers' socio emotional competence. *Early Education and Development, 31*(6), 819–837. https://doi.org/10.1080/10409289.2019.1692624

Sharma, D. (2022). Using developmental bibliotherapy design to improve self management skills of post-graduate students. *Journal of Poetry Therapy, 36*(2), 95–113.

Snow, K. L. (2006). Measuring school readiness: Conceptual and practical considerations. *Early Education and Development, 17*(1), 7–41. https://doi.org/10.1207/s15566935eed1701_2

Sofri, I., Czik, A., & Ziv, Y. (2023). Are you ready for a story? Kindergarten children's emotional competencies during a story-reading situation is associated with their readiness for school. *Education Sciences, 13*(12), 1169. https://doi.org/10.3390/educsci13121169

Sofri, I., Czik, A., & Ziv, Y. (2024). Parent–child emotional availability, children's early emotional reflectivity skills, and social behavior in kindergarten. *Family Relations*. https://doi.org/10.1111/fare.13131

Sofri, I., & Ziv, Y. (2024). Can you ride a bike? Mindful and alert story processing as a new assessment procedure for bibliotherapists. *Journal of Poetry Therapy, 37*(2), 87–104. https://doi.org/10.1080/08893675.2023.2216376

Southam-Gerow, M. A., & Kendall, P. C. (2002). Emotion regulation and understanding: Implications for child psychopathology and therapy. *Clinical Psychology Review, 22*(2), 189–222. https://doi.org/10.1016/S0272-7358(01)00087-3

Spira, E. G., & Fischel, J. E. (2005). The impact of preschool inattention, hyperactivity, and impulsivity on social and academic development: A review. *Journal of Child Psychology and Psychiatry, 46*(7), 755–773.

Stacks, A. M., & Oshio, T. (2009). Disorganized attachment and social skills as indicators of Head Start children's school readiness skills. *Attachment & Human Development, 11*(2), 143–164. https://doi.org/10.1080/14616730802625250

Steele, H., Steele, M., & Croft, C. (2008). Early attachment predicts emotion recognition at 6 and 11 years old. *Attachment & Human Development, 10*(4), 379–393. https://doi.org/10.1080/14616730802461409

Torre, J. B., & Lieberman, M. D. (2018). Putting feelings into words: Affect labeling as implicit emotion regulation. *Emotion Review, 10*(2), 116–124. https://doi.org/10.1177/1754073917742706

Wang, S., Cheung, D. S. K., Bressington, D., Li, Y., & Leung, A. Y. M. (2022). The development of an evidence-based telephone-coached bibliotherapy protocol for improving dementia caregiving appraisal. *International Journal of Environmental Research and Public Health, 19*(14), 8731.

Wasik, B. A., & Bond, M. A. (2001). Beyond the pages of a book: Interactive book reading and language development in preschool classrooms. *Journal of Educational Psychology, 93*(2), 243. https://doi.org/10.1037/0022-0663.93.2.243

Waters, S. F., Virmani, E. A., Thompson, R. A., Meyer, S., Raikes, H. A., & Jochem, R. (2010). Emotion regulation and attachment: Unpacking two constructs and their association. *Journal of Psychopathology and Behavioral Assessment, 32*(1), 37–47. https://doi.org/10.1007/s10862-009-9163-z

Welsh, J. A., Nix, R. L., Blair, C., Bierman, K. L., & Nelson, K. E. (2010). The development of cognitive skills and gains in academic school readiness for children from low-income families. *Journal of Educational Psychology, 102*(1), 43. https://doi.org/10.1037/a0016738

Yamashita, T. (2023). The experience of international students in interactive bibliotherapy: Functions of interactive bibliotherapy helping in environmental transitions. *Journal of Poetry Therapy, 36*(2), 114–130.

Yazici, E., & Bolay, H. (2017). Story based activities enhance literacy skills in preschool children. *Universal Journal of Educational Research, 5*(5), 815–823. https://doi.org/10.13189/ujer.2017.050528

Zaccaria, J. S., Moses, H. A., & Hollowell, J. S. (1978). *Bibliotherapy in rehabilitation, educational, and mental health settings: Theory, research, and practice*. Stipes.

Zimmermann, P. (1999). Structure and functions of internal working models of attachment and their role for emotion regulation. *Attachment & Human Development, 1*(3), 291–306. https://doi.org/10.1080/14616739900134161

Ziv, Y. (2013). Social information processing patterns, social skills, and school readiness in preschool children. *Journal of Experimental Child Psychology, 114*(2), 306–320. https://doi.org/10.1016/j.jecp.2012.08.009

Zoran, R. (2009) The third voice (in Hebrew). Jerusalem: Carmel publication.

Inbar Sofri is a bibliotherapist and clinician specializing in working with children and adolescents, including those with complex mental health challenges. She holds a PhD from the Laboratory for Early Childhood Development at the University of Haifa. Inbar combines clinical practice with research, focusing on the mental capacities that emerge through **storytelling** and bibliotherapy. She has extensive experience in therapeutic interventions in schools and special education settings, as well as in guiding parents and conducting research on child development and narrative-based therapeutic approaches.

Yair Ziv is a full professor and chair of the School of Therapy, Counseling, and Human Development at the University of Haifa. He is also the head of the Early Education and Development Lab. His research focuses on preschool children's social and emotional development. Specifically, he is interested in young children's social relationships and the ways in which these inform their social cognition. Prof. Ziv is a recipient of multiple research grants from competitive grant foundations. He has authored dozens of peer-reviewed articles and book chapters and currently serves as an associate editor of Early Childhood Research Quarterly.

Part II
Shared Book Reading Interventions at Home

Chapter 7
Tender Shoots: Nurturing Children's Socio-Emotional Competencies Through Shared Book-Reading

Amanda Clifford, Elizabeth Schaughency, Shika Das, and Elaine Reese

Contents

The preschool years are vital for children's socio-emotional and self-regulation development McCabe et al. (2004); Pons et al. (2004). Development during these early years predicts success across the lifespan (Moffitt et al., 2011). **Parent–child interactions** provide opportunities to foster preschoolers' positive socio-emotional development. For instance, **shared book-reading** is a developmentally appropriate interactional context where parents can have emotionally rich conversations with young children that support **socio-emotional learning** (Aram et al., 2013; Gilkerson et al., 2017; Schapira et al., 2021a, 2021b). Book-reading contains interesting story lines that hold children's interest while also providing a narrative about the causes of, experiences of, and resolutions to socio-emotional experiences. Story books that contain rich socio-emotional content can foster further socio-emotional conversations. Children may then apply their learning during book-reading to their own lives.

Other parent–child interactions, such as reminiscing about past events—where parents converse with children about their personal experiences—are also associated with children's socio-emotional development, including their emotion understanding and self-regulation skills (see Salmon & Reese, 2016 for a review). For instance, mothers taught to engage in high-quality reminiscing with their toddlers led to adolescents later reporting fewer emotional problems compared to adolescents in a reminiscing-as-usual control group (Mitchell & Reese, 2022). Young

A. Clifford (✉) · E. Schaughency · S. Das · E. Reese
Department of Psychology, University of Otago, Dunedin, New Zealand
e-mail: a.clifford@otago.ac.nz

R. Schapira, D. Aram (eds.), *Shared Book Reading and Children's Social-Emotional Competence*, https://doi.org/10.1007/978-3-032-14688-5_7

children face many frustrations, challenges, and successes each day. Rich and elaborative conversations about children's own past emotional experiences may draw their attention to new socio-emotional ideas. Talking about a shared positive experience may reinforce social connections, whereas talking about a negative experience may help them to resolve those emotions and foster children's understanding of challenging experiences (e.g., Fivush et al., 2003; Clifford et al., 2024; Laible, 2011). Reminiscing may allow parents and children to have productive conversations about emotional experiences with some emotional distance (Fivush et al., 2003). During these conversations, parents can provide emotional language labels to children. They can also draw attention to the causes, resolutions, and outcomes of children's socio-emotional experiences (Bird & Reese, 2006). In sharing these real-life stories, children gain the socio-emotional vocabulary and understanding to scaffold children's understanding in their real-life socio-emotional situations.

Although reminiscing can occur at any time of the day, such as during mealtime or a car ride, it also occurs in the context of **shared book-reading** when an adult invites conversation about a child's personal experience related to the book's theme (Timperley et al., 2021). We propose that one reason emotionally-rich **shared book-reading** conversations have been associated with children's developing cognitive, social, and emotional understanding (Aram et al., 2013; Curenton & Craig, 2011) could be due to this linking between book events and children's own emotional experiences. Importantly, although families differ in their practices, **shared book-reading** and reminiscing are both popular activities with many parents and children. In a sample of New Zealand families from a wide range of educational backgrounds, parents reported that they reminisced and shared books together nearly every day of the week (Riordan et al., 2022).

How Shared Book-Reading and Reminiscing Contribute to Children's Socio-Emotional Skills

Based on Vygotsky's (1978) socio-cultural theory, **parent–child interactions** help shape children's growing cognitive and emotional understanding. These interactions, such as those during **shared book-reading** and reminiscing, provide a space for parents and children to explore socio-emotional concepts and ideas (Reese, 2013). For instance, a systematic review of the benefits of **shared book-reading** found consistent associations with children's socio-emotional outcomes (Batini et al., 2021). Books often contain engaging and emotional events that are experienced by the book characters. Parents can elaborate on the emotional content of the book by asking questions and highlighting the experience of those book characters. For instance, Schapira and Aram (2019) found that parents' and children's socio-emotional utterances during book-reading were concurrently linked to children's performance on several socio-emotional measures. As mentioned above, parents can also use the book characters' experiences to foster reminiscing conversations about children's own emotional experiences (Reese, 2013).

These socio-emotional conversations of all types during book-reading can also predict children's later socio-emotional understanding. For example, Bernard and Deleau (2007) found that preschool children's ability to take perspectives during **shared book-reading** predicted children's performance on perspective-taking tasks 1 year later. In that study, children were presented with a series of scenarios where they were asked to consider their own and others' perspectives. For example, they were asked where a character thought an object would be located after it had been moved without the character's knowledge. This finding suggests that book-reading may provide the opportunity for children to practice taking the perspectives of others over time.

But what is it about **shared book-reading** that may be specifically helpful for children's **socio-emotional learning**? **Shared book-reading** may provide unique opportunities to develop socio-emotional understanding. Specifically, book-reading may ideally scaffold parents' and children's participation in socio-emotional conversations because they simultaneously elicit a focus on others' mental states as well as on the child's own mental states (Grover et al., 2023). For instance, books may already contain socio-emotional experiences, depictions of characters' emotions, and emotional language. Emotionally rich stories can help children engage in shared reading as these stories are interesting, engaging, and stimulating for young children (Batini et al., 2021). These stories can also be read repeatedly, allowing children to reinforce and extend their learning with the help of parents (Flack et al., 2018). Finally, a critical feature of **shared book-reading** is that through reminiscing with a parent or other adult, children may also be able to link the book characters' experiences with their personal experiences (Hindman et al., 2014). Therefore, parents can scaffold children's **socio-emotional learning** during book-reading in multiple ways by selecting books with socio-emotional themes, drawing attention to new or less familiar socio-emotional concepts, exploring characters' emotional and cognitive experiences, and linking characters' experiences to children's own experiences. **Shared book-reading** may also contain concrete and visible cues and reminders about emotional events. For all these reasons, **shared book-reading** can promote broad and deep exploration of the storyline and beyond in which parents and children can draw on their own socio-emotional experiences.

Weaving Together Rich Reading and Reminiscing

Separate bodies of research thus demonstrate the benefits of **shared book-reading** and shared reminiscing for children's socio-emotional skills (see Grover et al., 2023; Salmon & Reese, 2016 for reviews). Yet these contexts for socio-emotional conversations differ. Book-reading, for example, provides parents with ready-made emotional narratives experienced by the stories' characters, whereas reminiscing is specifically about the child's own experiences. Reminiscing outside the book-reading context requires parents to generate and discuss a narrative without the support of characters' depicted emotional expressions or text relating to emotions.

Drawing upon two separate lines of experimental research comparing different styles of **shared book-reading** (Reese & Cox, 1999) and reminiscing (Reese & Newcombe, 2007), we developed an integrated method called *Rich Reading and Reminiscing* (RRR) in the hope that the benefits from **shared book-reading** and reminiscing would be even stronger if combined rather than promoted separately. Specifically, we sought to enhance parents' extra-textual talk during book-reading, followed by extended reminiscing conversations on children's positive and negative experiences related to emotion themes in the book (Reese, 2013; Reese et al., 2023; Riordan et al., 2022). After a baseline assessment of parents' naturally occurring book-reading and reminiscing styles, parents in the experimental condition received an educational session about engaging in rich oral language interactions during and after **shared book-reading**. Then, for the following 6 weeks, they received prompted books that highlighted opportunities to engage in extra-textual conversations during book-reading, followed by a related reminiscing conversation. After 6 weeks of practice with RRR, parents and children engaged in richer conversations about the storylines of books and about children's personal experiences compared to parents and children in the two control groups (Riordan et al., 2022). One year after participating in RRR, children independently retold narratives from new books in more accurate and detailed ways (Reese et al., 2023).

Critically, these benefits of RRR extended to children's socio-emotional skills. Clifford et al. (2024) found that the preschool children who participated with parents in the same 6-week RRR preventive intervention demonstrated benefits for later socio-emotional competencies as rated by their primary-school teachers when compared to a parallel book-reading condition that focused on phonological awareness. Importantly, parents in both conditions read the same set of books but were encouraged to focus on different aspects of these stories (e.g., characters' emotions, inferences, and reminiscing vs sound play). These findings suggest that supporting parents to engage in emotion-rich conversations during and after **shared book-reading** may support children's socio-emotional development.

However, our previous analyses only explored the role of mental-state talk during separate reminiscing conversations at pre- and post-tests, not during **shared book-reading**, for parent and teacher ratings of children's socio-emotional competencies at 1-year follow-up (Clifford et al., 2024). RRR produced long-term benefits for teacher ratings of children's socio-emotional competencies, and RRR increased parents' mental-state talk during later reminiscing conversations with children about *positive* events. However, it was only parent–child reminiscing about *negative* events that was concurrently linked to children's socio-emotional skills. This finding is in line with prior reminiscing research showing a special role of parent–child reminiscing about negative events for children's socio-emotional development (Leyva et al., 2020). However, our earlier analyses did not examine the role of socio-emotional content of the conversations that occurred during **shared book-reading** in relation to socio-emotional competencies at 1-year follow-up (Clifford et al., 2024). Thus, we may have underestimated the role of parent–child conversations for children's socio-emotional skills because we did not capture the reminiscing and other emotional talk that occurs during **shared book-reading**. The main aim of this chapter is to conduct a parallel analysis of the mental-state talk (including emotions, evaluations, and cognitions) during **shared book-reading** in the same sample of parents and children 1 year after participating in RRR in relation to children's socio-emotional competencies.

In our earlier evaluation of the benefits for RRR for mental-state talk during **shared book-reading** from pre- to immediate post-test 6 weeks later, parents in RRR used more cognitive language (e.g., think, remember, and know) than those in SSS (*Strengthening Sound Sensitivity*, module focused on phonological awareness) and ABC *(Activity Based Control*, a non-reading-based control module containing developmentally appropriate activities), and parents and children in both book-reading conditions used more mental-state talk overall than those in ABC 7 months later (Das, 2018). Furthermore, children with the greatest increase in parent–child emotional language use during **shared book-reading** were more likely to have higher scores in behavioral inhibition and socio-emotional problem-solving at post-test. One year after post-test, parents and children who had participated in RRR continued to share books by focusing primarily on the meaning of the storyline, whereas parents in SSS continued to share books by focusing on sounds and print (Timperley et al., 2022). Yet, this analysis did not test whether parents and children in RRR talked more specifically about emotions and other mental states during book-reading at 1-year follow-up, which is the main focus of the present analysis. It is possible that the book components of RRR prompted and scaffolded parents to continue to engage in emotionally and cognitively rich conversations during book-reading in the longer term.

Many interventions or initiatives during the preschool period aim to provide benefits for children's wellbeing (Mashburn et al., 2018). However, given the rapid development and many changes that happen in young children's lives during their early years, it is important that interventions are evaluated longitudinally. First, the benefits of interventions may not be seen immediately but may develop over time. We hypothesize that supporting parents in emotionally rich interactions will help children develop critical socio-emotional knowledge. In turn, the reminiscing component of RRR may help children to apply this knowledge in their day-to-day lives. However, this process can take time and may not be captured fully by socio-emotional measures at immediate post-test. These sleeper effects—where long-term benefits only become visible after time—have been identified in the parent–child reminiscing literature, especially for socio-emotional benefits. For instance, in an intervention designed to encourage parents' emotionally rich reminiscing with preschoolers, benefits for children's emotion understanding were not evident until 6 months after the intervention, presumably because socio-emotional skills take time to develop (Van Bergen et al., 2009). Second, sometimes, benefits seen at post-test may fade out over time. For example, the benefits of some early childhood initiatives are lost when children start school (Bailey et al., 2017, 2020). School provides rich opportunities for children to learn about the socio-emotional world.

Therefore, nonparticipating children may catch up to participating peers given exposure to schooling. As a result, with some interventions, there is no added benefit to participating during the preschool years. Only with long-term follow-ups can these different patterns of intervention effects be seen.

The present study is part of the longer-term follow-up of the oral language and literacy initiative for parents and preschoolers called *Tender Shoots*, which is a longitudinal randomized controlled trial combining **shared book-reading** and related oral-language interactions to foster children's development (Clifford et al., 2024; Reese et al., 2023; Riordan et al., 2022; Schaughency et al., 2023; Timperley et al., 2022). During the implementation phase, participating parents of preschool children were given brief education sessions to understand shared oral language interactions as opportunities for developmental learning and how to have enhanced book-reading and reminiscing interactions with their children, followed by study resources to support implementation for 6 weeks. The present study aimed to evaluate the socio-emotional content of parent–child book-reading interactions specifically and relations with children's socio-emotional competencies 1 year following participation in Tender Shoots. The *Rich Reading and Reminiscing* (RRR) condition aimed to support oral language and socio-emotional talk during shared book-reading and reminiscing. Two active controls were included. The first was a book-reading condition called *Strengthening Sound Sensitivity* (SSS) with a specific focus on phonological awareness (see Schaughency et al., 2023). The second was an *Activity-Based Control* (ABC) where children were given a range of developmentally appropriate activities to engage in with their parents. We hypothesized that (1) preschool participation in RRR would have longer-term benefits for parents' and children's mental-state language during **shared book-reading** 1 year later compared to SSS and ABC; and (2) parent and child mental-state talk, including emotional, evaluative, and cognitive talk during book-reading, would be positively correlated with children's self-regulation and socio-emotional skills.

Method

Parents with 3–5-year-old children attending one of four early childhood centers in Aotearoa New Zealand were invited to participate (see Riordan et al., 2022 for details). At baseline, a total of 72 parent–child dyads were randomly assigned to one of three modules: RRR (*Rich Reading and Reminiscing*), SSS (*Strengthening Sound Sensitivity*), and an Active Control ABC (*Activity-Based Control*). Children were recruited from their early childhood centers, and most families spoke primarily English at home. At 1-year follow-up ($N = 69$), children were identified by their parents as New Zealand European (97%), New Zealand Māori (14%), and from other groups (15%) using a total response method. All children spoke English, and five children spoke more than one language (e.g., te reo Māori, Pacific, Asian, Middle Eastern, and other European languages). Participating parents included 67 mothers and 2 fathers. Parents endorsed age bands ranging between 21–25 and

51–55 years (Mode age: 36–40). Parents were predominantly New Zealand European (84%); 15% were New Zealand Māori; and 10% were from other groups using a total response method. Parent education varied from intermediate-level education (US middle school equivalent) to graduate degrees. Most parents reported some level of tertiary qualification (e.g., polytechnic qualification).

Measures

To assess the possible benefits of the **shared book-reading** and reminiscing intervention, children completed a battery of oral language, self-regulation, and socio-emotional measures at four timepoints before participating with their parents (baseline) and at three time points after participating with their parents (immediate post-test; 7-month follow-up, while children were still in preschool; 1-year follow-up, when children were in their first year of primary school) (Fig. 7.1). Parent–child **shared book-reading** interactions with different books from those in the intervention phase took place at three of these time points (baseline, immediate post-test, and 1-year follow-up). Research assistants and graduate psychology students assessed children's self-regulation and socio-emotional understanding in two 40-min assessments at the child's early childhood or primary school settings.

Measures Administered at all Time Points

Head–Toes–Knees–Shoulders (HTKS; McCabe et al., 2004) This "Simon says"-like activity provides a measure of children's self-regulation via their attention, inhibitory control, working memory, and cognitive flexibility (McClelland & Cameron, 2012). The task includes three sections with more complex rules as children progress through each level. At level 1, children are taught a rule where they are required to do the opposite action to what they are instructed, for example, "when I say touch your head, I want you to touch your toes". If children respond correctly, they move to the next level where all four behavioral rules are introduced (head is paired with toes, and knees are paired with shoulders). Finally, the third level involves switching the behavioral rule pairings (heads with knees, and shoulders with toes).

Scoring was completed as described by Clifford et al. (2024), using all 30 items across three sections to reduce floor effects with young preschool participants. Children were given a score of 0/2 for an incorrect response, 1/2 for a self-corrected response, and 2/2 for a correct response. The scores across the three levels were summed together to provide a total score between 0 and the highest possible score of 60.

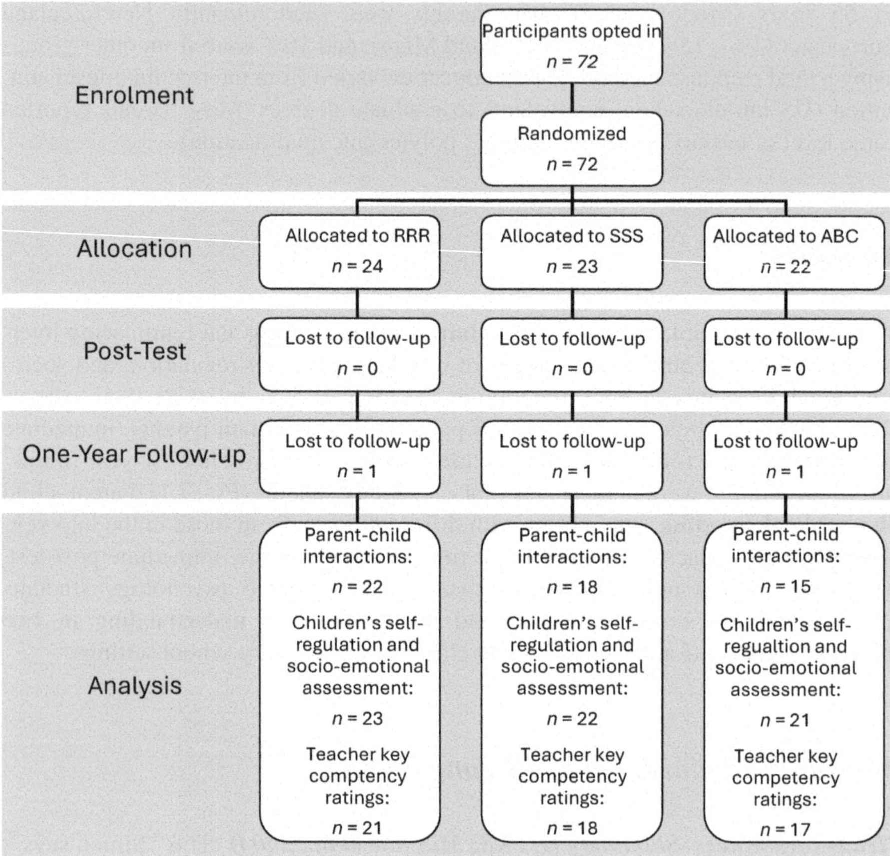

Fig. 7.1 Participant retention from recruitment to 1-year follow-up

One-Year Follow-Up Socio-Emotional Measures

At the 1-year follow-up, developmentally appropriate socio-emotional measures were added including the *Desire and Belief Task* and teacher ratings of children's socio-emotional competencies (see Clifford et al., 2024). Assessments took place at children's schools.

Desire and Belief Task (Pons et al., 2004)

Children completed the desire and belief components of the *Test of Emotional Comprehension* (Pons et al., 2004). Both tasks represent important phases in socio-emotional development as children transition to school. Children were presented with two brief scenarios including how characters felt about lettuce; they were then asked how a character would feel if presented with a box of lettuce. Children were then asked to select how each character would feel from the following options: happy, scared, sad, or just alright.

Children then completed a false belief task. They were presented with a rabbit eating a carrot and then shown a fox hiding behind a bush unbeknownst to the rabbit. Children were then asked if the rabbit could see the fox and how the rabbit would be feeling from four options presented: happy, scared, sad, or just alright. Children were given credit for every correct response they gave.

Across both measures, using scoring described in Pons (2004), the distribution of scores suggested possible floor effects (Barrett-Young, 2016). Because children's responses appeared to include emotional terms felt to be more commonly used in New Zealand, children's responses were re-scored to be given credit if their response was of the correct emotional valence. The distribution of scores for the re-scored desire and belief task was similar to that reported by Pons et al. (2003).

Teachers' Ratings of Children's Socio-Emotional Competencies Children's socio-emotional skills were also measured by their primary-school teachers using four competencies from the New Zealand Curriculum (Ministry of Education, 2015). Teachers were asked to rate participating children relative to their same-aged peers on (a) managing self; (b) using language to communicate; (c) participating and contributing; and (d) relating to others. The scale had five points ranging from far less-developed (−2) to typically developed (0) to very well-developed (+2). As the preventive intervention was delivered during the preschool years, primary-school teachers had no specific knowledge of children's participation, including intervention conditions.

Parent–Child Observational Measures

At each timepoint, parent–child dyads were asked to complete two separate interaction tasks: **shared book-reading** (Timperley et al., 2022) and reminiscing (Clifford et al., 2024). Parents were given new narrative picture books for the book-reading task and invited to select one shared positive and one shared negative event for the reminiscing task. Task order was counterbalanced. Parents were asked to engage in these activities as they would normally; researchers were not present in the room. When completed, parents received a $10 voucher. Interactions were audio-recorded and transcribed and coded. The focus of the current chapter is on the mental-state talk during the **shared book-reading** task at 1-year follow-up, controlling for pretest mental-state talk during book-reading.

Shared Book-Reading

Parents were asked to read two unfamiliar narrative picture books at pretest and posttest. One book was a rhyming book and the other a nonrhyming book (see Riordan et al., 2018, 2022). At 1-year follow-up, parents were asked to read a single narrative book (see Timperley et al., 2022). Each book followed an animal character encountering an emotionally challenging situation that required resolution such as being lost in the dark (Pretest: Ferguson's Night Fright (Morrell & Isaacson, 2013*); Plain Giraffe (Huisman,* 2012*); 1-year follow-up: Esau the Paw (Gurney,* 2014).

Coding

Audio-recordings were transcribed verbatim and then coded by two postgraduate students on 25% of the remaining transcripts to achieve reliability. Transcriptions were first coded for the presence of extratextual talk focused on either meaning or phonological features (see Timperley et al., 2022). For the present analyses, extratextual utterances were further coded for the presence of socio-emotional content. Based on Bird and Reese's (2006) emotion coding scheme, each mental-state word or reference was assigned a code for the presence of emotion (e.g., *happy, scared*), evaluative (e.g., *favorite, worst*), or cognitive (e.g., *think, know, remember*) content.

Intervention Conditions

Book-Reading Conditions (RRR and SSS)

Following baseline assessment, parents in the book-reading conditions received education on RRR or SSS. Parents learned the rationale for the skills targeted—book-reading and other **parent–child interactions** as contexts for learning—and how to enrich book-reading and other oral language interactions with their children. To support implementation, in the week following these sessions, parents and children received a treasure box with two prompted books (see Riordan et al., 2022). These books were commercially available and designed for preschool-aged children. They received new books every week for 6 weeks. Prompts in each set of books were specific to the goals of the condition (e.g., meaning-focused or phonological awareness). Parents were encouraged to read each book to their child three times. To foster scaffolding across successive readings, each book contained color-coded prompts, with prompts becoming more complex across repeated readings. Participants recorded each reading on a child stamp chart.

Rich Reading and Reminiscing (RRR)

In RRR, prompts inserted in each book focused on oral language, cognitive, and **socio-emotional learning** during **shared book-reading** and elaborative reminiscing. Across readings, parents were asked to draw attention to emotional terms and experiences within the book, including relating book experiences to the children's own experiences. At the conclusion of each reading, there was a suggested reminiscing task that invited parents to discuss in depth an emotional experience in the book that linked to a child's own experience. The reminiscing conversation could take place later that day or the next day if parents wished. To encourage reminiscing across a range of emotions for each book, suggested experiences focused on shared activities after the first reading (e.g., a time you cooked together), emotionally negative events after the second reading (e.g., a time your child was scared or frightened), and emotionally positive events after the third reading (e.g., a time your child had fun playing chase). All post-reading reminiscing prompts related to the theme of the book.

Strengthening Sound Sensitivity (SSS)

In SSS, prompts focused on phonological awareness and sound play. Over successive readings, prompts directed parents to highlight sound talk. This included exploring rhyme and beginning phonemic awareness (e.g., alliteration). At the end of each reading, parents were directed to engage in a sound-related activity such as songs, nursery rhymes, or word play that built upon phonological concepts introduced during shared reading.

Activity-Based Control (ABC)

To parallel the design of RRR and SSS, in the activity-based control, children and parents also received a treasure box and weekly activities for children to complete with their parents. Activities were selected to build areas identified as developmentally important in a focus group of parents of preschool-aged children (Schaughency et al., 2016). Activities incorporated fine motor skills and school transition tasks including health and nutrition, self-care, and music.

Results

Table 7.1 presents the means and standard deviations for the shared book-reading variables at 1-year follow-up.

Prior to analyses, data distributions were checked for violations to assumptions of normality. Variables were generally normally distributed, with most variables

Table 7.1 Descriptive statistics for shared book-reading mental-state talk of parents and children at 1-year follow-up

	RRR		SSS		ABC	
	M	*SD*	*M*	*SD*	*M*	*SD*
Parent						
Emotion	7.65	10.43	2.88	4.38	2.71	5.42
Cognitive	9.05	11.83	4.25	5.01	2.29	2.87
Evaluative	5.38	7.03	3.00	4.29	2.12	2.64
Child						
Emotion	3.15	4.08	1.25	1.73	1.56	2.22
Cognitive	3.40	4.55	1.88	2.28	1.56	2.06
Evaluative	2.30	3.34	1.25	2.14	0.81	1.33

Note. RRR = Rich Reading and Reminiscing; SSS = Strengthening Sound Sensitivity; ABC = Activity-Based Control. Means reflect average frequencies of parent and child utterances for each variable by condition

within ranges recommended for parametric statistics (skew <3.00, kurtosis <10; Kline, 2011). To account for those variables that did have a skew and kurtosis above these thresholds (parent cognitive and affective talk), nonparametric tests were completed where appropriate. To examine differences in parent–child shared book-reading by condition, ANCOVAs with bootstrapping were conducted. The same **shared book-reading** variable at pretest was added as a covariate. Due to the small sample size, findings are interpreted when $p < 0.10$, when 95% confidence intervals did not include zero, supplemented by effect sizes.

Table 7.2 presents the results of ANCOVAs comparing mental-state talk variables during **shared book-reading** by condition at the 1-year follow-up, controlling for the corresponding talk variable at pretest. The results showed main effects by condition (at $p < 0.10$ when 95% CIs did not include zero) for parents' content of the shared book-reading variables, with parents in RRR using more emotion language (e.g., *sad, scared*) and cognitive language (e.g., *think, know*) compared to parents in either SSS or ABC conditions. Parents in RRR also used more evaluative language (e.g., *nice, yucky*) than parents in ABC. Children who participated in RRR used more emotional language than children in SSS or ABC. Effect sizes were moderate to large across all mental-state talk categories for the RRR comparisons. In contrast, pairwise comparisons revealed no significant differences detected between SSS and the ABC control. Thus, parents and children continued to use more mental-state talk during **shared book-reading** 1 year after participating in RRR compared to the two control conditions, even when they had been exposed to the same books during the intervention phase as in SSS.

Table 7.2 Results of ANCOVAs comparing 1-year follow-up mental-state talk for parents and children during book-reading by condition

	RRR vs SSS				RRR vs ABC				SSS vs ABC			
	Mean difference	BCa 95% CI	*p*	*d*	Mean difference	BCa 95% CI	*p*	*d*	Mean difference	BCa 95% CI	*p*	*d*
Parent												
Emotion	7.07	1.79, 13.25	0.05	0.95	6.39	1.03, 12.75	0.046	0.86	−0.67	−4.12, 2.35	0.63	0.09
Cognitive	7.40	2.48, 13.52	0.06	0.99	7.47	3.08, 12.96	0.04	0.99	0.07	−3.78, 3.18	0.97	0.01
Evaluative	3.05	−0.09, 7.01	0.13	0.57	3.57	0.48, 7.40	0.097	0.68	0.53	−1.61, 2.55	0.63	0.10
Child												
Emotion	2.61	0.52, 4.91	0.048	0.87	2.14	0.18, 4.54	0.08	0.72	−0.46	−1.87, 1.14	0.51	0.16
Cognitive	2.11	−0.25, 4.82	0.15	0.64	1.64	−0.15, 3.72	0.16	0.50	−0.47	−2.33, 1.18	0.63	0.14
Evaluative	1.24	−0.60, 2.91	0.24	0.49	1.41	−0.08, 3.10	0.12	0.56	0.17	−1.24, 1.80	0.81	0.07

Note. RRR = Rich Reading and Reminiscing; SSS = Strengthening Sound Sensitivity; ABC = Activity-Based Control

Table 7.3 Pearson's correlations between parent–child book-reading mental-state talk and children's self-regulation and socio-emotional competencies

	HTKS60	Desire and belief	Managing self	Relating to others	Using Language to communicate	Participating and contributing
Parent						
Emotion	0.000	0.020	0.084	−0.204	−0.111	−0.172
Cognitive	−0.005	−0.109	−0.045	−0.273	−0.075	−0.167
Evaluative	0.009	−0.86	−0.028	−0.260	−0.045	−0.186
Child						
Emotion	0.051	0.050	0.054	−0.237	−0.207	−0.162
Cognitive	−0.017	−0.083	0.058	−0.273	−0.214	−0.035
Evaluative	0.014	−0.214	−0.157	−0.405**	−0.211	−0.215

**$p < 0.01$ (two-tailed)

Note. HTKS60—Head–Toes–Knees–Shoulders task

Correlations Between Shared Book-Reading Variables and Children's Self-Regulation and Socio-Emotional Variables at 1-Year Follow-Up

Our secondary aim was to conduct correlational analyses across conditions for the role of parent–child mental-state talk during book-reading for children's concurrent self-regulation and socio-emotional competencies. At 1-year follow-up, correlations between parent–child book-reading mental-state talk variables and children's concurrent self-regulation or socio-emotional variables ranged from negligible to modestly negative (see Table 7.3). Unexpectedly, teachers' ratings of children's ability to relate with others was negatively associated with parents' cognitive ($r = -0.273$, $p = 0.057$) and evaluative talk ($r = -0.260$, $p = 0.072$) and children's cognitive ($r = -0.273$, $p = 0.061$) and affective talk ($r = -0.405$, $p = 0.004$). We discuss potential reasons for these patterns below.

Discussion

In these analyses, we explored whether participating in an emotion-rich oral language preschool preventive intervention had an impact 1 year later, after children had started primary school. At this 1-year follow-up, we found benefits of the Rich Reading and Reminiscing module of *Tender Shoots* for parents' and children's mental-state talk during **shared book-reading**. Specifically, we saw higher levels for both parents' and children's emotional talk and parents' cognitive and evaluative talk compared to another shared reading control group (SSS) and a nonreading control group (ABC). These findings demonstrate that parents and children engaged in emotionally and cognitively enriched conversations during **shared book-reading** with new books and without specific prompts after a year had passed and children had started school. Thus, our light-touch 6-week scaffolded intervention in the preschool years had a long-term impact on the mental-state talk during parent–child book-reading a year later. Of particular interest is that we saw long-term benefits for parents' and children's emotion talk. Discussing emotional experiences can be a particularly challenging activity for parents and for children.

In our previous 1-year follow-up analyses with this sample that focused only on reminiscing conversations, we found benefits of RRR only for parents' evaluative talk during the positive-event reminiscing task (Clifford et al., 2024). In the present analyses, we found more consistent long-term benefits of earlier participation in RRR for parents' and children's emotion talk and for parents' cognitive and evaluative talk during the **shared book-reading** task. Across both sets of analyses, moderate to large effect sizes were observed of RRR for increasing mental-state talk during **shared book-reading**. These findings suggest that parents and children may have found it easier to maintain emotion-rich conversations during **shared book-reading** compared to reminiscing. Importantly, the benefits of RRR for parent–child book-reading interactions remained despite many important developmental and social changes that happen when children start school.

In our earlier analyses (Clifford et al., 2024), we also found that children who participated in RRR had higher teacher ratings on some measures of socio-emotional competencies than children in the other conditions at 1-year follow up, suggesting that RRR had supported young children's **socio-emotional learning**. In turn, these socio-emotional competencies were correlated with both parents' and children's socio-emotional talk during reminiscing but only when reminiscing about negative events. The present study aimed to explore the role of mental-state talk during **shared book-reading** for children's **socio-emotional learning**. However, despite the observed benefits of RRR for parents' and children's mental-state talk during **shared book-reading** at 1-year follow up, these forms of talk were not positively correlated with children's self-regulation or socio-emotional competencies as hypothesized. Recall that these null findings are in contrast to those from an earlier follow-up 7 months after participating in RRR, before most children had started primary school, when we found concurrent positive correlations between parents' and children's mental-state talk during book-reading and children's socio-emotional competencies (Das, 2018). Perhaps, participation in RRR was able to temporarily boost children's socio-emotional skills before school entry. These patterns also counter previous work that has found concurrent positive associations between parent–child book-reading and children's socio-emotional competencies during the preschool years (see Grover et al., 2023; Schapira & Aram, 2019). In fact, in the present analyses, children's cognitive talk during book-reading was *negatively* correlated with teachers' ratings of children's relating to others, in line with our findings that parents' cognitive talk during reminiscing was negatively related to teachers' ratings of managing self (Clifford et al., 2024).

These null and sometimes negative correlations between parent–child mental-state talk and children's socio-emotional skills in primary school are surprising, suggesting a complex and dynamic relationship. Parenting surveys in

English-speaking countries (e.g., Merga & Ledger, 2018) consistently show a decline in parent-reported shared book-reading with children once they enter primary school and begin formal reading instruction. In New Zealand, children begin reading instruction in their first year of school. Thus, perhaps the parents and children in our study were no longer regularly sharing picture books together. If they were not engaging in this activity as often, their reading style would not continue to shape their children's socio-emotional competencies as much, even if their style *when they do read* is similar to how it was when they finished the program. There is no corresponding evidence that reminiscing declines in primary school; instead, reminiscing becomes more elaborate and frequent over time (Reese et al., 2010, 2020). Together, these age-related shifts in **shared book-reading** and reminiscing could explain the puzzling pattern of concurrent negative correlations with children's socio-emotional competencies.

We must also bear in mind that the 1-year follow-up was the first time in the study that we obtained teacher ratings of children's socio-emotional skills. School provides children with an increased number of experiences, likely including frequent **socio-emotional learning** opportunities. These opportunities could lead non-participating children to quickly catch up to their participating peers. Thus, other processes—such as school-based social learning—may be more strongly related to the socio-emotional competencies measured here. Navigating peer relationships, classroom routines, and emerging academic learning all contribute to children's developing socio-emotional competencies.

Yet, the home environment is still important to children's socio-emotional functioning even after they enter primary school. For instance, we found that parent–child reminiscing during the negative event at 1-year follow-up was positively correlated with children's socio-emotional competencies, in contrast to the book-reading talk presented here (Clifford et al., 2024). It is possible we may have seen associations more similar to the reminiscing findings had we selected a picture book with a story that focused specifically on negative emotion experiences. These sorts of stories may elicit different kinds of emotional talk, and perhaps these types of talk could be concurrently associated with children's socio-emotional development as is the case with reminiscing (Shapira et al., 2021a, 2021b). Participation in Rich Reading and Reminiscing may have helped to guide parents to think about including socio-emotional conversations during and after **shared book-reading**.

Strengths and Limitations

Importantly, we were able to support parents and children to continue to engage in emotion-rich conversations 1 year after a brief period of supported participation during the preschool years. Although our sample size was small, the benefits presented in this chapter are consistent. By including SSS as an additional reading control group, we were able to demonstrate the added benefits of promoting emotion-rich conversations during book-reading above and beyond the book content. Reading books with socio-emotional themes may help children's learning, and explicitly drawing attention to these themes through additional prompts appears to help support children to engage in more of this mental-state talk themselves.

The current study provides insight into how both **shared book-reading** and reminiscing may support children's participation in rich oral language interactions. Rich conversations can happen alongside book-reading and support children's **socio-emotional learning**. Methods to enhance children's learning during these shared stories can have benefits for children's emotion talk even 1 year later. Therefore, story books that focus on encouraging these rich conversations in meaningful ways can enhance children's learning.

Future Directions

Although the present study focused on parents, these are not the only important adults who engage in book-reading with children. Future studies should explore how educators, teachers, or other caregivers can be supported in engaging in emotion-rich book-reading. Here in Aotearoa New Zealand and in developed countries worldwide (OECD, 2023), most children are enrolled in some form of childcare in the first 5 years of life. Therefore, these important adults may be able to support or further enhance children's **socio-emotional learning**.

References

Aram, D., Fine, Y., & Ziv, M. (2013). Enhancing parent–child shared book reading interactions: Promoting references to the book's plot and socio-cognitive themes. *Early Childhood Research Quarterly, 28*(1), 111–122. https://doi.org/10.1016/j.ecresq.2012.03.005

Bailey, D. H., Duncan, G. J., Cunha, F., Foorman, B. R., & Yeager, D. S. (2020). Persistence and fade-out of educational-intervention effects: Mechanisms and potential solutions. *Psychological Science in the Public Interest, 21*(2), 55–97. https://doi.org/10.1177/1529100620915848

Bailey, D., Duncan, G. J., Odgers, C. L., & Yu, W. (2017). Persistence and fadeout in the impacts of child and adolescent interventions. *Journal of Research on Educational Effectiveness, 10*(1), 7–39. https://doi.org/10.1080/19345747.2016.1232459

Barrett-Young, A. (2016). Correlations between narrative retell and socio-emotional skills in New Zealand 5-year-olds. Unpublished undergraduate honours' thesis, University of Otago.

Batini, F., Luperini, V., Cei, E., Izzo, D., & Toti, G. (2021). The association between reading and emotional development: A systematic review. *Journal of Education and Training Studies, 9*(1), 12–50. https://doi.org/10.11114/jets.v9i1.5053

Bernard, S., & Deleau, M. (2007). Conversational perspective-taking and false belief attribution: A longitudinal study. *British Journal of Developmental Psychology, 25*(3), 443–460. https://doi.org/10.1348/026151006X171451

Bird, A., & Reese, E. (2006). Emotional reminiscing and the development of an autobiographical self. *Developmental Psychology, 42*(4), 613–626. https://doi.org/10.1037/0012-1649.42.4.613

Clifford, A. E., Schaughency, E., Das, S., Riordan, J., Carroll, J. L., & Reese, E. (2024). Tender Shoots: Effects of a preschool shared reading and reminiscing initiative on parent-child interactions and for socio-emotional and self-regulation outcomes after school entry. *Learning and Individual Differences, 112*, 102443. https://doi.org/10.1016/j.lindif.2024.102443

Curenton, S. M., & Craig, M. J. (2011). Shared-reading versus oral storytelling: Associations with preschoolers' prosocial skills and problem behaviours. *Early Child Development and Care, 181*(1), 123–146. https://doi.org/10.1080/03004430903292208

Das, S. A. (2018). *Rich Reading and Reminiscing: Benefits of Parent-Preschooler Interactions for Children's Developing Language, Behavioural Regulation, and Socio-Emotional Competencies. Unpublished PhD thesis, University of Otago, Dunedin, New Zealand.*

Flack, Z. M., Field, A. P., & Horst, J. S. (2018). The effects of shared storybook reading on word learning: A meta-analysis. *Developmental Psychology, 54*(7), 1334.

Fivush, R., Berlin, L., McDermott Sales, J., Mennuti-Washburn, J., & Cassidy, J. (2003). Functions of parent-child reminiscing about emotionally negative events. *Memory, 11(2), 179–192.*

Hindman, A. H., Skibbe, L. E., & Foster, T. D. (2014). Exploring the variety of parental talk during shared book reading and its contributions to preschool language and literacy: Evidence from the Early Childhood Longitudinal Study-Birth Cohort. *Reading and Writing, 27(2), 287–313.*

Huisman, A. (2012). *Plain Giraffe.* CreateSpace Independent.

Gilkerson, J., Richards, J. A., & Topping, K. J. (2017). The impact of book reading in the early years on parent–child language interaction. *Journal of Early Childhood Literacy, 17*(1), 92–110. https://doi.org/10.1177/1468798415608907

Gurney, C. (2014). *Esau the Paw*. Scholastic New Zealand Limited.

Grøver, V., Snow, C. E., Evans, L., & Strømme, H. (2023). Overlooked advantages of interactive book reading in early childhood? A systematic review and research agenda. *Acta Psychologica, 239*, 103997.

Kline, R. B. (2011). *Methodology in the Social Sciences: Principles and practice of structural equation modeling. Guilford Press.*

Leyva, D., Reese, E., Laible, D., Schaughency, E., Das, S., & Clifford, A. (2020). Measuring parents' elaborative reminiscing: Differential links of parents' elaboration to children's autobiographical memory and socioemotional skills. *Journal of Cognition and Development, 21(1), 23–45.*

Mashburn, A., LoCasake-Crouch, J., & Pears, K. (2018). Kindergarten transition and readiness: Promoting cognitive, social-emotional, and self-regulatory development (1st ed). Springer. https://doi.org/10.1007/978-3-319-90200-5.

McCabe, L. A., Cunnington, M., & Brooks-Gunn, J. (2004). The development of self-regulation in young children: Individual characteristics and environmental contexts. In R. F. Baumeister & K. D. Vohs (Eds.), *Handbook of self-regulation: Research, theory, and applications* (pp. 340–356). The Guilford Press.

McClelland, M. M., & Cameron, C. E. (2012). Self-regulation in early childhood: Improving conceptual clarity and developing ecologically valid measures. *Child Development Perspectives, 6*(2), 136–142. https://doi.org/10.1111/j.1750-8606.2011.00191.x

Merga, M. K., & Ledger, S. (2018). Parents' views on reading aloud to their children: Beyond the early years. *The Australian Journal of Language and Literacy, 41*(3), 177–189.

Ministry of Education. (2015). The New Zealand Curriculum. Wellington, NZ: Ministry of Education. https://nzcurriculum.tki.org.nz/The-New-Zealand-Curriculum%0A.

Moffitt, T. E., Arseneault, L., Belsky, D., Dickson, N., Hancox, R. J., Harrington, H., et al. (2011). A gradient of childhood self-control predicts health, wealth, and public safety. *Proceedings of the National Academy of Sciences of the United States of America, 108*(7), 2693–2698. https://doi.org/10.1073/pnas.1010076108

Morrell, N., & Isaacson, M. (2013). *Ferguson's Night Fright*. Natalie Morrell.

OECD. (2023). https://www.oecd.org/en/about/programmes/early-childhood-education-and-care-ecec.html.

Laible, D. (2011). Does it matter if preschool children and mothers discuss positive vs. negative events during reminiscing? Links with mother-reported attachment, family emotional climate, and socioemotional development. *Social Development, 20*(2), 394–411.

Mitchell, C., & Reese, E. (2022). Growing memories: Coaching mothers in elaborative reminiscing with toddlers benefits adolescents' turning-point narratives and wellbeing. *Journal of Personality, 90*(6), 887–901.

Pons, F., Harris, P. L., & De Rosnay, M. (2004). Emotion comprehension between 3 and 11 years: Developmental periods and hierarchical organization. *European Journal of Developmental Psychology, 1*(2), 127–152. https://doi.org/10.1080/17405620344000022

Pons, F., Lawson, J., Harris, P. L., & De Rosnay, M. (2003). Individual differences in children's emotion understanding: Effects of age and language. *Scandinavian Journal of Psychology, 44*(4), 347–353. https://doi.org/10.1111/1467-9450.00354

Reese, E., & Cox, A. (1999). Quality of adult book reading affects children's emergent literacy. *Developmental Psychology, 35*(1), 20–28.

Reese, E., Macfarlane, L., McAnally, H., Robertson, S. J., & Taumoepeau, M. (2020). Coaching in maternal reminiscing with preschoolers leads to elaborative and coherent personal narratives in early adolescence. *Journal of Experimental Child Psychology, 189*, 104707.

Reese, E., & Newcombe, R. (2007). Training mothers in elaborative reminiscing enhances children's autobiographical memory and narrative. *Child Development, 78*(4), 1153–1170.

Riordan, J., Reese, E., Das, S., Carroll, J., & Schaughency, E. (2022). *Tender Shoots*: A randomized controlled trial of two shared-reading approaches for enhancing parent-child interactions and children's oral language and literacy skills. *Scientific Studies of Reading, 26*(3), 183–203. https://doi.org/10.1080/10888438.2021.1926464

Riordan, J., Reese, E., Rouse, S., & Schaughency, E. (2018). Promoting code-focused talk: The rhyme and reason for why book style matters. *Early Childhood Research Quarterly, 45*, 69–80. https://doi.org/10.1016/j.ecresq.2018.05.004

Salmon, K., & Reese, E. (2016). The benefits of reminiscing with young children. *Current Directions in Psychological Science, 25(4), 233–238.* https://doi-org.ezproxy.otago.ac.nz/10.1177/0963721416655100

Schapira, R., & Aram, D. (2019). Shared book reading at home and preschoolers' socio-emotional competence. *Early Education and Development, 31*(6), 819–837. https://doi.org/10.1080/10409289.2019.1692624

Schapira, R., Deitcher, D. B., & Aram, D. (2021a). Variability and stability in parent-child discourse during and following repeated shared book reading. *Reading and Writing, 34*(1), 273–300. https://doi.org/10.1007/s11145-020-10072-y

Schapira, R., Bergman Deitcher, D., & Aram, D. (2021b). Mothers' discourse during shared reading of books relating to 'positive' and 'negative' emotions in different genres. *Journal of Research in Reading, 44*(4), 897–909.

Schaughency, E., Riordan, J., Das, S., Carroll, J., & Reese, E. (2016). Embracing the spirit of ako: Growing partnerships between parents, early childhood educators and researchers. *Early Childhood Folio, 20*(2), 31–36. https://doi.org/10.18296/ecf.0028

Schaughency, E., Linney, K., Carroll, J., Das, S., Riordan, J., & Reese, E. (2023). Tender Shoots: A parent-mediated randomized controlled trial with preschool children benefits beginning reading 1 year later. *Reading Research Quarterly, 58*(3), 450–470.

Timperley, S., Schaughency, E., McDonald, R. R., & Reese, E. (2021). Rhymes and relatability: How storybook style and content relate to home-based educators' extra-textual talk. *Early Education and Development, 32*(8), 1240–1259.

Timperley, S., Schaughency, E., Riordan, J., Carroll, J., Das, S., & Reese, E. (2022). Tender Shoots: Effects of a preschool shared book reading preventive intervention on parent–child reading and parents' involvement in the first year of school. *School Mental Health, 14*(2), 238–253. https://doi.org/10.1007/s12310-022-09505-6

Reese, E. (2013). *Tell me a story: Sharing stories to enrich your child's world.* Oxford University Press.

Reese, E., Leyva, D., Sparks, A., & Grolnick, W. (2010). Maternal elaborative reminiscing increases low-income children's narrative skills relative to dialogic reading. *Early Education and Development, 21*(3), 318–342.

Reese, E., Barrett-Young, A., Gilkison, L., Carroll, J., Das, S., Riordan, J., & Schaughency, E. (2023). T ender Shoots: A parent book-reading and reminiscing program to enhance children's oral narrative skills. *Reading and Writing, 36*(3), 541–564.

Van Bergen, P., Salmon, K., Dadds, M. R., & Allen, J. (2009). The effects of mother training in emotion-rich, elaborative reminiscing on children's shared recall and emotion knowledge. *Journal of Cognition and Development, 10*(3), 162–187. https://doi.org/10.1080/15248370903155825

Vygotsky, L. S. (1978). *Mind and society: The development of higher psychological processes*. Harvard University Press.

Amanda Clifford is a senior lecturer at the University of Otago. Her research focuses on family health and wellbeing and parent–child interactions. Her PhD explored how educators and parents talk with children about socio-emotional events.

Elizabeth Schaughency is an honorary senior lecturer at the University of Otago. Her research explores children's development in social contexts and bridges research and practice by exploring how families and schools may support children's developmental outcomes.

Shika Das is the clinical lead at a specialist education school in London, embedding neurodiverse-affirming and trauma-informed practice into the curriculum and learning environment. Her work focuses on inclusive education, mental wellbeing, and holistic development for neurodivergent pupils.

Elaine Reese is a professor of psychology at the University of Otago. Her research focuses on the role of social interactions, especially during **shared book-reading** and reminiscing, for child and adolescent development.

Chapter 8
Fostering Social–Emotional Development in Deaf and Hard-of-Hearing Children Through Storybook Reading

Evelien Dirks and Loes Wauters

Contents

One in 1000 children is born **deaf** or hard of hearing (DHH) (van der Zee et al., 2022). DHH children are at greater risk of experiencing challenges in their language and **social–emotional** development compared to their typical hearing peers (e.g., Tomblin et al., 2015; Stevenson et al., 2015). This is largely due to restricted access to spoken language caused by their hearing loss. While hearing aids and cochlear implants improve access to spoken language, they cannot fully restore typical

E. Dirks (✉)
Dutch Foundation of the Deaf and Hard-of-Hearing Child (NSDSK), Amsterdam, The Netherlands

Behavioural Science Institute and Radboud University, Nijmegen, The Netherlands
e-mail: edirks@nsdsk.nl

L. Wauters
Tranzo, Tilburg University, Tilburg, The Netherlands

Royal Kentalis, Utrecht, The Netherlands
e-mail: l.wauters@kentalis.nl

R. Schapira, D. Aram (eds.), *Shared Book Reading and Children's Social-Emotional Competence*, https://doi.org/10.1007/978-3-032-14688-5_8

hearing. Research shows that, on average, DHH children still lag behind their hearing peers in language development (Tomblin et al., 2015; Lund, 2016). Moreover, the majority of DHH children (more than 90%) are born to hearing parents (Mitchell & Karchmer, 2004; Van der Zee & Dirks, 2022) who often have no prior experience with **deaf**ness or sign language, making it difficult for them to provide a rich (sign) language environment from the start.

Language is vital for children's **social–emotional** development. It allows them to express thoughts, emotions, and desires, facilitating meaningful interactions with peers and caregivers. Through language, children learn to understand others, regulate their own emotions, and build relationships (Fields-Olivieri et al., 2024). Without adequate language development, children may struggle with social connections and experience frustration, affecting their overall well-being. Therefore, supporting language acquisition from an early age is crucial for healthy social and emotional growth. To promote the language and **social-emotional** development of DHH children, it is crucial to detect hearing loss as early as possible. Early detection allows for timely intervention, which has proven to be effective in enhancing their language, communication, **social–emotional** skills, and overall well-being (Bongioletti et al., 2024; Grey et al., 2022; Meinzen-Derr et al., 2011; Yoshinaga-Itano et al., 2021). A Family-Centered Early Intervention (FCEI) approach is particularly effective as it emphasizes the involvement of the family in the intervention process, recognizing that parents and caregivers play a pivotal role in the child's development (Moeller et al., 2024).

Family-Centered Early Intervention for DHH Children

The primary objective of FCEI is to support parents in promoting their DHH children's language development and overall well-being. This approach is built on the principles of family–professional partnerships, which leverage family strengths while considering different lifestyles, cultures, and environments (Moeller et al., 2024). FCEI programs provide parents with essential knowledge about hearing loss, **deaf**ness, communication strategies, hearing technology, child development, and the importance of early language exposure. In addition, FCEI programs equip parents with practical skills to support their child's development, including skills such as sign language, communication strategies, and language-evoking strategies. Courses such as interactive **storybook reading** are often included in FCEI programs to enhance language acquisition and **parent–child interaction** (Dirks & Wauters, 2015). Strengthening the parent–child relationship is a cornerstone of FCEI, given the importance of these interactions for DHH children's language development (Curtin et al., 2021; Holzinger et al., 2022). Home visits by FCEI professionals provide opportunities to foster these interactions in an environment that is comfortable and familiar for families. Research showed that children who enrolled in FCEI before 6 months of age have better developmental outcomes than those enrolled later (Grey et al., 2022; Yoshinaga-Itano et al., 2021).

In addition to language and communication, FCEI also aims to promote the **social–emotional** development of DHH children. This aspect of child development receives significant attention within FCEI programs, given the unique challenges that DHH children face in their social and emotional growth (Stevenson et al., 2015). Both in the home visits and in courses at the FCEI center, parents are informed about the **social–emotional** challenges DHH children may encounter and are equipped with skills to foster their child's **social–emotional** development.

Social–Emotional Development in DHH Children

DHH children need to learn to navigate a world that is predominantly designed for hearing individuals. This is more difficult for them because they often have restricted access to auditory information compared to their hearing peers. Everyday interactions, such as playing with peers at the playground, following conversations in noisy environments, understanding speech without visual cues, and picking up subtle auditory signals, pose challenges, whereas access to these interactions is taken for granted by hearing people. The language delays that DHH children often experience further intensify these difficulties, impacting their ability to engage in social interactions. Limited vocabulary and delays in conversational skills and pragmatics (Bongioletti et al., 2024; Lund, 2016; Walker et al., 2019; Werfel et al., 2022) can hinder their ability to express themselves clearly, understand others, and participate in conversations. This can lead to feelings of frustration and difficulties in building and maintaining friendships. Research shows that DHH children experience more difficulties in social interactions than their typical hearing peers (Stevenson et al., 2015).

Emotion Recognition

Recognizing and responding to emotional cues significantly enhance social interactions (Izard et al., 2001). Children who understand emotions better are generally more liked by their peers (Denham et al., 1990). The ability to differentiate between facial expressions and interpret vocal cues is essential for understanding emotions during social interactions (Izard et al., 2001). For DHH children, interpreting emotions in spoken language may be difficult due to limited access to auditory cues like tone, intonation, and pitch (Chatterjee et al., 2015; Everhardt et al., 2020; Hopyan-Misakyan et al., 2009). These cues are vital for conveying emotional content. Without them, DHH children may misinterpret conversations, affecting social interactions.

In addition to their difficulties in recognizing vocal cues, DHH children also struggle with interpreting the facial expressions of emotions (Ludlow et al., 2010; Most & Michaelis, 2012; Wang et al., 2016; Wiefferink et al., 2013). In the study by Wiefferink et al., **deaf** children with a CI (2.5–5 years of age) showed difficulties in discriminating and identifying the four basic emotions (happy, sad, angry, and fear). The authors attribute the difficulties in emotion identification and discrimination partly to the quantity and quality of the interactions between DHH children and their parents.

Theory of Mind

Another important aspect of **social–emotional** functioning is the ability to take another person's perspective. **Theory of Mind** (ToM) is the ability to understand that other people have their own thoughts, beliefs, desires, and intentions, which may be different from one's own (Wellman, 2018). This skill is essential for **social–emotional** development, as it helps children interpret and predict others' actions, understand their perspectives, and navigate social interactions effectively. ToM begins to emerge in early childhood and is a key factor in successful communication, collaboration, and relationship-building. ToM plays an important role in predicting social skills (Peterson, 2016) and acceptance among peers (Slaughter et al., 2015). Several studies showed that DHH children lag behind their typical hearing peers in their ToM development (Jones et al., 2015; Ketelaar et al., 2012; Netten et al., 2017; Peterson, 2016; Peterson et al., 2005; Sundqvist & Heimann, 2014). For example, in the study by Ketelaar and colleagues, various aspects of ToM, including intention, desire, and belief understanding, in a sample of 72 **deaf** children with CIs and 69 typical hearing children aged 1 to 5 years were examined. The findings revealed that while **deaf** children with CIs demonstrated intention-understanding skills comparable to typical hearing children, they lagged behind in understanding desires and false beliefs, even after accounting for language abilities. This suggests that although CI improves language abilities, it does not fully address delays in ToM development. The researchers emphasize the importance of enhancing the quality of mental-state conversations between parents and **deaf** children with CIs to support ToM development.

Mental-State Talk

Delays in ToM development in DHH children are partly attributed to limited access to conversational experiences during early childhood (Jones et al., 2015; Ketelaar et al., 2012; Peterson & Siegal, 1995; Vaccari & Marschark, 1997). Engaging in family conversations about thoughts, intentions, and desires plays a vital role in fostering ToM development in DHH children. Mental-state language refers to talking about mental states such as thoughts, beliefs, desires, emotions, and intentions. This language helps typical hearing children understand and reflect on their own and others' inner experiences, enhancing their **social–emotional** skills and predicting ToM development (see meta-analysis by Tompkins et al., 2018). Research has shown that the use of mental-state language by parents is also linked to DHH children's ToM (Moeller & Schick, 2006; Pluta et al., 2023). However, typically hearing parents of DHH children engage less often in mental-state talk with their DHH children compared to parents of typical hearing children (Dirks et al., 2020; Moeller & Schick, 2006; Morgan et al., 2014; Walker et al., 2017). These parents may have difficulties communicating about abstract concepts such as thoughts and emotions in sign language because they have not yet mastered this language in the early years of their DHH child. However, research indicates that even when parents communicate with their DHH children in spoken language, a language they already master, they engage in less mental-state talk compared to parents of typical hearing children (Dirks et al., 2020; Morgan et al., 2014; Walker et al., 2017).

Pluta et al. (2023) examined the use of mental-state talk during **storybook reading** in association with DHH children's ToM abilities. The results showed that parents' use of mental-state language was positively related to DHH children's ToM abilities. They differentiated between parent's emotional and cognitive mental-state language use and found that cognitive references were related to children's early ToM skills and emotional references to both early and basic ToM skills. The use of emotional references seems to be of specific relevance to the ToM skills of DHH children. This is likely because emotional states (e.g., happiness, sadness) rather than cognitive mental states (thoughts) are often accompanied by observable expressions (e.g., smiling, crying), making it easier for parents to draw the child's attention to others' internal mental states (Pluta et al., 2023). The findings of Pluta et al. underscore the importance of mental-state language in mitigating developmental delays and the need for targeted interventions to support ToM development in DHH children, particularly through enhancing parental mental-state practice. One of those interventions could be **storybook reading**.

The Role of Storybook Reading in Social–Emotional Development

The context of **storybook reading** plays a crucial role in fostering **social–emotional** development, including ToM (Symons et al., 2005; Tompkins, 2015). By engaging in discussions about the characters' thoughts, feelings, and actions during book-reading, parents can help children understand and reason about mental states, thereby enhancing their social sensitivity and adaptive behaviors. This interactive approach, known as dialogic reading or interactive **storybook reading**, encourages children to ask questions and engage in conversations about the mind, which is essential for their **social–emotional** growth (Huebner & Meltzoff, 2005; Mol et al., 2008).

Research has investigated the impact of **storybook reading** on **social–emotional** outcomes in hearing children and noted positive results (e.g., Aram & Aviram, 2009; Baker, 2013; Williams et al., 2015). For instance, increased frequency of **storybook reading** is linked to improved emotion regulation (Baker, 2013; Williams et al., 2015), enhanced prosocial behavior (Wong et al., 2022), reduced behavior problems, and better engagement and joint attention during parent–child interactions (Baker, 2013). A systematic review by Batini et al. (2021) on the association between reading and emotional development indicated that reading is associated with improved emotional well-being and stability from early infancy through to the end of high school.

Reading storybooks to children enhances their emotional vocabulary as these books include a variety of emotion words. Cassidy et al. (1998) found that about 80% of U.S. children's books include mental terms related to thoughts, desires, emotions, and intentions. Dyer et al. (2000) examined references to mental states, including emotions, in English storybooks intended for children aged 3 to 6 years. They aimed to analyze books commonly read to young children. It was found that these books, on average, included at least one mental state reference every three sentences.

The different characters in storybooks have different feelings, intentions, and thoughts. Through reading these books, children are exposed to mental-state words and can correspond these to the characters' emotional states. They learn to identify and label different feelings, which enhances their emotion recognition skills. The socio-emotional discussions conducted by parents during and after reading sessions within the family setting significantly influence children's comprehension of the causes of emotions (Schapira & Aram, 2019). By reading storybooks with children, they get the opportunity to step into the shoes of different characters and see the world from their perspectives (Symons et al., 2005). This promotes their ToM development and thus their understanding that different people have different needs and desires (Adrián et al., 2007). In sum, **storybook reading** may be an effective way to promote children's social emotional development.

The number of books in the home of a child is a predictor of a child's reading performance (Park, 2008) and ToM abilities (Adrian et al., 2005; Tompkins, 2022). Although there are no published studies on the number of books in the homes of families with children who are DHH, a Dutch study on interactive reading by Dirks and Wauters (see Wauters et al., 2021) found that parents of 23 DHH children aged between 20 and 46 months reported having an average of 116 adult books (ranging from 0 to 500) and 35 children's books (ranging from 3 to 100). This average number of books is higher than the mean average reported in the study by Park (2008) on the number of books in the homes of 4th graders among 25 countries. Fifteen of the 25 countries in this study had an average of 26–100 books. In 10 countries, only 0–25 books were available in homes on average. In both studies, there was a significant variation between households, with some having no or very few books and others having up to 500 books.

Challenges in Storybook Reading with DHH Children

Although the number of available books in the homes of DHH children seems to be comparable to that of typical hearing children, research has shown that typical hearing parents do not frequently read to their DHH children (Marschark & Harris, 1996). When they do, there are notable differences compared to parents of hearing children. Stobbart and Alant (2008) examined the home literacy experiences of preschool DHH children with their hearing parents and found that these parents tend to focus more on the text rather than engaging their child in a conversation about the story. Research by Aram et al. (2006) among 30 kindergartners revealed that typical hearing parents tend to be more dominant, while DHH children are less responsive and active during **storybook reading** sessions. The parents in the study by DesJardin et al. (2014) used more lower-level facilitative language techniques during shared book-reading than parents of typically hearing children. These findings align with other studies on **parent–child interaction**s, which indicate shorter interactions and a more directive approach from parents (Pressman et al., 1999; Curtin et al., 2021). In addition, these findings indicate that parents, specifically those of DHH children, may need guidance and training in applying interactive reading strategies during book-reading with their child.

Several studies have shown positive effects of focused intervention on the applied strategies by parents of both hearing (Huebner, 2000; Huebner & Meltzoff, 2005) and DHH children (Fung et al., 2005; Dirks & Wauters, 2018). In addition to reported changes in parental behavior, a meta-analysis of nine programs also showed an impact on typical hearing children's expressive language skills (Mol et al., 2008).

Fostering Social–Emotional Development in Deaf and Hard-of-Hearing Children

Interactive Reading Program for Parents of DHH Children

Even though interactive reading programs have proven to be successful, they may need specific adaptations when it comes to reading with DHH children, as the mostly hearing parents of these children face some challenges in the communication and attention strategies during book-reading. Dirks and Wauters (2015, 2018) used an adaptation of the interactive reading program of DeBruin-Parecki (2007) to train parents of 2- to 4-year-old DHH children in interactive **storybook reading** with their child. The goal of the program was to improve parents' interactive reading behavior so that their children could profit more from **storybook reading** opportunities in their language and **social–emotional** development. All parents received FCEI, and the program was provided by two professionals within the FCEI center. The program consists of three group sessions of 2 h each, over a period of 6 weeks. The trainers model the interactive reading strategies, and parents practice

Table 8.1 Interactive reading program

Session	Content
1	– Importance of interactive storybook reading – Steps of interactive storybook reading – Storybook reading with children who are DHH
2	– Interactive reading strategies
3	– Choice of appropriate books – Reviewing videos of interactive reading at home

these strategies during the sessions. Strategies that are being taught are: let the child hold the book and turn the pages, follow the child's lead, introduce the book based on the cover, use materials/toys, allow the child to observe, process and respond, elaborate on the child's ideas, praise and reinforce, ask open-ended questions, point to pictures, relate book content to child experiences, use facial expressions and body posture to bring the book characters to life, use voicing and signs, reflect on the story, and re-read the story. Table 8.1 contains an overview of the sessions in the program.

In the first session, parents learn about interactive **storybook reading** and its importance for children's language, literacy, and **social–emotional** development. Also, the challenges of reading storybooks with DHH children are discussed, such as positioning during reading, attracting and maintaining the child's attention, and communication. Parents received two storybooks and accompanying materials/toys. They also received fact sheets with suggestions for interactive reading: a general fact sheet on steps for interactive **storybook reading**, and a specific fact sheet for each book with examples on how to introduce the story, questions parents could ask, and activities to do after reading the story. Parents were asked to use these materials to practice interactive reading at home with their child.

In the second session, interactive reading behaviors are the central theme. Strategies to attract and maintain DHH children's attention are taught, such as tapping a child's arm, allowing the child enough time to process and respond, following a child's lead, using language that aligns with the child's attentional focus, asking open-ended questions, and making signs in a child's visual field are modeled and practiced. Special attention is given to the use of signs, body posture, facial expressions, and voice, as these are valuable tools that parents can utilize during interactive reading with their DHH child. The creative use of mimicry, body posture, and voice brings the characters to life and helps convey the emotions and feelings of the characters. For a happy character, parents can use a cheerful tone and energetic body movements to depict the character's excitement. For a sad character, on the other hand, they can use slumped shoulders and a sad expression. These techniques make the story more engaging and help the child understand and connect with the character's emotions. Additionally, incorporating role-taking (taking the character's perspective) during reading can be helpful in modeling emotions and social interactions. Using distinct voices and expressions and getting into the character's skin help the child understand different perspectives and emotions.

In the third session, attention is given to the choice of appropriate books given the child's age and his or her interest in certain characters or themes. The focus of this session, however, is on watching and reviewing video-recordings that parents made at home during **storybook reading** with their child. Parents share their experiences with each other and the trainers. The discussions center on the application of interactive reading techniques learned during the course and the children's responses, highlighting what worked well and what could be improved. The feedback is positive and constructive, providing both tips for enhancement and praise for success. This collaborative environment fosters a deeper understanding and reinforces the techniques taught during the sessions.

In their study on the effect of the program, Dirks and Wauters (2018) found that parents who participated in the interactive reading program enhanced their interactive reading practices, as measured by the Responsive Adult–Child Engagement During Joint Book Reading Scale (RACED-JBR, DesJardin et al., 2014). Following the interactive reading program, parents asked more open-ended questions, made more efforts to align with their child's interests, and elaborated more on their child's input than before. An important finding when it comes to the possible impact of **storybook reading** on children's **social–emotional** development is that parents increased their use of engagement strategies after the program. These strategies include the following behaviors: sustaining interest and attention through eye contact, facial expressions, laughing, and touch; providing positive feedback; utilizing emotional language and intonation; making continued effort to engage the child in the interaction; and fostering and maintaining close proximity to the child. These positive findings remained stable even 4 months after the program. Although parental interactive reading behavior was not specifically scored on the use of mental-state talk, the changes in engagement may be of specific importance for the **social–emotional** development of children.

In addition to the measurement of parent behavior, parents indicated that they had learned new skills in the program and received valuable tips to apply during **storybook reading** with their child at home. At post-test, the majority of parents reported that they led their child be more in the lead (turn the pages (73%), set the pace (71%)), that they told stories based on the illustrations instead of reading the literal text (62%), asked questions to their child (73%), and related the story to the child's experiences (65%%). In the evaluation of the program, parents also mentioned that learning in interaction with other parents during the program was very useful.

Language for ToM Program

In another study by Dirks and colleagues (see Dirks, 2025), the effect of a parent program to promote **social–emotional** development and ToM, in particular, in DHH children was examined. Because of the challenges of ToM development in DHH children and the finding that their parents expose them to less mental-state language, the authors developed a program to promote ToM in 2-to-4-year-old DHH children: the Language for ToM program (Dirks & Ketelaar, 2020). The aim of this intervention is to increase parents' use of mental-state language during daily activities with their DHH child and to provide them with strategies that promote their child's **social–emotional** development. The program is offered to families enrolled in FCEI. In the program, the focus is on helping parents to enhance their DHH children's understanding of others' feelings and thoughts through modeling and guidance. This includes directing children's attention to others' emotions and explaining the causes behind them. By observing their parents express and manage emotions, and comfort others, children learn valuable **social–emotional** skills. Additionally, when parents explain the causes of emotions, it enhances children's understanding and perspective-taking abilities. Discussing a child's own feelings and thoughts also promotes their **social–emotional** development, particularly in emotion recognition and self-regulation. Parents in the program receive ToM's bag, which includes materials to encourage mental-state discussions between parents and children. The bag contains two storybooks, an emotion dice, emotion puzzles, and a perspective-taking game. All materials were developed for the program.

Over the course of three 2-h group sessions at a FCEI center, parents are provided with information on the significance of ToM and the use of ToM language (mental-state language), along with practical strategies for its application. The intervention is led by two FCEI practitioners, one of whom is proficient in sign language. Table 8.2 provides an overview of the sessions.

In the first session, parents are introduced to the concepts of ToM and ToM language. They gain insights into the importance of ToM language for ToM development and become more aware of its use in their home environment. Parents practice using emotion words, with guidance from the sign teacher on incorporating emotion signs. To encourage interaction, various group assignments are included. For example, during the session, parents are asked to write down as many emotion words as they can recall within 1 min. Afterward, they discuss how often they use these words in everyday conversations with their child and explore reasons why some words are used more naturally than others. Materials such as books, puzzles, and games are

Table 8.2 Language for the ToM program

Session	Content
1	– What is ToM and why is it so important? – ToM development in DHH children; challenges and opportunities – What is ToM language (mental state language)?
2	– Reflecting on the home assignment – Sharing tips and experiences – Perspective taking – Use of mental-state language during daily activities – Storybook reading
3	– Reflecting on the home assignment – Sharing tips and experiences – Watching and discussing videos of parents

used to practice ToM language during sessions and at home. Homework assignments are given to reinforce the lessons. Parents are asked to play the "You and Me" game with their child between sessions. In this game, children learn to reflect on what they like and dislike and the need to think about the preferences of others, helping them understand that people can have different ideas and tastes. The game consists of small cards with pictures of toys, food, and activities. Children can place these cards on a "like" or "dislike" board to show their preferences.

The second session focuses on perspective-taking and understanding that others may have different intentions, desires, and thoughts. Parents are taught to think aloud, exposing children to more ToM language. **Storybook reading** is a crucial part of session 2, where parents are taught the importance of **storybook reading** for their child's **social–emotional** development. Parents learn that storybooks are rich in emotional vocabulary, providing numerous opportunities to discuss and explore various emotions. They are made aware that storybook characters often have different viewpoints and experiences, which can be used as a basis for discussions with their child. During the session, parents can practice with various storybooks and are asked to explore the different perspectives of the characters. For example, "the dog wants to play with the ball, but the elephant wants to swim". They are also encouraged to observe the facial expressions of the characters and their body language.

Engaging in these discussions helps children develop empathy by understanding and appreciating these varied perspectives. Additionally, the illustrations in books provide numerous opportunities to explore emotions, such as examining the characters' facial expressions and body language. Mimicking emotions and body postures is a fun exercise for children to experience how emotions are expressed. This activity not only makes learning about emotions enjoyable but also helps children better understand and recognize different emotional states.

During the session, parents also participate in an exercise where they search for mental-state language and emotional expressions in existing storybooks. This exercise helps parents become more aware of the abundance of emotions that appear in a storybook. By actively searching for and identifying emotional expressions and mental-state language, parents can see just how frequently emotions are depicted in storybooks. This heightened awareness allows parents to better understand the emotional content of the stories and use it as a tool to discuss and explore emotions with their children. As a result, parents can more effectively use storybooks to support their child's **social–emotional** development. Various books that focus on emotions or specifically feature **deaf** and **hard-of-hearing** characters are highlighted during the sessions. These books serve as valuable resources for parents to use in their efforts to enhance their children's **social–emotional** development. By incorporating these books into their reading routines, parents can provide their children with relatable characters and scenarios that help them better understand and express their own emotions. Between sessions 2 and 3, parents are asked to read a storybook with their child at home and practice the strategies learned during the session.

In the final session, parents are encouraged to share their own video-recordings of ToM activities with the other parents in the group. They provide each other with positive feedback on successful interactions in which ToM language is used. This session also addresses strategies for gaining and maintaining attention, as well as selecting appropriate storybooks.

The effects of the Language for ToM program on parents' emotion communication and their use of mental state and the children's ToM abilities are currently being examined. A total of 48 children between 2 and 5 years of age and their parents participated in the study, and their interactions were examined before and twice after the parents participated in the program. **Parent–child interaction**s are recorded at home during two activities: free play and **storybook reading**. The storybook was a wordless storybook because past research indicated that these books elicit more mental-state language than storybooks with text (Ziv et al., 2013). Besides parent–child activities, children's ToM abilities will be examined. Preliminary findings showed that parents and children used more emotion words during the storybook activity than during free play before they participated in the program, although the number of emotion words used was quite low in both activities. In addition, preliminary findings, based on a parent questionnaire, showed an increase in the frequency of discussing emotions with their child after participating in the program.

Parents' evaluations about the program ($n = 32$) were positive. Almost all parents completely agreed (63%) or somewhat agreed (28%) with the statement: "I think that after the course, I am able to use more ToM language with my child." Additionally, nearly all parents believed they would apply the tips and advice from the course: 66% completely agreed with this statement, and 28% somewhat agreed. In response to the statement, "I would recommend this course to other parents," two-thirds of the parents completely agreed, while one-third somewhat agreed. Doing the assignments during the sessions was appreciated and evaluated as meaningful by 30 parents. The majority of the parents ($n = 28$) found it meaningful to make video-recordings of an interaction moment with their child and to share and discuss these recordings, and particularly their use of mental-state language, with the other parents during the last session.

The study is ongoing, and the analysis of interactions during play and **storybook reading** activities, where these interactions are transcribed and coded for mental-state language, will indicate the impact of the program on both parental mental-state language and children's **social–emotional** abilities.

Conclusions

Due to limited access to auditory information, DHH children are at risk in their language and **social–emotional** development. Although existing interventions for DHH children predominantly focus on promoting language development, considerably less attention is given to fostering their **social–emotional** growth, even though this group is at heightened risk for challenges in this area. A scoping review of early interventions for parents of DHH infants by Wright et al. (2021) found that, among the 54 studies included, none specifically aimed to support parents in nurturing their child's **social–emotional** development. This finding underscores the importance of addressing the **social–emotional** development of DHH children within early intervention programs, as well as the need for interventions that support parents in fostering these competencies from an early age.

In this chapter, we described two interventions: an interactive **storybook reading** program that includes elements addressing **social–emotional** themes, and the Language for ToM program, which targets **social–emotional** development with an integrated use of book-reading to support this goal. In both programs, parents were guided to use storybooks to foster their children's development. They became more aware of emotion-related vocabulary in storybooks, the different facial expressions of book characters, and their different perspectives. They also recognized that relating the story to their child's prior emotional experiences can support their child's emotional understanding. Both programs were positively evaluated by parents; they reported that they had learned from them and were applying the learned strategies in their interactions with their child during book-reading.

Moving forward, it would be valuable to integrate these two programs into a single intervention that explicitly uses shared **storybook reading** as a tool to foster **social–emotional** development in DHH children. Such an integrated program could more effectively support both language and emotional understanding, strengthening the foundations for strong interaction skills and emotional well-being.

References

Adrian, J. E., Clemente, R. A., Villanueva, L., & Rieffe, C. (2005). Parent–child picture-book reading, mothers' mental state language and children's theory of mind. *Journal of Child Language, 32*(3), 673–686. https://doi.org/10.1017/S0305000905006963

Adrián, J. E., Clemente, R. A., & Villanueva, L. (2007). Mothers' use of cognitive state verbs in picture-book reading and the development of children's understanding of mind: A longitudinal study. *Child Development, 78*(4), 1052–1067. https://doi.org/10.1111/j.1467-8624.2007.01052.x

Aram, D., & Aviram, S. (2009). Mothers' storybook reading and kindergartners' socio-emotional and literacy development. *Reading Psychology, 30*(2), 175–194. https://doi.org/10.1080/02702710802275348

Aram, D., Most, T., & Mayafit, H. (2006). Contributions of mother-child storybook telling and joint writing to literacy development in kindergartners with hearing loss. *Language, Speech, and Hearing Services in Schools, 37*(3), 209–223. https://doi.org/10.1044/0161-1461(2006/023)

Baker, C. E. (2013). Fathers' and mothers' home literacy involvement and children's cognitive and social emotional development: Implications for family literacy programs. *Applied Developmental Science, 17*, 184–197. https://doi.org/10.1080/10888691.2013.836034

Batini, F., Luperini, V., Cei, E., Izzo, D., & Toti, G. (2021). The association between reading and emotional development: A systematic review. *Journal of Education and Training Studies, 9*(1), 12–48. https://doi.org/10.11114/jets.v9i1.5053

Bongioletti, J., Doble, M., & Purcell, A. (2024). Conversation and pragmatics in children who are hard-of-hearing: A scoping review. *Journal of Deaf Studies and Deaf Education, 29*(4), 456–466. https://doi.org/10.1093/deafed/enae011

Cassidy, K. W., Ball, L. V., Rourke, M. T., Werner, R. S., Feeny, N., & Chu, J. Y. (1998). Theory of mind concepts in children's literature. *Applied PsychoLinguistics, 19*(3), 463–470. https://doi.org/10.1017/S0142716400010274

Chatterjee, M., Zion, D. J., Deroche, M. L., Burianek, B. A., Limb, C. J., Goren, A. P., et al. (2015). Voice emotion recognition by cochlear-implanted children and their normally-hearing peers. *Hearing Research, 322*, 151–162. https://doi.org/10.1016/j.heares.2014.10.003

Curtin, M., Dirks, E., Cruice, M., Herman, R., Newman, L., Rodgers, L., & Morgan, G. (2021). Assessing parent behaviours in parent–child interactions with deaf and hard of hearing infants aged 0–3 years: A systematic review. *Journal of Clinical Medicine, 10*(15), 3345. https://doi.org/10.3390/jcm10153345

DeBruin-Parecki, A. (2007). *Let's read together: Improving literacy outcomes with the adult-child interactive reading inventory (ACIRI)*. Brookes.

Denham, S. A., McKinley, M., Couchoud, E. A., & Holt, R. (1990). Emotional and behavioral predictors of preschool peer ratings. *Child Development, 61*(4), 1145–1152. https://doi.org/10.1111/j.1467-8624.1990.tb02848.x

DesJardin, J. L., Doll, E. R., Stika, C. J., Eisenberg, L. S., Johnson, K. J., Ganguly, D. H., et al. (2014). Parental support for language development during joint book reading for young children with hearing loss. *Communication Disorders Quarterly, 35*(3), 167–181. https://doi.org/10.1177/1525740113518062

Dirks, E. (2025). Fostering parent-child interaction in families of deaf and hard of hearing children. In R. Herman & C. Ens (Eds.), *Communication interventions with deaf people*. Oxford University Press.

Dirks, E., Stevens, A., Kok, S., Frijns, J., & Rieffe, C. (2020). Talk with me! Parental linguistic input to toddlers with moderate hearing loss. *Journal of Child Language, 47*(1), 186–204. https://doi.org/10.1017/S0305000919000667

Dirks, E., & Ketelaar, L. (2020). Language for ToM (Taal voor ToM) manual.

Dirks, E., & Wauters, L. (2015). Enhancing emergent literacy in preschool deaf and hard-of-hearing children through interactive reading. In H. Knoors & M. Marschark (Eds.), *Educating deaf learners: Creating a global evidence base* (pp. 415–441). Oxford University Press. https://doi.org/10.1093/acprof:oso/9780190215194.003.0018

Dirks, E., & Wauters, L. (2018). It takes two to read: Interactive reading with young deaf and hard-of-hearing children. *Journal of Deaf Studies and Deaf Education, 23*(3), 261–270. https://doi.org/10.1093/deafed/eny005

Dyer, J. R., Shatz, M., & Wellman, H. M. (2000). Young children's storybooks as a source of mental state information. *Cognitive Development, 15*(1), 17–37. https://doi.org/10.1016/S0885-2014(00)00017-4

Everhardt, M. K., Sarampalis, A., Coler, M., Başkent, D., & Lowie, W. (2020). Meta-analysis on the identification of linguistic and emotional prosody in cochlear implant users and vocoder simulations. *Ear and Hearing, 41*(5), 1092–1102. https://doi.org/10.1097/AUD.0000000000000863

Fields-Olivieri, M. A., Kim, Y., Jennings, K. J., & Cole, P. M. (2024). The role of language in the development of emotion regulation. In M. A. Bell (Ed.), Child development at the intersection of emotion and cognition (2nd ed., pp. 31–50). *American Psychological Association*. https://doi.org/10.1037/0000406-003

Fung, P. C., Chow, B. W. Y., & McBride-Chang, C. (2005). The impact of a dialogic reading program on deaf and hard-of-hearing kindergarten and early primary school-aged students in Hong Kong. *Journal of Deaf Studies and Deaf Education, 10*(1), 82–95. https://doi.org/10.1093/deafed/eni005

Grey, B., Deutchki, E. K., Lund, E. A., & Werfel, K. L. (2022). Impact of meeting early hearing detection and intervention benchmarks on spoken language. *Journal of Early Intervention, 44*(3), 235–251. https://doi.org/10.1177/10538151211025210

Holzinger, D., Hofer, J., Dall, M., & Fellinger, J. (2022). Multidimensional family-centred early intervention in children with hearing loss: A conceptual model. *Journal of Clinical Medicine, 11*(6), 1548. https://doi.org/10.3390/jcm11061548

Hopyan-Misakyan, T. M., Gordon, K. A., Dennis, M., & Papsin, B. C. (2009). Recognition of affective speech prosody and facial affect in deaf children with unilateral right cochlear implants. *Child Neuropsychology, 15*(2), 136–146. https://doi.org/10.1080/09297040802403682

Huebner, C. E. (2000). Promoting toddlers' language development through community-based intervention. *Journal of Applied Developmental Psychology, 21*(5), 513–535. https://doi.org/10.1016/S0193-3973(00)00052-6

Huebner, C. E., & Meltzoff, A. N. (2005). Intervention to change parent-child reading style: A comparison of instructional methods. *Journal of Applied Developmental Psychology, 26*(3), 296–313. https://doi.org/10.1016/j.appdev.2005.02.006

Izard, C., Fine, S., Schultz, D., Mostow, A., Ackerman, B., & Youngstrom, E. (2001). Emotion knowledge as a predictor of social behavior and academic competence in children at risk. *Psychological Science, 12*(1), 18–23. https://doi.org/10.1111/1467-9280.00304

Jones, A. C., Gutierrez, R., & Ludlow, A. K. (2015). Confronting the language barrier: Theory of mind in deaf children. *Journal of Communication Disorders, 56*, 47–58. https://doi.org/10.1016/j.jcomdis.2015.06.005

Ketelaar, L., Rieffe, C., Wiefferink, C. H., & Frijns, J. H. M. (2012). Does hearing lead to understanding? Theory of mind in toddlers and preschoolers with cochlear implants. *Journal of Pediatric Psychology, 37*(9), 1041–1050. https://doi.org/10.1093/jpepsy/jss086

Ludlow, A., Heaton, P., Rosset, D., Hills, P., & Deruelle, C. (2010). Emotion recognition in children with profound and severe deafness: Do they have a deficit in perceptual processing? *Journal of Clinical and Experimental Neuropsychology, 32*(9), 923–928. https://doi.org/10.1080/13803391003596447

Lund, E. (2016). Vocabulary knowledge of children with cochlear implants: A meta-analysis. *Journal of Deaf Studies and Deaf Education, 21*(2), 107–121. https://doi.org/10.1093/deafed/env060

Marschark, M., & Harris, M. (1996). Success and failure in learning to read: The special (?) case of deaf children. In C. Cornoldi & J. Oakhill (Eds.), *Reading comprehension difficulties: Processes and intervention* (pp. 279–300). Lawrence Erlbaum.

Meinzen-Derr, J., Wiley, S., & Choo, D. I. (2011). Impact of early intervention on expressive and receptive language development among young children with permanent hearing loss. *American Annals of the Deaf, 155*(5), 580–591. https://doi.org/10.1353/aad.2011.0010

Mitchell, R. E., & Karchmer, M. A. (2004). Chasing the mythical ten percent: Parental hearing status of deaf and hard of hearing students in the United States. *American Annals of the Deaf, 4*(2), 138–163. https://doi.org/10.1353/sls.2004.0005

Moeller, M. P., & Schick, B. (2006). Relations between maternal input and theory of mind understanding in deaf children. *Child Development, 77*(3), 751–766. https://doi.org/10.1111/j.1467-8624.2006.00901.x

Moeller, M. P., Szarkowski, A., Gale, E., Smith, T., Birdsey, B. C., Moodie, S. T., et al. (2024). Family-centered early intervention deaf/hard of hearing (FCEI-DHH): Guiding values. *Journal of Deaf Studies and Deaf Education, 29*(SI), SI8–SI26. https://doi.org/10.1093/deafed/enad038

Mol, S. E., Bus, A. G., de Jong, M. T., & Smeets, D. J. H. (2008). Added value of dialogic parent-child book readings: A meta-analysis. *Early Education and Development, 19*(1), 7–26. https://doi.org/10.1080/10409280701838603

Most, T., & Michaelis, H. (2012). Auditory, visual, and auditory-visual perceptions of emotions by young children with hearing loss versus children with normal hearing. *Journal of Speech, Language, and Hearing Research, 54*(4), 1148–1162. https://doi.org/10.1044/1092-4388(2011/11-0060

Morgan, G., Meristo, M., Mann, W., Hjelmquist, E., Surian, L., & Siegal, M. (2014). Mental state language and quality of conversational experience in deaf and hearing children. *Cognitive Development, 29*, 41–49. https://doi.org/10.1016/j.cogdev.2013.10.002

Netten, A. P., Rieffe, C., Soede, W., Dirks, E., Korver, A. M., Konings, S., et al. (2017). Can you hear what I think? Theory of mind in young children with moderate hearing loss. *Ear and Hearing, 38*(5), 588–597. https://doi.org/10.1097/aud.0000000000000427

Park, H. (2008). Home literacy environments and children's reading performance: A comparative study of 25 countries. *Educational Research and Evaluation, 14*(6), 489–505. https://doi.org/10.1080/13803610802576734

Peterson, C. C. (2016). Empathy and theory of mind in deaf and hearing children. *Journal of Deaf Studies and Deaf Education, 21*(2), 141–147. https://doi.org/10.1093/deafed/env058

Peterson, C. C., & Siegal, M. (1995). Deafness, conversation and theory of mind. *Journal of Child Psychology and Psychiatry, 36*(3), 459–474. https://doi.org/10.1111/j.1469-7610.1995.tb01303.x

Peterson, C. C., Wellman, H. M., & Liu, D. (2005). Steps in theory-of-mind development for children with deafness or autism. *Child Development, 76*(2), 502–517. https://doi.org/10.1111/j.1467-8624.2005.00859.x

Pluta, A., Krysztofiak, M., Zgoda, M., Wysocka, J., Golec, K., Gajos, K., Dołyk, T., Wolak, T., & Haman, M. (2023). Theory of mind and parental mental-state talk in children with CIs. *Journal of Deaf Studies and Deaf Education, 28*(3), 288–299. https://doi.org/10.1093/deafed/enad004

Pressman, L., Pipp-Siegel, S., Yoshinaga-Itano, C., & Deas, A. (1999). Maternal sensitivity predicts language gain in preschool children who are deaf and hard of hearing. *Journal of Deaf Studies and Deaf Education, 4*(4), 294–304. https://doi.org/10.1093/deafed/4.4.294

Schapira, R., & Aram, D. (2019). Shared book reading at home and preschoolers' socio-emotional competence. *Early Education and Development, 31*(6), 819–837. https://doi.org/10.1080/10409289.2019.1692624

Slaughter, V., Imuta, K., Peterson, C. C., & Henry, J. D. (2015). Meta-analysis of theory of mind and peer popularity in the preschool and early school years. *Child Development, 86*(4), 1159–1174. https://doi.org/10.1111/cdev.12372

Stevenson, J., Kreppner, J., Pimperton, H., Worsfold, S., & Kennedy, C. (2015). Emotional and behavioural difficulties in children and adolescents with hearing impairment: A systematic review and meta-analysis. *European Child & Adolescent Psychiatry, 24*, 477–496. https://doi.org/10.1007/s00787-015-0697-1

Stobbart, C., & Alant, E. (2008). Home-based literacy experiences of severely to profound deaf preschoolers and their hearing parents. *Journal of Developmental and Physical Disabilities, 20*, 139–153. https://doi.org/10.1007/s10882-007-9085-1

Sundqvist, A., & Heimann, M. (2014). The development of theory of mind: Considerations for deaf children with cochlear implants. *Otorinolaringologia, 64*(4), 179–189. https://doi.org/10.1016/j.ijporl.2013.12.039

Symons, D. K., Peterson, C. C., Slaughter, V., Roche, J., & Doyle, E. (2005). Theory of mind and mental state discourse during book reading and story-telling tasks. *British Journal of Developmental Psychology, 23*(1), 81–102. https://doi.org/10.1348/026151004X21080

Tomblin, J. B., Harrison, M., Ambrose, S. E., Walker, E. A., Oleson, J. J., & Moeller, M. P. (2015). Language outcomes in young children with mild to severe hearing loss. *Ear and Hearing, 36*, 76S–91S. https://doi.org/10.1097/AUD.0000000000000219

Tompkins, V. (2015). Mothers' cognitive state talk during shared book reading and children's later false belief understanding. *Cognitive Development, 36*, 40–51. https://doi.org/10.1016/j.cogdev.2015.08.004

Tompkins, V. (2022). Relations between the home literacy environment and young children's theory of mind. *Cognitive Development, 62*, 101179. https://doi.org/10.1016/j.cogdev.2022.101179

Tompkins, V., Benigno, J. P., Kiger Lee, B., & Wright, B. M. (2018). The relation between parents' mental state talk and children's social understanding: A meta-analysis. *Social Development, 27*(2), 223–246. https://doi.org/10.1111/sode.12280

Vaccari, C., & Marschark, M. (1997). Communication between parents and deaf children: Implications for social-emotional development. *Journal of Child Psychology and Psychiatry, 38*(7), 793–801. https://doi.org/10.1111/j.1469-7610.1997.tb01597.x

Van der Zee, R. B., Uilenburg, N. N., van der Ploeg, C. P. B., & Dirks, E. (2022). Prevalence of hearing loss in Dutch newborns; results of the nationwide well-baby newborn hearing screening program. *Applied Sciences, 12*(4), 2035. https://doi.org/10.3390/app12042035

van der Zee, R. B., & Dirks, E. (2022). Diversity of child and family characteristics of children with hearing loss in family-centered early intervention in The Netherlands. *Journal of Clinical Medicine, 11*(8), 2074. https://doi.org/10.3390/jcm11082074

Walker, E. A., Ambrose, S. A., Oleson, J., & Moeller, M. P. (2017). False belief development in children who are hard of hearing compared with peers with normal hearing. *Journal of Speech, Language, and Hearing Research, 60*(12), 3487–3506. https://doi.org/10.1044/2017_JSLHR-L-17-0121

Walker, E., Redfern, A., & Oleson, J. (2019). Linear mixed model analysis to examine longitudinal trajectories in vocabulary depth and breadth in children who are hard of hearing. *Journal of Speech, Language, and Hearing Research, 62*(3), 525–542. https://doi.org/10.1044/2018_JSLHR-L-ASTM-18-0250

Wang, Y., Su, Y., & Yan, S. (2016). Facial expression recognition in children with cochlear implants and hearing aids. *Frontiers in Psychology, 7*, 1–6. https://doi.org/10.3389/fpsyg.2016.01989

Wauters, L., DesJardin, J., & Dirks, E. (2021). Supporting school readiness skills and home literacy environment in young children who are deaf and hard of hearing. In S. R. Easterbrooks & H. M. Dostal (Eds.), *The handbook of deaf studies in literacy* (pp. 201–215). Oxford University Press. https://doi.org/10.1093/oxfordhb/9780197508268.013.15

Wellman, H. M. (2018). Theory of mind: The state of the art. *European Journal of Developmental Psychology, 15*(6), 728–755. https://doi.org/10.1080/17405629.2018.1435413

Werfel, K. L., Reynolds, G., & Fitton, L. (2022). Oral language acquisition in preschool children who are deaf and hard-of-hearing. *The Journal of Deaf Studies and Deaf Education, 27*(2), 166–178. https://doi.org/10.1093/deafed/enab043

Wiefferink, C. H., Rieffe, C., Ketelaar, L., De Raeve, L., & Frijns, J. H. M. (2013). Emotion understanding in deaf children with a cochlear implant. *Journal of Deaf Studies and Deaf Education, 18*(2), 175–186. https://doi.org/10.1093/deafed/ens042

Williams, K. E., Barrett, M. S., Welch, G. F., Abad, V., & Broughton, M. (2015). Associations between early shared music activities in the home and later child outcomes: Findings from the longitudinal study of Australian children. *Early Childhood Research Quarterly, 31*, 113–124. https://doi.org/10.1016/j.ecresq.2015.01.004

Wong, T. K., Konishi, C., & Kong, X. (2022). A longitudinal perspective on frequency of parent–child activities and social–emotional development. *Early Child Development and Care, 192*(3), 458–469. https://doi.org/10.1080/03004430.2020.1765773

Wright, B., Hargate, R., Garside, M., Carr, G., Wakefield, T., Swanwick, R., Noon, I., & Simpson, P. (2021). A systematic scoping review of early interventions for parents of deaf infants. *BMC Pediatrics, 21*, 467. https://doi.org/10.1186/s12887-021-02893-9

Yoshinaga-Itano, C., Mason, C. A., Wiggin, M., Grosse, S. D., Gaffney, M., & Gilley, P. M. (2021). Reading proficiency trends following newborn hearing screening implementation. *Pediatrics, 148*(4), e2020048702. https://doi.org/10.1542/peds.2020-048702

Ziv, M., Smadja, M. L., & Aram, D. (2013).** Mothers' mental-state discourse with preschoolers during storybook reading and wordless storybook telling. *Early Childhood Research Quarterly, 28*(1), 177–186. https://doi.org/10.1016/j.ecresq.2012.05.005

Evelien Dirks is the program director of the Deaf and Hard of Hearing Research and Development Program at the Dutch Foundation of the Deaf and Hard-of-Hearing Child. She is also an endowed professor at Tranzo, Tilburg University, Tilburg, the Netherlands. Her research studies the development of young deaf and hard-of-hearing in the context of parent–child interaction.

Loes Wauters is the program director of the Deaf and Hard of Hearing Research Program at the Kentalis Academy, Royal Kentalis, Utrecht, the Netherlands,. She is also an endowed professor at the Behavioral Science Institute, Radboud University, Nijmegen, the Netherlands. Her research studies the development of deaf and hard-of-hearing children and adolescents, with a focus on their literacy skills.

Chapter 9
Talk About Emotions and Other Mental States During Shared Book-Reading Interactions Between Adults and Children Across Diverse Risk Contexts

Pamela W. Garner, Julia M. Shadur, and Hideko H. Bassett

Contents

Effective participation in social interactions is dependent upon **social understanding**, which refers to the awareness of various mental states such as emotions, beliefs, perceptions, intentions, and other cognitive processes (Aram & Aviram, 2009; Garner & Parker, 2018; Garner et al., 2019; Ziv et al., 2014). This understanding is essential for how individuals interpret, predict, judge, and respond to others' words and actions (Yager & Ehmann, 2006; Wellman et al., 2001). Given that the caregiving context is a primary influence on young children's **social understanding**, this chapter aims to provide a narrative review that summarizes and interprets existing research on adults' mental-state talk (MST). In particular, we focus on **shared book-reading** (SBR) as a key forum for fostering early mental-state discourse and supporting the development of **social understanding** (Flack et al., 2018) with children experiencing various biological and **contextual risks**. This review is not intended to be a comprehensive summary of all existing studies but rather focuses on the selection of key research, given the space limitations and the scope of the chapter. In light of the limited research on MST among at-risk populations, we first provide a broader discussion of joint attention, particularly within the framework of shared book-reading (SBR), as a meaningful context for MST and the development of complex **social understanding** and competence (Kristen et al., 2011; Sodian &

P. W. Garner (✉) · J. M. Shadur · H. H. Bassett
George Mason University, Fairfax, VA, USA
e-mail: pgarner1@gmu.edu

R. Schapira, D. Aram (eds.), *Shared Book Reading and Children's Social-Emotional Competence*, https://doi.org/10.1007/978-3-032-14688-5_9

Kristen-Antonow, 2015; Stout et al., 2021; Vaughan Van Hecke et al., 2007). Joint attention is relevant to SBR because books often serve as a focal point for shared attention and discourse about mental states that extend beyond the text. By contextualizing SBR within the broader literature on samples from vulnerable populations, our review sheds light on how varying levels of child and parental risk influence its practices. We further discuss the potential impact of MST during SBR on children's **social understanding** and related developmental outcomes. Following that, we explore the feasibility of a research design and data collection method for an observational study that considers SBR among young children and their mothers receiving residential addiction treatment—a clinical population typically challenging to recruit and rarely explored in the research on SBR. Although the sample size is much too small to be considered pilot data or to yield preliminary outcomes, our results suggest the viability of research in this area, which could help us refine our research focus on this topic. Finally, we will discuss how future research can be encouraged, emphasizing the need for further exploration into SBR within at-risk caregiving environments and its potential impact on the development of **social understanding**.

Shared Book-Reading and Mental-State Talk and Understanding

Children begin to comprehend and talk about mental states during their second year of life (Bartsch & Wellman, 1995; Garner, 2003) and show significant advancement in this area during the early childhood years (e.g., Ontai & Thompson, 2002). This elevated **social understanding** is related positively to children's empathy development, prosocial responsiveness (Ekerim-Akbulut et al., 2020; Findlay et al., 2006; Paulus et al., 2015), and social skills (Garner et al., 1994). **Social understanding** is considered integral to enriching learning experiences in early caregiving environments and contributes to cognitive and social preparedness for school (Astington & Pelletier, 2013; Fine et al., 2003; Gal-Szabo et al., 2019; Garner et al., 1997, 2023; Garner & Toney, 2020; Miller et al., 2013; Scrimgeour et al., 2016). Especially relevant to our discussion is that young children may use their understanding of social and behavioral cues to interpret the mental states of others (Baldwin & Moses, 2001). One context in which this process is particularly evident is SBR, where parents label emotions and mental states significantly more frequently than during other types of adult-supported interactions (Drummond et al., 2014; Gest et al., 2006; Grøver et al., 2023). Parents' MST during SBR is also linked to children's later complex understanding of mental states (Adrián et al., 2007; Taumoepeau & Ruffman, 2006) and empathy development (Schapira & Aram, 2020). Although SBR about mental states has demonstrated clear value for children's social--emotional learning, the impact of these benefits can be further amplified with appropriate adult scaffolding and guidance. One effective scaffolding strategy sometimes used during SBR interactions is dialogic reading, where the reader asks questions, encourages active involvement, elaborates on the text, connects content to children's real-life experiences, and offers praise for their participation (Bassett et al., 2020; Lonigan & Whitehurst, 1998; Silkenbeumer et al., 2018).

Developing mental-state understanding can be particularly challenging for some young children (Lane & Bowman, 2021). Given the role of SBR in fostering early **social understanding**, it is essential to examine how shared learning processes may vary or be influenced by different risk contexts. Children experiencing risk may encounter unique obstacles in understanding and discussing mental states, which can stem from their own or the adult readers' personal experiences, physical conditions, cognitive factors, psychological challenges, and/or other environmental or contextual influences (e.g., Adamson et al., 2014; Dowdall et al., 2020; Mol et al., 2009; Towson et al., 2021). In the sections that follow, we review studies examining SBR behaviors and mental-state discussions among caregivers and children facing various risk contexts, with a discussion of the impacts on and implications for children's **social understanding** and related outcomes.

Joint Attention, Early Social Understanding, and Shared Book-Reading: Developmental Challenges and Considerations

The ability to engage in joint attention is associated with the development of social, cognitive, and language competence and impacts the learning of social information over time (DeMayo et al., 2019). Infants who frequently initiate joint attention with an adult are more likely to be rated by their parents as having a strong understanding of mental states by the time they reach preschool age (Brandone & Stout, 2023). As a foundational social skill, joint attention—the ability for two individuals to synchronize their focus on the same object or event (Siposova & Carpenter, 2019; Sodian & Kristen-Antonow, 2015)—is considered a clear indicator of early **social understanding** and emotion regulation ability (Bruinsma et al., 2004; Morales et al., 2005). For the most part, research in this area most often focuses on shared visual attention to an object or an event. However, in a process labeled as "joint attention to mental content," O'Madagain and Tomasello (2021) remind us that interaction partners can jointly attend to mental states during shared toy play, adult–child conversations, and SBR. For children, engaging in SBR requires attending to the reader and the book being read (Ambarchi et al., 2024). Although children at risk for atypical development present with both strengths and challenges in the domain of **social understanding** (e.g., Rosello et al., 2020), some of them struggle to develop joint attention to objects and/or people.

Autism Spectrum Disorder (ASD)

In terms of categories of risk, we begin with a discussion of ASD, as a large body of literature on joint attention focuses on these children, presumably because challenges in social communication and interaction are a defining feature of the disorder (Pierce et al., 2019). Children with ASD present distinct patterns of joint attention as compared to typically developing (TD) children (Bruinsma et al., 2004; Paparella et al., 2011). For example, Wicks et al. (2022) reported that, in the context of SBR, children with ASD show similar joint attention to print but less frequent joint attention to pictures as compared to their TD peers. These differences underscore the significance of shared attention in early development and may reflect broader cognitive and social processes that encompass mental-state understanding. Despite these findings, research investigating joint attention during SBR within this population is limited (Ambarchi et al., 2024). Children with ASD reference mental states of story characters less often than TD children and provide fewer justifications for these states during storytelling tasks (Hutchins et al., 2017; Siller et al., 2014). Slaughter et al. (2007) found that mothers of ASD-diagnosed children show some similarities to mothers of TD children in the use of different kinds of mental-state terms during SBR, albeit there is some question as to whether this language represents these children's actual awareness of their own and/or other's internal states (Racine & Carpendale, 2007). One notable finding that also emerged from this research was that mothers of children diagnosed with ASD are less likely to elaborate on story characters' mental states, a practice that was more strongly associated with advanced **social understanding** for the ASD-diagnosed group. Likewise, among children with ASD, mothers' use of emotion-based verbs and words is associated with greater **social understanding** and emotion regulation skills in their children (Nader--Grosbois et al., 2022). Additionally, parents' dialogic reading practices during SBR, including asking questions and discussing storylines, are associated with increased verbal engagement among preschoolers with ASD (Westerveld et al., 2020).

Down Syndrome

As the most widely acknowledged genetic cause of intellectual disabilities, children with Down syndrome also show delays in the acquisition of joint attention skills, mental-state talk (MST), and **social understanding** as compared to TD children of a similar developmental age (Legerstee & Fisher, 2008). For instance, young children with Down syndrome exhibit significantly fewer mental-state utterances overall and use fewer self-referential mental-state expressions and context-specific mental-state expressions during SBR and play tasks with their mothers relative to their cognitively and demographically matched peers (Beeghly & Cicchetti, 1997). These findings may extend into later childhood (Reilly et al., 1990). As compared to their TD peers, children diagnosed with Down syndrome are also more responsive to their mothers' direct versus suggestive requests to jointly attend to an object (Landry et al., 1994).

Prematurity, Perinatal, and Other Birth-Related Factors

Children born prematurely or to adolescent mothers or prenatally exposed to cocaine also sometimes struggle to develop joint attention skills and mental-state understanding. With respect to prematurity, children born extremely preterm and/or with low birth weight or other associated medical conditions show deficits in exploratory and communicative joint attention responses as compared to low-risk preterm and full-term (FT) children (Garner et al., 1991). These children also respond with low interest and fewer positive affective displays when their mothers attempt to share their attention with a toy (Garner & Landry, 1992, 1994; Landry et al., 1996). In their review on this topic, Zmyj et al. (2017) suggested that preterm children's difficulties in initiating joint attention with others and responding to others' efforts to engage them in joint attention could contribute to later impairments in social cognition, which could adversely affect their social interaction skills. Support for this hypothesis can be gleaned from research showing that children born prematurely tend to have more difficulty interpreting emotions and other mental states compared to their full-term counterparts (Campbell et al., 2015; Telford et al., 2016; Williamson & Jakobson, 2014a, 2014b). As another risk factor related to prematurity, children who experience gestational cocaine exposure (Puthuraya et al., 2023) show lower social and joint attention engagement (Claussen et al., 2002). In the same way, children with fetal alcohol spectrum disorders have lower social skills, empathy, and performance on social–cognitive tasks compared to their TD peers (Stevens et al., 2015). However, mothers' positive social behaviors are not always associated with their ability to achieve joint attention with these children during social interactions (Mattson et al., 2022).

Child Maltreatment

Child maltreatment also increases the likelihood of difficulties establishing joint attention and developing **social understanding** during SBR and other types of social interactions. This is not surprising considering that child maltreatment is associated with structural and functional changes in the human brain, particularly in the regions promoting **social understanding** (e.g., Dahmen et al., 2018). A meta-analysis revealed that social–emotional skills, including empathy, tend to be impaired in children exposed to parental maltreatment (Luke & Banerjee, 2013), challenges that have been implicated in the development of negative peer relationships (Sebastian et al., 2012). Research also shows that maltreated toddlers use significantly fewer mental-state words and types than non-maltreated toddlers and are less likely to attribute mental states to themselves or others. This same study demonstrated that maltreated toddlers exhibit significant limitations in their MST (Beeghly & Cicchetti, 1994). Additionally, young children in foster care with a history of maltreatment show significant deficits in emotion understanding and theory of mind as compared to matched controls who were not in foster care and had not experienced maltreatment (Pears & Fisher, 2005). The harmful effects of child maltreatment can also persist into parenthood. As evidence, caregivers who experienced maltreatment in their own childhood tend to demonstrate less supportive emotion socialization behaviors with their children. However, caregivers who use more cognitive-processing language when discussing mental states are less likely to engage in nonsupportive emotion-specific parenting behaviors, suggesting a potential disruption of the intergenerational transmission of parental maltreatment (Milan et al., 2021). Despite the growing body of research on joint attention and **social understanding** in various contexts, there is still limited knowledge regarding how these processes operate during SBR between adults and children experiencing abuse or neglect.

Parental Stressors and Adversity

As a starting point, economic stress is known to affect the development of joint attention, MST, and **social understanding**. For example, a recent study found that experiencing low income is associated with lower engagement in joint attention tasks among infants (Reilly et al., 2021). Among economically disadvantaged mothers and children, references to socioemotional issues during mother–child conversation correlate with children's **social understanding** and prosocial behavior (Aram et al., 2017). Research with low-income children attending Head Start has shown that teachers' MST in the context of SBR to a group is associated positively with language competence, especially when the child is the referent of the talk (Barnes & Dickinson, 2018). Teachers' questions and comments about mental state are associated with emotional excerpts from the selected book. Children were also highly responsive to teachers' discussions about emotions, and a reciprocal association existed between children's and teachers' talk about emotions (Alvarenga et al., 2020).

In another study, low-income children participated in SBR with books that included mental-state themes or that did not include mental states (control). The children in the control group condition continued with their daily classroom activities. Pre- and post-tests indicated that children who participated in the book-reading session with or without mental-state themes improved in **social understanding** from pre- to post-test as compared to the no-treatment control group. Children who read books that included mental-state themes showed greater improvements in **social understanding** than those in the non-mental-state themes condition (Cates & Nicolopoulou, 2019). Additionally, an intervention aimed at enhancing MST and SBR practices among caregivers from impoverished backgrounds showed that caregivers in the treatment group engaged in more discussions of characters' behaviors and mental states, which was positively associated with improvements in children's mental-state understanding (Fine et al., 2014).

As another risk factor, caregiver psychopathology may also influence SBR practices, MST, and young children's social–emotional understanding. For example, parents' mental health status is associated with SBR frequency with their infants as well as their perceived value of a reading-based parenting intervention (Rogers et al., 2024). Caregivers' mood disorders may also be associated with children's perceptions of emotions, as significant symptoms of maternal depression are associated with children's increased bias to perceive sadness (Martin et al., 2015). However, there is mixed support for the association between parental psychopathology, SBR, and joint attention. In a sample of mothers with clinical depression as compared to nondepressed mothers, there were no significant differences in joint attention (Henderson & Jennings, 2003). In a different study, Schechter et al. (2010) found that a composite variable that included parent–child relationship dysfunction, atypical maternal behavior, and child separation distress was associated with less time spent in joint attention during social interactions. However, differences in joint attention were observed within the depressed-mothers subsample, such that mothers with depression as well as comorbid disorders showed better joint attention with infants compared to mothers who experienced depression alone. Likewise, young children of mothers with a history of major depressive disorder show deficits in **social understanding**, which is associated with poorer MST (Shamblaw et al., 2019). Driscoll and Easterbrooks (2007) also found that young mothers with a history of maltreatment and greater symptoms of depression are prone to exhibiting parenting profiles characterized by less consistent and less sensitive patterns of joint attention during their play with their children.

Child-based risk status and children's emotional and behavioral symptoms may also be associated with different patterns of parental book-reading behaviors. In a low-income sample of preschoolers, mothers of children identified as having internalizing and/or externalizing symptoms and in need of intervention services were less likely to use emotion-based MST, showed less frequent use of types of negative emotion-based words, and were more likely to use cognition-based language during SBR. In the sample overall (clinical and nonclinical), mothers who made more causal connections to mental states in their narratives tended to have children who exhibited greater social competence, fewer behavior problems, and more interactive play (Bekar et al., 2018).

Parental addiction is also another contributing risk factor that can impact joint attention skills, **social understanding**, and MST. However, limited research has explored the impact of parental substance use disorders on SBR and parent–child interactions, with mixed results. Some research shows no differences in social or mental-state perception abilities among young adults with parents who have alcohol use disorders (Kopera et al., 2014). The associations among parental addiction, parenting behaviors, and child outcomes are likely more nuanced. Specifically, researchers have called for work that examines variability *within* families impacted by addiction rather than characterizing a collective group of caregivers as one "high-risk" group or only comparing caregivers with and without substance use disorders

(Shadur & Hussong, 2019). In line with this framework, findings from a sample of mothers with toddlers exposed to cocaine prenatally showed that children whose caregivers engaged in more in-tune behaviors, shared book control, and answering questions showed higher expressive language scores 1 year later as compared to their peers whose mothers were less responsive (Cross et al., 2011). Still, the effects of parental substance use on young children's **social understanding** remains an area for future research.

Recent efforts have focused on other ways in which caregivers with substance use disorders support their children's social–emotional development, particularly in teaching and responding to emotions. Mothers with substance use disorders, for instance, report engaging in "emotion-coaching" behaviors, characterized by more positive and supportive reactions to their children's emotions, similar to the patterns of emotion socialization found in low-risk community samples. However, these mothers report significantly higher levels of both supportive and nonsupportive emotion socialization behaviors with their young children (Shadur & Hussong, 2019). Furthermore, greater impairment due to substance use disorder symptoms is linked to less supportive emotion socialization behaviors, which, in turn, is associated with poorer emotion regulation among young children (Shadur & Hussong, 2020). Studies examining within-person variability also show that the context of active substance use differentially influences maternal emotion socialization behaviors, with less supportive and inconsistent behaviors during active substance use, and more supportive and consistent behaviors during sobriety (Shadur & Hussong, 2019). Feasibility data from our own laboratory points to the positive and resilient elements of caregiving behaviors among mothers in recovery who were in residential addiction treatment where they lived with their young children. Consenting respondents included three mothers in addiction treatment who engaged in a videotaped SBR task where they read a wordless picture book with mental-state themes. In accord with an iterative coding process, frequency counts and qualitative thematic analysis revealed that mothers in recovery used similar SBR practices as mothers with no history of substance use, including visible shared enjoyment behaviors, joint attention, maternal use of dialogic reading practices, such as asking questions, reciprocity, and positive responsiveness to children's cues and bids. Results provide proof of concept for the study design, demonstrating that a larger empirical study on SBR among mothers with substance use disorders is warranted.

Conclusions

Caregivers play a crucial role in fostering young children's social–emotional development, with their **shared book-reading** (SBR) practices serving as a key mechanism for building children's understanding of social dynamics. Although psychological, environmental, biological, and other **contextual risk** factors may present challenges, these families also possess significant resilience-promoting factors with regard to SBR that can be strengthened with intentional and well-developed support. The implications for intervention emphasize the need for individualized, strengths-based programs that address families' unique needs and focus on context-specific behaviors. A key shift in the field is a growing focus on within-group and within-person variability rather than treating high-risk families and/or children as a homogeneous group. Expanding the focus beyond mothers is also critical to understanding how SBR influences **social understanding** across various caregiver–child dynamics, including gender differences in both children and caregivers.

Research on SBR must also consider the nuances of culture, race, and racial/ethnic identity. Race-based biases in narratives and the selection of books are important factors to examine when considering how SBR impacts **social understanding**, especially for children of color. Although many minoritized households are already having conversations about race, it is important for families with White children to also engage in these discussions to reduce bias (see Hagan et al., 2024). SBR offers a rich opportunity for these race-based dialogues. A recent study showed that White preschoolers engaged in a "race-conscious book-reading curriculum" at school were more likely to initiate race-related discussions with their caregivers at home (Botto & Kerr, 2024). While promising, this child-driven approach highlights the importance of also incorporating parent-driven strategies that use race-conscious SBR narratives. Still, the growing body of work on SBR and its impact on child–caregiver interactions and **social understanding** point to clear targets for intervention and prevention. Caregiver-focused interventions can be effective in increasing interactive reading at home and improving social–emotional outcomes across various risk contexts.

Interventions targeting SBR and related practices have proven particularly effective in high-risk families. For example, one study found that an intervention that enhanced MST during SBR led to improvements in young children's **social understanding** (Fine et al., 2014). Interventions aimed at improving caregiver–child interactions through SBR have also been associated with improvements in parenting warmth, sensitivity, and child engagement (Canfield et al., 2020; Hockenberger et al., 1999). In a recent study, Kogan (2024) evaluated the impact of a dialogic reading approach combined with direct instruction of mental-state words during SBR on preschoolers' emotion vocabulary and found increases between pre- and post-session scores for MST and demonstrated a positive correlation between student engagement and MST. In yet another study, Grazzani and Ornaghi (2011) randomly assigned children to an intervention where they read stories enriched with mental-state terms and played games that encouraged the use of mental-state terms. Children in the intervention group showed a greater understanding of mental-state language. In a different study, Wang and Shao (2025) found that children who participated in an SBR intervention focused on mental-state discourse showed more advanced school readiness 18 months after completion of the program. An app-based intervention among preschoolers with low socioeconomic status involved reading of a wordless book, supported by audio and theory-of-mind prompts, which resulted in marginally greater meaningful narrative responses compared to the more basic set of reading prompts (Rubegni et al., 2021). Participation in a dialogic book-reading intervention is also associated with increased perspective-taking skills, likely through heightened awareness of story characters' mental states (Yurdakul et al., 2025). Ultimately, the caregiving context and SBR offer critical opportunities to shape children's **social understanding**. While intervention studies show promising results, ongoing research is needed to refine and tailor these approaches that meet the unique needs of children and families in diverse risk contexts. Future SBR interventions should focus on identifying family strengths and enhancing protective factors to promote resilience, benefiting both children and caregivers.

References

Adamson, L. B., Bakeman, R., Deckner, D. F., & Nelson, P. B. (2014). From interactions to conversations: The development of joint engagement during early childhood. *Child Development, 85*(3), 941–955. https://doi.org/10.1111/cdev.12189

Adrián, J. E., Clemente, R. A., & Villanueva, L. (2007). Mothers' use of cognitive state verbs in picture-book reading and the development of children's understanding of mind: A longitudinal study. *Child Development, 78*(4), 1052–1067. https://doi.org/10.1111/j.1467-8624.2007.01052.x

Alvarenga, P., Zucker, T. A., Tambyraja, S., & Justice, L. (2020). Contingency in teacher-child emotional state talk during shared book reading in early childhood classrooms. *Early Education and Development, 31*(8), 1187–1205. https://doi.org/10.1080/10409289.2020.1722786

Ambarchi, Z., Boulton, K. A., Thapa, R., Arciuli, J., DeMayo, M. M., Hickie, I. B., et al. (2024). Social and joint attention during shared book reading in young autistic children: A potential marker for social development. *Journal of Child Psychology and Psychiatry, 65*(11), 1441–1452. https://doi.org/10.1111/jcpp.13993

Aram, D., & Aviram, S. (2009). Mothers' storybook reading and kindergartners' socio-emotional and literacy development. *Reading Psychology, 30*(2), 175–194. https://doi.org/10.1080/02702710802275348

Aram, D., Deitcher, D. B., Shoshan, T. S., & Ziv, M. (2017). Shared book reading interactions within families from low socioeconomic backgrounds and children's social understanding and prosocial behavior. *Journal of Cognitive Education and Psychology, 16*(2), 157–177. https://doi.org/10.1891/1945-8959.16.2.157

Astington, J. W., & Pelletier, J. (2013). Theory of mind, language, and learning in the early years: Developmental origins of school readiness. In B. D. Homer & C. S. Tamis-LeMonda (Eds.), *The development of social cognition and communication* (pp. 205–230). Psychology Press.

Baldwin, D. A., & Moses, L. J. (2001). Links between social understanding and early word learning: Challenges to current accounts. *Social Development, 10*(3), 309–329. https://doi.org/10.1111/1467-9507.00168

Barnes, E. M., & Dickinson, D. K. (2018). Relationships among teachers' use of mental state verbs and children's vocabulary growth. *Early Education and Development, 29*(3), 307–323. https://doi.org/10.1080/10409289.2018.1440844

Bartsch, K., & Wellman, H. M. (1995). *Children talk about the mind*. Oxford University Press.

Bassett, H. H., Denham, S. A., Mohtasham, M., & Austin, N. (2020). Psychometric properties of the book-readings for an affective classroom education (BRACE) coding system. *Reading Psychology, 41*(4), 322–346. https://doi.org/10.1080/02702711.2020.1768980

Beeghly, M., & Cicchetti, D. (1994). Child maltreatment, attachment, and the self system: Emergence of an internal state lexicon in toddlers at high social risk. *Development and Psychopathology, 6*(1), 5–30. https://doi.org/10.1017/S095457940000585X

Beeghly, M., & Cicchetti, D. (1997). Talking about self and other: Emergence of an internal state lexicon in young children with Down syndrome. *Development and Psychopathology, 9*(4), 729–748. https://doi.org/10.1017/S0954579497001417

Bekar, O., Steele, M., Shahmoon-Shanok, R., & Steele, H. (2018). Mothers' mental state talk and preschool children's social-behavioral functioning: A multidimensional account. *Journal of Infant, Child & Adolescent Psychotherapy, 17*(2), 119–133. https://doi.org/10.1080/15289168.2018.1456890

Botto, I., & Kerr, M. L. (2024). Book talk: Promoting race-conscious conversations in White families through a preschool-based reading curriculum. *Journal of Child and Family Studies, 33*, 3130–3143. https://doi.org/10.1007/s10826-024-02904-0

Brandone, A. C., & Stout, W. (2023). The origins of theory of mind in infant social cognition: Investigating longitudinal pathways from intention understanding and joint attention to preschool theory of mind. *Journal of Cognition and Development, 24*(3), 375–396. https://doi.org/10.1080/15248372.2022.2146117

Bruinsma, Y., Koegel, R. L., & Koegel, L. K. (2004). Joint attention and children with autism: A review of the literature. *Mental Retardation & Developmental Disabilities Research Reviews, 10*(3), 169–175. https://doi.org/10.1002/mrdd.20036

Campbell, C., Horlin, C., Reid, C., McMichael, J., Forrest, L., Brydges, C., et al. (2015). How doyou think she feels? Vulnerability in empathy and the role of attention in school-aged children born extremely preterm. *British Journal of Developmental Psychology, 33*(3), 312–323. https://doi.org/10.1111/bjdp.12091

Canfield, C. F., Miller, E. B., Shaw, D. S., Morris, P., Alonso, A., & Mendelsohn, A. L. (2020). Beyond language: Impacts of shared reading on parenting stress and early parent–child relational health. *Developmental Psychology, 56*(7), 1305–1315. https://doi.org/mutex.gmu.edu/10.1037/dev0000940

Cates, C. B., & Nicolopoulou, A. (2019). The effects of bookreading with and without mental state themes on preschoolers' theory of mind. In E. Veneziano & A. Nicolopoulou (Eds.), *Narrative, literacy and other skills* (pp. 129–149). John Benjamins Publishing Company. https://doi.org/10.1075/sin.25.07cat

Claussen, A. H., Mundy, P. C., Mallik, S. A., & Willoughby, J. C. (2002). Joint attention and disorganized attachment status in infants at risk. *Development and Psychopathology, 14*(2), 279–291. https://doi.org/10.1017/S0954579402002055

Cross, J. R., Fletcher, K. L., & Neumeister, K. L. S. (2011). Social and emotional components of book reading between caregivers and their toddlers in a high-risk sample. *Journal of Early Childhood Literacy, 11*(1), 25–46. https://doi.org/10.1177/1468798410390894

Dahmen, B., Puetz, V. B., Scharke, W., von Polier, G. G., Herpertz-Dahlmann, B., & Konrad, K. (2018). Effects of early-life adversity on hippocampal structures and associated HPA axis functions. *Developmental Neuroscience, 40*(1), 13–22. https://doi.org/10.1159/000484238

DeMayo, M. M., Young, L. J., Hickie, I. B., Song, Y. J. C., & Guastella, A. J. (2019). Circuits for social learning: A unified model and application to autism Spectrum disorder. *Neuroscience and Biobehavioral Reviews, 107*, 388–398. https://doi.org/10.1007/s40489-017-0119-z

Dowdall, N., Melendez-Torres, G. J., Murray, L., Hartford, L., & Cooper, P. J. (2020). Shared picture book-reading interventions for child language development: A systematic review and meta-analysis. *Child Development, 91*, e383–e399. https://doi.org/10.1111/cdev.13225

Driscoll, J. R., & Easterbrooks, M. A. (2007). Young mothers' play with their toddlers: Individual variability as a function of psychosocial factors. *Infant and Child Development, 16*(6), 649–670. https://doi.org/10.1002/icd.515

Drummond, J., Paul, E. F., Waugh, W. E., Hammond, S. I., & Brownell, C. A. (2014). Here, there and everywhere: Emotion and mental state talk in different social contexts predicts empathic helping in toddlers. *Frontiers in Psychology, 5*, 361. https://doi.org/10.3389/fpsyg.2014.00361

Ekerim-Akbulut, M., Şen, H. H., Beşiroğlu, B., & Selçuk, B. (2020). The role of theory of mind, emotion knowledge and empathy in preschoolers' disruptive behavior. *Journal of Child and Family Studies, 29*(2020), 128–143. https://doi.org/10.1007/s10826-019-01556-9

Findlay, L. C., Girardi, A., & Coplan, R. J. (2006). Links between empathy, social behavior, and social understanding in early childhood. *Early Childhood Research Quarterly, 21*(3), 347–359. https://doi.org/10.1016/j.ecresq.2006.07.009

Fine, Y., Aram, D., & Ziv, M. (2014). Promoting low-SES kindergartners' reference to mental states through parental mediation during interactive storybook reading. *Megamot, 49*(3), 415–445.

Fine, S. E., Izard, C. E., Mostow, A. J., Trentacosta, C. J., & Ackerman, B. P. (2003). First grade emotion knowledge as a predictor of fifth grade self-reported internalizing behaviors in children from economically disadvantaged families. *Development and Psychopathology, 15*(2), 331–342. https://doi.org/10.1017/S095457940300018X

Flack, Z. M., Field, A. P., & Horst, J. S. (2018). The effects of shared storybook-reading on word learning: A meta-analysis. *Developmental Psychology, 54*(7), 1334–1346. https://doi.org/10.1037/dev0000512

Gal-Szabo, D. E., Spinrad, T. L., Eisenberg, N., & Sulik, M. J. (2019). The relations of children's emotion knowledge to their observed social play and reticent/uninvolved behavior in preschool: Moderation by effortful control. *Social Development, 28*(1), 57–73. https://doi.org/10.1111/sode.12321

Garner, P. W. (2003). Child and family correlates of toddlers' emotional and behavioral responses to a mishap. *Infant Mental Health Journal, 24*(6), 580–596. https://doi.org/10.1002/imhj.10076

Garner, P. W., Bolt, E., & Roth, A. N. (2019). Emotion-focused curricula models and expressions of and talk about emotions between teachers and young children. *Journal of Research in Childhood Education, 33*(2), 180–193. https://doi.org/10.1080/02568543.2019.1577772

Garner, P. W., Jones, D. C., Gaddy, G., & Rennie, K. M. (1997). Low-income mothers' conversations about emotions and their children's emotional competence. *Social Development, 6*(1), 37–52. https://doi.org/10.1111/j.1467-9507.1997.tb00093.x

Garner, P. W., Jones, D. C., & Miner, J. L. (1994). Social competence among low-income preschoolers: Emotion socialization practices and social cognitive correlates. *Child Development, 65*(2), 622–637. https://doi.org/10.1111/j.1467-8624.1994.tb00772.x

Garner, P. W., & Landry, S. H. (1992). Preterm infants' affective responses in independent versus toy-centered play with their mothers. *Infant Mental Health Journal, 13*(3), 219–230. https://doi.org/10.1002/1097-0355(199223)13:3<219::AID-IMHJ2280130308>3.0.CO;2-9

Garner, P. W., & Landry, S. H. (1994). Effects of maternal attention-directing strategies on preterm infants' affective expressions during joint toy play. *Infant Behavior and Development, 17*(1), 15–22. https://doi.org/10.1016/0163-6383(94)90018-3

Garner, P. W., Landry, S. H., & Richardson, M. A. (1991). The development of joint attention skills in very-low-birth-weight infants across the first 2 years. *Infant Behavior and Development, 14*(4), 489–495.

Garner, P. W., & Parker, T. S. (2018). Young children's picture-books as a forum for the socialization of emotion. *Journal of Early Childhood Research, 16*(3), 291–304. https://doi.org/10.1177/1476718X18775760

Garner, P. W., Shadur, J. M., & Dunsmore, J. C. (2023). Mothers' beliefs about emotions and authoritarian parenting as predictors of young children's behavioral problems. *Mental Health & Prevention, 30*, 200264. https://doi.org/10.1016/j.mhp.2023.200264

Garner, P. W., & Toney, T. (2020). Financial strain, maternal attributions, emotion knowledge and children's behavioral readiness for school. *Journal of Applied Developmental Psychology, 67*, 101122. https://doi.org/10.1016/j.appdev.2020.101122

Gest, S. D., Holland-Coviello, R., Welsh, J. A., Eicher-Catt, D. L., & Gill, S. (2006). Language development sub-contexts in Head Start classrooms: Distinctive patterns of teacher talk during free play, mealtime, and book-reading. *Early Education and Development, 17*(2), 293–315. https://doi.org/10.1207/s15566935eed1702_5

Grazzani, I., & Ornaghi, V. (2011). Emotional state talk and emotion understanding: A training study with preschool children. *Journal of Child Language, 38*(5), 1124–1139. https://doi.org/10.1017/S0305000910000772

Grøver, V., Snow, C. E., Evans, L., & Strømme, H. (2023). Overlooked advantages of interactive book-reading in early childhood? A systematic review and research agenda. *Acta Psychologica, 239*, 103997.

Hagan, C., Halberstadt, A., Cooke, A., & Garner, P. W. (2024). White parents' racial socialization: Questionnaire validation and associations with children's friendships. *Journal of Family Issues, 45*(2), 350–373. https://doi.org/10.1177/0192513X221150973

Henderson, E. N., & Jennings, K. D. (2003). Maternal depression and the ability to facilitate joint attention with 18-month-olds. *Infancy, 4*(1), 27–46.

Hockenberger, E. H., Goldstein, H., & Sirianni Haas, L. (1999). Effects of commenting during joint book reading by mothers with low SES. *Topics in Early Childhood Special Education, 19*(1), 15–27. https://doi.org/10.1177/027112149901900102

Hutchins, T. L., Deraway, C., Prelock, P., & O'Neill, A. (2017). Mothers' and children's story-telling: A study of dyads with typically developing children and children with ASD. *Journal of Autism and Developmental Disorders, 47*, 1288–1304. https://doi.org/10.1007/s10803-016-3022-z

Kogan, A.-M. (2024), Using dialogic reading and direct instruction of emotion words to increase emotion vocabulary knowledge in the preschool classroom. *Journal of Research in Innovative Teaching & Learning*, Vol. ahead-of-print No. ahead-of-print. https://doi.org/10.1108/JRIT-12-2023-0192

Kopera, M., Glass, J. M., Heitzeg, M. M., Wojnar, M., Puttler, L. I., & Zucker, R. A. (2014). Theory of mind among young adult children from alcoholic families. *Journal of Studies on Alcohol and Drugs, 75*(5), 889–894. https://doi.org/mutex.gmu.edu/10.15288/jsad.2014.75.889

Kristen, S., Sodian, B., Thoermer, C., & Perst, H. (2011). Infants' joint attention skills predicttoddlers' emerging mental state language. *Developmental Psychology, 47*(5), 1207–1219. https://doi.org/10.1037/a0024808

Landry, S. H., Garner, P. W., Pirie, D., & Swank, P. R. (1994). Effects of social context and mothers' requesting strategies on Down's syndrome children's social responsiveness. *Developmental Psychology, 30*(2), 293–302. https://doi.org/10.1037/0012-1649.30.2.293

Landry, S. H., Garner, P. W., Swank, P. R., & Baldwin, C. D. (1996). Effects of maternal scaffolding during joint toy play with preterm and full-term infants. *Merrill-Palmer Quarterly*, 177–199.

Lane, J. D., & Bowman, L. C. (2021). How children's social tendencies can shape their theory of mind development: Access and attention to social information. *Developmental Review, 61*. https://doi.org/10.1016/j.dr.2021.100977

Legerstee, M., & Fisher, T. (2008). Coordinated attention, declarative and imperative pointing in infants with and without Down syndrome: Sharing experiences with adults and peers. *First Language, 28*, 281–312. https://doi.org/10.1177/0142723708091045

Lonigan, C. J., & Whitehurst, G. J. (1998). Relative efficacy of parent and teacher involvement in a shared-reading intervention for preschool children from low-income backgrounds. *Early Childhood Research Quarterly, 13*(2), 263–290. https://doi.org/10.1016/S0885-2006(99)80038-6

Luke, N., & Banerjee, R. (2013). Differentiated associations between childhood maltreatment experiences and social understanding: A meta-analysis and systematic review. *Developmental Review, 33*, 1–28. https://doi.org/10.1016/j.dr.2012.10.001

Martin, S. E., Williamson, L. R., Kurtz-Nelson, E. C., & Boekamp, J. R. (2015). Emotion understanding (and misunderstanding) in clinically referred preschoolers: The role of child language and maternal depressive symptoms. *Journal of Child and Family Studies, 24*, 24–37. https://doi.org/10.1007/s10826-013-9810-6

Mattson, J. T., Thorne, J. C., & Kover, S. T. (2022). Parental interaction style, child engagement, and emerging executive function in fetal alcohol spectrum disorders (FASD). *Child Neuropsychology, 28*(7), 853–877. https://doi.org/10.1080/09297049.2021.2023122

Milan, S., Carlone, C., & Dáu, A. L. B. T. (2021). Emotion socialization in mothers who experienced maltreatment: Mentalizing the past may help the present. *Journal of Family Psychology, 35*(6), 851–856. https://doi.org/10.1037/fam0000839

Miller, M. R., Müller, U., Giesbrecht, G. F., Carpendale, J. I., & Kerns, K. A. (2013). The contribution of executive function and social understanding to preschoolers' letter and math skills. *Cognitive Development, 28*(4), 331–349. https://doi.org/10.1016/j.cogdev.2012.10.005

Mol, S. E., Bus, A. G., & De Jong, M. T. (2009). Interactive book-reading in early education: A tool to stimulate print knowledge as well as oral language. *Review of Educational Research, 79*(2), 979–1007. https://doi.org/10.3102/0034654309332561

Morales, M., Mundy, P., Crowson, M., Neal, A. R., & Delgado, C. (2005). Individual differences in infant attention skills, joint attention, and emotion regulation behaviour. *International Journal of Behavioral Development, 29*(3), 259–263. https://doi.org/10.1080/01650250444000432

Nader-Grosbois, N., Jacobs, E., Mazzone, S., & Poirier, N. (2022). Mothers' socialization of emotions and theory of mind and emotion regulation in children with autism spectrum disorders. *Psychology, 13*(1), 177–219. https://doi.org/10.4236/psych.2022.131011

O'Madagain, C., & Tomasello, M. (2021). Joint attention to mental content and the social origin of reasoning. *Synthese, 198*(5), 4057–4078. https://doi.org/10.1007/s11229-019-02327-1

Ontai, L. L., & Thompson, R. A. (2002). Patterns of attachment and maternal discourse effects on children's emotion understanding from 3 to 5 years of age. *Social Development, 11*(4), 433–450. https://doi.org/10.1111/1467-9507.00209

Paparella, T., Goods, K. S., Freeman, S., & Kasari, C. (2011). The emergence of nonverbal joint attention and requesting skills in young children with autism. *Journal of Communication Disorders, 44*(6), 569–583. https://doi.org/10.1016/j.jcomdis.2011.08.002

Paulus, M., Licata, M., Kristen, S., Thoermer, C., Woodward, A., & Sodian, B. (2015). Social understanding and self-regulation predict pre-schoolers' sharing with friends and disliked peers: A longitudinal study. *International Journal of Behavioral Development, 39*(1), 53–64. https://doi.org/10.1177/01650254145379

Pears, K. C., & Fisher, P. A. (2005). Emotion understanding and theory of mind among maltreated children in foster care: Evidence of deficits. *Development and Psychopathology, 17*(1), 47–65. https://doi.org/10.1017/S0954579

Pierce, K., Gazestani, V. H., Bacon, E., Barnes, C. C., Cha, D., Nalabolu, S., et al. (2019). Evaluation of the diagnostic stability of the early autism spectrum disorder phenotype in the general population starting at 12 months. *JAMA Pediatrics, 173*(3), 578–587. https://doi.org/10.1001/jamapediatrics.2019.0624

Puthuraya, S., Karnati, S., Othman, H., Sripathi, R., Nandakumar, V., & Aly, H. (2023). Neonatal outcomes of preterm infants with in-utero exposure to drugs of substance use: US national data. *Pediatrics & Neonatology, 64*(1), 53–60. https://doi.org/10.1016/j.pedneo.2022.03.021

Racine, T., & Carpendale, J. I. (2007). Shared practices, understanding, language and joint attention. *British Journal of Developmental Psychology, 25*(1), 45–54. https://doi.org/10.1348/026151006X162613

Reilly, J., Klima, E. S., & Bellugi, U. (1990). Once more with feeling: Affect and language in atypical populations. *Development and Psychopathology, 2*(4), 367–391. https://doi.org/10.1017/S0954579400005782

Reilly, E. B., Stallworthy, I. C., Mliner, S. B., Troy, M. F., Elison, J. T., & Gunnar, M. R. (2021). Infants' abilities to respond to cues for joint attention vary by family socioeconomic status. *Infancy, 26*(2), 204–222. https://doi.org/10.1111/infa.12380

Rogers, K. M., Frosch, C. A., Vilches, S. L., & Sjolseth, S. R. (2024). Partnering with reach out and read to understand families' experiences with books and their babies. *Family Relations, 73*(5), 3378–3397. https://doi.org/10.1111/fare.13071

Rosello, B., Berenguer, C., Baixauli, I., García, R., & Miranda, A. (2020). Theory of mind profiles in children with autism spectrum disorder: Adaptive/social skills and pragmatic competence. *Frontiers in Psychology, 11*, 567401. https://doi.org/10.3389/fpsyg.2020.567401

Rubegni, E., Dore, R., Landoni, M., & Kan, L. (2021). "The girl who wants to fly": Exploring the role of digital technology in enhancing dialogic reading. *International Journal of Child-Computer Interaction, 30*. https://doi.org/10.1016/j.ijcci.2020.100239

Schapira, R., & Aram, D. (2020). Shared book reading at home and preschoolers' socio-emotional competence. *Early Education and Development, 31*(6), 819–837. https://doi.org/10.1080/10409289.2019.1692624

Schechter, D. S., Willheim, E., Hinojosa, C., Scholfield-Kleinman, K., Turner, J. B., McCaw, J., et al. (2010). Subjective and objective measures of parent-child relationship dysfunction, child separation distress, and joint attention. *Psychiatry, 73*(2), 130–144.

Scrimgeour, M. B., Davis, E. L., & Buss, K. A. (2016). You get what you get and you don't throw a fit!: Emotion socialization and child physiology jointly predict early prosocial development. *Developmental Psychology, 52*(1), 102–116. https://doi.org/10.1037/dev0000071

Sebastian, C. L., McCrory, E. J., Cecil, C. A., Lockwood, P. L., De Brito, S. A., Fontaine, N. M., & Viding, E. (2012). Neural responses to affective and cognitive theory of mind in children with conduct problems and varying levels of callous-unemotional traits. *Archives of General Psychiatry, 69*(8), 814–822. https://doi.org/10.1001/archgenpsychiatry.2011.2070

Shadur, J. M., & Hussong, A. M. (2019). Conceptualization and measurement of parent emotion socialization among mothers in substance abuse treatment. *Journal of Child and Family Studies, 28*(2), 325–342. https://doi.org/10.1007/s10826-018-1269-z

Shadur, J. M., & Hussong, A. M. (2020). Maternal substance use and child emotion regulation: The mediating role of parent emotion socialization. *Journal of Child and Family Studies, 29*(6), 1589–1603. https://doi.org/10.1007/s10826-019-01681-5

Shamblaw, A. L., Benson, J. E., Harkness, K. L., & Sabbagh, M. A. (2019). Maternal depression and children's false belief understanding. *Social Development, 28*(4), 927–941. https://doi.org/10.1111/sode.12369

Silkenbeumer, J. R., Schiller, E., & Kartner, J. (2018). Co- and self-regulation of emotions in the preschool setting. *Early Childhood Research Quarterly, 44*(1), 72–81. https://doi.org/10.1016/j.ecresq.2018.02.014

Siller, M., Swanson, M. R., Serlin, G., & Teachworth, A. G. (2014). Internal state language in the storybook narratives of children with and without autism spectrum disorder: Investigating relations to theory of mind abilities. *Research in Autism Spectrum Disorders, 8*(5), 589–596. https://doi.org/10.1016/j.rasd.2014.02.002

Siposova, B., & Carpenter, M. (2019). A new look at joint attention and common knowledge. *Cognition, 189*, 260–274. https://doi.org/10.1016/j.cognition.2019.03.019

Slaughter, V., Peterson, C. C., & Mackintosh, E. (2007). Mind what mother says: Narrative input and theory of mind in typical children and those on the autism spectrum. *Child Development, 78*(3), 839–858. https://doi.org/10.1111/j.1467-8624.2007.01036.x

Sodian, B., & Kristen-Antonow, S. (2015). Declarative joint attention as a foundation of theory of mind. *Developmental Psychology, 51*(9), 1190–1200. https://doi.org/10.1037/dev0000039

Stevens, S. A., Dudek, J., Nash, K., Koren, G., & Rovet, J. (2015). Social perspective taking and empathy in children with fetal alcohol spectrum disorders. *Journal of the International Neuropsychological Society, 21*(1), 74–84. https://doi.org/10.1017/S1355617714001088

Stout, W., Karahuta, E., Laible, D., & Brandone, A. C. (2021). A longitudinal study of thedifferential social-cognitive foundations of early prosocial behaviors. *Infancy, 26*(2), 271–290. https://doi.org/10.1111/infa.12381

Taumoepeau, M., & Ruffman, T. (2006). Mother and infant talk about mental states relates to desire language and emotion understanding. *Child Development, 77*(2), 465–481. https://doi.org/10.1111/j.1467-8624.2006.00882.x

Telford, E. J., Fletcher-Watson, S., Gillespie-Smith, K., Pataky, R., Sparrow, S., Murray, I. C., et al. (2016). Preterm birth is associated with atypical social orienting in infancy detected using eye tracking. *Journal of Child Psychology and Psychiatry, 57*(7), 861–868. https://doi.org/10.1111/jcpp.12546

Towson, J. A., Akemoglu, Y., Watkins, L., & Zeng, S. (2021). Shared interactive book-reading interventions for young children with disabilities: A systematic review. *American Journal of Speech-Language Pathology, 30*(6), 2700–2715. https://doi.org/10.1044/2021_AJSLP-20-00401

Vaughan Van Hecke, A., Mundy, P. C., Acra, C. F., Block, J. J., Delgado, C. E., Parlade, M. V., et al. (2007). Infant joint attention, temperament, and social competence in preschool children. *Child Development, 78*(1), 53–69. https://doi.org/10.1111/j.1467-8624.2007.00985.x

Wang, Z., & Shao, Y. (2025). Picture book reading improves children's learning understanding. *British Journal of Developmental Psychology, 43*(1), 12–35. https://doi.org/10.1111/bjdp.12479

Wellman, H. M., Cross, D., & Watson, J. (2001). Meta-analysis of theory-of-mind development: The truth about false belief. *Child Development, 72*(3), 655–684. https://doi.org/10.1111/1467-8624.00304

Westerveld, M. F., Paynter, J., & Wicks, R. (2020). Shared book reading behaviors of parents and their verbal preschoolers on the autism spectrum. *Journal of Autism and Developmental Disorders, 50*(8), 3005–3017. https://doi.org/10.1007/s10803-020-04406-6

Wicks, R., Westerveld, M., Stainer, M., & Paynter, J. (2022). Prompting visual attention to print versus pictures during shared book reading with digital storybooks for preschoolers with ASD compared to TD peers. *Autism Research, 15*(2), 254–269. https://doi.org/10.1002/aur.2623

Williamson, K. E., & Jakobson, L. S. (2014a). Social attribution skills of children born preterm at very low birth weight. *Development and Psychopathology, 26*(4), 889–900. https://doi.org/10.1017/S0954579414000522

Williamson, K. E., & Jakobson, L. S. (2014b). Social perception in children born at very low birthweight and its relationship with social/behavioral outcomes. *Journal of Child Psychology and Psychiatry, 55*(9), 990–998. https://doi.org/10.1111/jcpp.12210

Yager, J. A., & Ehmann, T. S. (2006). Untangling social function and social cognition: A review of concepts and measurement. *Psychiatry, 69*(1), 47–68. https://doi.org/10.1521/psyc.2006.69.1.47

Yurdakul, Y., Beyazit, U., & Ayhan, A. B. (2025). The effect of dialogic book reading on preschool children's perspective taking skills. *Early Childhood Education Journal, 53*, 49–62. https://doi.org/10.1007/s10643-023-01567-8

Ziv, M., Smadja, M. L., & Aram, D. (2014). Mothers' and teachers' mental-state discourse with preschoolers during storybook-reading. *Journal of Cognitive Education and Psychology, 13*(1), 103–119. https://doi.org/10.1891/1945-8959.13.1.103

Zmyj, N., Witt, S., Weitkämper, A., Neumann, H., & Lücke, T. (2017). Social cognition in children born preterm: A perspective on future research directions. *Frontiers in Psychology, 8*. https://doi.org/10.3389/fpsyg.2017.00455

Pamela W. Garner is a Professor of Childhood Studies in the School of Integrative Studies and the Human Development and Family Science Program at George Mason University. She conducts research on the social and emotional development of children from minoritized groups and investigates the contributions of parents and teachers to young children's social emotional learning.

Julia M. Shadur is an Associate Professor of Childhood Studies in the School of Integrative Studies and the Human Development and Family Science Program at George Mason University. She conducts research on social–emotional development and emotion regulation in at-risk and underrepresented populations with a focus on emotion socialization.

Hideko H. Bassett, Ph.D. is an Assistant Professor in the School of Integrative Studies, where she teaches courses on child development and socialization, family processes, and interdisciplinary studies. Her research explores socialization of young children's emotional competence.

Part III
Interventions in Educational Settings

Chapter 10
Feeding Two Birds with One Scone: How Read-Alouds in Prekindergarten Classrooms Support Socioemotional and Language Development for Children from Low-Income Homes

Erica M. Barnes

Contents

Children between the ages of 3 and 6 typically experience enormous language and socioemotional development. Many children in these formative ages spend time in prekindergarten (preK) classrooms, which provide unique learning opportunities that promote linguistic and socioemotional growth. Instructional settings, such as classroom **read-alouds**, have long been associated with rich learning opportunities (Noble et al., 2019). Classroom **read-alouds** are socially constructed events whereby an adult reads aloud a text, often a storybook, to a group of young children who are not yet able to read the text independently (van Kleeck, 2003). A wealth of research notes the relations of **read-alouds** and children's **language development** (Noble et al., 2019). An emerging body of research shows relations with children's socioemotional growth (Grøver et al., 2023). Not all children profit equally, though. Differences in learning have been noted for children with varying language abilities as well as children from different socioeconomic levels (SES) (Marulis & Neuman, 2013). This research indicates **read-alouds** are helpful for children's language and

E. M. Barnes (✉)
University at Albany, Albany, NY, USA
e-mail: ebarnes@albany.edu

R. Schapira, D. Aram (eds.), *Shared Book Reading and Children's Social-Emotional Competence*, https://doi.org/10.1007/978-3-032-14688-5_10

socioemotional learning (SEL) along with a need for considering SES when evaluating effectiveness.

In this chapter, we review the literature demonstrating the associations among SES and children's language and socioemotional development. We begin by discussing the inter-relations across these three factors, with a particular emphasis on reciprocal relationships between language and socioemotional growth. We then describe and report our findings from the studies of a preK curriculum that emphasizes language and socioemotional development. Finally, we discuss our findings in relation to future research and practice to highlight how we can metaphorically feed two birds with one scone by considering both language and socioemotional topics in preK **read-alouds** serving children from low-income homes (see Fig. 10.1).

Relations of SES, Language, and SEL

SES has a profound effect on language and socioemotional development. Sadly, children from low-income homes are exposed to more violence, instability, household chaos, and family separations (Evans, 2004). Abundant research notes the negative impacts of poverty on children's developmental outcomes, such as brain structure and physical and mental health, as well as emotional, cognitive, behavioral, and **language development** (Blair & Raver, 2012, Shonkoff et al., 2012). Specifically, many studies note a relation between SES and language for young children, such that children from low-income homes are more likely to demonstrate lower language abilities on standardized assessments (Levine et al., 2020). Neuroimaging studies have noted significant SES differences in brain volume in areas related to language and executive functioning (Farah et al., 2006). Some studies attribute this lower language with limited linguistic input in children's homes, as children raised in lower income homes tend to hear less language and therefore

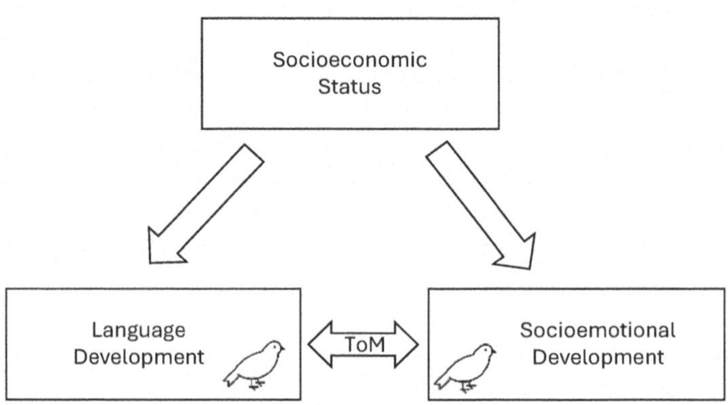

Fig. 10.1 Relations among socioeconomic status, language development, and socioemotional development

learn fewer words (e.g., Golinkoff et al., 2019; Pace et al., 2017). Knowing more words allows children to develop conceptual knowledge and categorizations, which results in more robust and efficient word learning and general understanding (e.g., Golinkoff & Hirsh-Pasek, 2008; Neuman, 2011). Knowing fewer words can impede children's abilities to express thoughts, feelings, and emotions, as well as their abilities to control their impulses (Roben et al., 2013).

Additionally, SES relates to children's SEL, particularly externalizing behaviors. Externalizing behaviors include aggression, lack of self-control, acting out, and defiance. A second-order meta-analysis found small effects for externalizing behaviors and overall SES (Korous et al., 2018), such that children from low-income homes are more likely to demonstrate problematic behaviors than their peers from more affluent homes. Children from low-SES homes tend to have lower scores on language assessments and demonstrate more difficulty with externalizing and internalizing behaviors (LeTourneau et al., 2011).

Interestingly, language and socioemotional development are related. Language allows children to understand verbal cues in social situations and resolve conflict through language (e.g., "use their words") (Lloyd-Esenkava et al., 2021), thus likely inhibiting problematic behavior. Research demonstrates relations between problematic behaviors and low language, such that children with lower language abilities tend to exhibit more problematic behaviors (Chow & Wehby, 2018; Vissers & Koolen, 2016). Children with speech and language impairments (SLI) are reported to experience emotional, behavioral, and social difficulties (Yew & O'Kearney, 2013; Helland et al., 2014). Specifically, prekindergartners with SLI show delays in or less development of social skills and tend to be rated lower on social competence by their parents and teachers than children with typical language (McCabe, 2005).

Theory of Mind

Of particular importance to children's socioemotional and **language development** is the emergence of **theory of mind** (ToM). ToM is the ability to understand others have thoughts and feelings that differ from one's own and may have incorrect perceptions or false beliefs. ToM is useful for understanding or interpreting others' actions and ideas; therefore, it is enormously important for SEL. The development of ToM is also essential for **language development** as it allows for efficient communication between interlocutors, as effective communication involves a meeting of the minds (Baldwin & Moses, 2001). Understanding one's inner self as well as others' is pivotal for the production and interpretation of communication. Language, particularly mental-state language, draws attention to the internal states of the self and others and allows for naming of emotions and thoughts. Language is also essential for understanding and regulating inner states. ToM and language abilities facilitate social communication, regulation of one's inner world, and understanding of other's inner worlds, behaviors, and motivations (Vissers & Koolen, 2016).

Therefore, the mutual development of ToM and language may also facilitate socio-emotional growth.

ToM tends to develop between the ages of 3 and 6 and is strongly related to linguistic competence (Milligan et al., 2007). A study involving 5-year-old children reported robust correlations between vocabulary growth and the development of ToM (Strasser & Del Rio, 2014), indicating that children are more likely to possess more developed ToM when they have larger funds of vocabulary. Unsurprisingly, language and ToM development are entangled from early childhood to adolescence (Tager-Flusberg, 2000). Importantly, children with SLI or slower **language development** will follow a typical trajectory for developing ToM but with a lower final level of ToM and development that occurs at a slower pace (Spanoudis, 2016).

Discussions focusing on the mind (e.g., emotions, feelings, and thoughts) are likely to promote the understanding that one's mind or point of view differs from others', allowing for social perspective-taking, which is associated with SEL. These discussions can stimulate reflection on social experiences, which can promote ToM through considering and enhancing the accuracy of mental-state attributions (e.g., Vissers & Koolen, 2016). Mental-state language is related to ToM as it introduces the language of the mind. Conversations involving mental-state language (e.g., emotions) likely facilitate ToM development (Ornaghi et al., 2014), especially when conversations are explanatory (Tenenbaum et al., 2008). Mental-state verbs (MSV), which are verbs that express memories, knowledge, feelings, ideas, or thoughts (Shatz et al., 1983), are often used to describe general cognitive processes or the contents of the mind (Olson & Asington, 1993). Children acquire MSV through engagements with more mature speakers within linguistically rich environments (Tomasello, 2000). Acquiring MSV allows children to more clearly describe internal states, which allows for more precise communication and facilitates understanding of others' motivations, which can be useful for the interpretation of social situations. Therefore, ToM development plays a crucial linking role between SEL and **language development** in young children.

Classroom Read-Alouds

Classroom **read-alouds** are ripe with opportunities for children to develop their language and socioemotional skills. In preK classrooms, **read-alouds** are typically comprised of three components: the text, the teacher's comments and discussion meant to engage children, and children's responses to the text (van Kleeck, 2003). From a constructivist perspective, the conversations between the adult and child are seen as experiences which promote the construction of meaning in a shared context (Halliday, 2004).

The text read-aloud serves as the focal point for instruction and discussion. Children's books introduce rare vocabulary, complex syntax or syntax rarely encountered in casual conversation (e.g., passive voice), and topical content that encourages knowledge development (van Kleeck, 2003), all of which are associated with academic and/or socioemotional gains. Often, children's storybooks focus on socioemotional topics such as social understandings (e.g., friendships), emotions, and conflict resolution (Dyer-Seymour et al., 2004). Such texts encourage discussion of mental states such as feelings, desires, emotions, bodily states, and cognition.

Teachers scaffold children's SEL opportunities during **read-alouds** by modeling language for problem-solving, using and explaining mental-state terms, drawing attention to characters' actions and reactions, and encouraging children to engage in problem-solving and conflict resolution (Grøver et al., 2023). A recent review found that experimental and correlational studies report **read-alouds** have positive or mixed effects on children's understandings of internal states and internal state language, socioemotional topics, socio-cognitive themes, and perspective-taking skills (Grøver et al., 2023). Specifically, the inclusion of emotionally focused books, discussion of characters' perspectives/emotions, the identification of misunderstandings between characters, and the extension of book topics to children's experiences were related to children's socioemotional growth.

Additionally, **read-alouds** can be rich with mental-state language and MSV. Research supports children's acquisition of MSV through **read-alouds**, with findings indicating increased use of mental-state terms by parents is associated with children's development of ToM (Ruffman et al., 2002; Symons et al., 2005), which may be associated with linguistic capability more generally (Milligan et al., 2007). Importantly, parental use of mental-state talk may vary based on SES, with parents from different SES levels producing different types and amounts of mental-state talk, and these differences relating to children's development of ToM (Ebert et al., 2017). Research on MSV use conducted in early childhood classrooms is nascent yet promising. Ziv et al. (2014, 2015) and Barnes and Dickinson (2018) found teachers' use of mental-state talk in prekindergarten settings to relate to children's language and/or socioemotional growth.

Opening the World of Learning Curriculum

PreK curricula can promote instruction that facilitates children's language and socioemotional growth. *Opening the World of Learning* (OWL: Schickedanz & Dickinson, 2005) is a full-year comprehensive curriculum that emphasizes early literacy and **language development** across a full instructional day. Six thematically based instructional units build conceptual knowledge in a systematic manner through daily, whole-class **read-alouds**, and small and large group instructions focusing on science, social studies, and socioemotional topics. Thematic content is spread across a series of 48 narrative picture books during **read-alouds**, with each text being read four times. The accompanying Teachers' Guide provides support for developing conversations around vocabulary and thematic content during each read-aloud in a scaffolded manner across the four readings of the text.

Several instructional themes in the curriculum involve socioemotional topics such as friends and family. The Friends unit encourages children to talk about what makes a good friend, what friendship means, and how to resolve conflict with friends. The storybooks aligned with this unit address these topics through engaging narratives that include diverse casts of characters. Teachers are encouraged to help their students identify characters' feelings, make connections to similar personal experiences, and discuss how to see a situation from another person's point of view (i.e., develop empathy). For example, one picture book in the Friends unit, *Matthew and Tilly* (Jones, 1995), introduces children to conflict resolution when the two friends in the text get into an argument. One character accidentally breaks their crayons, and together, the two characters learn how to resolve conflict to preserve their friendship through apologizing. This text serves as a platform for engaging discussions that promote word learning and socioemotional development.

The curriculum also provides suggestions for discussion topics that emphasize **socioemotional learning**. For example, following the initial reading of *Matthew and Tilly*, the Teachers' Guide provides the following discussion prompt, "Do you think that Tilly really thought Matthew had broken her crayon on purpose, or was she just so upset that she said he had?" Teachers are encouraged to scaffold children's understandings of accidents and the consequences of blaming others in moments of anger. During a second reading of *Matthew and Tilly*, teachers are encouraged to reconstruct the story with the children using the text's illustrations. The Teachers' Guide encourages teachers to help children connect the depicted events with Matthew's and Tilly's feelings. These discussions encourage children to consider differing points of view and provide concrete representations of characters displaying feelings and emotions, which may promote the development of ToM. Topics introduced during **read-alouds** are carried over into other instructional settings across the day. For example, children are encouraged to draw and talk about pictures of their friends during small group time.

Studies of OWL

In this chapter, we draw on findings from our research team's longitudinal study of Head Start prekindergarten classrooms located in the Southeastern portion of the United States to examine the relations among socioemotional and **language development** for children from low-income homes. These classrooms took part in a randomized control trial funded by the Institute of Education Sciences, U.S. Department of Education,[1] evaluating the effects of a language and literacy-focused intervention curriculum (OWL) in comparison with business as usual. Our earlier work examining **read-alouds** in OWL classrooms found significant, positive results for children's vocabulary growth, particularly when children were

[1] The research reported here was supported by the Institute of Education Sciences, U.S. Department of Education, through Grant R324E060088A to David K. Dickinson and Ann Kaiser at Vanderbilt University. The opinions expressed are those of the authors and do not represent views of the U.S. Department of Education.

exposed to more nonverbal supports (Barnes et al., 2023), instructional comments (Barnes et al., 2017), and academic language (Barnes & Dickinson, 2017). Here, we present findings focusing on teachers and students assigned to the OWL curriculum condition. We explore three important themes in our analysis. First, we examine correlations among children's receptive vocabulary and social skills ratings to detect possible relations among language and SEL within our sample of children from low-income homes. Next, we examine differences in socioemotional growth for children with differing levels of language ability. Finally, we examine relations among teachers' use of MSV during **read-alouds** and children's socioemotional skills.

We followed 31 Head Start teachers (98% female, 91.5% Black) across one school year as they implemented the OWL curriculum. These teachers averaged 16 years of classroom experience, with 11 of those years in Head Start prekindergarten setting. Head Start serves children between the ages of 3 and 5 from low-income homes in the United States. Teachers were trained in the OWL curriculum in the year prior to implementation and received ongoing coaching and professional development during the implementation year. Teachers were videorecorded in the fall (start) of the school year during a typical whole-class read-aloud where they read one or two of the OWL curriculum books. All videos were transcribed and analyzed using CHILDES (MacWhinney, 2000).

Children in the classrooms of these teachers were pretested at the onset of the school year using the Preschool Language Scale 4 (PLS: Zimmerman et al., 2002) to determine their initial language status for analyses purposes. Children were categorized as low language if their PLS-4 global language standard score fell below 75 ($n = 125$) and typical language if their global language standard score was above 85 ($n = 110$). Children with scores between 76 and 84 were not included in the analysis to intentionally create a gap between the two groups. All children in both groups had scores typical of children enrolled in Head Start (Puma et al., 2012) but were below the mean of 100 for the assessment.

Additionally, children were administered assessments of nonverbal intelligence, receptive vocabulary, and socioemotional development at the beginning (fall) and end (spring) of the school year. In the analyses described below, we utilized Leiter-R (Roid & Miller, 1996), Peabody Picture Vocabulary Test (PPVT: Dunn et al., 1997), and the Social Skills Rating Scale (SSRS: Gresham & Elliott, 1990). Leiter-R is a standardized assessment of children's nonverbal intelligence that involves game-like tasks to assess attentional, cognitive, and neuropsychological abilities. Leiter-R was used as a control measure given children may process the verbal and nonverbal information presented during **read-alouds** in different ways. PPVT is a standardized assessment of children's receptive vocabulary. Children are asked to match a stimulus word with one of four provided pictures. The SSRS is a norm-referenced assessment that asks teachers to rate student behaviors on a 3-point scale (0 = Never, 1 = Sometimes, 2 = Very Often). The Social Skills scale contains five subscales that evaluate cooperation, assertion, responsibility, empathy, and self-control. The Behaviors scale includes three subscales that evaluate externalizing problem behaviors, internalizing problems, and hyperactivity. Our analyses utilize the summed

Table 10.1 Descriptive statistics

	Minimum	Maximum	Mean	SD
SSRS social skills T0[a]	64	130	97.35	14.18
SSRS problem behavior T0[a]	85	139	94.94	11.31
SSRS social skills T1[a]	65	130	105.25	14.15
SSRS problem behavior T1[a]	85	142	94.37	10.96
MSV types	1	18	8.16	3.88
Desire types	0	5	1.29	1.36
Bodily state types	0	2	0.55	0.77
Emotion types	0	2	0.45	0.69
Cognitive types	1	14	5.87	2.71

[a]Denotes standard score. T0 = pretest (fall of school year). T1 = post-test (spring of school year)

total of the subscales to broadly evaluate social skills and behaviors. Descriptive data of students' scores are provided in Table 10.1.

We began our analyses by exploring possible relations among children's receptive vocabulary and their social skills using bivariate correlations. Children's end-of-year PPVT scores were significantly related to their end-of-year social skills scores, as measured by the SSRS ($r = 0.242$, $p < .001$). Children with higher receptive vocabulary scores tended to have higher social skill ratings at the end of 1 year of preK when instructed in classrooms utilizing the OWL curriculum. Similarly, we found a significant relation for children's problem behaviors and their end-of-year receptive vocabulary ($r = -0.171$, $p = 0.009$). In this case, children with lower end-of-year PPVT scores had higher ratings of problem behaviors (i.e., more problem behaviors), as measured by the SSRS. These findings align with the literature base indicating relations of children's language and socioemotional development and add to the findings to note these relationships are present in children from low-income homes.

As a second step for investigating children's SEL development across 1 year of Head Start prekindergarten, we compared the average growth for social skills and problem behaviors between children categorized as low and typical language. All children demonstrated growth in social skills as rated by the SSRS at the end of the school year. Children in the low language group grew 7.36 points, while children categorized as typical language grew by 8.36 points. Children considered low language had a substantial reduction in problem behaviors in comparison with those in the typical language group across the preK year. Children categorized as low language experienced approximately double the growth in problematic behavior ratings ($M = -1.65$) compared with their typical language peers ($M = -0.86$). Negative changes in ratings indicate decreases in problematic behaviors. Children in the typical language group had relatively consistent scores, which is desirable for this measure given their scores were in the average range.

Given our initial findings, we next sought to determine if teachers' use of MSV during **read-alouds** functions as a potential mechanism for evoking socioemotional growth in children from low-income homes with varying language abilities. We examined teachers' talk to determine their use of MSV, which are markers of socioemotional language, hypothesizing teachers' use of MSV would positively relate to children's socioemotional growth. MSV can refer to desire, cognition, bodily states, or emotions. A modified version of Bretheron and Beegley's (1982) list of MSV that included inflected verb endings was utilized in the analyses. Desire MSV relate to individuals' wants and needs (e.g., wishes, hopes, and wants), whereas bodily state MSV referred to the five senses (e.g., hearing, seeing, tasting, touching, and smelling). Cognitive MSV pertained to knowledge, thoughts, or beliefs held by individuals. Emotion MSV referred to expressions of feelings (e.g., satisfies, loathes, and enjoys). Transcripts were run through the CHILDES program to detect exact matches to our list of MSV using the FREQ command. Total word types (number of different words) were calculated for all categories of MSV. All instances of MSV were hand-checked within the transcripts to ensure consistency with our definitions of each category.

Analyses reveal that teachers used relatively few MSV in their extratextual talk during **read-alouds**, which were 10 minutes in length on average. Most teachers produced roughly one MSV per minute within the read aloud, which included discussion before, during, and after the reading of the text. Teachers were more likely to use cognitive MSV (think and wonder) than other types of MSV, with teachers producing the fewest emotion MSV on average (see Table 10.1).

We hypothesized that teachers' use of MSV would have positive effects on children's socioemotional development, as assessed by the SSRS. Data were checked for outliers and normality prior to hypothesis testing. Some attrition was experienced, as is typical for children enrolled in Head Start given this population tends to be more mobile than other preK populations (Zill et al., 2003). Data was therefore assumed to be missing at random. Cases with missing data were eliminated listwise from the data set. Full information maximum likelihood was utilized for data analysis to incorporate all available information at each step of the analysis. Intra-class correlation coefficients were calculated for each outcome (social skills and problem behaviors), with each demonstrating substantial variance at the classroom (teacher) level. We therefore created two level models where children were nested within classrooms. Baseline models for social skills and problem behaviors were developed and tested as intercept-only models. Pre-test scores (fall social skills or problem behaviors) were added and tested for significance. Random-effects models were deemed insufficient due to little variations between classrooms in terms of association between MSV and children's learning. Therefore, a random intercept and fixed slope model was employed. This approach fixed the relationship between outcome measures and predictors. Estimated marginal means were generated and tested for statistical significance. Children's nonverbal intelligence, as measured by Leiter-R, was entered as a child-level covariate (grand mean-centered). Teacher's MSV types, the variable of interest, were entered at the classroom level (grand mean-centered).

Teachers' use of MSV types, a composite variable composed of all types of MSV, during **read-alouds** was significantly related to children's social skill growth controlling for fall social skills scores (pre-test) and nonverbal intelligence, as measured by Leiter-R for children in the low language group ($b = 0.77$, $p = 0.036$) but

Table 10.2 Relations among teachers' MSV use and children's SSRS scores

	Low language			Typical Language		
	Estimate	SE	p	Estimate	SE	p
MSV						
Intercept	40.46	7.98	<0.001	42.04	9.29	<0.001
SSRS Fall	−0.46	0.07	<0.001	−0.49	0.08	<0.001
MSV	0.77	0.35	0.036	0.21	0.34	0.54
Leiter-R	0.15	0.13	0.251	0.34	0.15	0.026
Emotion MSV						
Intercept	43.48	7.35	<0.001	42.93	8.92	<0.001
SSRS Fall	−0.46	0.06	<0.001	−0.48	0.08	<0.001
MSV	5.28	1.87	0.009	1.76	1.66	0.297
Leiter-R	0.16	0.13	0.218	0.33	0.15	0.035

not for children in the typical language group ($b = 0.21$, $p = 0.540$). To further probe this relationship, a second model was built to evaluate the effect of emotion MSV on children's social skill growth controlling for fall social skills (pre-test) and nonverbal intelligence, as measured by Leiter-R. Teachers' use of emotion MSV during **read-alouds** was significantly related to social skill growth for children in the low language group ($b = 5.28$, $p = 0.009$) but not for children in the typical language group ($b = 1.76$, $p = 0.297$). No significant relations were found for either group on the problem behavior scales of the SSRS. No significant relations were found for other types of MSV with either problem behaviors or social skills ratings on the SSRS. The detailed results of these analyses are presented in Table 10.2.

Our findings indicate a relation of teachers' use of MSV with children's social skills, such that increases in teachers' use of MSV were associated with increases on the social skills ratings for children categorized as low language. Similarly, increases in teachers' use of emotion MSV were associated with increases on the social skills ratings for children categorized as low language. These findings are of particular importance given these children entered preK with the double disadvantage of coming from low-income homes with low language scores, yet they experienced socioemotional growth when in classrooms where teachers produced more MSV during **read-alouds**. Teachers who include more MSV, specifically emotion MSV, may be providing a springboard for socioemotional growth for children with low language from low-income homes, therefore potentially offering up a means for bridging the gap between children with differing language abilities from low-income homes.

We conducted post-hoc analyses of our transcripts to identify instances of teacher talk that included MSV within discussions pertaining to socioemotional topics. Transcript analyses reveal that teachers often discussed socioemotional topics when utilizing MSV in their extratextual talk. For example, the following discussion took place during a read-aloud of *Matthew and Tilly*.

Teacher: Look how they're standing (points to illustration). Look at Matthew and look at Tilly. See how she's standing?

Child: Yeah!
Teacher: She's standing like she is really hurt and acting real mean because he broke her crayon. She was angry.

In this example, the teacher utilizes the illustrations to further children's story comprehension when a character is displaying a strong emotional reaction to a tense social situation. The teacher points to the illustration to draw attention to characters' body postures in a manner that emphasizes how the body can be used to display an emotion. She furthers this by noting the character has hurt feelings and names the character's emotion as anger. Another teacher takes a moment to act out the scene to demonstrate a physical enactment of emotion and social interaction.

Teacher: You know us ladies, we have to do the thing like... (Teacher stands up and puts her hand on her hip and extends her hand, palm facing the students in a 'halt' gesture.)
Teacher: Do you understand? Read the hand! (pretending to be Tilly telling Matthew to stop).
Teacher: (talking to students) See, look at her. (points to illustration in book).
Teacher: She got her hands on her hips (points to illustration in book).
Teacher: She is really upset with Matthew because he broke her brand-new purple crayon.

Here, the teacher embodies the character by re-enacting the scene from the text while simultaneously gesturing to explain what the character's movements and language imply. She pairs physical enactment with speech to support students' understandings of the social interaction, modeling how bodies can be used to demonstrate emotions. This extratextual support provides multiple means for children to develop deeper socioemotional understanding by specifically linking behaviors to emotions. Interestingly, our earlier work pertaining to nonverbal supports indicates that teachers who frequently use nonverbal supports (e.g., pointing gestures) also provide frequent support for understanding characters' motives and feelings ($r = 0.577$, $p < 0.001$) (Barnes & Dickinson, 2012).

Teachers also utilize **read-alouds** as a means for discussing conflict resolution, also through the text *Matthew and Tilly*. The following discussion took place after the teacher had concluded her read-aloud.

Teacher: Don't we do things that we don't mean to do?
Child: Yes!
Teacher: But when we don't mean to do them, don't we apologize?
Child: Yeah!
Teacher: How do you apologize to someone?
Child: I'm sorry.
Teacher: And it helps you and them to feel better, doesn't it?

This teacher bridges the conflict resolution in the text to children's personal experiences by asking them if they have experienced similar situations. She reinforces important emotional state language such as apologize, sorry, and feel better.

A child is even able to provide an example of an apology that can serve as a language model for other children in the classroom. This example demonstrates how storybooks can serve as productive launching points for discussions that integrate vocabulary terms with socioemotional topics, potentially resulting in growth in children's social skills and word learning.

Conclusions

Our studies investigating **read-alouds** in Head Start preK classrooms using the OWL curriculum indicate children from low-income homes with varying funds of language demonstrate language and socioemotional growth. This dual growth is unsurprising given the interrelationship between language and socioemotional development, yet of particular importance given the long-ranging effects early language and socioemotional development have on later achievement. Hearing MSV during **read-alouds** may prime children to focus on and learn about emotions and behaviors, which may result in SEL. Learning words that name emotions and feelings is an important first step in SEL. These findings are particularly important given our preK children had the double disadvantage of coming from low-income homes with below-average language scores. We therefore view **read-alouds** as the metaphorical scone that feeds the two birds, namely **language development** and SEL. Enhancing effective practices, such as the use of MSV in supportive talk, is a worthwhile endeavor given the potential to positively impact both language and socioemotional development of children from low-income homes.

Mental-state language can be challenging for children to learn given it is not highly imageable or concrete. Verbs such as *feel*, *think*, and *wonder* are abstract and challenging to define in child-friendly language. Pairing mental-state language with supportive book reading (e.g., illustrations and extratextual talk) may provide a constellation of supports for learning the language of emotions, which can lead to SEL. Indeed, the complexity hypothesis asserts that providing redundant information during complex tasks, particularly through nonverbal means such as gesture, can be beneficial for learners (McNeil et al., 2000), especially for novices (Kalyuga et al., 2003). Understanding others' feelings and points of view can be enormously challenging for young children; therefore, including MSV in conceptually rich, analytical engagements, such as **read-alouds**, may promote word learning (Neuman & Celano, 2006) and SEL for children from low-income homes. MSV appear relatively late in children's expressive vocabulary, typically emerging between the ages of 2 and 4 when children are in prekindergarten settings (Shatz et al., 1983). This parallels the emergence of ToM; hence, assisting children with learning the language of the mind may enhance or facilitate ToM, and vice versa. Young children may spend substantial time in preK classrooms; hence, prekindergarten curricula that encourage mental-state talk during **read-alouds** may enhance children's understanding of mental states and ToM and subsequently lead to SEL. We encourage the field to continue exploring the effects of mental-state talk in preK **read-alouds**, particularly for children with low-language ability from low-income homes given the potential of this practice to accelerate children's language and socioemotional growth.

Our findings are an important step in considering how read-alouds may foster socioemotional and language growth, however, some limitations bear noting. Our study did not include measures of ToM, hence we were unable to test any hypotheses regarding the interplay among ToM, language, and socioemotional growth. Future studies may evaluate children's ToM development as a potential mediating factor. Additionally, children in our study experienced the OWL curriculum across the entire school day. Other instructional settings included socioemotional topics that may have positively impacted children's SEL and reductions of problematic behaviors; hence, it is possible other settings in addition to read-alouds contributed to student outcomes. Future research should attempt to isolate the effects to read-alouds. **Read-alouds**, while an important part of the preK day, are relatively brief in nature; hence, extending socioemotional topics and discussions across the instructional day merits additional exploration.

In conclusion, our work indicates discussion of socioemotional topics during **read-alouds** in preK classrooms may yield socioemotional and language growth for children from low-income homes. As our findings and Grøver et al.' (2023) review indicate, **read-alouds** are a valuable source of nourishment for the socioemotional and language growth of young children. SEL can lead to a reduction in problematic behaviors, which may result in more learning opportunities for young children from low-income homes.

References

Baldwin, D. A., & Moses, L. J. (2001). Links between social understanding and early word learning: Challenges to current accounts. *Social Development, 10*(3), 309–329. https://doi.org/10.1111/1467-9507.00168

Barnes, E. M., & Dickinson, D. K. (2012, November). *Is book reading a unified construct? Examining the relationship of teachers' book reading styles and use of extra-textual discussions.* Literacy Research Association Annual Conference, San Diego, CA.

Barnes, E. M., & Dickinson, D. K. (2017). The relationship of Head Start teachers' academic language use and children's receptive vocabulary. *Early Education and Development, 28*(7), 794–809. https://doi.org/10.1080/10409289.2017.1340069

Barnes, E. M., & Dickinson, D. K. (2018). Relationships among teachers' use of mental state verbs and children's vocabulary growth. *Early Education and Development, 29*(3), 307–323. https://doi.org/10.1080/10409289.2018.1440844

Barnes, E. M., Dickinson, D. K., & Grifenhagen, J. F. (2017). The role of teachers' comments during book reading in children's vocabulary growth. *Journal of Educational Research, 110*(5), 515–527. https://doi.org/10.1080/00220671.2015.1134422

Barnes, E. M., Hadley, E. B., Lawson-Adams, J., & Dickinson, D. K. (2023). Non-verbal supports for word learning; Prekindergarten teachers' gesturing practices during shared book reading. *Early Childhood Research Quarterly, 64*(3), 302–312. https://doi.org/10.1016/j.ecresq.2023.04.005

Blair, C., & Raver, C. C. (2012). Child development in the context of adversity: Experiential canalization of brain and behavior. *American Psychologist, 67*, 309–318. https://doi.org/10.1037/a0027493

Bretherton, I., & Beeghly, M. (1982). Talking about internal states: The acquisition of an explicit theory of mind. *Developmental Psychology, 18*(6), 906. https://doi.org/10.1037/0012-1649.18.6.906

Chow, J. C., & Wehby, J. H. (2018). Associations between language and problem behavior: A systematic review and correlational meta-analysis. *Educational Psychology Review, 30*, 61–82. https://doi.org/10.1007/s10648-016-9385-z

Dunn, L., Williams, K. T., Wang, J. J., & Booklets, N. (1997). Peabody Picture Vocabulary Test-(PPVT-III) Form IIIA: American Guidance Service, Inc.

Dyer-Seymour, J., Shatz, M., Wellman, H., & Saito, M. (2004). Mental state expressions in US and Japanese children's books. *International Journal of Behavioral Development, 28*, 546–552. https://doi.org/10.1080/01650250444000261

Ebert, S., Peterson, C., Slaughter, V., & Weinert, S. (2017). Links among parents' mental state language, family socioeconomic status, and preschoolers' theory of mind development. *Cognitive Development, 44*, 32–48.

Evans, G. W. (2004). The environment of childhood poverty. *American Psychologist, 59*, 77–92. https://doi.org/10.1037/0003-066X.59.2.77

Farah, M. J., Shera, D. M., Savage, J. H., Betancourt, L., Giannetta, J. M., Brodsky, N. L., & Malmud, E. H. (2006). Childhood poverty: Specific associations with neurocognitive development. *Brain Research, 1110*, 166–174. https://doi.org/10.1016/j.brainres.2006.06.072

Golinkoff, R. M., & Hirsh-Pasek, K. (2008). How toddlers begin to learn verbs. *Trends in Cognitive Science, 12*, 397–403. https://doi.org/10.1016/j.tics.2008.07.003

Golinkoff, R. M., Hoff, E., Rowe, M. L., Tamis-LeMonda, C., & Hirsh-Pasek, K. (2019). Language matters: Denying the existence of the 30-million-word gap has serious consequences. *Child Development, 90*(3), 985–992.

Gresham, F. M., & Elliott, S. N. (1990). *Social skills rating system manual*. AGS.

Grøver, V., Snow, C. E., Evans, L., & Stromme, H. (2023). Overlooked advantages of interactive book reading in early childhood? A systematic review and research agenda. *Acta Psychologica, 239*, 1–20. https://doi.org/10.1016/j.actpsy.2023.103997

Halliday, M. A. K. (Ed.). (2004). *The place of dialogue in children's construction of meaning* (5th ed.). International Reading Association.

Helland, W. A., Lundervold, A. J., Heimann, M., & Posseurud, M. B. (2014). Stable associations between behavioral problems and language impairments across childhood: The importance of pragmatic language problems. *Research in Developmental Disabilities, 35*(5), 943–951. https://doi.org/10.1016/j.ridd.2014.02.016

Jones, R. C. (1995). *Matthew and Tilly*. Picture Puffins.

Kalyuga, S., Ayres, P., Chander, P., & Sweller, J. (2003). The expertise reversal effect. *Educational Psychologist, 38*(11), 23–31.

van Kleeck, A. (2003). Research on book sharing: Another critical look. In A. van Kleeck, S. A. Stahl, & E. B. Bauer (Eds.), *On reading books to children: Parents and teachers*. Erlbaum.

Korous, K. M., Causadias, J. M., Bradley, R. H., & Luthar, S. S. (2018). Unpacking the link between socioeconomic status and behavior problems: A second-order meta-analysis. *Development and Psychopathology, 30*, 1889–1906. https://doi.org/10.1017/S0954579418001141

Letourneau, N., Duffett-Leger, L., Levac, L., Watson, B., & Young-Morris, C. (2011). Socioeconomic status and child development: A meta-analysis. *Journal of Emotional and Behavioral Disorders, 21*, 211–224. https://doi.org/10.1177/1063426611421007

Levine, D., Pace, A., Luo, R., Hirsh-Pasek, K., Golinkoff, R. M., de Villiers, J., Iglesias, A., & Wilson, M. S. (2020). Evaluating socioeconomic gaps in preschoolers' vocabulary, syntax, and language process skills with the Quick Interactive Language Screener (QUILS). *Early Childhood Research Quarterly, 50*, 114–128. https://doi.org/10.1016/j.ecresq.2018.11.006

Lloyd-Esenkaya, V., Forrest, C. L., Jordan, A., Russell, A. J., & Clair, M. C. S. (2021). What is the nature of peer interactions in children with language disorders? A qualitative study of parent and practitioner views. *Autism & Developmental Language Impairments, 6*, 1–17.

MacWhinney, B. (2000). *The CHILDES Project: Tools for analyzing talk, Volume II: The database* (Vol. 2). Erlbaum.

Marulis, L. M., & Neuman, S. B. (2013). How vocabulary interventions affect young children at risk: A meta-analytic review. *Journal of Research on Educational Effectiveness, 6*(3), 223–262. https://doi.org/10.1080/19345747.2010.755591

McCabe, P. C. (2005). Social and behavioral correlates of preschoolers with specific language impairment. *Psychology in the Schools, 42*, 373–387. https://doi.org/10.1002/pits.20064

McNeil, N. M., Alibali, M. W., & Evans, J. L. (2000). The role of gesture in children's comprehension of spoken language: Now they need it, now they don't. *Journal of Nonverbal Behavior, 24*(2), 131–150. https://doi.org/10.1023/A:1006657929803

Milligan, K., Astington, J. W., & Dack, L. A. (2007). Language and theory of mind: Meta-analysis of the relation between language ability and false-belief understanding. *Child Development, 78*(2), 622–646. https://doi.org/10.1111/j.1467.8624.2007.01018.x

Neuman, S. B. (2011). Lessons from my mother: Reflections on the National Early Literacy Panel Report. *Educational Researcher, 39*(4), 301–304. https://doi.org/10.3102/0013189X10370475

Neuman, S. B. & Celano, D. (2006). The knowledge gap: Implications of leveling the playing field for low-income and middle-income children. *Reading Research Quarterly, 41(2), 176–201.* https://doi.org/10.1S9S/RRQ.41.2.2

Noble, C., Salab, G., Petera, M., Lingwood, J., Rowlanda, C., Gobeta, F., & Pinea, J. (2019). The impact of shared book reading on children's language skills: A meta-analysis. *Educational Research Review, 28*, 100290. https://doi.org/10.1016/j.edurev.2019.100290

Olson, D. R., & Astington, J. (1993). Thinking about thinking: Learning how to take statements and hold beliefs. *Educational Psychologist, 28*(1), 7–23.

Ornaughi, V., Brockmeier, J., & Grazzani, I. (2014). Enhancing social cognition by training emotion understanding: A primary school study. *Journal of Experimental Child Psychology, 119*, 26–39. https://doi.org/10.1016/j.jecp.2013.10.005

Pace, A., Luo, R., Hirsh-Pasek, K., & Golinkoff, R. M. (2017). Identifying pathways between socioeconomic status and language development. *Annual Review of Linguistics, 3*, 285–308. https://doi.org/10.1146/annurev-linguistics-022516-034226

Puma, M., Bell, S., Cook, R., Heid, C., Broene, P., Jenkins, F., … Downer, J. T. (2012). *Third grade follow-up to the Head Start impact study: Final report.* Retrieved from Washington, DC: Office of Planning, Research and Evaluation, Administration for Children and Families.

Roben, C. K., Cole, P. M., & Armstrong, L. M. (2013). Longitudinal relations among language skills, anger expression, and regulatory strategies in early childhood. *Child Development, 84*, 891–905.

Roid, G. H., & Miller, L. J. (1996). *Leiter international performance scale-revised.* Wood-Dale.

Ruffman, T., Slade, L., & Crowe, E. (2002). The relation between child and mothers' mental state language and theory-of-mind understanding. *Child Development, 73*, 734–751.

Schickedanz, J., & Dickinson, D. K. (2005). *Opening the world of learning: A comprehensive early literacy program.* Pearson Early Learning.

Shatz, M., Wellman, H. M., & Silber, S. (1983). The acquisition of mental verbs: A systematic investigation of the first reference to mental state. *Cognition, 14*(3), 301–321. https://doi.org/10.1016/0010-0277(83)90008-2

Shonkoff, J. P., Garner, A. S., Siegel, B. S., Dobbins, M. I., & Earls, M. F. (2012). The lifelong effects of early childhood adversity and toxic stress. *Pediatrics, 129*, e232–e246.

Spanouis, G. (2016). Theory of mind and specific language impairments in school-age children. *Journal of Communication Disorders, 6*(1), 83–96. https://doi.org/10.1016/j.jcomdis.2016.04.003

Strasser, K., & del Río, F. (2014). The role of comprehension monitoring, theory of mind, and vocabulary depth in predicting story comprehension and recall of kindergarten children. *Reading Research Quarterly, 49*(2), 169–187. https://doi.org/10.1002/RRQ.68

Symons, D. K., Peterson, C., Slaughter, V., Roche, J., & Doyle, E. (2005). Theory of mind and mental state discourse during book reading and story-telling tasks. *British Journal of Developmental Psychology, 23*, 81–102.

Tager-Flusberg, H. (2000). The challenge of studying language development in children with autism. In L. Menn & N. Bernstein Ratner (Eds.), *Methods for studying language production (pp. 313–332). Erlbaum.* https://doi.org/10.4324/9781410601599

Tenenbaum, H. R., Alfieri, L., Brooks, P. J., & Dunne, G. (2008). The effects of explanatory conversations on children's emotion understanding. *British Journal of Developmental Psychology, 26*, 249–263. https://doi.org/10.1348/026151007x231057

Tomasello, M. (2000). First steps toward a usage-based theory of language acquisition. *Cognitive Linguistics, 11*(1/2), 61–82.

Vissers, C., & Koolen, S. (2016). Theory of mind deficits and social emotional functioning in preschoolers with specific language impairment. *Frontiers in Pscyhology, 7*, 1734. https://doi.org/10.3389/fpsyg.2016.01734

Yew, S. G., & O'Kearney, R. (2013). Emotional and behavioural outcomes later in childhood and adolescence for children with specific language impairments: Meta-analyses of controlled prospective studies. *Journal of Child Psychology and Psychiatry, 54*, 516–524. https://doi.org/10.1111/jcpp.12009

Zill, N., Resnick, G., Kim, K., O'Donnell, K., Sorongon, A., McKey, R. H., … D'Elio, M. A. (2003). *Head Start FACES 2000: A whole-child perspective on program performance. Fourth progress report.* Washington, DC.

Zimmerman, I. L., Steiner, V. G., & Pond, R. E. (2002). *PLS-4: Preschool language scale-4*. The Psychological Corporation.

Ziv, M., Smadja, M., & Aram, D. (2014). Mothers' and teachers' mental-state discourse with preschoolers during storybook reading. *Journal of Cognitive Education and Psychology, 13*(1), 103–119.

Ziv, M., Smadja, M., & Aram, D. (2015). Preschool teachers' reference to theory of mind topics in three storybook contexts: Reading, reconstruction and telling. *Teaching and Teacher Education, 45*, 14–24.

Erica M. Barnes, PhD, is an Associate Professor in the Department of Literacy Teaching and Learning at the University at Albany, 1400 Washington Ave., Albany, NY, USA 12222. Her research investigates teacher–child interactions in early childhood classrooms that promote language and literacy growth, with an emphasis on the developmental trajectories of children with varying levels of language abilities from underserved populations.

Chapter 11
A Shared Book-Reading Intervention Program to Promote Preschoolers' Empathy

Rotem Schapira

Contents

Empathy consists of two components: cognitive **empathy** and emotional **empathy**. Cognitive **empathy** is the ability to recognize and understand others' emotions, while emotional **empathy** is the ability to share in someone else's emotion and simultaneously feel separate from the other (Uzefovsky & Knafo-Noam, 2016). **Empathy** contributes to a child's development: **Empathy** fosters better academic performance and supports emotional well-being and mental health. **Empathy** enhances the ability to form and maintain healthy relationships, lays the groundwork for future economic stability and contributes to overall improvement in life satisfaction and well-being (e.g., Depow et al., 2021). **Empathy** serves as a fundamental driver of prosocial behavior (Eisenberg, 2000; Malti et al., 2009), fostering positive social interactions and reducing antisocial tendencies and related health risks (Malti & Ongley, 2014).

R. Schapira (✉)
The Academic College Levinsky-Wingate, Tel Aviv, Israel

Tel Aviv University, Tel Aviv, Israel
e-mail: rotem.schapira@l-w.ac.il

R. Schapira, D. Aram (eds.), *Shared Book Reading and Children's Social-Emotional Competence*, https://doi.org/10.1007/978-3-032-14688-5_11

Empathy has been consistently linked to promoting meaningful interactions and strengthening connections with others (Rumble et al., 2010). This perspective is supported by evidence indicating that **empathy** contributes to the development of friendships, conflict resolution, and moral behaviors (Spinrad & Eisenberg, 2014). Conversely, lower levels of **empathy** have been associated with increased aggression, bullying, and emotional detachment (Nickerson et al., 2008). Additionally, research highlights the role of **empathy** in education, demonstrating its ability to enhance classroom engagement, foster a sense of belonging, and promote intrinsic motivation for learning (Barr & Higgins-D'Alessandro, 2007). Researchers propose that **empathy** encompasses fundamental precursor skills, including self-awareness, cognitive perspective-taking, and emotional regulation, which collectively motivate prosocial behavior (Eisenberg et al., 2006).

Gender differences in **empathy** emerge as early as toddlerhood and continue to develop throughout early childhood (Rochat, 2023). Girls in the **preschool** years tend to exhibit higher levels of affective **empathy**, displaying greater sensitivity to others' emotions and distress (Christov-Moore et al., 2014; Eisenberg et al., 2015). These differences are reinforced by caregiver interactions, as parents are more likely to engage daughters in emotionally expressive conversations and encourage prosocial behaviors such as comforting and helping (Fabes et al., 1994; Ornaghi et al., 2020). This reinforces gender-role expectations, as caregivers scaffold social sensitivity in girls, perceiving them as more attuned to emotional cues (McClure, 2000). At ages 5–9, females generally exhibit higher mentalizing abilities, such as understanding false beliefs and predicting others' behavior (Hughes et al., 2005). These early-emerging gender differences continue to shape social interactions, peer relationships, and moral reasoning throughout early childhood (Rochat, 2023). Understanding these early developmental patterns is essential for supporting balanced emotional growth and **empathy** development in both boys and girls during the critical formative years of early childhood.

Early childhood is a meaningful period for emotional socialization, frequently through interactions with caregivers at home and in early education settings (Denham, 2007). Educators play a vital role as emotional socializers, as young children spend extended hours in **preschool**. Educators can develop and promote emotional skills by modeling, by responding contingently to children's emotions, and by teaching through emotionally meaningful conversations (Ciucci et al., 2018; Denham et al., 2017, 2020). With frequent opportunities to express and understand emotions, early education settings significantly influence children's emotional development, making teachers essential to their social and emotional growth (e.g., Denham, 2023).

Grusec and Davidov (2010) identified five domains of socialization: protection, reciprocity, control, group participation, and guided learning. The current study focused on guided learning. This domain refers to situations where a more knowledgeable person, such as a teacher, provides explanations, examples, and encouragement to help the child acquire and practice social and emotional skills. Instead of learning alone, the child receives structured support to develop new skills in social–emotional competence. According to Vygotsky's theoretical approach

(1978), the scaffolding provided by adults (experts) is a crucial factor in fostering high cognitive functioning in children. This support is based on social interactions and the use of psychological tools and symbols, such as language. Within the "zone of proximal development" (Vygotsky, 1978), children engage in tasks they cannot yet complete independently but can achieve with guidance. Through this interactive process, learning is reinforced as children advance beyond their current abilities. In this context, emotion discourse, mediated by the "expert" adult, plays a vital role in enhancing children's social–emotional competence, as it unfolds through language and dialogue between the teacher and the children.

Using Emotion Discourse to Promote Children's Empathy

Language is an important medium for enhancing young children's emotional competence because children come to understand emotions via dialogue about emotional events in the real world and the world of fiction (e.g., films and books). Discourse with, and support from, an adult helps children understand aspects of their everyday lives, including emotions, intentions, reasons, and motives. Discourse on emotions enables children to depart from the "here and now," and cope with and learn about social–emotional experiences that they encounter in their lives (e.g., Thompson et al., 2003). For instance, talking about the causes and consequences of emotions contributes to an increase in children's emotion knowledge (Denham & Kochanoff, 2002). Recently, Reschke et al. (2023) showed that young children's emotion talk during discourse with their parents is significantly related to their emotion knowledge, highlighting the importance of child participation in the discourse.

Emotion discourse can occur in various contexts in children's daily lives, such as play, reminiscing about an event, and sharing book-reading. Much of the literature on emotion discourse has explored the context of reminiscing (conversations about past events) and reminiscing-based interventions (Kisa et al., 2023; Waters et al., 2019). Most studies have focused on parental reminiscing (Neale & Pino-Pasternak, 2017). However, insights from this body of research may contribute to understanding the contribution of **preschool** educators' reminiscing discourse to emotional development. Studies indicated that parent–child reminiscing contributes to children's emotional development (Laible & Song, 2006; Leyva et al., 2021) and that training parents in emotion discourse during reminiscing is associated with increases in children's emotion knowledge (Valentino et al., 2019). In a review of the benefits of reminiscing with children, Salmon and Reese (2016) emphasized that children of parents who discussed the past in an elaborative emotional way had more insights into their own and others' feelings. Pavlova and her colleagues (2021) examined how parent–child reminiscing about pain relates to 4-year-old **preschool**ers' empathic behaviors, showing that parents who used more neutral emotion language (e.g., 'How did you feel?') had children who exhibited greater empathic concern in response to another's pain. Similarly, children who provided more explanations while reminiscing about past painful events also demonstrated increased empathic concern for others' pain." The evidence from research on reminiscing indicates that emotion discourse can promote children's emotional development and **empathy**. Recent studies have also examined this contribution in other contexts, such as shared book-reading (SBR). Nevertheless, further investigation is needed to clarify how such discourse operates within SBR and to explore its broader educational implications.

Shared Book-Reading

SBR is a daily activity that allows adults to engage in rich conversations that promote child development in areas such as language (e.g., Mol et al., 2008), social cognition (e.g., Aram et al., 2017), and emotion understanding (e.g., Grazzani & Ornaghi, 2011). SBR often includes discussion of both the "visible" aspects of the storybook, such as the plot, illustrations, and the characters (e.g., Price et al., 2009), as well as the more "hidden" aspects that go beyond the "here and now," such as relating to social or emotional features, or connecting the book to the child's life (e.g., Hindman et al., 2014). This is in keeping with Bruner's (1986, 1990) dual landscape model, according to which narratives include two "landscapes"—the action level and the consciousness level. The former is focused on more general aspects of the book, including the plot and the characters' behaviors, while the latter is focused on deeper aspects, including socio-emotional aspects, such as thoughts, beliefs, desires, emotions, and intentions that underlie characters' behaviors. Studies demonstrate that parents vary in how much they relate to the different landscapes in books, as well as the number and types of questions they ask, expansions or elaborations that they use, and the like (Aram et al., 2013; Tompkins et al., 2017). This emphasis on the inner world of characters also resonates with bibliotherapy literature, which highlights how engaging with stories can foster processes of identification, emotional reflection, and insight, thereby supporting children's socio-emotional development.

A growing body of research emphasizes the importance of SBR for young children's emotional competence in both the home and **preschool** contexts (e.g., Brownell et al., 2013; Garner & Parker, 2018). For example, Schapira and Aram (2020) found that parent–child conversation during SBR related to **preschool**ers' emotional competences and **empathy**. That is, elaborations on the characters' emotions and connecting to the child's emotional life relate to their emotional outcomes. Bassett et al. (2020) found that **preschool** teachers' dialogue relating to emotions during SBR was especially beneficial to children who had lower emotion knowledge at the beginning of the school year. At the same time, there is limited research on SBR interventions implemented by **preschool** teachers to foster children's emotional development and **empathy**. Few intervention studies in the **preschool** context found the contribution of SBR intervention and emotion discourses to social and emotional development. For instance, Ornaghi et al. (2015) found that a training group that focused on conversation surrounding book-reading outperformed a control group focused on free play, in children's emotion understanding and prosocial orientation, and that this effect remained stable 4 months later. In addition, an intervention by Voltmer and von Salisch (2022), which trains teachers in dialogic reading of picture books with emotional content and engaging in reminiscing about shared emotional events during mealtimes, contributed to an improvement of children's emotion knowledge when comparing the intervention and the control group. As far as we know there is no study that investigates the contribution of shared book-reading intervention to **preschools' empathy**.

When exploring the relation between SBR and young children's emotional development, it is essential to consider key factors that can foster emotional dialogue: repeated reading of the same book multiple times and the book genre. Repeated readings of a book help the child to become a more active participant and provide opportunities to move from the discussion of the plot into the consciousness level that includes discussion of emotions (e.g., McArthur et al., 2005; Sipe, 2002; Schapira et al., 2021). Characteristics of different children's book genres impact the discourse during SBR. For example, mothers used didactic books for detailed conversations with their children. The simpler structure of the book may have facilitated the discourse about emotions. Mothers related more to anger and sadness compared to love and happiness. This may indicate that they feel they have to explain and teach their children about 'negative' emotions and how to cope with them, whereas positive emotions may be more implicitly understood (Schapira et al., 2021). Also, studies found differences in discourse while reading books with different main characters (human vs. animal). For example, the discourse in a book with human characters was richer than that in a book with animal characters. When reading the book with the human characters, parents elaborated more, asked more questions, related more to their children's lives, and used more mental words. These findings demonstrate the importance of the characteristics of the characters in the book to the nature of the discourse between adults and children during book-reading.

The Current Study

This study investigates the impact of an SBR intervention, implemented by **novice preschool teachers**, all in their first year of teaching, on children's **empathy**. Its novelty lies in working with novice teachers as part of their Bachelor's degree program, particularly during their first year of teaching, which serves as an internship. Additionally, the study emphasizes the role of emotional discourse between **preschool** teachers and small groups of children during repeated SBR sessions using both narrative and didactic books—two genres that differ in structure and purpose. Narrative books typically unfold within a specific setting, featuring a plot and character-driven events that aim to engage the reader through storytelling, without necessarily conveying an explicit moral message. Didactic books are designed to teach a specific lesson or value. While they may also contain characters and a storyline, their structure is generally simpler, presenting a clear problem and resolution, and often includes an explicit educational or moral theme (Kelly & Moses, 2018; Silveira Barbosa et al., 2018; Skinner et al., 2016).

The current study builds on the growing body of literature highlighting **discourse during SBR to enhance children's social-emotional competence, particularly empathy**. It examines the impact of an SBR-based intervention, implemented by **novice preschool teachers**, that emphasizes emotionally rich conversations using both narrative and didactic books. The study aims to evaluate whether such emotionally attuned SBR sessions promote higher levels of **empathy** among **preschoolers** compared to book reading without dialogue at all. It further investigates gender differences in **empathy** and the differential effects of the program on males and females. Based on prior findings, the first hypothesis is that children in the intervention group will show greater gains in **empathy** than those in the control group. The second hypothesis is that females will initially exhibit higher **empathy** levels than males, but that males—who tend to begin with lower **empathy** scores—will benefit more substantially from the intervention. This study thus seeks to explore not only the overall effectiveness of emotion discourse in early educational contexts but also its potential to foster emotional development among children who start from lower baselines in socio-emotional competencies.

Method

Participants included 77 **preschool**ers (M = 54.95, SD = 23.19); there were 34 males and 43 females. Ten **novice preschool teachers**, all in their first year of teaching, conducted the intervention. Each teacher was randomly assigned to work with an intervention group and a control group, each consisting of four children.

Two books were selected, each representing a different approach to emotional learning: the narrative book *The Rabbit Listened* by Cori Doerrfeld and the didactic book *The Color Monster* by Anna Llenas. These books were chosen for their rich emotional content and their distinct pedagogical styles. *The Rabbit Listened* offers an emotionally nuanced story that emphasizes the power of **empathy** and attentive listening, while *The Color Monster* provides a structured, color-coded framework for identifying and naming basic emotions.

Procedure The program lasted six weeks, with one weekly small-group meeting led by each novice teacher. Across the program, two books were read, and each book was presented in three consecutive sessions. In the **intervention group**, each session lasted approximately 30 min and included both SBR and guided emotional discourse. Following Bruner's holistic model (1986, 1990), the first reading emphasized the plot and characters (e.g., "*The tower Taylor built came crashing down*"). The second and third readings fostered deeper discussion about the characters' emotions (e.g., "*What does Taylor feel? What did the rabbit do to help Taylor?*")

and connections to children's own experiences (e.g., *"Have you ever felt proud? Would you like to tell us about it?"*).

Prior to the intervention, the novice teachers were introduced to the books and trained to conduct emotionally meaningful discussions. Training emphasized the use of open-ended questions, emotional elaborations, and responsive scaffolding, in line with effective emotion socialization principles (Bassett et al., 2020). For example: *"It's okay to feel frustrated—what do you think helped Taylor feel better?"* Such emotionally attuned responses aimed to help children reflect on feelings, link them to personal experiences, and develop **empathy**. In the **control group**, children also attended six weekly sessions, each lasting about 10 min. They listened to the same books but without emotional discourse or supportive conversation. Prior to and following the repeated reading meetings, the teachers evaluated the children's **empathy** (Strayer & Roberts, 2004) and language (Snow et al., 1989), which served as a control variable.

Empathy (Strayer, 1989; Strayer & Roberts, 2004)

This measure reflects children's ability to identify another's emotions, match their emotions to those of another, and explain their attributions. Children view 10 brief film vignettes referring to sadness, happiness, and anger from the television show "The Secret Life of Four-Year-Olds' '(e.g., a vignette showing a girl who is sad when separating from her parent when going to **preschool**). After watching each segment, the child is interviewed and asked: (1) How does the character in the film feel? What is the intensity of the character's feeling (low or high)? Why does he or she feel this way? (2) How do you feel after watching the segment? What is the intensity of your feeling (low or high)? And why? Children's answers are assessed on a 19-point scale that integrates the degree of affective sharing experienced (i.e., the degree of match between the child's own and the character's emotion) with the child's cognitive attribution for their own emotions. Affect match is coded on a 4-point scale, ranging from 0 = child felt no emotion (the same as usual) to 3 = the child's emotion and intensity are the same as the character's. The cognitive level of each attribution is coded on a 7-point scale, from a low level (0) = inaccurate identification of character's emotion, through medium level (3) = attributions based on events only (e.g., "The basement was scary"), to the highest level (7) = explicit statement of role taking (e.g., "I would be sad, too, in her place when my father leaves"). The effect match and cognitive attribution responses are integrated to yield an **empathy** continuum, with scores ranging from 0 to 19. Scores are derived for each clip and then averaged to form an overall **empathy** score. Inter-item reliability was Cronbach's α = 0.81. Reliability between two coders was Cohen's kappa = 0.75.

Expressive Vocabulary: Definitions Task (Snow, 1989)

The Hebrew adaptation of a definitions task (Aram & Levin, 2004) will be used to assess children's expressive vocabulary level. The task includes 14 lexical items (e.g., bicycle) presented in a fixed order. Children are asked for the meaning: "What is a bicycle?" Children's descriptions (e.g., "the bird chirps"), synonyms ("cap is also a hat"), comparisons (e.g., "A donkey is like a horse"), and functional characteristics (e.g., "You bang a nail into the wall") are summed across all 14 nouns. This serves as the definitions' score. Inter-item reliability was Cronbach's $\alpha = 0.91$.

Results

To verify the impact of the intervention on children's **empathy**, repeated measures analyses were conducted using generalized estimating equations (GEE). Time (pre- and post-intervention), group condition (intervention vs. control), and gender were included as fixed effects, with language ability entered as a covariate. In addition to the main effects, interaction terms between time and group and between time and gender were tested to examine differential changes in **empathy** across groups and genders over time. **Empathy** was assessed at two time points (pre- and post-intervention) for both the intervention and control groups. GEE was selected to account for the correlated nature of repeated measurements within individuals, providing population-averaged estimates while accommodating within-subject dependencies. An unstructured working correlation matrix was specified to avoid imposing assumptions about the pattern of correlations across time points. **Empathy** was modeled assuming a normal distribution and an identity link function. Wald chi-square tests were used to assess the significance of main effects and interactions. All analyses were conducted using [insert your statistical software and version, e.g., SPSS version 28.0]. Descriptive statistics are presented in Table 11.1.

The results indicated a significant main effect of time, $b = -0.38$, SE = 0.64, 95% CI [−1.62, 0.87], Wald $\chi^2(1) = 7.63$, $p = 0.006$, with **empathy** levels increasing from pre- to post-intervention. Specifically, mean **empathy** scores increased from 4.57 (SE = 0.48) to 5.90 (SE = 0.69) in the control group, and from 5.88 (SE = 0.60) to 7.15 (SE = 0.78) in the intervention group, suggesting overall improvement across both groups. An independent-samples t-test showed that **empathy** scores in the

Table 11.1 Empathy scores by group and gender (pre- and post-intervention)

	Pretest *M* (SE)	Post-test *M* (SE)
Empathy—Intervention	5.88 (0.60)	7.15 (0.78)
Empathy—Control	4.57 (0.48)	5.90 (0.69)
Empathy—Males	4.40 (0.50)	6.58 (0.73)
Empathy—Females	6.06 (0.59)	6.46 (0.76)
Language (overall)	1.10 (0.30)	–

pretest were higher in the intervention group than in the control group. This difference was not significant in the two-tailed test ($p = 0.063$) but reached significance in the one-tailed test ($p = 0.031$), Cohen's $d = 0.43$ (see Fig. 11.1 for a visual representation of the changes).

No significant main effects were observed for group, $b = -1.25$, SE = 1.05, 95% CI [−3.31, 0.81], Wald $\chi^2(1) = 2.53$, $p = 0.111$, or gender, $b = 0.12$, SE = 1.06, 95% CI [−1.96, 2.20], Wald $\chi^2(1) = 0.93$, $p = 0.334$. The time × group interaction was not significant (B = −0.06, SE = 0.94, p = 0.951), indicating that the increase in **empathy** did not differ between the intervention and control groups. A marginally significant time × gender interaction was found, $b = -1.78$, SE = 0.98, 95% CI [−3.70, 0.15], Wald $\chi^2(1) = 3.27$, $p = 0.071$, suggesting a tendency for males to improve more in **empathy** over time compared to females. Pairwise comparisons revealed that females had significantly higher **empathy** scores than males at pre-intervention ($p = 0.036$); however, post-intervention, males showed greater gains in **empathy**, surpassing females ($p = 0.024$). Specifically, males initially showed lower empathic abilities than females and greater progress in both groups after the intervention program (see Fig. 11.2). Pairwise comparisons revealed that females had significantly higher **empathy** scores than males at pre-intervention ($p = 0.036$); however, post-intervention, males showed greater gains in **empathy**, surpassing females ($p = 0.024$). These findings indicate that while no overall gender effect was found, differences emerged across time, with females starting higher but males showing steeper improvement.

There was a connection between language and **empathy** ($b = 3.40$* (1.62), 95% CI 0.21, 6.59]). Content analysis showed that the **novice preschool teachers** shared that the SBR intervention program taught them about emotion discourse to promote **empathy**, and they made use of it in diverse situations in the **preschool** setting. See Fig. 11.3 for a visual representation of the relationship between language ability and **empathy**.

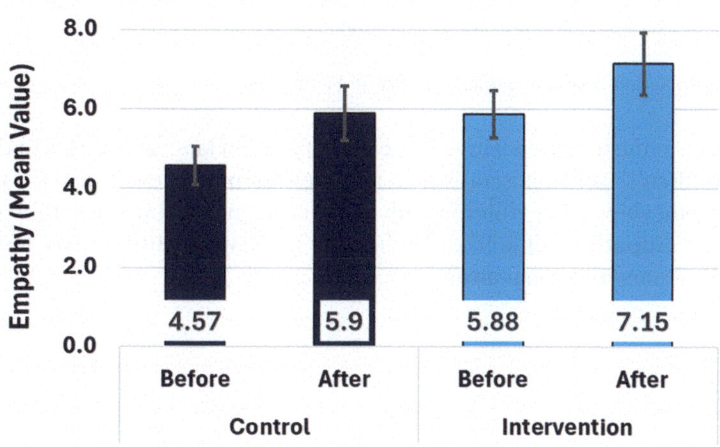

Fig. 11.1 Empathy scores by group and time

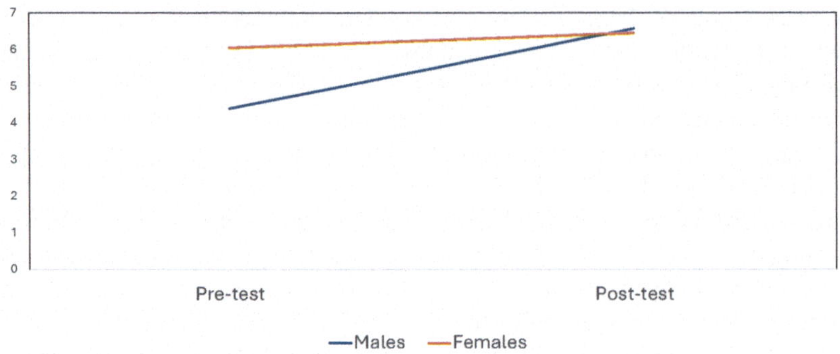

Fig. 11.2 Changes in empathy by gender from pre- to post-intervention

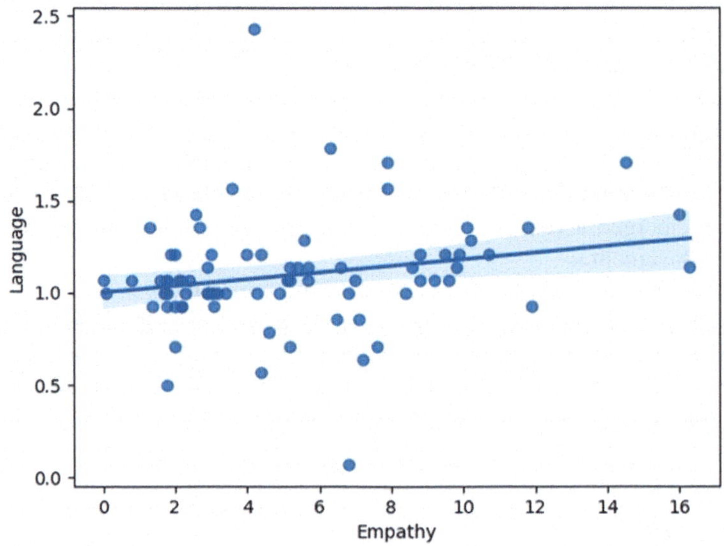

Fig. 11.3 Association between language ability and empathy

Figure 11.3 illustrates a positive association between language ability and **empathy**. As children's language scores increase, their **empathy** levels also tend to rise. The scatterplot shows that children with stronger language skills generally demonstrate higher **empathy**, while those with lower language ability display more variability in their empathic responses.

Discussion

This study examined the effects of short intervention program emphasizing emotional discourse during SBR on **preschoolers' empathy**, while also considering the role of gender and language ability. Novice teachers implemented the intervention through repeated reading of two emotionally rich picture books, combined with guided emotional discourse. **Empathy** was measured before and after the intervention in both the intervention and control groups. The findings provide support for the contribution of guided SBR sessions to the development of **empathy** in early childhood, while also highlighting important mechanisms and contextual factors that shape these outcomes.

Intervention Impact and Parallel Gains Across Groups

The main finding—a significant effect of time—demonstrated that children in both the intervention and control groups improved in **empathy** from pre- to post-intervention. Importantly, the group × time interaction was not statistically significant, indicating that gains were observed across both groups rather than being uniquely attributable to the guided SBR sessions.

A plausible explanation for these parallel gains lies in the structure of the intervention, in which each novice teacher worked with both an intervention and a control group. Although teachers were instructed to apply emotional discourse strategies only in the intervention sessions, it is reasonable to assume that the knowledge and practices they acquired during training could not be fully restricted. Thus, emotional discourse strategies may have been generalized and used spontaneously in daily **preschool** interactions with all children.

These informal applications—during play, transitions, and routines—could have supported emotional growth in the control group as well. This interpretation highlights the dual role of the teachers as learners of new practices and as active socializers of emotion, a process that was not fully under the researcher's control. It also resonates with Denham et al. (2017) and Ciucci et al. (2018), who emphasized early childhood teachers' broader role as emotional socializers, and underscores the ecological validity of emotion-focused interventions. These results further align with socio-constructivist theories (Vygotsky, 1978; Grusec & Davidov, 2010), which emphasize the role of adult scaffolding and language-mediated interaction in shaping children's understanding of emotions and others' perspectives. Moreover, SBR may have functioned not only as a structured literacy activity but also as a vehicle for emotional co-regulation and joint attention—affordances that novice teachers may have internalized and replicated in spontaneous interactions. It is also possible that the novice teachers, who practiced emotional discourse in the context of book-reading, extended this skill to a variety of naturally occurring situations throughout the **preschool** day. In this sense, shared book-reading became a meaningful opportunity for both teachers and children to engage in emotionally rich dialogue, fostering professional growth in the educators and emotional development in the children alike. The process of learning and practicing emotional discourse during the intervention may have contributed to the teachers' emerging professional identity as emotionally attuned educators. This aligns with recent studies on teacher identity development, which highlight how emotionally meaningful experiences in training promote internalization and generalization of pedagogical strategies (Zinsser et al., 2015; Jennings & Frank, 2015). In particular, emotionally grounded interactions with children—such as those practiced during SBR—can deepen teachers' emotional self-awareness and sensitivity to children's needs (Zinsser et al., 2023). Finally, the spillover effect observed here may point to the powerful role of emotional discourse itself—regardless of whether it is embedded in book-reading or in other social contexts. At the same time, the findings also underscore the inherent value of book-reading per se. Even children in the control group, who only listened to the books without guided discourse, showed gains in **empathy**. Notably, the control group started with lower baseline **empathy** scores, which may have provided them with greater room for improvement compared to the intervention group. This suggests that exposure to emotionally rich narratives can foster children's socio-emotional development, a conclusion consistent with previous studies linking the frequency of shared book-reading to children's emotional understanding and social competence (e.g., Aram & Aviram, 2009; Martin et al., 2022). From this perspective, the study highlights both the potential and the methodological challenge: it is difficult to fully separate intervention from control conditions when teachers are simultaneously acquiring and applying new practices. The presence of emotionally responsive, language-rich interactions may be a key mechanism through which **empathy** develops in young children, especially when modeled consistently by trusted adults.

Gender Differences and the Role of Emotional Discourse

A marginally significant time × gender interaction emerged, with boys showing greater improvements in **empathy** over time than girls (see Fig. 11.2). Given the relatively small group sizes in this study, the marginal effect should be interpreted with caution, as larger samples might have yielded clearer patterns. Although girls initially exhibited higher **empathy** levels (consistent with prior findings, e.g., Christov-Moore et al., 2014; Ornaghi et al., 2020), boys surpassed them post-intervention. These findings are aligned with prior studies suggesting that boys—who often begin with lower levels of emotional understanding—may benefit more from explicit, structured emotion discourse (Bassett et al., 2020). In this study, the combination of repeated readings of emotionally rich texts and scaffolded dialogue may have provided boys with opportunities to recognize, label, and reflect on emotions in a supportive, nonthreatening context. Narrative texts may serve as "emotionally safe spaces" where boys can explore and engage with emotions without threatening dominant masculine norms (Bosacki, 2008). This reflects a compensatory mechanism: children with lower empathic abilities at baseline—here, boys—reap greater benefits from interventions that emphasize emotional scaffolding. These results highlight the potential of structured emotional discourse to narrow gender gaps in **empathy** during early childhood and underscore the importance of tailoring emotional learning strategies to meet the needs of different learners.

Link Between Language and Empathy

A significant association between language and **empathy** suggests that children with stronger language abilities demonstrated higher levels of **empathy** (see Fig. 11.3). This finding aligns with previous research highlighting the interdependence of language development and socio-emotional competence (Kalland & Linnavalli, 2023; Ruffman et al., 2006). As language enables children to articulate emotional states, consider others' perspectives, and engage in mental-state discourse, it is not surprising that children with more advanced language skills displayed more empathic behavior. Moreover, the association between language and **empathy** underscores the developmental potential of books as cultural tools—comprising both spoken and written language—to promote young children's emotional and social development. Shared book-reading provides a symbolic and dialogic space in which children can explore emotional experiences, reflect on characters' feelings, and practice perspective-taking through adult-guided language use. This interpretation resonates with Vygotsky's (1978) sociocultural framework, which views language and storytelling as key mediators of higher-order psychological processes such as **empathy**.

Limitations

Despite these encouraging findings, the study has several limitations. First, the dual-role structure of novice teachers working with both intervention and control groups likely limited the ability to detect between-group differences. This overlap may have diluted the intervention's unique effect and introduced unintentional contamination of the control group. Future studies should consider assigning different teachers to each group or using classroom-level randomization.

Second, the relatively small group sizes and the brief duration of the intervention (six weeks), coupled with the absence of follow-up assessments, constrain the generalizability of the findings. While the program was intentionally short, it should be regarded as a preliminary step that highlights the potential of longer-term interventions to yield stronger and more sustainable effects.

Third, **empathy** was measured via teacher-reported scales rather than direct observations of empathic behavior. Although teacher ratings provide valuable insight, combining them with observational or physiological measures would allow for a more comprehensive understanding of the intervention's impact.

Educational Implications and Future Directions

This study highlights the importance of integrating emotional discourse into early childhood teacher education. When novice teachers are equipped with tools to scaffold emotional understanding, they can foster **empathy** development even beyond the boundaries of structured programs. Professional development should explicitly train educators in emotionally attuned communication, offering concrete strategies for initiating and sustaining meaningful emotional dialogue across diverse **preschool** contexts. The findings also suggest that emotionally rich shared reading experiences are uniquely powerful for cultivating **empathy**—particularly when paired with intentional, guided conversations. These contexts allow children to engage with emotional content through language and narrative structure, facilitating reflection and perspective-taking. The program's greater benefit for boys and for children with lower language skills underscores the need for differentiated and targeted interventions that help narrow early socio-emotional gaps.

Future research could explore the distinct impact of book features—such as narrative versus didactic structure, emotional valence (e.g., sadness vs. joy), and character type (human vs. animal)—on **empathy** outcomes, as proposed by Schapira et al. (2021). Longitudinal studies are also needed to assess whether gains in **empathy** are sustained over time and whether they translate into broader prosocial behavior and social integration.

Importantly, the positive outcomes observed in both groups suggest that novice teachers not only learned about emotional discourse but also internalized it, applying these tools across a range of daily **preschool** situations. This underscores the broader, indirect impact of emotionally focused teacher training—beyond the specific SBR intervention sessions.

Moreover, the program appeared particularly effective for children who initially displayed lower **empathy** levels. For these children, structured emotional discourse—delivered through emotionally rich stories—may serve as a critical support for developing emotional competencies. These findings reinforce the need for a comprehensive approach to socio-emotional development in early childhood education that goes beyond academic readiness.

Social-emotional learning (SEL) should be a core component of novice teacher training. Programs should include direct instruction, modeling, and practice in emotional discourse—both within and outside of book-reading. The ability to feel and express **empathy**, and to translate it into prosocial action, depends on the development of core emotional competencies: emotion understanding, regulation, and expressivity (Hay, 2019). When children develop deep emotional awareness and effective self-regulation, they are more likely to engage in caring, cooperative, and socially responsible behaviors—hallmarks of positive development in early childhood.

References

Aram, D., & Aviram, S. (2009). Mothers' storybook reading and kindergartners' socio-emotional and literacy development. *Reading Psychology, 30*(2), 175–194. https://doi.org/10.1080/02702710802275348

Aram, D., Fine, Y., & Ziv, M. (2013). Enhancing parent-child shared book reading interactions: Promoting references to the book's plot and socio-cognitive themes. *Early Childhood Research Quarterly, 28*(1), 111–122. https://doi.org/10.1016/j.ecresq.2012.03.005

Aram, D., & Levin, I. (2004). The role of maternal mediation of writing to kindergartners in promoting literacy in school: A longitudinal perspective. *Reading and Writing, 17*(4), 387–409. https://doi.org/10.1023/B:READ.0000032665.14437.e0

Aram, D., Ziv, M., Bergman Deitcher, D., & Sabag Shoshan, T. (2017). Shared book reading interactions within families from low socioeconomic backgrounds and children's social understanding and prosocial behavior. *Journal of Cognitive Education and Psychology, 16*(2), 157–177. https://doi.org/10.1891/1945-8959.16.2.157

Barr, J. J., & Higgins-D'Alessandro, A. (2007). Adolescent empathy and prosocial behavior in the multidimensional context of school culture. *The Journal of Genetic Psychology, 168*(3), 231–250. https://doi.org/10.3200/GNTP.168.3.231-250

Bassett, H. H., Denham, S. A., Mohtasham, M., & Austin, N. (2020). Psychometric properties of the book readings for an affective classroom education (BRACE) coding system. *Reading Psychology, 41*(4), 322–346. https://doi.org/10.1080/02702711.2020.1768980

Bosacki, S. L. (2008). *Children's emotional lives: Sensitive shadows in the classroom*. Peter Lang.

Brownell, C. A., Svetlova, M., Anderson, R., Nichols, S. R., & Drummond, J. (2013). Socialization of early prosocial behavior: Parents' talk about emotions is associated with sharing and helping in toddlers. *Infancy, 18(1), 91–119.* https://doi.org/10.1111/j.1532-7078.2012.00125.x

Bruner, J. S. (1986). *Actual minds, possible worlds*. Harvard University Press.

Bruner, J. S. (1990). *Acts of meaning*. Harvard University Press.

Christov-Moore, L., Simpson, E. A., Coudé, G., Grigaityte, K., Iacoboni, M., & Ferrari, P. F. (2014). Empathy: Gender effects in brain and behavior. *Neuroscience & Biobehavioral Reviews, 46*, 604–627. https://doi.org/10.1016/j.neubiorev.2014.09.001

Ciucci, E., Baroncelli, A., Toselli, M., & Denham, S. A. (2018). Personal and professional emotional characteristics of early childhood teachers and their proneness to communicate with parents and colleagues about children's emotions. *Child & Youth Care Forum, 47*, 303–316. https://doi.org/10.1007/s10566-017-9431-0

Denham, S. A. (2007). Dealing with feeling: How children negotiate the worlds of emotions and social relationships. *Cognition Brain & Behavior, 1*, 48. https://denhamlab.gmu.edu/Publications%20PDFs/Denham%202007.pdf

Denham, S. A. (2023). *Development of emotional competence in young children*. Guilford Publications.

Denham, S. A., Bassett, H. H., & Miller, S. L. (2017). Early childhood teachers' socialization of emotion: Contextual and individual contributors. *Child & Youth Care Forum, 46*, 805–824. https://doi.org/10.1007/s10566-017-9409-y

Denham, S. A., Ferrier, D. E., & Bassett, H. H. (2020). Preschool teachers' socialization of emotion knowledge: Considering socioeconomic risk. *Journal of Applied Developmental Psychology, 69*, 1–11. https://doi.org/10.1016/j.appdev.2020.101160

Denham, S., & Kochanoff, A. T. (2002). Parental contributions to preschoolers' understanding of emotion. *Marriage & Family Review, 34*(3–4), 311–343. https://doi.org/10.1300/J002v34n03_06

Depow, G. J., Francis, Z., & Inzlicht, M. (2021). The experience of empathy in everyday life. *Psychological Science, 32*(8), 1198–1213. https://doi.org/10.1177/0956797621995202

Eisenberg, N. (2000). Emotion, regulation, and moral development. *Annual Review of Psychology, 51*, 665–697. https://doi.org/10.1146/annurev.psych.51.1.665

Eisenberg, N., Fabes, R. A., & Spinrad, T. L. (2006). *Handbook of child psychology (Vol. 3, pp. 646–718). John Wiley & Sons.*

Eisenberg, N., Eggum-Wilkens, N. D., & Spinrad, T. L. (2015). The development of prosocial behavior. In D. A. Schroeder & W. G. Graziano (Eds.), *Oxford library of psychology. The Oxford handbook of prosocial behaviour* (pp. 114–136). Oxford University Press.

Fabes, R. A., Eisenberg, N., Karbon, M., Bernzweig, J., Speer, A. L., & Carlo, G. (1994). Socialization of children's vicarious emotional responding and prosocial behavior: Relations with mothers' perceptions of children's emotional reactivity. *Developmental Psychology, 30*, 44–55. https://doi.org/10.1037/0012-1649.30.1.44

Garner, P. W., & Parker, T. S. (2018). Young children's picture-books as a forum for socialization of emotion. *Journal of Early Childhood Research, 16*(3), 291–304. https://doi.org/10.1177/1476718X18775760

Grazzani, I., & Ornaghi, V. (2011). Emotional state talk and emotion understanding: A training study with preschool children. *Journal of Child Language, 38*(5), 1124–1139. https://doi.org/10.1017/S0305000910000772

Grusec, J. E., & Davidov, M. (2010). Integrating different perspectives on socialization theory and research: A domain-specific approach. *Child Development, 81*(3), 687–709. https://doi.org/10.1111/j.1467-8624.2010.01426.x

Hay, D. F. (2019). *Emotional development from infancy to adolescence: Pathways to emotional competence and emotional problems*. Routledge. https://doi.org/10.4324/9781315849454

Hindman, A. H., Skibbe, L. E., & Foster, T. D. (2014). Exploring the variety of parental talk during shared book reading and its contributions to preschool language and literacy: Evidence from the Early Childhood Longitudinal Study-Birth Cohort. *Reading and Writing, 27*, 287–313. https://doi.org/10.1007/s11145-013-9445-4

Hughes, C., Jaffee, S. R., Happé, F., Taylor, A., Caspi, A., & Moffitt, T. E. (2005). Origins of individual differences in theory of mind: From nature to nurture? *Child Development, 76*(2), 356–370. https://doi.org/10.1111/j.1467-8624.2005.00850_a.x

Jennings, P. A., & Frank, J. L. (2015). Inservice preparation for educators. In J. A. Durlak, C. E. Domitrovich, R. P. Weissberg, & T. P. Gullotta (Eds.), *Handbook of social and emotional learning: Research and practice (pp. 422–437). The Guilford Press.*

Kalland, M., & Linnavalli, T. (2023). Associations between social-emotional and language development in preschool children. Results from a study testing the rationale for an intervention. *Scandinavian Journal of Educational Research, 67*(5), 791–804. https://doi.org/10.1080/00313831.2022.2070926

Kelly, L. B., & Moses, L. (2018). Children's literature that sparks inferential discussions. *The Reading Teacher, 72*(1), 21–29. https://doi.org/10.1002/trtr.1675

Kisa, E. B., Sahin-Acar, B., & Ilgaz, H. (2023). Maternal storytelling and reminiscing styles in relation to preschoolers' perspective-taking abilities. *Cognitive Development, 66*, 101323. https://doi.org/10.1016/j.cogdev.2023.101323

Laible, D., & Song, J. (2006). Constructing emotional and relational understanding: The role of affect and mother-child discourse. *Merraill-Palmer Quarterly, 1982*, 44–69. https://doi.org/10.1353/mpq.2006.0006

Leyva, D., Catalan Molina, D., Suárez, C., Tamis-LeMonda, C. S., & Yoshikawa, H. (2021). Mother-child reminiscing and first-graders' emotion competence in a low-income and ethnically diverse sample. *Journal of Cognition and Development, 22*(4), 501–522. https://doi.org/10.1080/15248372.2021.1908293

Malti, T., Gummerum, M., Keller, M., & Buchmann, M. (2009). Children's moral motivation, sympathy, and prosocial behavior. *Child Development, 80*, 442–460. https://doi.org/10.1111/j.1467-8624.2009.01271.x

Malti, T., & Ongley, S. (2014). The development of moral emotions and moral reasoning. In M. Killen & J. Smetana (Eds.), *Handbook of moral development* (2nd ed., pp. 163–183). Psychology Press.

Martin, K. J., Beck, A. F., Xu, Y., Szumlas, G. A., Hutton, J. S., Crosh, C. C., & Copeland, K. A. (2022). Shared reading and risk of social-emotional problems. *Pediatrics, 149*(1), 1–11.

McArthur, D., Adamson, L., & Deckner, D. F. (2005). As stories become familiar: Mother-child conversations during shared reading. *Merrill-Palmer Quarterly, 51*(4), 389–411. https://doi.org/10.1353/mpq.2005.0025

McClure, E. B. (2000). A meta-analytic review of sex differences in facial expression processing and their development in infants, children, and adolescents. *Psychological Bulletin, 126*(3), 424–453. https://doi.org/10.1037/0033-2909.126.3.424

Mol, S. E., Bus, A. G., de Jong, M. T., & Smeets, D. J. H. (2008). Added value of dialogic parent–child book readings: A meta-analysis. *Early Education and Development, 19*(1), 7–26. https://doi.org/10.1080/10409280701838603

Neale, D., & Pino-Pasternak, D. (2017). A review of reminiscing in early childhood settings and links to sustained shared thinking. *Educational Psychology Review, 29*(3), 641–665. https://doi.org/10.1007/s10648-016-9376-0

Nickerson, A. B., Mele, D., & Princiotta, D. (2008). Attachment and empathy as predictors of roles as defenders or outsiders in bullying interactions. *Journal of School Psychology, 46*(6), 687–703. https://doi.org/10.1016/j.jsp.2008.06.002

Ornaghi, V., Conte, E., & Grazzani, I. (2020). Empathy in toddlers: The role of emotion regulation, language ability, and maternal emotion socialization style. *Frontiers in Psychology, 11*, 586862. https://doi.org/10.3389/fpsyg.2020.586862

Ornaghi, V., Grazzani, I., Cherubin, E., Conte, E., & Piralli, F. (2015). 'Let's Talk about Emotions!'. The effect of conversational training on preschoolers' emotion comprehension and prosocial orientation. *Social Development, 24*(1), 166–183. https://doi.org/10.1111/sode.12091

Pavlova, M., Graham, S. A., Peterson, C., Lund, T., Kennedy, M., Nania, C., & Noel, M. (2021). The socialization of young children's empathy for pain: The role of mother–and father–child reminiscing. *Journal of Pediatric Psychology, 46*(3), 314–323. https://doi.org/10.1093/jpepsy/jsaa107

Price, L. H., Van Kleeck, A., & Huberty, C. J. (2009). Talk during book sharing between parents and preschool children: A comparison between storybook and expository book conditions. *Reading Research Quarterly, 44*(2), 171–194. https://doi.org/10.1598/RRQ.44.2.4

Reschke, P. J., Clifford, B. N., Brown, M., Siufanua, M., Graver, H., Cooper, A. M., Porter, C. L., Stockdale, L. A., & Coyne, S. M. (2023). Links between parent–child conversations about emotions and changes in children's emotion knowledge across early childhood. *Child Development*. https://doi.org/10.1111/cdev.13960

Rochat, M. J. (2023). Sex and gender differences in the development of empathy. *Journal of Neuroscience Research, 101*(5), 718–729. https://doi.org/10.1002/jnr.25009

Ruffman, T., Slade, L., Devitt, K., & Crowe, E. (2006). What mothers say and what they do: The relation between parenting, theory of mind, language and conflict/cooperation. *British Journal of Developmental Psychology, 24*(1), 105–124. https://doi.org/10.1348/026151005X82848

Rumble, A. C., Van Lange, P. A., & Parks, C. D. (2010). The benefits of empathy: When empathy may sustain cooperation in social dilemmas. *European Journal of Social Psychology, 40*(5), 856–866. https://doi.org/10.1002/ejsp.659

Salmon, K., & Reese, E. (2016). The benefits of reminiscing with young children. *Current Directions in Psychological Science, 25*(4), 233–238. https://doi.org/10.1177/0963721416655100

Schapira, R., & Aram, D. (2020). Shared book reading at home and preschoolers' socio-emotional competence. *Early Education and Development, 31*(6), 819–837. https://doi.org/10.1080/10409289.2019.1692624

Schapira, R., Bergman Deitcher, D., & Aram, D. (2021). Variability and stability in parent–child discourse during and following repeated shared book reading. *Reading and Writing, 34*(1), 273–300. https://doi.org/10.1007/s11145-020-10072-y

Silveira Barbosa, M. C., Gobbato, C., & Boito, C. (2018). Play and interactions in didactic books for child education. *Acta Scientiarum. Education, 40*(2), 1–12.

Sipe, L. R. (2002). Talking back and talking over: Young children's expressive engagement during storybook read-aloud. *The Reading Teacher, 55*, 476–483. https://www.jstor.org/stable/20205086

Skinner, J., Livingston, T., & Oswald, H. (2016). *Play by design: The world of children's books*. Macmillan.

Spinrad, T. L., & Eisenberg, N. (2014). Empathy, prosocial behavior, and positive development in schools. In *Handbook of positive psychology in schools* (pp. 82–98). Routledge.

Strayer, J. (1989). What children know and feel in response to witnessing affective events. In C. Saarni & P. L. Harris (Eds.), *Children's understanding of emotion* (pp. 259–289). Cambridge University Press.

Strayer, J., & Roberts, W. L. (2004). *The empathy continuum scoring manual*. Simon Fraser University.

Thompson, R., Laible, D., & Ontai, L. (2003). Early understanding of emotion, morality, and self: Developing a working model. In R. V. Kail (Ed.), *Advances in child development and behavior* (pp. 139–172). Academic.
Tompkins, V., Bengochea, A., Nicol, S., & Justice, L. M. (2017). Maternal inferential input and children's language skills. *Reading Research Quarterly, 52*(4), 397–416. https://doi.org/10.1002/rrq.176
Uzefovsky, F., & Knafo-Noam, A. (2016). Empathy development throughout the lifespan. In J. Sommerville & J. Decety (Eds.), *Social cognition: Frontiers in developmental science series Psychology Press. Taylor and Francis Group.*
Valentino, K., Cummings, E. M., Borkowski, J., Hibel, L. C., Lefever, J., & Lawson, M. (2019). Efficacy of a reminiscing and emotion training intervention on maltreating families with preschool-aged children. *Developmental Psychology, 55*(11), 2365. https://psycnet.apa.org/doi/10.1037/dev0000792
Voltmer, K., & von Salisch, M. (2022). The feeling thinking talking intervention with teachers advances young children's emotion knowledge. *Social Development, 31*(3), 846–861. https://doi.org/10.1111/sode.12586
Vygosky, L. S. (1978). *Mind in society*. Harvard University Press. (Original work published 1930).
Waters, T. E., Camia, C., Facompré, C. R., & Fivush, R. (2019). A meta-analytic examination of maternal reminiscing style: Elaboration, gender, and children's cognitive development. *Psychological Bulletin, 145*(11), 1082–1102. https://doi.org/10.1037/bul0000211
Zinsser, K. M., Denham, S. A., Curby, T. W., & Shewark, E. A. (2015). Practice what you preach: Teachers' perceptions of emotional competence and emotionally supportive classroom practices. *Early Education and Development, 26, 899–919.* https://doi.org/10.1080/10409289.2015.1009320
Zinsser, K. M., Curby, T. W., Gordon, R. A., & Moberg, S. (2023). A unidimensional model of emotion-focused teaching in early childhood. *Learning Environments Research, 26*(3), 933–949. https://doi.org/10.1007/s10984-023-09461-1

Rotem Schapira, PhD, is a researcher, lecturer, and pedagogical counselor at the Academic College Levinsky-Wingate and the Bob Shapell School of Social Work at Tel Aviv University. Her work focuses on early childhood socio-emotional development, caregivers' emotional discourse, and evidence-based interventions such as shared book-reading to promote empathy, prosocial behavior, and values. She collaborates internationally and leads cross-cultural studies and intervention programs.

Chapter 12
Co-Woven Storytelling with Persona Dolls: Promoting Social Justice and Shared Life in Israel

Margalit Ziv and Tamar Verete

Contents

Introduction

Ten Israeli **Persona Dolls** (PDs)—child-like dolls, representing children from diverse backgrounds, "visit" Israeli kindergartens. Figure 12.1 displays the dolls. Just imagine how many diverse stories they can tell about their lives and communities. Here is one example: *Yasin and his grandmother arrived at the mall in Be′er Sheva. Yassin eagerly pulled his grandmother toward the toy store—she had*

M. Ziv (✉)
Kaye Academic College of Education, Beersheba, Israel
e-mail: margalitziv@gmail.com

T. Verete
David Yellin College of Education, Jerusalem, Israel
e-mail: Tamar.verete@gmail.com

R. Schapira, D. Aram (eds.), *Shared Book Reading and Children's Social-Emotional Competence*, https://doi.org/10.1007/978-3-032-14688-5_12

Fig. 12.1 The Israeli **Persona Dolls**. From left to right: Gil a Jewish boy from a Sephardi background, Shahar a Jewish Ethiopian descendant girl, Amir a Druz boy, Mila an Israeli Arab Christian girl, Naomi a Jewish Ultra-Orthodox religious girl, Rona a Jewish secular girl, Yasin, an Israeli Bedouin Muslim boy, Nur an Israeli Arab Muslim girl, Tom a Jewish boy from former Soviet Union, and Noam a Jewish religious boy (https://www.g4f.co.il/)

promised to buy him a tractor for his birthday. But as they entered, he noticed something unsettling. The embroidered dress and the veil that left only her eyes visible seemed to attract silent yet unmistakable stares from those around them. The store, which had moments earlier promised excitement, now felt unfamiliar and tense. Yassin no longer wanted the tractor; instead, he longed to leave and return home.

Yasin's moment of discomfort is not unique to the Bedouin, Muslim PD. It encapsulates the subtle, yet powerful ways in which children experience and internalize social hierarchies, biases, and exclusions. Children's literature plays a crucial role in shaping how young readers understand identity, belonging, and otherness (e.g., Wild, 2024). Yet, in societies where segregation is deeply embedded in social structures—including education, media, and cultural production—literature often reflects, rather than challenges, these divisions. In Israel, children's literature largely mirrors the country's stratified reality: secular Jewish children are rarely exposed to books portraying Orthodox Jewish life, and vice versa; Jewish children seldom encounter Palestinian narratives, and Israeli Palestinian children are equally unlikely to see themselves in Hebrew literature (Ḥaj Yaḥya, 2021). Stories that could serve as bridges between communities instead reinforce mutual ignorance and, consequently, deepen social biases.

In response to this challenge, we propose co-weaving literature—a new **storytelling** model, emerging from our work with the Persona Doll Approach (PDA). The PDA aims to educate children in the appreciation of diversity and shared life. Our model is situated within broader discussions on multicultural education, **education for shared life**, and social–emotional learning through book-reading with children. However, unlike conventional children's literature, which is primarily authored by adults for children, this approach integrates multiple voices—parents, social activists, educators, and children—into a collaborative narrative-creation process. Thus, Yasin's story, based on a real-life event, can be continued by children and adults from varied socio-cultural groups in Israel, creating diverse and varied versions of it. The different versions can then serve as the foundation for a written story,

Our metaphor of co-weaving **storytelling** has emerged from Bishop's metaphors of multicultural literature as mirrors, windows, and sliding glass doors. According to Bishop, for children to be enriched and empowered by literature, they must see themselves reflected in stories, encounter the lives of others, and access a world shaped by diverse voices, equity, and justice (Cahill & Joo, 2021). In our view, these metaphors aptly apply to the PDA.

To the best of our knowledge, the theoretical and practical link between Bishop's model and the PDA has not yet been explored. Thus, we will introduce both frameworks, highlighting their unique contributions and illustrating how Bishop's literary concepts extend into the narrative-based practices of the PDA. We also draw on additional theoretical foundations of the PDA and then zoom in to the context of Israeli society. We aim to show how the co-woven **storytelling** model not only reimagines the boundaries of children's literature but also cultivates intergroup understanding through lived, co-constructed narratives in a deeply divided society.

Narrative Encounters with Diversity: Integrating Bishop's Framework and the PDA

Bishop's seminal metaphors—mirrors, windows, and sliding glass doors—articulate the inclusive and transformative role of literature in young children's lives (Bishop, 1990). Books function as mirrors when they reflect children's identities, affirming their sense of self and belonging, as windows when they provide insight into the lives of others, fostering empathy and appreciation of diversity, and as sliding glass doors when they invite children to imaginatively enter new worlds and perspectives (Waller & Sullivan-Walker, 2023).

For children from marginalized backgrounds, mirror experiences are essential in countering invisibility and affirming identity (Mansour & Martin, 2020). For those from dominant groups, literature functions as a window into others' lives, challenging stereotypes and expanding worldviews. Bishop emphasized that children from majority cultures often find mirrors in books but suffer from limited exposure to others' realities—a gap multicultural literature aims to address.

Although Bishop's model was originally developed in the context of written texts, its conceptual power extends to the PDA—a **storytelling**-based, anti-bias pedagogy addressing identity, prejudice, and human rights (Morris, 2023; Smith, 2013; Jesuvadian & Wright, 2011). The PDA originated in the 1950s with Kay Taus, a U.S. nursery teacher, as a response to racial prejudice among white children in her classroom (Smith, 2013). Since then, the approach has been implemented in multiple countries, for example, South Africa (Smith, 2013), Australia (MacNaughton & Davis, 2001; Sheppard, 2021), Greece (Al-Jubeh & Vitsou, 2021), and Northern Ireland (FitzPatrick, 2023), with adaptations to local contexts. For instance, in South

Africa, PDs address racism, gender inequality, and linguistic exclusion; in Australia, they support positive attitudes toward Indigenous Australians; and in Greece, they help foster empathy toward Syrian refugees.

PDs provide mirrors by presenting composite stories drawn from authentic experiences, including those of marginalized children. These stories include culturally specific events, family dynamics, and emotional struggles. When children encounter a doll whose story resonates with their own, they gain affirmation, recognition, and a sense of belonging. PDs create mirrors in a dynamic manner that is shaped by educators' choices and children's interactions, creating space for identification and self-expression.

For children from different backgrounds, PD narratives function as windows, offering glimpses into unfamiliar lived experiences—often touching on topics absent from formal curricula, such as poverty, displacement, or discrimination. Furthermore, PDs function as sliding glass doors. As children listen, respond, and co-create the evolving story, they are invited to inhabit new perspectives imaginatively—not as passive observers but as active participants. This process cultivates agency, moral reasoning, empathy, and social engagement.

The teacher plays a pivotal role in this process. By voicing the doll's story and fostering a safe, open atmosphere, the educator enables children to explore complex issues while sharing their own thoughts and experiences. PDs are not puppets nor toys for dramatic play; they act as consistent classroom participants—joining children in **storytelling**, singing, playing, and reflection (Wilkinson & Wilkinson, 2022).

The PDA thus offers a dynamic and dialogically constructed pedagogy where mirrors, windows, and sliding glass doors are not static representations. Rather, the stories are actively embodied and co-constructed within the educational encounter.

Theoretical Foundations of the PDA

Along with its strong links to Bishop's approach, the PDA is firmly grounded in additional theoretical frameworks, which complement each other. One of its key foundations is the multicultural education theory developed by Banks (Banks, 1993, 2015). According to Banks, the ultimate goal of multicultural education is to foster social transformation and establish an equitable and just society. Within this framework, the education system is envisioned as a catalyst for change, operating through several interrelated processes: Content Integration—incorporating diverse perspectives and voices into the curriculum; Equity Pedagogy—employing teaching strategies that support the academic success of all students; Empowering School Culture—restructuring school systems to promote social justice and equity; Prejudice Reduction—facilitating the development of positive attitudes toward various social, racial, and cultural groups; and Social Justice and Action—encouraging students to actively engage in addressing societal inequalities.

Banks' approach to multicultural education aligns closely with Bishop's concept of multicultural literature. They share a social justice perspective and emphasize the importance of fostering socio-cultural understanding and equity among children. While Banks focuses on transforming educational practices at a systemic level, Bishop highlights the use of literature as a powerful medium for exposing children to diverse voices and experiences. Together, their perspectives underscore the significance of providing children with means to critically engage with and address societal inequities.

Another foundational pillar of the PDA is Developmental Psychology. The PDA provides developmentally appropriate content by addressing children's evolving attitudes toward in-groups and out-groups, as well as their linguistic, socio-emotional, cognitive, and moral capacities. During early childhood, children gradually become aware of similarities and differences among individuals based on characteristics such as skin color, language, gender, socioeconomic status, and nationality (Aboud & Doyle, 1996). They also develop an understanding of the social and personal implications of these differences (Nesdale et al., 2010). Additionally, this developmental period is marked by significant growth in children's theory of mind (Selcuk et al., 2023), empathy, and other social skills, enabling them to consider perspectives that differ from their own and to recognize situations involving injustice and unfairness (Aram & Ziv, 2024). Importantly, negative social attitudes toward outgroups are more likely to develop when children are exposed to negative cues from adults, peers, or when the out-group is perceived as threatening, highlighting the powerful role of environmental messages in shaping intergroup attitudes from an early age.

Social Psychology, particularly theories and concepts related to intergroup relations, provides another critical theoretical foundation for the PDA. Social Identity Theory highlights the human tendency to categorize the world into "us" (in-group) and "them" (out-group), emphasizing the inherent need to belong to social groups (Harwood, 2021). This categorization often results in a preference for in-groups, which, in certain contexts, can manifest as rejection, hostility, or even racism toward out-groups.

Furthermore, Social Dominance Theory posits that societies tend to organize themselves hierarchically, with power dynamics between groups. According to this theory, groups in positions of power frequently construct moral and intellectual justifications for maintaining discriminatory and unequal systems. Both theories underpin key processes addressed by the PDA, such as the development of stereotypes, biases, exclusion, discrimination, and racism (Nesdale & Lawson, 2011).

Diversity in Israeli Society

Israel was established in 1948 as the homeland of the Jewish people. Its Declaration of Independence affirms a commitment to freedom, justice, peace, and full equality of social and political rights for all citizens, regardless of religion, race, or sex (Knesset, 1948).

As of 2024, Israel's population is nearing 10 million. Jews make up approximately 74%, and Arabs make up 21%. The two groups differ in language, religion, culture, and residential patterns. Among Jewish citizens, 65% identify as secular (including traditional nonreligious), 25% as religious, and 10% as Orthodox. Within the Arab population, 93% are Muslim, 7% are Christian, and the remainder are from other faiths (Central Bureau of Statistics, 2023).

Most Jewish citizens are immigrants or descendants of immigrants who arrived over the past century. They belong to four major subgroups: Jews of European and American origin (Ashkenazim), Jews from Asian and African countries (Sephardim), post-1989 immigrants from the former Soviet Union, and Ethiopian immigrants who arrived in the late 1980s and early 1990s. These groups vary in traditions, religiosity, socioeconomic status, and political orientation. While this diversity contributes to cultural richness, it also generates inequality and social friction (Aram & Ziv, 2024).

The most fundamental divide, however, is between Israeli Jewish and Arab citizens, shaped by the protracted Israeli–Palestinian conflict (Bar-Tal et al., 2017). Contentious issues—particularly territorial disputes—have persisted since 1948. This chapter is being written amid the ongoing war that began on October 7, 2023, involving Israel, Hamas in Gaza, and Hezbollah in Lebanon.

Israel's sociocultural diversity is evident in its segmented education system, which includes four tracks: state secular, state religious, state Arab, and independent Orthodox. State schools follow a mandated core curriculum. Yet, state religious schools allocate 40% of instructional hours to religious studies. Arab schools teach in Arabic and incorporate Arab language, holidays, and traditions (Government of Israel, 1953). Independent Orthodox schools do not follow the Ministry of Education guidelines. A small number of bilingual schools offer a rare exception—providing joint education for Jewish and Arab children in both languages and promoting mutual understanding and dialogue (Bekerman & Horenczyk, 2004).

Segregation is also evident in children's literature. Each group is typically exposed only to books that reflect their own norms and lifestyle. Secular children rarely encounter stories about ultra-Orthodox life and vice versa; similarly, Jewish and Palestinian children do not encounter each other's literature (Segev, 2013). Books depicting shared spaces or interactions between Jews, Arabs, secular, and religious characters are rare (Yahya, 2024). Rather than fostering cross-group understanding, children's literature often reinforces social separation.

This systemic segregation and protracted intergroup tension contribute to the early emergence of intergroup bias. By age 5, Israeli children from both secular and religious backgrounds already exhibit in-group preferences and out-group biases, particularly toward Ethiopian and Arab peers (Nasie et al., 2021). They show a preference for playing with in-group members, attribute more positive traits to them, and express greater empathy for them.

In light of the multidimensional divisions within the Israeli society, its segregated education, and the early emergence of negative intergroup attitudes, there is a need for age-appropriate educational programs to alleviate children's biases and create an alternative, more inclusive, and hopeful worldview. The PDA has been implemented in Israel, to address this challenge.

Implementation of the PDA in Israel

When observing the 10 Israeli PDs sitting side by side (Fig. 12.1), one may recognize that such a scene is rare in Israeli reality. However, from the perspective of young children, this vision may seem possible and attainable. Bringing this vision to life is the goal we, the authors of this chapter, along with our like-minded colleagues, strive to achieve.

The first seven PDs in Israel—four girls and three boys—were created in 2018 by the Israeli NGO *Games for the Future* (G4F) (G4F website). Established in 2017, G4F aims to foster respect for diversity among young children. The organization now operates under the auspices of the A-Chord Center: Social Psychology for Social Change, at the Hebrew University of Jerusalem (https://www.achord.org.il/en.). Between 2023 and 2024, three additional dolls (two boys and one girl) were added, bringing the total to ten.

Each doll was designed through focus groups representing the diversity of Israeli society. Ultra-Orthodox, Bedouin, Ethiopian, and other community representatives shaped dolls that embody their group's cultural identity, values, and lived experiences (Verete et al., 2022). Measuring about 80 cm tall and made of soft fabric, the dolls are introduced not as group representatives but as unique individuals with distinct stories. They function as **storytelling** catalysts, helping children explore both familiar and unfamiliar cultural narratives (Ziv, 2023).

A study by Nasie et al. (2021) examined the PDA's impact on 109 kindergarteners from secular and religious Jewish communities. Over 4 weeks, children were introduced to four PDs from diverse backgrounds. The findings revealed increased knowledge of other groups and greater openness to interacting with out-group peers, especially Israeli Arabs and Jews of Ethiopian descent. Children also recognized a shared Israeli identity across the dolls. These results highlight the PDA's potential to reduce prejudice, while pointing to the need for further research on flexible, teacher-led implementation.

Teachers' Role and Perspectives

Recognizing teachers' central role in the PDA, approximately 300 Israeli educators have participated in comprehensive professional development courses. The 30–60-h courses focus on reflective practice (exploring teachers' sociocultural identities), theoretical and pedagogical foundations of the PDA, and challenges of implementation—offering space for open dialogue and shared inquiry (Ziv, 2023).

Teachers' perspectives are vital for understanding what works, how, and why. Accordingly, qualitative research has accompanied PDA's implementation in Israel, including interviews and analysis of teachers' documentation. In one study, 12 teachers were interviewed to explore the topics they introduced to children through the PDs' stories (Ziv, 2023). Teachers emphasized PDA's flexibility in responding to children's interests while gradually addressing complex topics. Stories often included personal anecdotes from the PDs' everyday lives and families, authentically and non-stereotypically incorporating cultural and community elements, as well as challenging societal issues. For example, one teacher shared a story about Tom who was anxious because his family had recently moved to a new apartment far from his Russian-speaking friends. Another teacher used Shahar's story to discuss racism, recounting how Shahar's brother was racially bullied by children at a playground. Teachers reported that children's curiosity was often the starting point as they asked questions about the PDs' lives and cultural customs, such as Nur's Ramadan traditions. These stories enhanced children's knowledge and sparked rich classroom discussions, promoted empathy, solidarity, and attempts to support the dolls.

Expanding the Scope and Impact of the PDA Stories—Co-Weaving Stories

Closely working with teachers increased our fascination with the rich, creative, collaborative **storytelling** that has emerged during the implementation of the PDA in Israel. Since the PDA's introduction to Israeli Kindergartens, educators have shared with us numerous original and authentic stories that the PDs shared with children. These narratives have revealed the potential that extends beyond their oral delivery to a specific group of children. By highlighting and integrating the diverse and meaningful components of these stories, we believe they could evolve into a unique genre of children's literature—one that offers children "mirrors" to see reflections of their own lives, "windows" to gain insight into others' experiences, and "sliding glass doors" to step into new perspectives and worlds.

As with any narrative structure, the PD **Storytelling** framework includes three key elements: the protagonist—the central character of the story; the conflict or dilemma—the challenge the protagonist faces, and the process of resolution—the journey toward solving the conflict. However, unlike traditional **storytelling** practices, where the storyteller solely guides the narrative, PD **Storytelling** is a unique, collaborative process, involving multiple participants.

The Five Voices in the Storytelling Fabric

In PDA **storytelling**, five distinct voices are interwoven to create each narrative. The first voice belongs to the focus groups—social activists, professionals, and parents from the doll's identity group—who collaboratively shape the doll's persona. This voice serves as the "warp" thread: a cultural backbone that grounds the doll's identity in authentic lived experiences.

The second voice is that of the teachers. Guided by pedagogical and personal considerations, the teacher selects a doll and introduces a "trigger story"—a short narrative that poses a dilemma, e.g., about Rona whose younger sister prefers to play with her brother's cars than draw with her. These stories may originate from the teacher, the existing PDA story collection, children's input, and/or real-life events. Once selected, the teacher adopts the doll's voice, setting aside the conventional adult-didactic stance.

The third voice is the PS's. Though voiced by the teacher, the doll expresses itself as a peer—not as an authority figure. Cultural elements emerge subtly through the doll's expressions rather than explicit labeling. For example, a Haredi doll might mention that only girls attend her kindergarten or that her brother studies in a Yeshiva—revealing her background through personal experience, not declaration.

The fourth voice is that of the children. Most children quickly recognize the difference between conversations with the teacher and dialogues with the PD. With the doll, they more often express unfiltered emotions, e.g., anger, embarrassment, and pride, without fear of judgment. The PD invites them to elaborate, allowing deeper layers of thought and feeling to emerge. These dynamics foster empathy, social justice, and inclusion (Dimitiradi, 2015). For example, in Yasin's story, the doll recounts his reluctance to buy the toy tractor due to embarrassment over his grandmother's traditional Bedouin dress. Children responded with emotional solidarity: "Ignore them and buy the tractor," or "That happened to me! My Ethiopian grandma wore her dress, and I hugged her and stuck my tongue out at the people staring."

Finally, the fifth voice is ours, the authors. Drawing on stories from classrooms across Israel, we document, edit, and share co-woven narratives with the broader educational community. These stories reflect the PDA's core principles and values: authentic dialogue, critical thinking about social power, empathy, equity, justice, and activism.

The following example illustrates how the five voices interact in practice: Focus groups shape Gil, a North African Jewish PD who loves to dance to Oriental music like his mother. The PD "says" that some peers mock him, saying he "dances like a girl." The teacher presents Gil's problem to the class, allowing the children to co-construct its resolution. Children respond with their own experiences and suggestions. In some cases, the PD selects one of their suggestions to conclude the tale—though the final thread often remains loose, encouraging further **storytelling**.

If we imagine the story as a piece of weaving, the final thread in the trigger story remains loose, inviting children to continue weaving the story further. Since every kindergarten group reacts differently, each **storytelling** session results in a unique narrative. When we, as writers, compile a written version of a story, we draw from multiple **storytelling** sessions across different kindergartens. We attempt to craft a short, engaging narrative based on the diverse versions we collect.

Themes That Have Emerged in the PD Storytelling

As Gil's story illustrates, each PD has a distinct cultural identity and a unique story, rooted in Israeli society. Yet the themes that emerge from their stories are often universal. Below, we outline key themes and provide illustrative examples that highlight the educational potential of the co-woven **storytelling** genre.

Everyday Kindergarten Conflicts

When the PD (through the teacher) introduces a familiar daily conflict in the trigger story, it encourages discussion—one that extends beyond the typical normative dialogue in the classroom. For example, is there a kindergarten where children don't argue over seating? *"That was my chair!" "You took my spot!" "I want to sit next to her!"* (Of course, conflicts over "place" are not limited to kindergarten—they lie at the heart of broader social and political disputes, both in Israel and beyond (Gurevitch, 2007).

Rona, the PD, shares: *"Yesterday, during circle time, she wanted to sit next to Lihi. But Michal and Sigal had already taken the seats beside her. She was so sad she couldn't even listen to the story. What should she do if this happens again?"* Children first offered standard solutions: "Ask nicely," "Take turns," "Save a seat." But when Rona pressed for more ideas, Shai suggested: *"Let's arrange the chairs like a zipper—Sigal can move her chair forward, Lihi moves back, and Rona can sit in the middle!"* Rona enthusiastically accepted the idea, sparking a broader classroom conversation about fairness and flexibility in seating arrangements. A story inspired by this moment might be titled *"The Kindergarten Where the Seating Changed Every Day."*

Shame

Shame often arises from internalized social norms and unmet expectations, especially around appearance, language, or economic status (Laurén & Malinen, 2021). A kindergarten teacher in an underprivileged community used Naomi, a Haredi PD, to introduce the topic: *"Naomi didn't want to join the Purim celebration. Her parents couldn't afford a new Queen Esther costume, so she had to wear a second-hand one from the Gemach. She felt ashamed."* The teacher explained that for years she had wanted to discuss economic hardship with children, but she had struggled to find the right way to approach the subject. When the PDs arrived in her classroom, she finally found a way—through Naomi.

Children responded with empathy, sharing similar experiences. They suggested practical solutions: saving money, making or borrowing a costume, or collecting bottles for deposits. Then, one girl offered a fresh take: *"Why be Queen Esther? She had to marry a stupid king. What's the point of being a queen if you don't love your king?"* She suggested Naomi dress as a doctor using classroom props. Naomi loved the idea. A written version of this story might be titled *"This Year, Naomi Won't Be Queen Esther."*

Fear and Anxiety

Like children everywhere, Israeli children experience fear and anxiety—but these feelings are intensified by the ongoing Israeli–Palestinian conflict. For Palestinian citizens of Israel, the fear is compounded by concern for loved ones on both sides of the border and the lack of adequate shelters in many communities (Huesmann et al., 2023).

During the current war, Noam, a religious PD, shared: *"There's no safe room in our apartment, so when the siren goes off, he runs with his family to the public shelter. He's scared to go to sleep because it might happen at night—and he's still scared even when they get there."*

Noam's story opened the door for children to share their own fears, like hearing alarms while in the shower, and the small comforts that help them cope: snacks, games, or music. One child suggested: *"Noam, what if every time there's a siren, your mom shows you a bit of The Lion King? Then you'll still be scared—but also excited to see what happens next."* Noam expanded on the idea: *"Or maybe a soccer game! I'll ask to watch a few minutes every time we go to the shelter."* A story based on this session might be titled *"Noam Looks Forward to Sitting in the Shelter."*

Standing Strong

This story did not begin with a teacher-planned trigger but emerged spontaneously when Marcel, the teacher, introduced Nur, a Muslim PD, to a Jewish kindergarten class. One child mocked her name, calling her "Nurofen" (a pain-relief medication), prompting laughter from the class. Marcel, visibly upset, removed Nur from the room.

During recess, Marcel confided in one of this chapter's authors. The incident had triggered a painful memory: on her first day of kindergarten, her teacher suggested her father change her name to a Hebrew one. Marcel, then a young child, feared her name was being taken from her. Fortunately, her father refused.

The Hebraization of names—both private and surnames—has a long history in Israel. Israel's first Prime Minister, David Ben-Gurion, demanded that public figures adopt Hebrew names, and government clerks often assigned new names to immigrants (Landman, 2018). Still today, Ethiopian families are encouraged to give their children Hebrew names deemed easier to pronounce.

The author encouraged Marcel to share her story with the children, explaining why Nur's name mattered and why the laughter hurt. The following story was shaped by the personal experiences of Nur and Marcel, as well as by the children's reflections and conversation after hearing Nur's voice.

Nur and Sveta: One Big Light

Nur knew everyone at Science Camp would speak Hebrew and that she would be the only Arab girl. Still, she was determined. One day, she would become a scientist and find cures for serious diseases—just like the ones her grandmother made from plants at home.

When Nur arrived with her father, she introduced herself: "My name is Nur." Some children laughed. The counselor turned to her father: "Maybe she should use a more familiar name—like Nurit? Then the kids won't laugh at her."

"My name is Nur, not Nurit!" Nur said, shaking her head.

Her father bent down and whispered in Arabic, "*Habibti, do you want to come home? I'm not sure this camp is right for you. Come back with me—you can go to camp in our village instead.*"

After her father left, Nur felt her eyes filled with tears. She curled up on a big cushion in the camp's library, resting her head on her knees. "*Why does the counselor want me to change my name? Maybe I* ***should*** *change it? If I have a different name, will I have two names—one for camp and one for home? No! My name is who I am. With a new name, I'll be someone else…*".

Suddenly, Nur felt the cushion shift—someone had sat down beside her. It was Orit. Quietly, Orit asked, "*Are you sure you don't want to change your name to Nurit?*"

Nur shook her head again, this time even more firmly.

Orit didn't say anything. She sat next to Nur in silence.

When the counselor called all the children to watch a science experiment, Nur lifted her head and turned to Orit.

"*Nur in Arabic means 'light'—just like your name,*" she said.

Orit's eyes widened. She leaned in and whispered, "*You know, back in Ukraine, my name was Sveta. Sveta means 'light' in Russian. When we moved to Israel, they changed my name to Orit. No one even asked if I wanted to change it. They just called me Orit. And that was that.*"

The two girls sat together in silence until the counselor called again, *"Nur and Orit, come join us*".

Nur turned to Orit and smiled. But Orit shook her head.

"From now on, my name is Sveta. Just Sveta." She said to the counselor and to the children. And the two girls sat side by side.

Discussion

Israeli society is both richly diverse and deeply divided, fraught by complex sociocultural and political realities. Children's literature in Israel rarely aligns with Bishop's model of *Mirrors, Windows, and Sliding Glass Doors*; instead, it often reinforces existing social hierarchies and mutual biases.

In response, we have proposed *co-woven* ***storytelling***—a new literary genre emerging from s**torytelling** with PDs. This approach reconfigures traditional adult–child power dynamics, transforming all participants into co-creators of narratives that foster empathy, agency, and social awareness.

Grounded in the premise that every child and community have a story to tell (Banks, 2015; Derman-Sparks et al., 2023), co-woven stories originate in children's lived experiences. Whether sparked by a commonly silenced voice or a seemingly minor classroom conflict, stories such as Naomi's shame over her costume, Gil's joy in dancing, or Rona's seating dilemma illustrate how children's emotions and social realities become meaningful points of entry. Sensitive issues—poverty, racism, war, language, and gender—are not avoided but embraced as opportunities for dialogue, problem-solving, and perspective-taking (Domingues, 2021).

At the heart of the model is a five-voiced narrative process. The identity group's voice shapes each doll's persona through cultural, linguistic, and familial lenses. The teacher introduces a culturally embedded "trigger story" and assumes the doll's voice to engage children. Children respond, reframe, and redirect the narrative, allowing their emotional insights to guide the story's development. Finally, authors and experts in PDA synthesize these contributions into written texts that preserve the dialogic richness of the live exchange. This polyphonic process creates a counter-narrative to dominant, linear, adult-authored literature. Co-woven stories become democratic texts, authored through interaction, grounded in diverse voices, and reflective of children's social worlds.

The above-mentioned process has the potential of profoundly supporting children's socio-emotional development and wellbeing. The process promotes empathy and encourages suggestions for creative and innovative resolutions to difficulties—all core components of healthy social development (Denham et al., 2007). Importantly, the dolls' mediated voices invite children to experience diversity in a nonthreatening manner. This often leads to moments of closeness and identification—even when the doll's identity differs markedly from the child's own. Such was the experience of Sveta, of Russian origin and Nur, from a Muslim family, who discovered their connection across difference and the power of their togetherness.

Furthermore, grounding stories in real-life experiences has promoted agency and social change within classrooms. In Rona's story, where she could not sit next to her friend, children not only empathized but suggested a "zipper" seating arrangement. The class adopted this idea, prompting a broader reconsideration of spatial norms. This example highlights the transformative potential of co-woven **storytelling** to reshape actual social practices, already in early childhood, in an age-appropriate manner.

Aligned with research on young children's awareness of social identity (e.g., Nesdale et al., 2010), the process supports both marginalized and dominant-group children. For marginalized children, it provides affirming representation and fosters self-worth and belonging. For dominant-group children, it cultivates critical awareness and emotional engagement with unfamiliar experiences. In this dialogic space, all children become co-authors of a narrative that reflects the society they inhabit and also portrays an improved version of the society they live in.

Bishop's Model in Action

Bishop's (1990) influential metaphors of mirrors, windows, and sliding glass doors provide a foundational lens through which to understand the PDA as a means for affirming identity, fostering empathy, and opening children to unfamiliar perspectives. Co-woven **storytelling** applies Bishop's literary metaphors in lived, participatory practice. Rather than relying solely on pre-authored texts, it offers a dynamic, child-centered form of narrative construction that is responsive to context, current events, and emotional nuance, making it particularly suited to diverse and divided communities, including in times of crisis.

In co-woven stories, children encounter reflections of their lives through open-ended, evolving dilemmas, voiced by PDs that represent authentic cultural identities, and real-life experiences and dilemmas. The mirrors are not static but co-created, allowing **children's voices**, emotions, and meaning-making to shape the story in real time.

As windows, the stories become dialogic encounters, rather than merely literary openings. When Jewish children engage with Nur's story of name-based exclusion, for instance, they are not only listening; they become witnesses and interlocutors in a conversation about identity, belonging, and injustice.

As sliding glass doors, co-woven stories empower children to access new social worlds as equal participants and agents in their construction. After being exposed to the experiences of mirrors and windows, children "enter" the sliding glass door with insights and perspectives that transform both the narrative space and the actual world. Stories become spaces in which children explore, challenge, and reimagine social realities, reinforcing the understanding that change is both imaginable and attainable.

Challenges, Recommendations, and Future Directions

Despite its potential, the co-woven **storytelling** model faces significant challenges. First, not all educators feel equipped or motivated to address emotionally or politically sensitive topics such as Arab–Jewish relations, gender identity, or socio-economic inequality (Ziv, 2023). This hesitation may stem from personal discomfort, varied worldviews and beliefs, institutional constraints, or fear of backlash, especially during times of conflict and war.

Second, the Ministry of Education in Israel has yet to establish a policy which clearly gives high priority to the issues of diversity and shared life (Bar-Tal & Rosen, 2009). Currently, much of the support for PDA development and implementation is provided by NGOs and educational foundations. Third, as explained at the beginning of the chapter, most mainstream publishers remain reluctant to produce books that reflect children's lived experiences with exclusion or social tension, limiting the dissemination of such stories.

To address these challenges, we recommend several steps. First, further research is needed—both on the PDA broadly and on the specific impacts of co-woven **storytelling**—on children's and adults' attitudes toward diversity and shared life. Such studies should be grounded in robust theoretical frameworks like those outlined in this chapter. A large-scale study is currently underway in Israeli–Palestinian early childhood settings, building on earlier findings (e.g., Nasie et al., 2021). These data will help advance both scholarship and practice.

A particularly promising direction to explore concerns the use of PDA stories to support children's emotional **resilience** during war. Early indications from the current conflict in Israel suggest that co-woven narratives reflecting children's fears and coping strategies may offer therapeutic value. This aspect of the model could inform trauma-sensitive educational practices globally and warrants further research.

Equally important is integrating coursework on multicultural pedagogy, shared society, and intergroup relations into both pre-service and in-service teacher education. Educators need structured, supported opportunities to explore their own identities and biases and to develop inclusive pedagogical strategies for **storytelling** and dialogue in early childhood classrooms.

Finally, partnerships with writers and illustrators should be fostered to introduce them to the co-woven model. Through collaboration with children and educators, artists can create developmentally appropriate engaging stories, amplifying **children's voices** and expanding the reach of this transformative approach.

Summary

The PDA, co-woven **storytelling**, inspired by Bishop's metaphors of mirrors, windows, and sliding glass doors, provides a new genre of children's stories and an innovative contribution to education for appreciation of diversity and shared life. It challenges segregated norms and creates a model of shared life rooted in dialogue, respect, and imagination. As children co-construct stories in real-life contexts, they are not only witnesses and/or victims but participate in acts of recognition, care, and activism. The continued development and dissemination of co-woven **storytelling** will require structural investment, creative alliances, and ongoing research. As the current social and political situation in Israel (and in many other locations) remains painful and uncertain, voices heard in these stories offer both healing and hope.

References

Aboud, F., & Doyle, A. (1996). Parental and peer influences on children's racial attitudes. *International Journal of Intercultural Relations, 20*, 371–383.

Al-Jubeh, D., & Vitsou, M. (2021). Empowering refugee children with the use of persona doll. *International Journal of Progressive Education, 17*(2), 210–227.

Aram, D., & Ziv, M. (2024). Introduction to the special issue ECE in Israel. *Early Child Development and Care, 294*, 645–654.

Banks, J. A. (1993). Multicultural education: Development, dimensions, and challenges. *The Phi Delta Kappan, 75*(1), 22–28.

Banks, J. A. (2015). *Cultural diversity and education: Foundations, curriculum, and teaching*. Routledge.

Bar-Tal, D., Diamond, A. H., & Nasie, M. (2017). Political socialization of young children in intractable conflicts: Conception and evidence. *International Journal of Behavioral Development, 41*(3), 415–425. https://doi.org/10.1177/0165025416652508

Bar-Tal, D., & Rosen, Y. (2009). Peace education in societies involved in intractable conflicts: Direct and indirect models. *Review of Educational Research, 79*(2), 557–575. https://doi.org/10.3102/0034654308330969

Bekerman, Z., & Horenczyk, G. (2004). Arab-Jewish bilingual coeducation in Israel: A long-term approach to intergroup conflict resolution. *Journal of Social Issues, 60*(2), 389–404. https://doi.org/10.1111/j.0022-4537.2004.00120.x

Bishop, R. S. (1990). Windows and mirrors: Children's books and parallel cultures. *California State University reading conference: 14th annual conference proceedings* (pp. 3–12).

Cahill, M. E. E., & Joo, S. (2021). Storytime programs as mirrors, windows, and sliding glass doors? Addressing children's needs through diverse book selection. *Information Science Faculty Publications., 88*. https://uknowledge.uky.edu/slis_facpub/88

Derman-Sparks, L., Lee Keenan, D., & Nimmo, J. (2023). *Leading anti-bias early childhood programs: A guide to change, for change*. Teachers College Press.

Central Bureau of Statistics. (2023). *Israel in figures–selected annual data 2022*. https://www.cbs.gov.il/he/publications/DocLib/isr_in_n/sr_in_n22e.pdf

Denham, S. A., Bassett, H. H., & Wyatt, T. (2007). The socialization of emotional competence. In *Handbook of socialization: Theory and research* (pp. 614–637).

Dimitiradi, S. (2015). Inclusionary education in early years through the use of personal dolls: A case from Greece. *Diversity, Needs and Inclusion in Early Years Education,* 61.

Domingues, M. (2021). Discarded identities/inspiring just sustainability with reuse persona dolls. *Sustainability, 13*(15), 8623.

Fitzpatrick, S. (2023). Developing a culture of respecting difference with young children, their families and communities in Northern Ireland. In J. D. Feder, S. Fitzpatrick, & M. Ziv (Eds.), *Foundations for a peaceful world: The transformative power of early childhood education to promote peace and social cohesion* (pp. 1–16). Early Years.

Government of Israel. (1953). *State education law*. Retrieved from http://www.nevo.co.il/law_html/Law01/152_024.htm
Gurevitch, Z. (2007). On Israeli and Jewish place. *Am Oved [Hebrew]*.
Ḥaj Yaḥya, A. (2021). Between particularism and pluralism: Children's literature as a multicultural agent. *Social identities, 27*(6), 660–681.
Harwood, J. (2021). Modes of intergroup contact: If and how to interact with the outgroup. *Journal of Social Issues, 77*(1), 154–170.
Huesmann, L. R., Dubow, E. F., Boxer, P., Smith, C., Shikaki, K., Landau, S. F., & Gvirsman, S. D. (2023). Consequences of exposure to war violence: Discriminating those with heightened risk for aggression from those with heightened risk for post-traumatic stress symptoms. *International Journal of Environmental Research and Public Health, 20*(12), 6067.
Jesuvadian, M. K., & Wright, S. (2011). Doll tales: Foregrounding children's voices in research. *Early Child Development and Care, 181*(3), 277–285. https://doi.org/10.1080/03004430903293172
Knesset. (1948). *Declaration of independence*. https://main.knesset.gov.il/en/about/pages/declaration.aspx
Landman, S. (2018). Through the onomastic: Reflecting cultural formation in the Jewish sector in Israel. *Immigration, 8*, 82–103. [Hebrew].
Laurén, K., & Malinen, A. (2021). Shame and silences: Children's emotional experiences of insecurity and violence in postwar Finnish families. *Social History, 46*(2), 193–220.
MacNaughton, G., & Davis, K. (2001). Beyond 'othering': Rethinking approaches to teaching young Anglo-Australian children about indigenous Australians. *Contemporary Issues in Early Childhood, 2*(1), 83–93.
Mansour, N., & Martin, M. H. (2020). What can Danish multicultural children's literature and African American children's literature learn from each other? Literary histories in dialogue. *Barnboken, 43*.
Nasie, M., Ziv, M., & Diesendruck, G. (2021). Promoting positive intergroup attitudes using persona dolls: A vicarious contact intervention program in Israeli kindergartens. *Group Processes & Intergroup Relations, 25*(5), 1269–1294.
Nesdale, D., Lawson, M. J., Durkin, K., & Duffy, A. (2010). Effects of information about group members on young children's attitudes towards the in-group and out-group. *British Journal of Developmental Psychology, 28*(2), 467–482.
Nesdale, D., & Lawson, M. J. (2011). Social groups and children's intergroup attitudes: Can school norms moderate the effects of social group norms? *Child Development, 82*(5), 1594–1606.
Morris, C. (2023). Teacher candidates, persona dolls, and class libraries. *Journal of Language and Literacy Education, 19*(2), 1–18.
Wild, N. R. (2024). The other side: Preschool children's experience of a read-aloud focused on social justice. *Early Childhood Education Journal, 53*, 1–8.
Segev, Y. (2013). Themes, trends, and current directions in Haredi and religious children's literature from the 1990s onward. *Orotreshet, 4*, 327–355. [Hebrew].
Selcuk, B., Gonultas, S., & Ekerim-Akbulut, M. (2023). Development and use of theory of mind in social and cultural context. *Child Development Perspectives, 17*(1), 39–45.
Sheppard, S. (2021). *Diversity doll training in Australia*. Sheppard Educational Resources.
Smith, C. L. (2013). Using personal dolls to learn empathy, unlearn prejudice. *The International Journal of Diversity in Education, 12*(3), 23.
Waller, R., & Sullivan-Walker, M. (2023). Homelessness in children's literature: A path to opening additional mirrors, windows and sliding glass doors. *The Reading Teacher, 77*(1), 137–140.
Wilkinson, C., & Wilkinson, S. (2022). Using persona dolls in research with children to combat the insider/outsider researcher status dilemma. *Children's Geographies, 20*(3), 375–380. https://doi.org/10.1080/14733285.2022.2051433
Yahya, A. H. (2024). Inclusion, equality and educational justice: Enhancing social-emotional learning through children's literature in a diverse and segregated society. *The International Journal of Information, Diversity, & Inclusion, 8*(1).

Verete, T., Ziv, M. & Kidron, R. (2022). *Fostering inclusion and curiosity toward socio-cultural diversity through the use of persona dolls*. http://www.gilrach.co.il/?p=8194
Ziv, M. (2023). Applying the persona doll approach in Israel to promote shared life and respect for diversity in early childhood. In J. D. Feder, S. Fitzpatrick, & M. Ziv (Eds.), *Foundations for a peaceful world: The transformative power of early childhood education to promote peace and social cohesion* (pp. 17–36). Early Years.

Margalit Ziv Associate Professor and a member of the steering committee of the Early Childhood M.Ed. program at Kaye Academic College of Education in Beer Sheva, Israel. Her research and practice focus on theory of mind, shared life and peace education, and additionally, promoting children's social understanding through shared book-reading. She serves as Director of *Horizons for Early Childhood*, an initiative that advances early childhood education within Israeli Arab communities, and as Pedagogical Director of *Games for the Future* at the Hebrew University's A-Chord Centre, which promotes shared life using the Persona Doll Approach. In addition, she is a member of the executive committee of the international *Network for Peace Building in Early Childhood.*

Tamar Verete -Zehavi is a social–political activist dedicated to advancing social justice, human rights, and shared life. Her activism is expressed in multiple arenas, including her educational work, as well as through her writing for children. She is a senior lecturer in early childhood education at the David Yellin Academic College of Education and a member of the pedagogical team of *Games for the Future* at the Hebrew University's A-Chord Centre, which promotes shared life across communities through the Persona Doll Approach. An award-winning children's author, Verete-Zehavi addresses socio-political issues in all her books and regularly lectures about them in schools across Israel

Chapter 13
Shared Book-Reading and the Promotion of Emotional Competence and Prosocial Conduct in Toddlerhood: The TEPP Program

Ilaria Grazzani and Alice Scotti

Contents

Introduction

Shared book-reading (SBR) generally refers to the practice of reading a book with a child in family or nonfamily settings (Murray et al., 2022; Schapira & Aram, 2020). Numerous studies have shown that SBR supports the development of various child competencies, including language (Flack et al., 2018) and cognitive (Aram et al., 2013) skills. Given the recognized importance of early support for psychological development (Tollan et al., 2023), the last 15 years have seen an increased focus on **nursery** and preschool settings, as key environments for promoting language and cognitive abilities (Noble et al., 2019).

I. Grazzani (✉) · A. Scotti
University of Milano-Bicocca, Milan, Italy
e-mail: ilaria.grazzani@unimib.it; a.scotti20@campus.unimib.it

R. Schapira, D. Aram (eds.), *Shared Book Reading and Children's Social-Emotional Competence*, https://doi.org/10.1007/978-3-032-14688-5_13

This chapter focuses on the educational practice of group-based SBR in **nursery** settings, specifically aligning with studies from our research group's laboratory[1] *on fostering* ***emotional competences*** *and prosocial behaviors in* ***toddlerhood***. While numerous studies and metanalyses (e.g., Dowdall et al., 2020) have highlighted the significant benefits of SBR for linguistic and cognitive development, our research has prioritized shared storybook-reading as a means of promoting socio-emotional skills.

Emotional competence spans the expression, regulation, and comprehension of emotions (Denham, 2023). These abilities begin to appear early in children' s development. For example, starting in the second year of life, children can use an adult's facial emotional cues to interpret unfamiliar situations (Klinnert et al., 1986). Similarly, from their second year, toddlers display the ability to recognize others' needs and desires, even when these are counterintuitive and different to their own wishes (Repacholi & Gopnik, 1997). From about 20 months, they start to use the emotional state language to refer to their own and others' emotions (Tompkins et al., 2018). By the end of the second year, they begin to label emotional expressions in pictures and associate emotions with their external antecedents. Still, more surprisingly, at around 2 years, children can correctly predict how interlocutors will behave even when this involves attributing them with a false belief (Buttelmann et al., 2009). Toddlers' early ability to read others' mind (Poulin-Dubois, 2020) enables them to engage in **prosocial conduct**—that is, to act on behalf of others without anticipating any immediate personal benefit (Eisenberg et al., 2015). Thus, at around 18 to 24 months, toddlers demonstrate prosocial behaviors by offering unsolicited help, sharing personal items such as toys and food, and comforting individuals in distress (Dunfield, 2014). Their engagement in prosocial behaviors depends, at least in part, on their understanding of others' mental states, such as their emotions, desires, and intentions.

Numerous studies have shown that early socio-emotional abilities are linked to and predict later positive outcomes, such as subjective wellbeing, better regulation of aggressive behaviors, and academic achievement (Eisenberg et al., 2015; Denham, 2023). Therefore, early support and enhancement of these abilities constitutes an important protective factor in development (Denham, 2023). Although **emotional competence**s and prosocial behaviors appear early in development, research highlights the significant contribution of *socialization processes* to positive developmental trajectories (Eisenberg, 2020; Song et al., 2022; Denham, 2023). Specifically, adults' use of modeling, contingency, and coaching styles has been extensively analyzed and shown to impact the development of **emotional competence** in preschool and school-age children. In particular, coaching refers to socializers' tendency to discuss emotions within a warm and supportive relationship. It involves guiding children in expressing and regulating their emotions, using emotion and affective talk to help them interpret their experiences and behavior. Notably, the deployment of

[1]We are deeply indebted to the invaluable contributions of the Lab-PSE team members (https://www.labpse.it/en/persone) to the research presented in this chapter.

coaching styles by teachers has been associated with enhanced emotion regulation and knowledge in children (Denham et al., 2020; Denham, 2023).

Focusing on promoting socio-**emotional competence**s, our research group has, over the last 15 years, conducted a series of training studies to assess the effectiveness of our intervention programs. The main feature of these programs, implemented in educational settings, is that they are based on *SBR and mentalistic conversations with small groups of children* guided by trained adults. Indeed, numerous authors have highlighted the impact of everyday conversational engagement on psychological development (see for instance the meta-analysis by Tompkins et al., 2018). Talking to others is considered an advanced form of social interaction that enhances children's awareness of their own and others' internal states, such as intentions, beliefs, desires, and emotions. From early childhood, conversations centered on explaining mental states and discussing them with other people play a key part in fostering children's understanding of the social world (Carpendale & Lewis, 2021). Studies have shown that reading aloud offers a unique context for initiating, fostering, and sustaining dialogue with children about emotions and other internal states (Brownell et al., 2013; Ziv et al., 2013). SBR facilitates the initiation of conversations between an adult and a group of children by providing a shared focus of interest and attention. Recent research has delved into how adults enjoy engaging with children's questions, comments, and observations while reading a book, and this fosters a positive cycle of motivation, interest, attention, and enriched conversational trajectories (Murray et al., 2022). In fact, when children feel that their comments are valued and listened to with genuine interest, this gratifies and encourages them and induces them to remain attentive for an even longer timespan.

Two of our initial studies on the impact of SBR on children's development were conducted in preschool settings (Ornaghi et al., 2011; Grazzani & Ornaghi, 2011). These studies involved a 2-month intervention during which children listened to stories enriched with mental-state talk and participated in language games and conversations designed to stimulate the use of emotional state language via the "word launching" technique. Compared to a control group, the children in the intervention group showed a significant increase in emotion comprehension ability. The validated program, including the stories and guidelines for teachers, is available in the study of Grazzani and Ornaghi (2022).

A subsequent intervention study was innovatively conducted with very young children in **nursery** settings to enhance their socioemotional skills (Agliati et al., 2015). The novelty of this study was that the practice described above, primarily implemented and tested in preschool context, was imported for the first time in **nursery** school. The effectiveness of this intervention with toddlers, based on SBR (*The Stories of Ciro & Beba*), followed by conversations on emotions, was corroborated by significant findings regarding the participants' **emotional competence** and resulted in the publication of an educational program (Agliati et al., 2015). Preliminary findings of this study, obtained through indirect measures, suggested an impact of the intervention on participants' prosocial disposition as well (Grazzani et al., 2016). This program, based on reading *The Stories of Ciro & Beba*, was widely applied in nurseries, and followed-up data were collected (Grazzani et al., 2019).

More recently, Brazzelli et al. (2021) and Scotti (2024) conducted further research in the **nursery** context using new stories and guidelines to test the efficacy of the PETT (*Prosocial Empathy Training Program*), which combines SBR with the conversation about inner states and prosocial dispositions. Analyzing data from a battery of prosocial tasks, these authors found a significant impact of PETT on participants' prosocial behaviors—namely sharing, helping, and comforting, which are the primary types of positive actions that typically emerge within the first 2 years of life (Dunfield, 2014).

The Current Study[2]

The new study presented here offers original features with respect to existing trainings using SBR and conversation on emotions. First of all, this study was conducted in a **nursery** school, while most of the existing research has been caried out within the family environment and the preschool context. Second, this study targeted an age group that has traditionally scarcely involved in this kind of activities; in fact, educators tend to consider toddlers incapable of participating in a group conversational activity on emotions and prosociality (Grazzani et al., 2020). Third, while the study by Grazzani et al. (2016) focused on **emotional competence** and the study by Brazzelli et al. (2021) on prosocial behavior, the present study sought to test the efficacy of the TEPP in a larger sample of toddlers, in terms of its impact on both **emotional competence** and prosocial skills.

Specifically, we evaluated the impact of a SBR and conversation-based intervention (TEPP: *Toddlers Emotion Prosociality Program*) on toddlers' **emotional competence** and prosocial behaviors. The engagement in **prosocial conduct**s, in fact, depends, at least in part, on an understanding of others' mental states, such as their emotions, desires, and intentions. Some studies have reported significant relationships between **emotional competence** (e.g., emotion knowledge) and specific aspects of prosociality (for an overview: Brazzelli et al., 2022).

As recent literature has shown that early social and **emotional competence**s are associated to later positive outcomes (Denham, 2023; Schapira & Grazzani, 2025), with the present study, we wished to contribute further to this research area exploring the impact of a new intervention at an early age, when children begin to speak and engage in conversation (Carpendale & Lewis, 2021). We included gender in the research design since the literature on toddlers' social and **emotional competence** reports mixed findings. Some studies have indicated that girls score higher than

[2] The content of this chapter is drawn from a large-scale project funded by the University of Milano-Bicocca (2023-ATE-0213) on the promotion of socio-emotional development in educational settings. Specifically, we present part of the data collected during the 2020–2021 and 2023–2024 academic years. We are grateful for the wonderful collaboration of the participating children, teachers, and my colleagues at Lab-PSE (www.labpse.it)

boys on measures of emotion knowledge (Sette et al., 2015), and other research found no gender differences (Ensor & Hughes, 2005; Grazzani et al., 2016).

The study included three conditions: (1) SBR with conversation about emotions and other mental states, (2) SBR with conversation about physical states and actions of protagonists, and (3) SBR without conversation. Based on previous findings, we hypothesized that the toddlers in Condition 1 would outperform their peers in Conditions 2 and 3 on the post-test measures.

Method

Participants

Participants were 151 toddlers (76 girls), whose mean age at pretest was 28.78 months (*SD* = 3.94; range: 22–37 months). All children were Italian speakers whose linguistic development fell between the tenth and the 95th percentile referring to the normative values reported in the manual of the tool used to evaluate language ability (see below). They attended 11 different nurseries (early childhood education centers) in two provinces of northern Italy. All participants were from low–medium SES backgrounds. The inclusion criteria for this study were: (1) the children were required to be aged between 22 and 38 months, and (2) parents were required to provide informed consent for their children's participation in the study.

The 27 teachers who participated in the study had a mean age of 47.11 years (range: 26–59), and 80% of them had more than 12 years of professional activity. They had at least a bachelor's degree, came from the same education centers, and followed the same pedagogical line, inspired by the ministerial education guidelines. Five centers (11 teachers and 58 children) were randomly assigned to Condition 1, three centers (8 teachers and 47 children) to Condition 2, and three centers (8 teachers and 46 children) to Condition 3. The teachers in Conditions 2 and 3 knew that they were part of a control group within a research project on socio-emotional development in early childhood. They were told that they would be offered the opportunity to learn about the intervention program the following school year.

Research Design

Following familiarization with the research settings, the study comprised three phases: pretest, training, and post-test. In Table 13.1, we present a summary of the research phases, the instruments administered, and the specific forms of intervention implemented with each of the three groups. The intervention began 2 weeks after the end of the pretest phase and lasted 2 months. The post-test phase started 2 months after completion of the intervention phase and lasted about 1 month. The

Table 13.1 Research phases as a function of group condition and tools used

	Pre-test	Intervention	Post-test
Condition 1 (SBR and conversation on emotions and inner states)	PinG (language ability) AKT (Affective Knowledge Test) PT (Prosocial Tasks)	Shared storybook reading Conversational training about inner states and prosocial behaviors (TEPP)	PinG (language ability) AKT (Affective Knowledge Test) PT (Prosocial Tasks)
Condition 2 (SBR and conversation on physical states)	The same instruments administered to the children in the Condition 1 group	Shared storybook reading Conversation about physical characteristics and practical actions of the characters	The same instruments administered to the children in the Condition 1 group
Condition 3 (SBR and no conversation)	The same instruments administered to the children in the Condition 1 group	Shared storybook reading Free play	The same instruments administered to the children in the Condition 1 group

research design was approved by the Ethics Committee of the University of Milano-Bicocca. The study was conducted in accordance with the ethical principles and code of conduct of the American Psychological Association.

Before collecting the data, two testers spent 2 weeks familiarizing with the **nursery** setting. We used standardized instruments to measure the variables under study, including a language assessment tool to verify the equivalence of the three groups in terms of their linguistic ability and to ensure that no participants were affected by language impairments.

Measures

All participants completed individual pretesting and post-testing on all measures, presented in a counterbalanced order, in a quiet area of the **nursery**.

PinG (Bello et al., 2010). This standardized Italian language tool was also administered to control for any initial differences in verbal ability across the three conditions. The PinG test consists of four subtests: *Noun Comprehension* (NC), *Noun Production* (NP), *Predicate Comprehension* (PC), and *Predicate Production* (PP), each of which comprises 20 lexical targets with two training items. We applied the standard scoring procedures outlined in the PinG manual. Cronbach's reliability coefficient was $\alpha = 0.84$ at pretest and $\alpha = 0.88$ at post-test.

AKT (Denham, 1986). We adopted the validated Italian version by Camodeca and Coppola (2010). This tool uses blank-faced puppets and felt discs depicting facial expressions that correspond to four basic emotions (happy, sad, angry, and afraid). Given the young age of the participants, we administered only three subtasks from the battery: the expressive knowledge task, the receptive knowledge task, and the situation knowledge task. The *expressive knowledge* task assesses children's ability to verbally label emotions. The tester points to each of the four faces in turn and asks the child to label it, using the prompt question: "How does he/she feel?" In the *receptive knowledge* task, the experimenter shuffles the faces and asks: "Where is the (emotion) face?". The child then nonverbally identifies each of the four emotional expressions by pointing. To prepare for the *situation knowledge* task, the tester first trains the child to identify the basic emotions, labeling each facial expression while using matching gestures, tone of voice, and body language. The situation knowledge task comprises eight vignettes, for each of which the child selects the appropriate face to represent the puppet's emotion (happiness, sadness, anger, or fear). Participants received a score of 2 for a correct response, a score of 1 for an incorrect response of the appropriate emotional valence (e.g., "good" or "smiling" for "happy"; "crying" for "sad"), and 0 for a completely inappropriate response (e.g., "happy" for "angry"). Each child received a total score from 0 to 32, and three sub-scores (expressive knowledge task: max. 8; receptive knowledge task: max. 8; situation knowledge task: max. 16). Reliability coefficients were $\alpha = 0.94$ at pretest and $\alpha = 0.93$ at post-test.

Prosocial Tasks (adapted from Dunfield & Kuhlmeier, 2013; Warneken & Tomasello, 2006, 2007). To assess the children's propensity to engage in prosocial behaviors, we devised three experimental situations. Participants were brought in individually and seated across from an experimenter at a small table positioned in the middle of a dedicated testing room at the **nursery**. They were then presented with a battery of three prosocial tasks (helping, sharing, and comforting tasks), each targeting a different domain of prosocial behavior. For the *helping tasks*, we slightly adapted Warneken and Tomasello's (2006) "out-of-reach" task. The experimenter picked up a small plastic toy (a card in the post-test session), playfully "walked" it across the table, and then dropped it over the far side while exclaiming "Oops!". The experimenter next extended her arm toward the toy. For the first 5 seconds, she focused her gaze on the toy, and then for the next 5 seconds, she alternated her gaze between the toy and the child. The trial concluded once the child responded or otherwise after a total of 10 seconds had elapsed. At no point did the experimenter directly ask the child for help. The "across-the-room" task was similar to the out-of-reach task, with the key distinction being that the jigsaw puzzle piece that the experimenter wished to recover was already at the other side of the room, and thus the child had never observed it in the experimenter's possession. When the child and experimenter had completed most of the puzzle, the experimenter would exclaim, "We're missing a piece!" The experimenter would then look around the room and, spotting the piece of the puzzle, say "Oh!" and reach toward the piece. Again, at this point, the experimenter looked directly at the puzzle piece for the first 5 seconds and then for the subsequent 5 seconds alternated her gaze between the puzzle piece and the child.

In the *sharing task*, participants were presented with two scenarios: the first involved sharing food, whereas the second involved sharing toys. In both tasks, the experimenter was given an empty container, while the participant received a box filled with colored pencils (markers in the post-test). Before handing the full container to the child, the experimenter displayed her own empty container to the toddler and said, “Look what I have”. The child then received his or her container. The experimenter put on a sad facial expression and held out her hand, palm up. For the first 5 seconds, the experimenter focused on her own container; then, for the following 5 seconds, she alternated her gaze between her container and the participant. At no point did she verbally request pencils. She acknowledged any items received with a neutral “Thank you”.

In the comforting tasks, participants were presented with two varieties of distress: physical and emotional distress. In the first, the experimenter banged her knee off the edge of the table, which in turn hit a metal bracket, making a loud noise. The experimenter then sat down with a look of distress on her face. She rubbed her knee, vocalizing pain (e.g., “Oh! My knee, I banged my knee”). For the first 5 seconds, the experimenter focused on her knee, before alternating her gaze between her knee and the participant for another 5 seconds. The experimenter never directly requested aid. The emotional comforting task was administered similarly to the physical trial. The experimenter showed the child her favorite toy. While the experimenter was playing with her toy, she tore a hole in the back of it. The experimenter looked at her toy and exclaimed in a sad voice “Oh! My toy, I broke my toy!” For the first 5 seconds thereafter, the experimenter looked at her toy with a sad expression on her face, and for the subsequent 5 seconds, she alternated her gaze between the toy and the child.

Each session was video-recorded and coded by two expert judges, who were blind to both the aim of the study and the group conditions. Each prosocial task was coded for the target behavior following the coding scheme used by Ketelaar et al. (2015). Specifically, two points were awarded for displaying the appropriate target behavior during the first 5 seconds, one point for producing the appropriate target behavior during the next 5 seconds, and 0 points for displaying nontarget behaviors only. Each child was assigned a total score from 0 to 6. Reliability coefficients for the global measure were $\alpha = 0.64$ at pretest and $\alpha = 0.79$ at post-test.

The Training Procedure and the Stories

We implemented a 2-month intervention that entailed three training sessions a week conducted with groups of four to six toddlers, organized by research condition. Each group included a mix of boys and girls who were familiar with one another and accustomed to participating in educational activities together. The teachers leading the intervention had received prior training over a 2-month period, during which they were provided with standardized criteria guidelines for delivering the story reading and moderating the subsequent conversational interaction. For example, they were instructed to read the text faithfully, without adding, omitting, or altering content. In addition, they were asked to avoid over-dramatizing or personalizing delivery while still reading in an engaging manner to sustain the children’s interest in the story.

During the training phase, the teachers received a manual outlining the key features of the intervention. Additionally, all participating teachers in each condition were videotaped while implementing the intervention, receiving feedback from the research team on their delivery of both the reading and conversation activities. To ensure fidelity, supervision of the video-recorded sessions continued throughout the entire research process.

The stories in the PETT program, specifically written for children aged 2 to 3, comprise four short tales collected in the book *Tom and Bea, Two Furry Friends* (Brazzelli & Grazzani, 2021). The teachers read the stories following the order in which they were collected in the book. The main characters, a dog named Tom and a cat named Bea, experience a series of adventures that elicit emotions such as fear, happiness, anger, and sadness. Each tale follows a classic story schema: a brief introduction is followed by a problematic situation that evokes a particular emotion, and action is undertaken to resolve the issue. In each story, the resolution centers on a prosocial act by a story character, such as comforting a distressed friend, offering practical help, or sharing resources. For example, in "*Bea's Ball of Wool*", Bea feels sad when her ball of wool rolls out of reach under the dresser. Seeing Bea's distress, Tom invites her to play with his ball of wool instead.

The *Tom and Bea* stories also feature a rich psychological lexicon (Bartsch & Wellman, 1995) that sets them apart from most books commonly used with or aimed at early childhood audiences. While the psychological terms are primarily emotional (e.g. "he gets angry"; "she is happy"; "they are bored"), they also include items related to perception ("he hears crying"), volition ("I was longing for an ice-cream"), and cognition ("deciding to").

Condition 1: SBR and conversation on inner states and prosocial behaviors. The training sessions followed a four-step procedure to implement the TEPP: (1) preparation of a suitable setting for the activity, (2) SBR, (3) conversation about the emotions and prosocial behaviors thematized in the story, and (4) a concluding phase. At each session, the children first listened to a brief story from *Tom and Bea*, an illustrated storybook developed by the authors, containing age-appropriate stories focused on prosocial behaviors (a sample story and conversation extracts are provided in the Appendix). Figure 13.1 highlights a moment from Step 3, where children are guided through a conversation about the adventures of Tom and Bea.

The key component of the experimental intervention procedure was the guided conversation about emotions and prosocial behaviors that took place immediately after the shared story-reading. During this discussion, the teacher encouraged the children to reflect on the story by focusing on the story characters' emotions and other inner states, as well as their prosocial actions such as helping, sharing, and comforting. The TEPP includes stimulus questions designed to individually engage all the children in the group, prompting them to share personal or observed experiences —— whether involving themselves, family members, friends, or familiar cartoon/story characters—related to the prosocial behaviors featured in the story.

Condition 2: SBR and conversation on physical states. A distinct four-step procedure was followed in Condition 2, differing significantly from Condition 1: specifically, after the SBR step, children in the Condition 2 group were engaged in conversations focused on the story characters' physical traits, the characteristics of the inanimate objects in the story, and the characters' observable actions. Teachers

Fig. 13.1 An SBR session in a nursery setting (Source: Scotti, 2024, p. 49)

assigned to Condition 2 were primarily trained in reading the illustrated story verbatim in an engaging manner, with additional guidance on discussing the story characters' physical features and overt actions.

Condition 3: SBR and play activities. Children in Condition 3 listened to the same stories as the other two groups but did not participate in any subsequent conversation or dialogue. Instead, they were offered a selection of toys, including Lego, building blocks, and jigsaw puzzles, and allowed to engage in free play. Teachers in Condition 3 received training only in reading and were similarly supervised throughout the research process.

Data Analysis

Data analysis was performed using IBM SPSS (2023). Before analyzing the data, we conducted standard data-cleaning procedures (Ewens & Brumberg, 2023), including analyses of missing values (three toddlers) and multivariate outliers (two toddlers). The final sample ($N = 151$) included children who participated in all the sessions of SBR and had scores for both testing phases.

We computed the main descriptive statistics and zero-order correlations before running a series of ANOVAs to check for statistically significant differences among the three groups at the pretest phase. Gender also was considered in the correlation matrix. Then, to assess the impact of the TEPP intervention on the competences under study, we conducted a series of multivariate analyses of variance for repeated measures with the following independent variables: time (pre and post) as a

Table 13.2 Pre- and post-test means and standard deviations for all variables by group condition

	Pretest			*Post-test*		
	Condition 1	Condition 2	Condition 3	Condition 1	Condition 2	Condition 3
Age in months	28.00 (3.60)	28.77 (3.83)	29.78 (4.28)	33.66 (3.57)	34.77 (3.83)	35.39 (4.30)
Language ability (PinG)	32.96 (17.64)	33.60 (18.07)	29.46 (18.06)	48.47 (13,8)	38.04 (17.11)	41.07 (15.45)
Emotional competence (AKT)	8.76 (6.50)	11.17 (5.6)	9.20 (642)	18.22 (6.80)	9.62 (6.81)	11.80 (6.9)
Prosocial behavior (prosocial tasks)	2.12 (2.16)	1.68 (1.88)	2.65 (2.50)	5.36 (3.20)	2.04 (1.80)	2.96 (3.00)

Note. Standard deviations are presented in round parentheses

within-subjects factor and experimental condition (Condition 1 vs. Condition 2 vs. Condition 3) as a between-subjects factor. Age entered in the model as a covariate factor.

Results

Descriptive and Correlational Analyses

Table 13.2 presents the descriptive statistics for all variables by group condition at both pre-and post-test. A series of ANOVAs indicated no significant pretest differences between groups in terms of children's age or performance on any of the administered measures.

The correlation matrix revealed significant associations at pre-test between age and AKT scores ($r = 0.448$; $p = 0.001$), age and PT scores ($r = 0.342$; $p = 0.001$), age and language ability ($r = 0.565$; $p = 0.001$), AKT and PT ($r = 0.352$; $p = 0.001$), AKT and language ability ($r = 0.740$; $p = 0.001$), and PT and language ability ($r = 0.394$; $p = 0.001$). Gender was not significantly correlated with any of the other study variables (gender*age: $r = 0.053$, $p = 0.516$; gender*AKT: $r = 0.041$, $p = 0.614$; gender*language: $r = 0.034$, $p = 0.693$) and was therefore excluded from subsequent analyses.

Multivariate Analysis

To investigate the effect of TEPP on toddlers' performance, we ran a multivariate analysis of variance for repeated measures, calculating effect sizes using partial eta-squared values (η^2). We remind that Time (pre and post) was a within-subjects factor, whereas experimental condition (Condition 1 vs. Condition 2 vs. Condition 3) was a between-subjects factor.

Considering the AKT scores (**emotional competence**), we found a significant main effect of Time (Wilks's $\lambda = 0.728$, $F = 55{,}4$, $p = <0.001$, $\eta^2 = 0.27$) as well as a significant Time x Group Condition interaction effect (Wilk's $\lambda = 0.600$, $F = 49{,}34$, $p = 0.001$, $\eta^2 = 0.40$) (see Fig. 13.2). More precisely, all groups showed significant higher scores as a function of Time from pre- to post-test phase. Regarding the interaction Time x Condition, multiple comparisons showed that children in Condition 1 who benefitted from TEPP (SBR + conversation on emotions and other inner states and on prosociality) significantly outperformed those in Condition 2 ($p = 0.025$) and Condition 3 ($p = 0.034$) in **emotional competence**, with no significant differences between Conditions 2 and 3.

Considering the PT scores (prosocial behaviors), the multivariate analysis of variance for repeated measures also revealed a significant main effect of Time (Wilks's $\lambda = 0.793$, $F = 38.61$, $p = 0.001$, $\eta^2 = 0.20$) and a significant Time x Group Condition interaction effect (Wilks's $\lambda = 0.763$, $F = 23.02$, $p = <0.001$, $\eta^2 = 0.37$) (Fig. 13.3). The three groups showed significant higher scores as a function of Time from the pre- to post-test phase. With regard to the significant interaction, multiple comparisons indicated that children in Condition 1 significantly outperformed those in Condition 2 ($p = <0.001$) on the prosocial task battery, with a trend toward significant difference between Conditions 1 and 3 ($p = 0.08$). In fact, the gain in scores from pre- to post-test was greater in Condition 2 than in Condition 3, but the difference between the two groups was not statically significant.

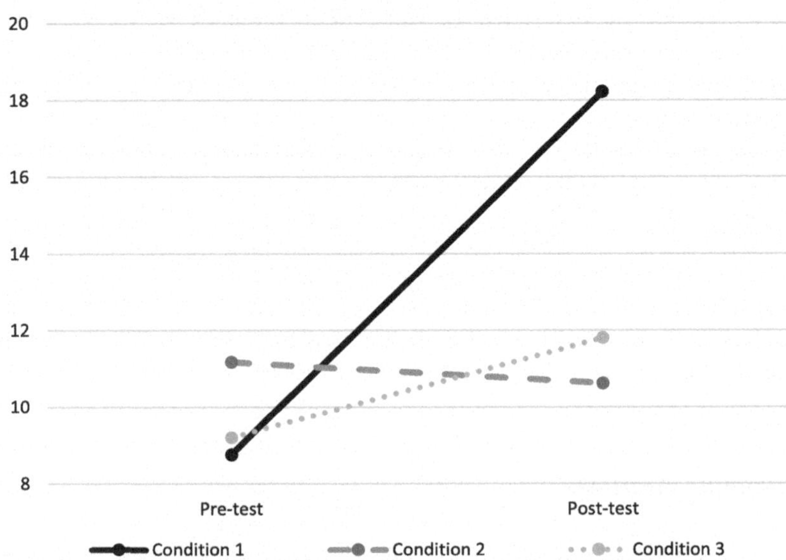

Fig. 13.2 Toddlers' pre to post-test improvement in emotional competence as a function of group condition

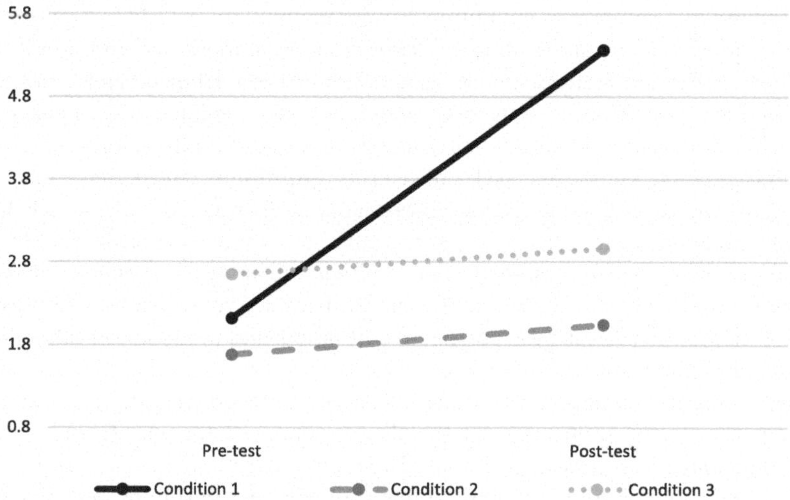

Fig. 13.3 Toddlers' pre to post-test improvement in prosociality as a function of group condition

Finally, for language ability, we also found both a significant Time effect (Willk's $\lambda = 0.506$, $F = 134.6$, $p = 0.001$, $\eta^2 = 0.494$) and a significant Time x Group Condition interaction effect (Willk's $\lambda = 0.836$, $F = 13.50$, $p = 0.001$, $\eta^2 = 0.164$). Multiple comparisons indicated that children in Condition 1 significantly outperformed those in Condition 2 ($p = 0.022$) and in Condition 3 ($p = 0.025$). The analyses showed no significant difference between Conditions 2 and 3. Lastly, age factor did not interact with any of the study variables.

Discussion

Our aim in this study was to provide further evidence on the effectiveness of TEPP in promoting both emotional and prosocial skills in toddlers aged 2 to 3, controlling for age effect. Previous research (Brazzelli et al., 2021) focused on prosocial behaviors in a smaller sample of children, while the present study, using a larger sample of participants, expanded the scope to include assessments of both **emotional competence** and **prosocial conducts** in toddlers.

With this objective in mind, we implemented a training study with three research conditions: (1) SBR and conversation on emotions, other inner states, and prosociality; (2) SBR and conversation on material and practical story content; (3) SBR and free play. The key feature of TEPP (Condition 1) is an innovative conversational approach tailored for young children. Specifically, during the intervention phase, the ad hoc guidelines helped teachers and toddlers to discuss inner states—particularly emotions—and explore prosocial responses to problems and others' needs.

We found that children in Condition 1 (implementation of TEPP) displayed significantly greater gains in the abilities under study than those in Condition 2 (SBR and conversation about physical states and actions of protagonists) and Condition 3 (SBR and no conversation, only play activities). As predicted, the experimental group children performed significantly better at post-test on the expressive, receptive, and situation knowledge tasks measuring **emotional competence** and were significantly more inclined to respond prosocially to the needs of others via helping, sharing, and comforting actions. The study outcomes were also corroborated by the medium–high effect sizes obtained in the multivariate analyses. It appears that children between 22 and 37 months of age are particularly receptive to activities that enhance their ability to take the perspective of others and to recognize others' feelings, desires, and needs.

These outcomes support the connection between conversation about inner states, particularly emotions, and the development of the **emotional competence** that underlies prosocial action (Brazzelli et al., 2022). This aligns with previous research conducted with older children in preschool settings (e.g., Ornaghi et al., 2011; Grazzani & Ornaghi, 2011; Giménez-Dasí et al., 2013; Grazzani & Valle, 2025). Indeed, in Condition 1, children not only listened to prosocial stories but also had the opportunity to discuss the story characters' emotional experiences. We suggest that conversation in group settings, based on the discussion of different emotions and other inner states, can increase young children's awareness and understanding of their own and others' feelings and needs, which in turn appears to strengthen their tendency to engage in prosocial action (Brownell et al., 2013).

Analysis of our video-recorded data (see Appendix, Extract 1—Condition 1) shows how the teacher's questions about internal experiences effectively guided the children's attention to inner states, helping them to explore both the causes of emotions and their various forms of expression (for example, a teacher says "*In this story, Bea feels very sad…. When do you feel sad?*" and Alessia responds "*I feel sad when my mom goes to work*", while Paul says "*I feel sad when my dad goes to work*", and Marie adds "*When I feel sad, I cry*"). Furthermore, the teachers in Condition 1 guided the conversations toward reflection on positive actions that can alleviate the emotional distress of others or help them to solve everyday problems (for example, during a conversation about a story on the theme of sharing toys with a friend, one child says "*I gave some of my Lego to Paul because he didn't get any, and we played together*").

In contrast, in Condition 2 (see Appendix, Extract 2), the teacher intentionally focused the conversation on the material and practical aspects of the stories, such as naming the toys present at the playground or recognizing the color of objects, thus precluding verbal exchanges concerning mental states, emotions, and prosociality. While this type of conversation promoted turn-taking in linguistic exchanges and presumably facilitated children's learning about objects and their functions, it did not encourage—at least in principle—the exchange of perspectives or deeper exploration of inner states (needs, desires, and emotions) that is fundamental to children developing social understanding.

Notably, children in Condition 1 demonstrated greater improvements in language proficiency compared to the other groups. This finding is particularly significant because while SBR alone typically enhances language skills, and accordingly both Groups 1 and 2 showed improved language abilities at post-test, the statistically significant time-by-condition interaction effect reveals that the experimental condition implementing TEPP was most effective at promoting such language-related gains. Indeed, in the course of the intervention period, the children in Condition 1 became gradually more active in conversing on emotions and other mental states, moving from an initial interest to details of the stories (e.g., illustrations) to acquisition of the capacity to talk about the story characters and, by extension, about their own inner states. This ties in with the idea that the training enhances the change of knowledge from implicit to explicit (Carpendale & Lewis, 2021), allowing toddlers to engage in processes of reflection on their own and others' internal states. At the beginning of the intervention, the toddlers were activating a mechanism of *repetition and imitation* of what they had just heard from their teachers (example: a teacher says: "…Paul, did you notice that Bea wants an ice-cream because it's very hot and she wants to cool off?" and Marie intervenes repeating: "…she wants the ice-crime"). However, toward the end of the intervention, the children began to adopt a mechanism of *discursive elaboration* of story content and to engage in reflection on their own and others' internal states (example: Carole says: "I'm happy too because my mum is coming…" and Matthew adds: "I'm happy when I come to Pete's because there are lots of toys there"; Bob says: "I don't lose my toy because I leave it in the locker, but I'm sad if Giulio takes it from me"…. while Clare adds: "I lose my small train but then Mum gives it to me and I am happy"). During the intervention phase, toddlers in Condition 2 were more engaged in conversation focused on physical features and actions in the study of the story and less encouraged to dwell on their emotions and those of characters in the stories (see Appendix).

Limitations and Educational Implications of the Study

A first key limitation of our research design is the absence of a follow-up phase to assess the long-term durability of the training effects. Nevertheless, our findings provide encouraging evidence for the educational value of promoting **emotional competence** and prosocial behavior in early childhood education settings. Second, the lack of teacher blinding to group assignment (experimental versus control) introduced potential bias, given that teachers' awareness of their condition may have influenced their behavior. Third, the fact that the three conditions were assigned on the center level is also a limitation because the sampling of participants was not random. Finally, a more nuanced analysis of the mental-state language used during conversation sessions could yield valuable qualitative insights to enhance future program effectiveness. Specifically, further examination is needed of children's contributions to the conversational exchanges (for example, appropriate vs off-topic comments) and teachers' linguistic styles (for example, the balance between open-ended and closed questions). Such detailed analyses could inform the development of more effective training protocols for education practitioners implementing the program in professional settings (Grazzani, 2024). In addition, further studies with a control group *without* SBR, including characters' emotions and other inner states, could provide more information about the effective role of SBR and conversation on emotions.

Despite these limitations, this intervention study makes a novel contribution to the existing literature. Specifically, it stands out as one of few studies examining how SBR and guided discussions about inner states (e.g., emotions) and prosocial behaviors can enhance social and emotional learning and prosocial orientation in 2- and 3-year-olds. Current research indicates that story-time discussions in daycare settings typically emphasize the physical and material characteristics of story content (Aram et al., 2013; Misailidi et al., 2013; see also Fine et al., 2019; Grazzani & Brockmeier, 2019). In contrast, the outcomes of this study add new findings to the existing literature to encourage policymakers and practitioners to design early childhood educational activities that focus on the relationship between internal experiences, emotions, and prosocial actions. The early promotion of these aspects can be a crucial protective factor in development.

Appendix

Sample story and conversation extracts from the different conditions

Story: Bea's Ball of Wool

Bea and Tom are playing with balls of wool. The wool is colourful and soft.

They are having fun rolling the balls around the house, running and jumping as they go!

"Tom, look how far I can throw mine!", says Bea. But Bea's ball rolls under the dresser.

She tries to get it back by going over to the dresser and stretching out her paw...

but it's no good, she cannot reach her ball of wool! Feeling disappointed, Bea goes back to her basket.

She is upset because she cannot play with her favourite toy anymore.

Bea looks longingly at Tom's ball of wool. Tom sees that Bea is looking very sad.

So, he goes over to his friend and asks her: "Do you want to play with me? We can play catch with my ball". Bea is happy and says OK.

The two friends begin to play with Tom's ball of wool, tossing it from one side of the room to the other. They are very careful now not to let it roll under the furniture!

Sample conversation (extract)

Condition 1—Conversation about inner states and prosocial behaviour:

Teacher: In this story, Bea feels very sad as she can't reach her ball of wool. When do you feel sad?

Alessia: I feel sad when my mom goes to work.

Teacher: And what about the rest of you?

Paul: When my dad goes to work, I feel sad.

Juli: I feel sad when my brother plays with my toys.

Marie: Me too. When I'm sad, I cry.

Carole: Me too, I start to cry, and I make a face like this.

Teacher: So, children, how did Bea feel when she couldn't play with her ball of wool?

Carole: Disappointed.

Paul: Sad.

Teacher: Yes, she was sad. But Tom decided to comfort his friend. He asked Bea if she wanted to play with him and with his ball of wool. …. Carole, what could you do if you saw that Anna was sad? Would you give her your toy to play with together? Would you give her your doll?

Carole: I'd tell my mom. When she came to pick me up, I'd tell her she must remind me to bring my doll.

Teacher: That is very nice….Anna would be very happy, I believe.

Anna: Happy.

Condition 2—Conversation about physical states:

Teacher: What are Tom and Bea playing at?

Leonardo: They are playing with a ball of wool.

Teacher: And where are they?

F: They are in their house.

Teacher: Mm. Tom and Bea are playing with a ball of wool. Look here, this is the sofa. What colour is this sofa?

R: Blue.

Teacher: Right, it's blue. What other objects do you see in the room?

N: The cupboard.

A: The cupboard.

E: In my kitchen, there is a cupboard.

Teacher: Oh, that's great. What can you find in your cupboard?

E: I find my cakes.

I: Me too.

References

Agliati, A., Grazzani, I., & Ornaghi, V. (2015). *La socializzazione emotiva nei contesti educativi per l'infanzia. Conversare sulle emozioni al nido (motion socialization in early childhood educational contexts. Conversation on emotions at nursey)*. Junior Spaggiari.

Aram, D., Fine, Y., & Ziv, M. (2013). Enhancing parent-child shared book reading interactions: Promoting references to the book's plot and socio-cognitive themes. *Early Childhood Research Quarterly, 28*(1), 111–122. https://doi.org/10.1016/j.ecresq.2012.03.005

Bartsch, K., & Wellman, H. (1995). *Children talk about the mind*. Oxford University Press.

Bello, A., Caselli, M. C., Pettenati, P., & Stefanini, S. (2010). *PinG. Parole in gioco (PinG. Words in play)*. Giunti Psychometrics.

Brazzelli, E., & Grazzani, I. (2021). *The stories of Tom and Bea. Two furry friends*. FronteRetro.
Brazzelli, E., Grazzani, I., & Pepe, A. (2021). Promoting prosocial behavior in toddlerhood: A conversation-based intervention at nursery. *Journal of Experimental Child Psychology, 204*, 105056. https://doi.org/10.1016/jecp.2020.105056
Brazzelli, E., Pepe, A., & Grazzani, I. (2022). Prosocial behavior in toddlerhood: The contribution of emotion knowledge, theory of mind, and language ability. *Frontiers in Psychology, 13*, 897812. https://doi.org/10.3389/fpsyg.2022.897812
Buttelmann, D., Carpenter, M., & Tomasello, M. (2009). Eighteen-month-old infants show false belief understanding in an active helping paradigm. *Cognition, 112*(2), 337–342. https://doi.org/10.1016/j.cognition.2009.05.006
Camodeca, M., & Coppola, G. (2010). Competenza socio-emotiva e difficoltà di relazione in età prescolare: Un approccio multi-informatore [Social-emotional competence and relationship dìfficulties in preschool years: A multi-informant approach]. In E. Baumgartner (Ed.), *Gli esordi della competenza emotiva. Strumenti di studio e di valutazione* (pp. 51–74). LED.
Brownell, C. A., Svetlova, M., Anderson, R., Nichols, S. R., & Drummond, J. (2013). Socialization of early prosocial behavior: Parents' talk about emotions is associated with sharing and helping in toddlers. *Infancy, 18*(1), 91–119. https://doi.org/10.1111/j.1532-7078.2012.00125.x
Carpendale, J., & Lewis, C. (2021). *What makes us human: How minds develop through social interaction*. Routledge.
Denham, S. A. (1986). Social cognition, prosocial behavior, and emotion in preschoolers: Contextual validation. *Child Development, 57*(1), 194–201. https://doi.org/10.2307/1130651
Denham, S. A. (2023). *The development of emotional competence in young children*. Guilford Press.
Denham, S. A., Ferrier, D. E., & Bassett, H. H. (2020). Preschool teachers' socialization of emotions knowledge: Considering socioeconomic risk. *Journal of Applied Developmental Psychology, 69*, 101160. https://doi.org/10.1016/j.appdev.2020.101160
Dowdall, N., Melendez-Torres, G. J., Murray, L., Gardner, F., Hartford, L., & Cooper, P. J. (2020). Shared picture book reading interventions for child language development: A systematic review and meta-analysis. *Child Development, 91*(2), e383–e399. https://doi.org/10.1111/cdev.13225
Dunfield, K. A. (2014). A construct divided: Prosocial behavior as helping, sharing, and comforting subtypes. *Frontiers in Psychology, 5*, 958. https://doi.org/10.3389/fpsyg.2014.00958
Dunfield, K. A., & Kuhlmeier, V. A. (2013). Classifying prosocial behavior: Children's responses to instrumental need, emotional distress, and material desire. *Child Development, 84*(5), 1766–1776. https://doi.org/10.1111/cdev.12075
Eisenberg, N. (2020). Findings, issues, and new directions for research on emotion socialization. *Developmental Psychology, 56*(3), 664–670. https://doi.org/10.1037/dev0000906
Eisenberg, N., Eggum-Wilkens, N. D., & Spinrad, T. L. (2015). The development of prosocial behavior. In D. A. Schroeder & W. G. Graziano (Eds.), *The Oxford handbook of prosocial behavior* (pp. 114–136). Oxford University Press.
Ensor, R., & Hughes, C. (2005). More than talk: Relations between emotion understanding and positive behaviour in toddlers. *British Journal of Developmental Psychology, 23*(3), 343–363. https://doi.org/10.1348/026151005X26291
Ewens, W. J., & Brumberg, K. (2023). *Introductory statistics for data analysis*. Springer.
Fine, Y., Aram, D., & Ziv, M. (2019). Enriching parent-child discourse during book sharing. In E. Veneziano & Nicolopoulou (Eds.), *Narrative, literacy and other skills. Studies in intervention* (pp. 223–244). John Benjamins Publishing Company.
Flack, Z. M., Field, A. P., & Horst, J. S. (2018). The effects of shared storybook reading on word learning: A meta-analysis. *Developmental Psychology, 54*(7), 1334–1346. https://doi.org/10.1037/dev0000512
Giménez-Dasí, M., Fernández-Sanchez, M., Quintanilla, L., & Daniel, M. F. (2013). Improving emotion comprehension and social skills in early childhood through philosophy for children. *Childhood and Philosophy, 9*(17), 63–89. https://doi.org/10.12957/child.philo.2017.26763
Grazzani, I. (2024). Promoting theory of mind and emotion understanding in preschool settings: An exploratory training study. *Frontiers in Psychology, 15*, 1439824. https://doi.org/10.3389/fpsyg.2024.1439824

Grazzani, I., & Brockmeier, J. (2019). Language games and social cognition: Revisiting Bruner. *Integrative Psychological and Behavioral Science, 53*(4), 602–610. https://doi.org/10.1007/s12124-019-09489-0

Grazzani, I., & Ornaghi, V. (2011). Emotional state talk and emotion understanding: A training study with preschool children. *Journal of Child Language, 38*(5), 1124–1139. https://doi.org/10.1017/S0305000910000772

Grazzani, I., & Valle, M. (2025). Training preschoolers with language games: enhancing theory of mind, emotion understanding, prosocial orientation and language ability. *European Journal of Developmental Psychology, 22*(5) 651–673. https://doi.org/10.1080/17405629.2025.2523752

Grazzani, I., Ornaghi, V., Agliati, A., & Brazzelli, E. (2016). How to foster toddlers' mental state talk, emotion understanding and prosocial behavior: A conversation-based intervention at nursery school. *Infancy, 21*(2), 199–227. https://doi.org/10.1111/infa.12107

Grazzani, I., Ornaghi, V., Agliati, A., & Brazzelli, E. (2020). Promoting toddlers' development of mental-state language and social cognition: The role of conversation at nursery school. In C. Cefai & R. Spiteri (Eds.), *Resilience in schools: Research and practice* (pp. 55–77). Centre for Resilience and Socio-Emotional Health, University of Malta Publisher.

Grazzani, I., Ornaghi, V., Agliati, A., Brazzelli, E., & Lucarelli, M. (2019). Enhancing mental state language and emotion understanding of toddlers' social cognition. In E. Veneziano & A. Nicolopoulou (Eds.), *Narrative, literacy and other skills. Studies in intervention* (pp. 109–127). John Benjamins Publishing Company.

Grazzani, I., & Ornaghi, V. (2022). *Children's development of social understanding*. Junior Spaggiari.

IBM SPSS. (2023). *Statistics for windows, version 29.0.2.0*. IBM Corp.

Ketelaar, L., Wiefferink, C. H., Frijns, J. H. M., Boekhof, E., & Rieffe, C. (2015). Preliminary findings of association between moral emotion and social behavior in young children with normal hearing and with cochlear implants. *European Child and Adolescent Psychiatry, 24*(11), 1369–1380. https://doi.org/10.1007/s00787-015-0688-2

Klinnert, M., Emde, R., Butterfield, P., & Campos, J. (1986). Social referencing: The infants' use of emotional signals from a friendly adult with mother present. *Developmental Psychology, 22*(4), 427–432.

Misailidi, P., Papoudi, D., & Brouzos, A. (2013). Mind what teachers say: Kindergarten teachers' use of mental state language during picture story narration. *Early Education and Development, 24*(8), 1161–1174. https://doi.org/10.1080/10409289.2013.765787

Murray, L., Rayson, H., Ferrari, P.-F., Wass, S. V., & Cooper, P. J. (2022). Dialogic book-sharing as a privileged intersubjective space. *Frontiers in Psychology, 13*, 786991. https://doi.org/10.3389/fpsyg.2022.786991

Noble, C. H., Sala, G., Peter, M. S., Lingwood, J., Rowland, C. F., Gobert, F. R., & Pine, J. M. (2019). The impact of shared book reading on children's language skills: A meta-analysis. *Educational Research Review, 28*, 100290. https://doi.org/10.1016/j.edurev.2019.100290

Ornaghi, V., Brockmeier, J., & Grazzani, I. (2011). The role of language games in children's understanding of mental states: A training study. *Journal of Cognition and Development, 12*(2), 239–259. https://doi.org/10.1080/15248372.2011.563487

Poulin-Dubois, D. (2020). Theory of mind development: State of the science and future directions. In S. Hunnius & M. Meyer (Eds.), *New perspective on early social-cognitive development* (pp. 141–166). Elsevier. https://doi.org/10.1016/bs.pbr.2020.05.021

Repacholi, B., & Gopnik, A. (1997). Early reasoning about desires: Evidence from 14 and 18 months-olds. *Developmental Psychology, 33*(1), 12–21. https://doi.org/10.1037/0012-1649.33.1.12

Schapira, R., & Aram, D. (2020). Shared book reading at home and preschoolers' socio-emotional competence. *Early Education and Development, 31*(6), 819–837. https://doi.org/10.1080/10409289.2019.1692624

Schapira, R., & Grazzani, I. (2025). Shared book reading and promoting social and emotional competences in educational settings: a narrative review. *Frontiers in Psychology*, https://doi.org/10.3389/fpsyg.2025.1622536

Scotti, A. (2024). *Promoting prosocial behaviors and socio-emotional competence: A conversational intervention with children aged 2 to 4*. Unpublished Master Thesis. Department of Psychology, University of Milano-Bicocca.

Sette, S., Bassett, H. H., Baumgartner, E., & Denham, S. A. (2015). Structure and validity of affect knowledge test (AKT) in a sample of Italian preschoolers. *The Journal of Genetic Psychology: Research and Theory on Human Development, 176*(5), 330–347. https://doi.org/10.1080/00221325.2015.1075466

Song, Y., Broekhuizen, M., & Dubas, J. S. (2022). A three-wave study on the development of prosocial behaviours across toddlerhood: The role of socialization. *Infant and Child Development*, e2289. https://doi.org/10.1002/icd.2289

Tollan, K., Jezrawi, R., Underwood, K., & Janus, M. (2023). A review on early intervention systems. *Current Developmental Disorders Reports, 10*(2), 147–153. https://doi.org/10.1007/s40474-023-00274-8

Tompkins, V., Benigno, J., Lee, B., & Wright, B. (2018). The relation between parents' mental state talk and children's social understanding: A meta-analysis. *Social Development, 27*, 223–246. https://doi.org/10.1111/sode.12280

Warneken, F., & Tomasello, M. (2006). Altruistic helping in human infants and young chimpanzees. *Science, 311*(5765), 1301–1303. https://doi.org/10.1126/science.1121448

Warneken, F., & Tomasello, M. (2007). Helping and cooperation at 14 months of age. *Infancy, 11*(3), 271–294. https://doi.org/10.1111/j.1532-7078.2007.tb00227.x

Ziv, M., Smadja, M.-L., & Aram, D. (2013). Mothers' mental-state discourse with preschoolers during storybook reading and wordless storybook telling. *Early Childhood Research Quarterly, 28*(1), 177–186. https://doi.org/10.1016/j.ecresq.2012.05.005

Ilaria Grazzani, PhD, is Full Professor of Developmental and Educational Psychology at the University of Milano-Bicocca and head of the Laboratory for Developmental and Educational Psychology (https://www.labpse.it/en/). She has been Visiting Researcher at OISE, University of Toronto, where she worked with Professor Keith Oatley and his emotion research team at the "Centre for Applied Cognitive Science". In recent years, her primary scientific focus has been on the development of social cognition in children, with a particular emphasis on theory of mind, emotion recognition, and emotional competence. She has coordinated a large European project (https: //www.promehs.org/) aimed at validating a program to promote social and emotional learning in schools (https://www.promehs.org/) and has conducted several evidence-based studies on the implementation of innovative early intervention programs across different educational settings. These interventions have been documented in multiple national and international publications.

Alice Scotti, M.Sc. is a psychologist graduated in Developmental and Educational Psychology. She works in a kindergarten and collaborates with the Laboratory for Developmental and Educational Psychology (https://www.labpse.it/en/) at the University of Milano-Bicocca.

Chapter 14
Impact of Shared Book-Reading on Children's Social–Emotional Competence: A Meta-Analysis of Intervention Studies

He Sun, Siew Chin Ng, and Alexa von Hagen

Contents

H. Sun (✉)
National Institute of Education, Nanyang Technological University, Singapore, Singapore
e-mail: he.sun@nie.edu.sg

S. C. Ng
Singapore University of Social Sciences, Singapore, Singapore
e-mail: scng@suss.edu.sg

A. v. Hagen
IDeA–Center for Research on Individual Development and Adaptive Education of Children at Risk, Frankfurt am Main, Germany

R. Schapira, D. Aram (eds.), *Shared Book Reading and Children's Social-Emotional Competence*, https://doi.org/10.1007/978-3-032-14688-5_14

Introduction

Children's **social–emotional competence** (SEC) has gained considerable attention over the past few decades from researchers, educators, and policymakers, as it plays a crucial role in supporting children's general well-being and mental health (Durlak et al., 2011). Sound SEC is associated with a number of developmental outcomes positively, including healthier lifestyle choices and greater life satisfaction (Shoshani & Slone, 2017). SEC is a multifaceted construct involving interrelated skills that allows people to successfully build relationships, recognize and manage emotions, and navigate social interactions. The Collaborative for Academic, Social, and Emotional Learning (CASEL) outlines five key competencies within SEC, including self-awareness, self-management, social awareness, relationship skills, and responsible decision-making (CASEL, 2019).

Aside from the CASEL framework which has been commonly referred to in classroom practices, scholars had dominantly investigated SEC mainly in the areas of prosocial skills (e.g., Yoder, 2014), social understanding (e.g., Ongley & Malti, 2014), emotional understanding (e.g., Garner et al., 2008), empathy (Aram et al., 2011), and perspective-taking (e.g., De Rosnay et al., 2004). In the home contexts, prior studies had looked into children's social understanding and prosocial behavior (e.g., Aram et al., 2017), as well as the use of emotion words (e.g., Bassett & Denham, 2014). These constructs informed us of the various ways of investigating SEC for young children. These skills correspond closely with CASEL's framework. For instance, empathy and perspective-taking are key aspects of social awareness. Other frameworks for understanding SEC include Denham's (2006) model of social and emotional competence, where social problem-solving, social behavior, emotion knowledge, emotional expression, and regulation of emotions were recognized as the basis for developing SEC. According to Denham's (2006) model, SEC arises from emotion knowledge, regulation, and social problem-solving, which are shaped by adult–child interactions in everyday contexts. Another influential model is Eisenberg's (2005) model of prosocial behavior. The model links children's emotional development to the emergence of empathy, moral reasoning, and helping behaviors, making it particularly applicable to understanding how stories and adult-led discussions shape children's social understanding. Saarni's (1999) emotional competence framework further underscores the importance of children's ability to recognize, interpret, and respond to emotional cues within social contexts—skills that are frequently activated during shared narrative experiences. Current guidelines for social–emotional development emphasize the importance of systematically nurturing SEC from an early age, as it is a period marked by rapid social and emotional growth (Fisak et al., 2011). Developing these skills early not only aids in children's immediate social adjustment but also provides a foundation for lifelong interpersonal success and well-being (Jones et al., 2015).

Shared Book-Reading and Social Emotional Competencies

Shared book-reading (SBR) provides a rich context for the development of these competencies (Ng & Sun, 2022; Sun, 2023; Sun et al., 2023). SBR refers to an interactive activity during which an adult reads and discusses a book with either nonreading children (van Kleeck et al., 1997) or beginning readers (Blewitt & Langan, 2016). Traditionally, SBR has been recognized as an effective method to facilitate children's development in vocabulary and reading comprehension (Sun et al., 2020, 2021). In recent years, researchers have increasingly emphasized the potential of SBR to support children's SEC (Sun, 2019), and it is now widely recommended as a natural and effective approach for fostering these skills (Dresser, 2013). The content of books provides children with valuable opportunities to explore mental states (Adrian et al., 2007), understand motivations behind behaviors (Bruner, 1990), develop prosocial skills (Zeece, 2004), and learn about emotions and emotion-related vocabulary (Green & Sun, 2024). For instance, Green and Sun (2024) examine the prevalence and diversity of emotion-specific vocabulary (e.g., happy, sad, furious) and emotion-related vocabulary (e.g., fabulous, friendship) in children's picture books, exploring how it differs from language exposure in typical spoken language settings. Their findings reveal that picture books contain a richer and more diverse range of emotion vocabulary compared to typical child-directed speech. Moreover, regular book-reading significantly enhances children's exposure to emotion-related terms, providing supplemental input beyond spoken interactions. This study underscores the great potential of picture book-reading to enrich children's emotional vocabulary and support the development of their emotional competence.

The impact of SBR on children's SEC extends beyond the content of the books to include the communications that take place during reading sessions (Aram & Shapira, 2012; Aram et al., 2017). Research has linked the frequency and quality of SBR activity to improved empathy skills (Aram & Shapira, 2012) and better social–emotional adjustment (Aram & Aviram, 2009). During SBR, adults often assume multiple roles, including reader, motivator, clarifier, and questioner (Sun et al., 2020; Sun & Verspoor, 2022; Sun & Batra, 2024), and introduce values and encourage socially appropriate behaviors in children. O'Connor et al. (2017) outlined a range of strategies for promoting SEC through **shared book-reading** in preschool classrooms. These strategies include selecting books that depict a variety of emotions, asking children perspective-taking questions, engaging them in problem-solving discussions, and encouraging reflection on emotional experiences. Such structured reading practices help children interpret characters' actions and feelings, recognize different viewpoints, and make moral and social judgments. During SBR, these adult–child conversations offer valuable opportunities for emotional scaffolding. For instance, Bruner (1990) emphasized how narratives allow children to connect actions and intentions with underlying motivations, facilitating deeper comprehension of social dynamics. Similarly, Aram and Shapira (2012) demonstrated that guided discussions during book-reading help children regulate their emotions and reflect on their real-life social experiences in a supportive setting.

Furthermore, SBR can play a crucial role in fostering children's **social–emotional competence** (SEC) in multilingual societies. When children encounter peers from different cultural backgrounds, they may feel curious yet uncertain about racial differences and related social issues. In such cases, SBR can serve as an effective tool to enhance their understanding of cultural and racial diversity, as children's literature often addresses these themes. SBR helps children explore complex social topics, encouraging them to appreciate diverse cultures and adopt open-minded attitudes toward others. Reading multicultural literature, for instance, can challenge racial biases, promote acceptance of individuals from different ethnicities, and nurture democratic attitudes toward diversity (Koss, 2015). The discussion based on such literature may touch upon such sensitive topics and help children understand how to interact with others appropriately. For instance, if a child expresses discomfort or makes negative comments about a classmate who speaks a different language or has a different accent, the adult can share stories of characters who navigate multilingual environments and celebrate the richness of speaking multiple languages. Discussions during or after SBR should focus on how speaking different languages can connect people across cultures and broaden their understanding of the world. Children should also be encouraged to reflect on the challenges faced by those who could not speak the societal dominant language, helping them develop empathy for those who may feel misunderstood or overlooked.

Beyond naturalistic adult–child interactions (Aram & Shapira, 2012; Aram et al., 2017; Ziv et al., 2014), several structured **shared book-reading** (SBR) intervention programs have been purposefully designed to promote children's **social–emotional competence** (SEC). For example, in educational settings, structured programs such as those examined by Bergman Deitcher et al. (2021) and Grazzani and Ornaghi (2011) have integrated SBR into school curricula to foster emotional literacy and prosocial skills. These programs typically involve training caregivers or educators to use specific strategies—such as open-ended questions, emotion-rich language, and reflective dialogue—during book-reading sessions. In the study by Bergman Deitcher et al. (2021), the researchers examined the effects of a brief, small-group SBR intervention on preschoolers' ability to express thoughts and emotions, as well as their social understanding. A total of 116 Arab–Israeli preschoolers were randomly assigned to either an intervention or a comparison group. Across five SBR sessions, children in the intervention group engaged with story texts enriched with emotional and mental-state vocabulary and participated in discussions about characters' thoughts, feelings, behaviors, and the consequences of their actions. In contrast, the comparison group focused solely on the plot, characters, and actions, without explicit discussion of mental states. Results indicated that children in the intervention group made significant gains in using emotion-related vocabulary, linking thoughts with emotions, identifying social problems, and proposing appropriate solutions. The interventions included in the current review build upon these foundational studies. Our meta-analysis aims to systematically synthesize their outcomes to evaluate the efficacy of SBR-based interventions in promoting various aspects of SEC across different contexts and populations.

In conclusion, SBR provides an important opportunity for children to explore different social scenarios and enhance their comprehension of others' emotions, thoughts, intentions, beliefs, and desires. Through narrative discussions, adults guide children in interpreting characters' mental states, labeling emotions, and drawing connections between the story and real-life experiences (Bruner, 1990; Adrian et al., 2007). This supports key mechanisms of SEC development, including mental-state reasoning and emotional perspective-taking. Parents and educators also model emotion language and scaffold children's reasoning about social situations, which foster empathy and social understanding (Aram & Shapira, 2012; Aram et al., 2017). These verbal exchanges during SBR allow adults to highlight moral lessons, discuss socially appropriate behaviors, and pose open-ended questions about characters' motivations and consequences of their actions (O'Connor et al., 2017). Taken together, these interactive features of SBR not only support language and literacy but also function as a developmentally appropriate pathway to enhance children's emotional and social learning.

The Present Study

Given the importance of SEC and the potential benefits of conducting SBR on SEC, this review aims to systematically examine the effects of SBR interventions on children's SEC and to explore how various factors (e.g., familial socioeconomic status (SES) and types of SEC) might moderate these effects. By addressing these dimensions, we intend to provide a nuanced evidence base that can guide parents, educators, researchers, and policymakers in the effective implementation of **shared book-reading** interventions to support social and emotional growth in children. The two specific research questions are as follows:

1. How do SBR interventions impact the SEC of children?
2. Do factors associated with participants (e.g., age and SES), interventions (e.g., setting), control participants (type of control intervention), and outcome measures of SEC (i.e., social and emotional skills, attitudes toward self and others, positive social behaviors, conduct problems, and emotional distress) moderate the impact of SBR interventions?

Methods

At the start of this systematic review, we developed a pre-registered protocol following the PRISMA statement (Moher et al., 2009) and registered it in the International Prospective Register of Systematic Reviews PROSPERO on the ninth of March of 2019 with the ID Number PROSPERO 2019 CRD42019127331

Eligibility of Studies

We defined the relevant terms for this systematic review with reference to participants, interventions, comparisons, and outcomes (PICO) in Table 14.1. For participants, we only included study reports that focused on participants from birth to 8 years of age, including infants, toddlers, children in nursery preschool, as well as primary school.

Regarding the design, to be included in the meta-analysis, a study had to measure the impact of SBR by comparing the experimental participants to a group of control participants. The control group could have either received no intervention at all or an alternative intervention (passive vs. active control group). We considered these factors within the moderator analysis. As for the outcomes, we only included studies that measured the effect of a SBR intervention on children's SEC. In terms of SEC, studies were included if the measures were obtained through standardized tests, experimental tasks, or questionnaires with scores specifically related to **social–emotional competence**.

Search Strategy

The search strategy that we used can be found in Appendices. We completed the search on November 7, 2019, without any limitations regarding the publication date of the studies.

Information Sources

We searched the following databases: PsychINFO, PsychARTICLES, MEDLINE, EMBASE, Wiley databases, Pubmed, ERIC, ProQuest dissertations and theses, Web of Science, and Directory of Open Access Journals (DOAJ). As recommended by a

Table 14.1 Eligibility criteria

PICO element	Signaling question	Inclusion	Exclusion
Participants	1. Does the study include participants from birth to 8 years of age?	YES	NO
Intervention	2. Does the study report on a shared book-reading intervention that consists of (a) at least one child participant, (b) an adult trainer, and (c) at least one picture-book (either narrative or informative text structure, eBook or wordless printed book or printed book with words)?	YES	NO
Outcomes	3. Does the study measure the effect of shared book-reading on at least one objective (experimental, standardized measures as opposed to self-, teacher- or parent-report) social–emotional competence outcome?	YES	NO

research librarian we consulted, we also added Bodeleian Education Library, databases included in the EPPI Centre, Campbell Collaboration, Cochrane Collaboration, OCLC Worldcat, and the Directory of Open Repositories to our information sources. Finally, we searched for gray literature by entering our search strategy in PsycExtra.

Selection Process

First, the titles and abstracts of the identified references were imported from the databases into Covidence. This software then automatically detected any duplicated references, while we dismissed further duplicates or reports of overlapping samples during the selection process. Two out of four reviewers independently screened the title and abstract of each identified reference based on the eligibility criteria mentioned above (see Table 14.1). If conflicts between the judgments of both reviewers arose, the judgment of a third reviewer was used to resolve the problem. When the title and abstract screening stage was completed, the full texts of all the references included were downloaded and imported into Covidence. Once again, two out of four reviewers independently screened the included full texts based on the eligibility criteria mentioned above (see Table 14.1), and conflicts were resolved by a third reviewer.

Data Extraction

We used a data extraction form configured in Covidence to extract the data of each of the included studies. One reviewer completed the extraction, and a second reviewer double-checked it. Once again, a third reviewer resolved disagreements.

Results

The initial search yielded 10,007 studies. After removing 1961 duplicates, 8046 studies underwent title and abstract screening, resulting in 344 studies selected for full-text review. Of these, 17 studies (references with * in the reference list) met the inclusion criteria and contained sufficient data for effect size calculation.

Impact of SBR Interventions on Children's SEC

The 17 studies included in this review provided data for 76 experimental–control group comparisons. All statistical analyses were performed in R (R Core Team, 2017), utilizing the *metafor* (Viechtbauer, 2010) and *clubSandwich* (Pustejovsky, 2020) packages. Following the method outlined by Morris (2008), standard mean changes (*SMC*) and variance estimates (*V*) were calculated from pre- and post-test data. Due to the absence of reported correlations in most cases, a correlation of $r = 0.8$ was assumed between pre- and post-test scores. Hedges' correction for small sample sizes was then applied to the resulting *SMC* and *V* values (Bornstein et al., 2009, pp. 27–29).

Given the potential dependency among effect sizes (e.g., multiple outcome measures per study), robust variance estimation (RVE) methods were employed, as recommended by Pustejovsky and Tipton (2020). Specifically, the correlated and hierarchical effects (CHE) working model was implemented, assuming a constant sampling correlation of $\rho = 0.6$. A random-effects meta-regression model was then computed, comparing the impact of SBR interventions on children's (a) social and emotional skills, (b) attitudes toward self and others, (c) positive social behaviors, and (d) conduct problems. Table 14.2 presents the results.

Analyses revealed a statistically significant effect of SBR interventions on all four outcome variables: (a) social and emotional skills ($SMC = 0.65$, $SE = 0.12$), (b) attitudes toward self and others ($SMC = 0.13$, $SE = 0.19$), (c) positive social behaviors ($SMC = 0.13$, $SE = 0.19$), and (d) conduct problems ($SMC = 0.33$, $SE = 0.31$). However, based on robust Wald tests comparing the size of overall effects, we cannot rule out the hypothesis that average effects are equal for all four outcomes ($p = 0.43$). While between-study heterogeneity (τ) was minimal (<0.01), within-study heterogeneity (ω) was substantial (0.76), with a significant residual heterogeneity observed (Q, $p < 0.0001$).

Impact of Participant, Intervention, and Design Characteristics on Intervention Efficacy

To further investigate the impact of different moderators at the protocol stage we planned to compute moderator analyses for 30 variables (see Methods section), if data from at least 10 studies was available for each variable (Littell et al., 2008).

Table 14.2 Estimated effects by outcome measure

Outcome measure	*N* of studies	*N* of effect sizes	Mean change between groups				Heterogeneity		
			SMC	*SE*	95% *CI*	*Z*			*Q*
Social and emotional skills	13	54	0.65	0.12	0.37–0.93	4.78			
Attitudes toward self and others	5	14	0.13	0.19	−0.62-0.88	0.59			
Positive social behaviors	4	6	0.13	0.19	−0.51-0.77	0.40			
Conduct problems	2	2	0.33	0.31	−3.54-4.20	0.59			
Total	17	76					<0.01	0.76	798.34***

Note. ***$p < 0.001$

This was the case for 11 moderators that were included in separate meta-regression models. Information on the remaining 19 moderators was insufficient to compute analyses. In Table 14.3, we present details on the above-mentioned analyses.

Overall, based on the results of robust Wald tests, we only found evidence supporting the impact of the frequency of intervention sessions on children's SEC ($p < 0.001$). More specifically, interventions with two ($SMC = 0.56$; $SE = 0.17$; $n_{studies} = 8$; $n_{effect.sizes} = 39$) and four sessions per week ($SMC = 1.53$; $SE < 0.01$; $n_{studies} = 1$; $n_{effect.sizes} = 4$) showed the largest effects.

For the 10 additional moderators we analyzed, based on the results of robust Wald tests, we cannot rule out the hypothesis that average effects are equal across subgroups ($p > 0.05$). Nevertheless, we identified the following descriptive tendencies that need to be confirmed by future meta-analyses as more primary research on the influence of these moderators becomes available.

Participant Characteristics

On a descriptive level, interventions that included participants of similar age groups showed a nonsignificant tendency to achieve a higher impact on children's SEC than interventions including participants from wider age ranges. As such, average effects for interventions with children from 0 to 3 years ($SMC = 0.68$; $SE < 0.01$; $n_{studies} = 1$; $n_{effect.sizes} = 5$; $p = 0.08$) and 4–6 years ($SMC = 0.73$; $SE = 0.19$; $n_{studies} = 8$; $n_{effect.sizes} = 36$; $p < 0.01$) tended to be larger than the effects for interventions with children from 0 to 6 years ($SMC = 0.28$; $SE = 0.15$; $n_{studies} = 5$; $n_{effect.sizes} = 17$; $p = 0.17$) and 4–8 years ($SMC = 0.04$; $SE = 0.28$; $n_{studies} = 3$; $n_{effect.sizes} = 13$; $p = 0.87$). In a similar way, descriptive results indicate a nonsignificant tendency that average effects are larger when interventions target participants from low SES levels ($SMC = 0.69$; $SE = 0.27$; $n_{studies} = 4$; $n_{effect.sizes} = 15$; $p = 0.03$) and other SES levels ($SMC = 0.75$; $SE = 0.31$; $n_{studies} = 4$; $n_{effect.sizes} = 17$; $p = 0.02$) separately as compared to mixed groups ($SMC = 0.26$; $SE = 0.37$; $n_{studies} = 3$; $n_{effect.sizes} = 21$; $p = 0.43$).

Intervention Characteristics

In relation to general characteristics of the intervention, we identified the following nonsignificant tendencies in the available evidence base. First, concerning intervention setting, we found a trend toward larger average effects for interventions delivered at home ($SMC = 0.84$; $SE = 0.48$; $n_{studies} = 4$; $n_{effect.sizes} = 15$; $p = 0.01$) as compared to the ones implemented at educational institutions ($SMC = 0.30$; $SE = 0.17$; $n_{studies} = 12$; $n_{effect.sizes} = 55$; $p = 0.19$) and in both settings ($SMC = 0.66$; $SE < 0.01$; $n_{studies} = 1$; $n_{effect.sizes} = 5$; $p = 0.25$). In coherence, the evidence points to the tendency that a higher impact of children's SEC could be achieved if the intervention is delivered by children's relatives ($SMC = 0.82$; $SE = 0.48$; $n_{studies} = 4$; $n_{effect.sizes} = 15$; $p < 0.01$), as compared to other professionals (e.g., teachers ($SMC = 0.41$; $SE = 0.14$; $n_{studies} = 7$; $n_{effect.sizes} = 23$; $p = 0.07$) or experimenters

Table 14.3 Moderator analyses

Moderator	*N* of studies	*N* of effect sizes	Mean changes between groups				Heterogeneity			HTZ-type Wald tests *p*
			SMC	*SE*	95% *CI*	*Z*			*Q*	
Participant Characteristics										
Age group	17	71					<0.01	0.79	767.45	0.35
0–3 years	1	5	0.68	<0.01	0.68–0.68	1.75				
0–6 years	5	17	0.28	0.15	−0.14-0.71	1.36				
4–6 years	8	36	0.73	0.19	0.22–1.25	4.14				
4–8 years	3	13	0.04	0.28	−3.56-3.64	0.17				
SES	11	53					0.34	0.87	718.52	0.69
Low	4	15	0.69	0.27	−0.21-1.58	2.18				
Others	4	17	0.75	0.31	−0.27-1.77	2.43				
Mixed groups	3	21	0.26	0.37	−4.44-4.97	0.79				
Intervention Characteristics										
Setting	17	75					0.37	0.82	747.37	0.25
Home	4	15	0.84	0.48	−0.71-2.39	2.53				
Educational institution	12	55	0.30	0.17	−0.14-0.73	1.31				
Mixed	1	5	0.66	<0.01	0.66–0.66	1.16				
Frequency	14	66					<0.01	0.80	705.48	<0.001***
1 session/week	1	10	−0.10	<0.01	−0.10-(−0.10)	−0.33				
2 sessions/week	8	39	0.56	0.17	0.06–1.05	3.25				
3 sessions/week	2	3	−0.13	<0.01	−0.13-(−0.13)	−0.22				
4 sessions/week	1	4	1.53	<0.01	1.53–1.53	2.87				
5 sessions/week	2	10	0.67	0.01	0.50–0.84	2.34				
Total weeks	12	57					0.41	0.79	618.91	0.58
6 weeks or less	7	33	0.35	0.18	−0.14-0.84	1.32				

(continued)

Table 14.3 (continued)

Moderator	*N* of studies	*N* of effect sizes	Mean changes between groups				Heterogeneity			HTZ-type Wald tests *p*
			SMC	*SE*	95% *CI*	*Z*			*Q*	
More than 6 weeks	5	24	0.61	0.41	−0.75-1.98	2.03				
Interaction type	17	70					0.35	0.70	704.77	0.21
Dialogic	16	68	0.55	0.15	0.16–0.82	3.24				
Non-interactive	1	2	0.25	0.43	NA-NA	0.46				
Material theme	16	62					0.21	0.77	634.55	0.88
SEC-oriented	12	41	0.50	0.15	0.16–0.84	3.01				
Non-SEC-oriented	2	6	0.36	0.22	−2.05-2.77	0.98				
Mixed	2	15	0.19	0.33	−3.75-4.13	0.70				
Number of participants	16	71					0.33	0.77	770.37	0.66
Individual	5	17	0.79	0.39	−0.29-1.87	2.81				
Small group	3	19	0.32	0.28	−0.92-1.56	1.14				
Large group	8	35	0.39	0.15	−0.04-0.82	1.68				
Relation of child trainer	17	73					0.30	0.76	791.81	0.70
Experimenter	6	35	0.33	0.22	−0.36-1.03	1.43				
Professional	7	23	0.41	0.14	0.04–0.78	1.83				
Relative	4	15	0.82	0.48	−0.73-2.37	2.74				
SBR type	17	73					0.28	0.76	793.15	0.53
SBR only	13	53	0.53	0.16	0.17–0.89	3.28				
SBR with other activities	4	20	0.31	0.28	−0.95-1.58	1.20				
Study Design Characteristics										
Control group	17	76					0.27	0.74	805.36	0.41
Active control	11	39	0.56	0.16	0.20–0.92	3.47				
Passive control	6	37	0.33	0.21	−0.41-1.07	1.52				

(*SMC* = 0.33; *SE* = 0.22; $n_{studies}$ = 6; $n_{effect.sizes}$ = 35; $p = 0.15$)). Another related finding indicates that interventions that were delivered individually (SMC = 0.79; SE = 0.39; $n_{studies}$ = 5; $n_{effect.sizes}$ = 17; $p < 0.01$) showed a tendency toward higher impact as compared to small-group (SMC = 0.32; SE = 0.28; $n_{studies}$ = 3; $n_{effect.sizes}$ = 19; $p = 0.25$) and large-group interventions (SMC = 0.39; SE = 0.15; $n_{studies}$ = 8; $n_{effect.sizes}$ = 35; $p = 0.09$). Concerning intervention dose, on average, we observed a trend that a total duration of more than 6 weeks (*SMC* = 0.61; *SE* = 0.41; $n_{studies}$ = 5; $n_{effect.sizes}$ = 24; $p = 0.04$) achieved better results as compared to shorter interventions lasting 6 weeks or less (*SMC* = 0.35; *SE* = 0.18; $n_{studies}$ = 7; $n_{effect.sizes}$ = 33; $p = 0.19$).

Turning to characteristics related to the intervention content, programs that solely focused on SBR activities (SMC = 0.53; SE = 0.16; $n_{studies}$ = 13; $n_{effect.sizes}$ = 53; $p < 0.01$) revealed a nonsignificant trend to be more efficient than interventions that also included other activities (SMC = 0.31; SE = 0.28; $n_{studies}$ = 4; $n_{effect.sizes}$ = 20; $p = 0.23$). Also, interventions that provided many opportunities for interactions among trainers and participants and emphasized a dialogic character (SMC = 0.55; SE = 0.15; $n_{studies}$ = 16; $n_{effect.sizes}$ = 68; $p = 0.11$) tended to achieve better results than the ones that did not emphasize these aspects (SMC = 0.25; SE = 0.43; $n_{studies}$ = 1; $n_{effect.sizes}$ = 2; $p = 0.44$). Finally, considering the theme of the materials included in the intervention, as it would be expected, an exclusive focus on SEC-oriented themes (*SMC* = 0.50; *SE* = 0.15; $n_{studies}$ = 12; $n_{effect.sizes}$ = 41; $p < 0.01$) seems to lead to a higher impact on children's SEC as compared to a focus on other non-SEC-related themes (*SMC* = 0.36; *SE* = 0.22; $n_{studies}$ = 2; $n_{effect.sizes}$ = 6; $p = 0.33$) or a combination of both (*SMC* = 0.19; *SE* = 0.33; $n_{studies}$ = 2; $n_{effect.sizes}$ = 15; $p = 0.49$).

Study Design Characteristics

In relation to study design characteristics, we observed a tendency toward higher effects when interventions were compared to active control groups (SMC = 0.56; SE = 0.16; $n_{studies}$ = 12; $n_{effect.sizes}$ = 39; $p < 0.01$) than to passive control groups (SMC = 0.33; SE = 0.21; $n_{studies}$ = 6; $n_{effect.sizes}$ = 37; $p = 0.13$). It is important to keep in mind that the above-described findings only reflect tendencies that did not reach statistical significance and must therefore be further investigated in future research.

Discussion

Our review aimed to investigate whether SBR interventions influence the SEC of children and the extent to which this relationship is moderated by factors such as participant characteristics, intervention strategies, and study design. Unlike general book-reading routines, the interventions analyzed in this study were intentionally designed to promote SEC, often including adult training, guided discussion strategies, and targeted book selections. Our findings therefore speak directly to the effectiveness of programmatic SBR interventions. The findings of this meta-analysis offer valuable insights into the effectiveness of SBR interventions, while also identifying areas for future research and practical application. The results underscore the complexities involved in implementing SBR to enhance its impact on SEC.

In response to the first research question, our findings indicated that SBR positively impacted on children's SEC, with statistically significant average effects observed for social and emotional skills (*SMC* = 0.65), attitudes toward self and others (*SMC* = 0.13), positive social behaviors (*SMC* = 0.13), and conduct problems (*SMC* = 0.33). However, we found no evidence of differences across competency domains, thereby suggesting that SBR benefits multiple areas of SEC in similar ways without favoring one over another. This finding is consistent with many studies that reported benefits of SBR on children's SEC (e.g., Aram et al., 2017, Green & Sun, 2024). Studies have also been increasingly supporting the use of SBR to promote SEC (e.g., Ng & Sun, 2022; Sun et al., 2023; Ziv et al., 2014) even without books that explicitly relay messages relating to social and emotional situations (Ng & Sun, 2022). Hence, this finding further supported the impact of SBR and the importance of its utility in this area of development. As international frameworks highlight the importance of social and emotional learning to contribute to lifelong successes (OECD, 2015), it is recommended for both teachers and parents to conduct SBR as an activity at school and at home to inculcate these skills from a young age.

With regard to the moderators, we only found evidence of a significant impact of the frequency of interventions sessions. Interventions that were conducted two (*SMC* = 0.56) or four times (*SMC* = 1.53) per week yielded the largest effects. This finding highlights the importance of frequency of SBR where it was found to be positively correlated with children's socioemotional adjustment and empathy skills (Aram & Shapira, 2012), prosocial behavior (Sun, 2019), and emotional understanding (Garner et al., 2008). Our finding reveals that reading two or four times per week yielded the strongest effects when compared against interventions conducted one, three, or five times per week. Our results align with the research on cognitive consolidation and learning transfer. According to distributed practice principles, moderate and spaced repetition optimizes encoding new information without cognitive overload (Cepeda et al., 2006). In the case of SBR, this frequency likely balances novelty, reflection time, and emotional engagement, thereby allowing children to absorb, revisit, and generalize socio-emotional themes presented in the books. Too few sessions may limit exposure, while excessive repetition could reduce engagement or diminish opportunities for deep, varied discussion.

For the remaining intervention and design characteristics, although not statistically significant, our results revealed important trends that may influence the efficacy of SBR. First, interventions conducted at home tended to be more effective than those implemented in educational settings. Additionally, readings delivered by relatives (SMC = 0.84) demonstrated stronger effects compared to those conducted by teachers (SMC = 0.41) or experimenters (SMC = 0.33). These findings suggest that one-on-one interactions in familiar settings with trusted interlocutors may be more conducive to SEC-related discussions, which might be explained by the nature of parent–child interactions. In the home setting, caregivers typically engage in one-on-one shared reading, offering emotionally secure and personalized exchanges. According to Attachment Theory (Bowlby, 1982), emotionally secure relationships with familiar caregivers create an optimal context for children to internalize emotion-related discourse. These trusted relationships foster a sense of safety, which in turn enhances children's receptivity to discussions about emotions, social behavior, and moral understanding. Moreover, family members may naturally tailor conversations to their child's specific emotional needs based on their experience, which is more difficult for teachers to do in group-based school settings.

Second, interventions lasting more than 6 weeks (*SMC* = 0.61) tended to be more effective than shorter ones (*SMC* = 0.35), indicating that consistent SBR may be optimal for promoting SEC. In terms of content, interventions that exclusively targeted SBR (*SMC* = 0.53) or emphasized interactive reading (*SMC* = 0.55) yielded better SEC outcomes. Books with SEC-oriented topics (*SMC* = 0.50) also proved more impactful, underscoring the importance of aligning reading content with desired outcomes. Regarding intervention design, active control designs (*SMC* = 0.56) exhibited higher effect sizes than passive control designs (*SMC* = 0.33). Passive control groups refer to participants who receive no intervention or continue with regular activities, whereas active control groups participate in alternative, structured activities that do not involve the intervention of interest (in this case, non-SBR activities). The finding that SBR interventions showed stronger effects in comparison with active controls is notable because it indicates that SBR has a unique effect above and beyond general adult–child engagement or classroom routines. Moreover, effects observed with active controls tend to be more conservative and methodologically rigorous, as they account for potential placebo or expectancy effects. Therefore, the observed benefits of SBR under these more stringent conditions underscore the robustness of the intervention's impact on SEC.

In terms of child characteristics, the analysis of age and SES indicated a tendency to moderate the impact of SBR interventions on SEC. Studies focusing on younger children, specifically those aged 0–3 years (*SMC* = 0.68) and 4–6 years (*SMC* = 0.73), showed larger effects compared to studies with broader or mixed-age groups (e.g., 0–6 years). This may be because interventions tailored to specific developmental stages can more precisely align with children's cognitive, linguistic, and emotional capabilities. In contrast, interventions targeting wider age spans often need to generalize content and strategies, which may dilute their developmental appropriateness and reduce individual engagement. Furthermore, studies involving children from low SES backgrounds (*SMC* = 0.69) or other specific SES levels (*SMC* = 0.75) demonstrated greater effects than those with mixed SES groups. These findings highlight the importance of tailoring SBR interventions to meet the unique needs of specific demographic groups, particularly those at higher risk of developmental challenges. The results regarding age also emphasize that **early childhood** is a critical period for SEC development, suggesting that stakeholders should leverage this window to maximize the benefits of SBR. Our findings are consistent with developmental theories identifying **early childhood** as a sensitive period for socio-emotional growth (Denham, 2006; Saarni, 1999). During this period, children's neural and emotional systems are highly malleable, and they are especially responsive to adult modeling of emotional language and behavior. **Shared book-reading** offers structured yet emotionally resonant opportunities for children to engage in emotion labeling, perspective-taking, and regulation—all of which are foundational components of SEC. Thus, introducing SBR interventions during **early childhood** may be especially impactful due to the developmental receptiveness of this age group.

Our findings have important implications for the future design and practice of SBR in supporting children's SEC development. Adequate exposure to SBR is crucial, and we recommend that both parents and teachers conduct SBR sessions two to four times per week for a duration of more than 6 weeks. Additionally, it is essential to encourage verbal exchanges about socio-emotional situations during SBR. Our results reveal that the quality of SBR sessions—particularly the inclusion of emotion talk—is essential for promoting SEC. Caregivers and educators are encouraged to explicitly discuss characters' feelings, use emotion vocabulary, and pose open-ended questions about emotional events in the story. These interactions support children's ability to identify, interpret, and regulate emotions, which are core components of emotional competence (Denham, 2006; Saarni, 1999). Our findings align with more recent evidence demonstrating the effectiveness of SBR interventions in promoting children's emotional and social understanding. For instance, Schapira and Aram (2020) found that kindergarteners who participated in SBR sessions focused on emotional discourse showed significant improvements in emotion recognition and empathy. The study highlighted the role of adult-guided discussion, particularly when focused on labeling emotions, reflecting on motives, and drawing parallels between the story and real-life experiences. These findings reinforce the importance of caregiver mediation in helping children build **social–emotional competence** through book-based conversations.

These practices should begin as early as possible at home, with family members serving as facilitators, and focus on SEC-oriented content. Tailored interventions targeting younger children and at-risk populations, with an emphasis on dialogic reading techniques, may further optimize the impact of SBR on SEC. Those interventions should especially focus on children from low socioeconomic status (SES) backgrounds who may face barriers to regular reading engagement. In home settings, providing parents—particularly those with limited time or literacy resources—with accessible training, sample scripts, or ICT-based support (e.g., narrated eBooks and WhatsApp parent guides) can help them initiate meaningful SBR interactions. Encouraging involvement from extended family members, such as grandparents or older siblings, can also expand the child's emotional learning network. In school settings, designated time during the week for focused SBR with at-risk children can ensure equitable access to high-quality reading experiences. Community-based initiatives that partner with local volunteers or public libraries can also support broader implementation.

Conclusion

This study provides meta-analytic evidence on the effectiveness of intervention-based **shared book-reading** (SBR) programs in enhancing young children's **social–emotional competence**. The results highlight that when SBR is implemented through structured and intentional intervention formats, it significantly benefits children's emotional understanding, social behaviors, and conduct. Our findings demonstrate the positive impact of SBR on SEC across various domains and emphasize the importance of intervention frequency, with two to four readings per week proving to be the most effective. These results have significant implications for parents, teachers, education specialists, and policymakers dedicated to fostering children's social and emotional development. By conducting regular SBR practices at home and in school, adults can leverage its benefits to nurture socially adept and resilient children, paving the way for their happiness and well-being throughout their lives.

Despite the significant findings and implications of our study, it is worth noting that there was significant within-study heterogeneity in our results, suggesting that some important moderating factors were not included. Future studies should address these important gaps in the literature remain. First, longitudinal studies are needed to examine the lasting impact of SBR on SEC over time and across developmental transitions, such as entry into formal schooling. Most existing studies rely on short-term pre–post designs, leaving questions about sustained effects unanswered. Second, cross-cultural research on SBR is limited. Given the culturally embedded nature of storytelling practices and parent–child communication styles, future work should explore how SBR influences SEC across different linguistic, cultural, and socio-economic contexts. Understanding these differences can inform culturally responsive intervention design. Third, book content and thematic focus deserve closer attention. Future studies should systematically compare how different types of narratives (e.g., those emphasizing conflict resolution, empathy, or moral dilemmas) contribute to specific SEC outcomes. Studies could also investigate how books featuring diverse characters or addressing issues such as inclusion, identity, or resilience affect children's social attitudes and emotional understanding. By addressing these areas, future research can refine both the theoretical grounding and practical implementation of SBR interventions for social–emotional development.

Appendices

Appendix A

Search Strategy

(child* OR preschool OR kindergarten* OR nurser*) AND (book* OR storybook* OR shar* OR interactive OR dialogic* OR story OR joint) AND (read* OR "listen* to story*" OR "read* aloud") AND (parent* OR teacher* OR adult* OR trainer* OR enrichment) AND (socio-emotional OR socioemotional OR interpersonal OR inter-personal OR emotion* OR prosocial OR pro-social OR moral OR (social AND (adjust* OR alienate* OR emotion* OR attitude* OR cognition OR competence* OR development OR interaction OR isolation OR learn* OR participation OR problem* OR skill* OR awareness OR management)) OR (self AND (regulate* OR control OR efficacy OR evaluate* OR inhibition OR awareness OR esteem OR perception OR manage* OR respect) OR intrapersonal OR intra-personal OR conduct OR acting out OR aggress* OR empathy OR hostility OR impulsive*) AND (skill* OR understand* OR well-being OR well-being OR behavior* OR develop* OR knowledge OR competence* OR cognition OR intelligence OR perform* OR adjust* OR disorder* OR difficult* OR problem OR relation* OR interaction) OR (peer AND (relation* OR acceptance OR rejection OR pressure) OR resilience* OR theory of mind OR mental state vocabulary).

References

Adrian, J. E., Clemente, R. A., & Villanueva, L. (2007). Mothers' use of cognitive state verbs in picture-book reading and the development of children's understanding of mind: A longitudinal study. *Child Development, 78*(4), 1052–1067. https://doi.org/10.1111/j.1467-8624.2007.01052.x

Aram, D., & Aviram, S. (2009). Mothers' storybook reading and kindergartners' socio-emotional and literacy development. *Reading Psychology, 30*, 175–194. https://doi.org/10.1080/02702710802275348

*Aram, D., Fine, Y., & Ziv, M. (2013a). Enhancing parent–child shared book reading interactions: Promoting references to the book's plot and socio-cognitive themes. *Early Childhood Research Quarterly, 28*(1), 111–122. https://doi.org/10.1016/j.ecresq.2012.03.005.

Aram, D., & Shapira, R. (2012). Parent-child shared book reading and children's language, literacy, and empathy development. *Rivista Italiana di Educazione Familiare, 2*, 55–65.

Aram, D., Deitcher, D. B., Shoshan, T. S., & Ziv, M. (2017). Shared book reading interactions within families from low socioeconomic backgrounds and children's social understanding and prosocial behavior. *Journal of Cognitive Education and Psychology, 16*(2), 157–177. https://doi.org/10.1891/1945-8959.16.2.157

Aram, D., Ziv, M., & Fine, Y. (2011). *Shared book reading as a context for promoting children's social cognition*. Il contributo di Eric Carle alla crescita dei bambini nel nido e nella scuola dell'infanzia.

Bassett, H. H., & Denham, S. A. (2014). *Parent-child affect communication task (PACT)*. George Mason University.

Bergman Deitcher, D., Aram, D., Khalaily-Shahadi, M., & Dwairy, M. (2021). Promoting preschoolers' mental-emotional conceptualization and social understanding: A shared book-reading study. *Early Education and Development, 32*(4), 501–515. https://doi.org/10.1080/10409289.2020.1772662

*Bhavnagri, N. P., & Samuels, B. G. (1996). Children's literature and activities promoting social cognition of peer relationships in preschoolers. *Early Childhood Research Quarterly, 11*(3), 307–332. https://doi.org/10.1016/S0885-2006(96)90010-1.

*Bierman, K. L., Welsh, J. A., Heinrichs, B. S., Nix, R. L., & Mathis, E. T. (2015). Helping head start parents promote their children's kindergarten adjustment: The research-based developmentally informed parent program. *Child Development, 86*(6), 1877–1891. https://doi.org/10.1111/cdev.12448.

Blewitt, P., & Langan, R. (2016). Shared book reading and language development in young children: What predicts responsiveness? *Reading Research Quarterly, 51*(4), 373–390. https://doi.org/10.1002/rrq.139

Bornstein, M., Hedges, L. V., Higgins, J., & Rothstein, H. R. (2009). *Introduction to meta-analysis*. Wiley.

Bowlby, J. (1982). Attachment and loss: Vol. 1. Attachment (2nd ed.). Basic Books.

Bruner, J. S. (1990). *Acts of meaning*. Harvard University Press.

*Casey, E. M. (2010). *Exploring the influences of multicultural literature and teacher-child discussions on improving racial attitudes in pre-kindergarten children: A mixed-methods approach.* [Doctoral dissertation, University of Arkansas]. ProQuest Dissertations & Theses.

*Cates, C. B., & Nicolopoulou, A. (2019). The effects of bookreading with and without mental state themes on preschoolers' theory of mind. In E. Veneziano & A. Nicolopoulou (Eds.), *Narrative, literacy and other skills* (pp. 129–149). John Benjamins Publishing Company. https://doi.org/10.1075/sin.25.07cat.

Cepeda, N. J., Pashler, H., Vul, E., Wixted, J. T., & Rohrer, D. (2006). Distributed Practice in Verbal Recall Tasks: A Review and Quantitative Synthesis. *Psychological Bulletin, 132*(3), 354–380. https://doi.org/10.1037/0033-2909.132.3.354

Collaborative for Academic Social and Emotional Learning (CASEL). (2019). *What is social and emotional learning?* Retrieved from http://www.casel.org/what-is-sel/

Denham, S. A. (2006). Social-Emotional Competence as Support for School Readiness: What Is It and How Do We Assess It? *Early Education and Development, 17*(1), 57–89. https://doi.org/10.1207/s15566935eed1701_4

De Rosnay, M., Pons, F., Harris, P. L., & Morrell, J. M. B. (2004). A lag between understanding false belief and emotion attribution in young children: Relationship with linguistic ability and mothers' mental-state language. *British Journal of Developmental Psychology, 22*(2), 197–218. https://doi.org/10.1348/026151004323044573

Dresser, R. (2013). The role of children's literature in social-emotional learning. *Young Children, 68*(5), 32–38.

Durlak, J. A., Weissberg, R. P., Dymnicki, A. B., Taylor, R. D., & Schellinger, K. B. (2011). The impact of enhancing students' social and emotional learning: A meta-analysis of school-based universal interventions. *Child Development, 82*(1), 405–432. https://doi.org/10.1111/j.1467-8624.2010.01564.x

Eisenberg, N., Cumberland, A., Guthrie, I. K., Murphy, B. C., & Shepard, S. A. (2005). Age Changes in Prosocial Responding and Moral Reasoning in Adolescence and Early Adulthood. *Journal of Research on Adolescence, 15*(3), 235–260. https://doi.org/10.1111/j.1532-7795.2005.00095.x

*Esteban, M., Sidera, F., Serrano, J., Amadó, A., & Rostan, C. (2017a). Improving social understanding of preschool children: Evaluation of a training program. *Electronic Journal of Research in Educational Psychology, 8*(2), 841–860. https://doi.org/10.25115/ejrep.v8i21.1386.

Fisak, B., Richard, D., & Mann, A. (2011). The prevention of anxiety in children and adolescents: A meta-analytic review. *Prevention Science, 12*(3), 255–268. https://doi.org/10.1007/s11121-011-0210-0

Garner, P. W., Dunsmore, J. C., & SouthamGerrow, M. (2008). Mother–child conversations about emotions: Linkages to child aggression and prosocial behavior. *Social Development, 17*(2), 259–277. https://doi.org/10.1111/j.1467-9507.2007.00424.x

Grazzani, I., & Ornaghi, V. (2011). Emotional state talk and emotion understanding: A training study with preschool children. *Journal of Child Language, 38*(5), 1124–1139.

Green, C., & Sun, H. (2024). Emotion vocabulary in children's picture books: A corpus study modelling the lexical input to children with accompanying pedagogical resources. *Early Education and Development.* https://doi.org/10.1080/10409289.2024.2423259

Jones, S. M., Greenberg, M., & Crowley, M. (2015). Early social-emotional functioning and public health: The relationship between kindergarten social competence and future wellness. *American Journal of Public Health, 105*(11), 2283–2290. https://doi.org/10.2105/AJPH.2015.302630

Koss, M. D. (2015). Diversity in contemporary picturebooks: A content analysis. *Journal of Children's Literature, 41*(1), 32–42.

*Larsen, N. E., Lee, K., & Ganea, P. A. (2018). Do storybooks with anthropomorphized animal characters promote prosocial behaviors in young children? *Developmental Science, 21*(3). https://doi.org/10.1111/desc.12590.

Littell, J. H., Corcoran, J., & Pillai, V. (2008). *Systematic reviews and meta-analysis*. Oxford University Press.

Moher, D., Liberati, A., Tetzlaff, J., & Altman, D. G. (2009). Preferred reporting items for systematic reviews and meta-analyses: The PRISMA statement. *Annals of Internal Medicine, 151*(4), 264–269. https://doi.org/10.7326/0003-4819-151-4-200908180-00135

Morris, S. B. (2008). Estimating effect sizes from pretest-posttest-control group designs. *Organizational Research Methods, 11*(2), 364–386. https://doi.org/10.1177/1094428106291059

Ng, S. C., & Sun, H. (2022). Promoting social-emotional learning through shared book reading: Examining teacher's strategies and children's responses in kindergarten classrooms. *Early Education and Development, 33*(8), 1326–1346. https://doi.org/10.1080/10409289.2021.1974232

O'Conner, R., De Feyter, J., Carr, A., Luo, J. L., & Romm, H. (2017). *A review of the literature on social and emotional learning for students ages 3–8: Teacher and classroom strategies that contribute to social and emotional learning (part 3 of 4) (REL 2017–247)*. U.S. Department of Education, Institute of Education Sciences, National Center for education evaluation and regional assistance, regional educational laboratory mid-Atlantic. http://ies.ed.gov/ncee/edlabs/(open in a new window)

Ongley, S. F., & Malti, T. (2014). The role of moral emotions in the development of children's sharing behavior. *Developmental Psychology, 50*(4), 1148–1159. https://doi.org/10.1037/a0035191

*Ornaghi, V., Brazzelli, E., Grazzani, I., Agliati, A., & Lucarelli, M. (2017b). Does training toddlers in emotion knowledge lead to changes in their prosocial and aggressive behavior toward peers at nursery? *Early Education and Development, 28*(4), 396–414. https://doi.org/10.1080/10409289.2016.1238674.

Organisation for Economic Co-operation and Development (OECD). (2015). Skills for social progress: The power of social and emotional skills. *OECD skills studies*. OECD Publishing.

*Peskin, J., & Astington, J. W. (2004). The effects of adding metacognitive language to story texts. *Cognitive Development, 19*(2), 253–273. https://doi.org/10.1016/j.cogdev.2004.01.003.

*Poventud, L. S. (2013). *Developing social-emotional vocabulary through storybook reading*. [Doctoral dissertation, University of Florida]. ProQuest Dissertations and Theses Global. http://libservy.nie.edu.sg/login.php?url=https://search.proquest.com/docview/1547360316?accountid=28158

Pustejovsky, J. (2020). clubSandwich: Cluster-robust (Sandwich). *Variance estimators with small-sample corrections*. R package version 0.5.2. https://CRAN.R-project.org/package=clubSandwich

Pustejovsky, J. E., & Tipton, E. (2020). Meta-analysis with robust variance estimation: Expanding the range of working models. *MetaArXiv*. https://doi.org/10.31222/osf.io/vyfcj

R Core Team. (2017). *R: A language and environment for statistical computing*. R Foundation for Statistical Computing. URL https://www.R-project.org/

*Ribeiro, N. N. (2012). *Atribuição de estados mentais e consciência metatextual: Efeitos de uma pesquisa-intervenção com a literatura infantil*. Unpublished doctoral dissertation.

*Riquelme, E., & Montero, I. (2013b). Improving emotional competence through mediated reading: Short-term effects of a children's literature program. *Mind, Culture, and Activity, 20*(3), 226–239. https://doi.org/10.1080/10749039.2013.781185.

Saarni, C. (1999). *The development of emotional competence*. Guilford Press.

Schapira, R., & Aram, D. (2020). Shared book reading focusing on emotional understanding among kindergarteners: Can we narrow the gap between low and mid SES children? *Early Childhood Research Quarterly, 51*, 384–395. https://doi.org/10.1016/j.ecresq.2019.12.007

*Seung-Mcfarland, S. (2008). *Using bibliotherapy to positively impact the emergent racial identity of African American children.* [Doctoral dissertation, Seton Hall University].ProQuest Information & Learning.

*Shanty, L. M. (2016). *Preschool children's emotion knowledge: Storybooks as a learning tool.* [Doctoral dissertation, University of Maryland, Baltimore County]. ProQuest Dissertations and Theses Global.

Shoshani, A., & Slone, M. (2017). The drama of media violence: Psychological desensitization or emotional coping? *American Psychologist, 72*(3), 215–226. https://doi.org/10.1037/a0040415

Sun, H. (2019). Home environment, bilingual preschooler's receptive mother tongue language outcomes, and social-emotional and behavioral skills: One stone for two birds? *Frontiers in Psychology, 10,* 1640. https://doi.org/10.3389/fpsyg.2019.01640

Sun, H. (2023). Harmonious bilingual experience and child wellbeing: A conceptual framework. *Frontiers in Psychology, 14,* 1282863. https://doi:10.3389/fpsyg.2023.1282863.

Sun, H., & Batra, R. (2024). Contextualized and decontextualized questions on bilinguals' heritage language learning and reading engagement. *Reading and Writing: An Interdisciplinary Journal, 37,* 973–1009. https://doi.org/10.1007/s11145-022-10332-z

Sun, H., & Verspoor, M. (2022). Mandarin vocabulary growth, teacher qualifications and teacher talk in child heritage language learners. *International Journal of Bilingual Education and Bilingualism, 25*(6), 1976–1991. https://doi.org/10.1080/13670050.2020.1835813

Sun, H., Bornstein, M. H., & Esposito, G. (2021). The specificity principle in young dual language learners' English development. *Child Development, 92*(5), 1752–1768. https://doi.org/10.1111/cdev.13558

Sun, H., Ng, S. C., & Peh, A. (2023). Shared book Reading and children's social-emotional learning in Asian schools. In R. B. King, I. S. Caleon, & A. B. I. Bernardo (Eds.), *Positive psychology and positive education in Asia: Understanding and fostering Well-being in schools* (pp. 293–309). Springer. https://doi.org/10.1007/978-981-99-5571-8_16

Sun, H., Toh, W. M., & Steinkrauss, R. (2020). Instructional strategies and linguistic features of kindergarten teachers' shared book reading: The case of Singapore. *Applied PsychoLinguistics, 41*(2), 427–456. https://doi.org/10.1017/S0142716420000053

*Terry, M. (2011). *Exploring the additive benefit of parental nurturance training on parent and child shared reading outcomes: A pilot intervention study.* [Doctoral dissertation, Texas A&M University]. ProQuest Dissertations & Theses.

*Tompkins, V. (2015). Improving low-income preschoolers' theory of mind: A training study. *Cognitive Development, 36,* 1–19. https://doi.org/10.1016/j.cogdev.2015.07.001.

van Kleeck, A., Gillam, R., Hamilton, L., & McGrath, C. (1997). The relationship between narrative skills and language skills in preschool and early elementary-age children. *Journal of Speech, Language, and Hearing Research, 40*(5), 1173–1184. https://doi.org/10.1044/jslhr.4005.1173

Viechtbauer, W. (2010). Conducting meta-analyses in R with the metafor package. *Journal of Statistical Software, 36*(3), 1–48. https://doi.org/10.18637/jss.v036.i03

*Yen, C.-C., & Tsai, M.-J. (2016). Effects of parent-child emotion talk skills intervention on kindergartners' emotional understanding and emotion regulation. *Bulletin of Educational Psychology, 48*(1), 113–132.

Yoder, N. (2014). *Teaching the whole child: Instructional practices that support social and emotional learning in three teacher evaluation frameworks.* American Institutes for Research, Center on Great Teachers and Leaders.

Zeece, P. D. (2004). Promoting empathy and developing caring readers. *Early Childhood Education Journal, 31,* 193–199. https://doi.org/10.1023/B:ECEJ.0000012314.00539.12

Ziv, M., Smadja, M., & Aram, D. (2014). Mothers' and teachers' mental-state discourse with preschoolers during storybook reading. *Journal of Cognitive Education and Psychology, 13*(1), 103–119. https://doi.org/10.1891/1945-8959.13.1.103

He Sun, PhD, is Associate Professor at the National Institute of Education, Nanyang Technological University, Singapore. Her research focuses on child bilingualism and ICT (e.g., eBooks, AI), individual differences in bilingual/second/foreign language learning, and fostering harmonious bilingual experience. Her work appears in leading journals, including *Bilingualism: Language and Cognition*, *Child Development*, *Studies in Second Language Acquisition*, and *International Journal of Bilingual Education and Bilingualism*, and has been featured in media such as *The Straits Times* and *CNA*. She serves as Associate Editor of *Journal of Child Language*, Consulting Editor of *Child Development*, and sits on IASCL's Executive Committee.

Siew Chin Ng, PhD, is a Lecturer in early childhood education at the Singapore University of Social Sciences in Singapore. Her research interests include early childhood curriculum, adult–child interaction, and teacher professional learning. She has worked as an early childhood educator and is currently a researcher and teacher educator for early childhood education program. Siew Chin is keen to rethink current ways of doing in order to promote novel understanding and contribute to meaning-making with the world.

Alexa von Hagen, PhD, is an independent researcher in educational psychology specializing in child bilingualism, learning difficulties, socio-emotional and language development. With expertise in systematic review methodology, she bridges research and educational practice. She earned an International Doctorate in Experimental Approaches to Language and Brain in 2019, followed by postdoctoral positions in Singapore and Germany. Currently based in Frankfurt, she collaborates on projects with international teams in Australia, Uruguay, the UK, and Paraguay. Her work focuses on how children learn and thrive in multilingual and diverse contexts, supporting inclusive and effective educational practices worldwide

Index

R. Schapira, D. Aram (eds.), *Shared Book Reading and Children's Social-Emotional Competence*, https://doi.org/10.1007/978-3-032-14688-5

The manufacturer's authorised representative in the EU is Springer Nature Customer Service Centre GmbH, Europaplatz 3, 69115 Heidelberg, Germany. If you have any concerns regarding our products, please contact ProductSafety@springernature.com

Printed and bound by CPI Group (UK) Ltd, Croydon, CR0 4YY
21/09/2026
02220010-0007